Human Capital

Gary S. Becker

Human Capital

*A Theoretical and Empirical Analysis,
with Special Reference to Education*

Third Edition

The University of Chicago Press
Chicago and London

This book is published by arrangement with the National Bureau of Economic Research

The University of Chicago Press, Chicago 60637
The University of Chicago Press, Ltd., London
© 1964, 1975, 1993 by The National Bureau of Economic Research
All rights reserved. Published 1993
Printed in the United States of America
02 01 00 99 98 97 96 95   2 3 4 5
ISBN: 0–226–04119–0 (cloth)
         0–226–04120–4 (paper)

Library of Congress Cataloging in Publication Data
Becker, Gary Stanley, 1930–
    Human Capital : a theoretical and empirical analysis, with spe-
cial reference to education / Gary S. Becker.—3rd ed.
        p.   cm.
    Includes index.
    1. Education—Economic aspects—United States. 2. Manpower
policy—United States. 3. Human capital—United States. I. Title.
LC66.B4   1993
331.11′423—dc20   93-24690
                                                                              CIP

⊗The Paper used in this publication meets the minimum requirements of the American National Standard for Information Sciences—Permanence of Paper for Printed Library Materials, ANSI
Z39.48–1984.

Relation of the Directors to the Work and Publication of the National Bureau of Economic Research

1. The object of the National Bureau of Economic Research is to ascertain and to present to the public important economic facts and their interpretation in a scientific and impartial manner. The Board of Directors is charged with the responsibility of ensuring that the work of the National Bureau is carried on in strict conformity with this object.

2. The President of the National Bureau shall submit to the Board of Directors, or to its Executive Committee, for their formal adoption all specific proposals for research to be instituted.

3. No research report shall be published by the National Bureau until the President has sent each member of the Board a notice that a manuscript is recommended for publication and that in the President's opinion it is suitable for publication in accordance with the principles of the National Bureau. Such notification will include an abstract or summary of the manuscript's content and a response form for use by those Directors who desire a copy of the manuscript for review. Each manuscript shall contain a summary drawing attention to the nature and treatment of the problem studied, the character of the data and their utilization in the report, and the main conclusions reached.

4. For each manuscript so submitted, a special committee of the Directors (including Directors Emeriti) shall be appointed by majority agreement of the President and Vice Presidents (or by the Executive Committee in case of inability to decide on the part of the President and Vice Presidents), consisting of three Directors selected as nearly as may be one from each general division of the Board. The names of the special manuscript committee shall be stated to each Director when notice of the proposed publication is submitted to him. It shall be the duty of each member of the special committee to read the manuscript. If each member of the manuscript committee signifies his approval within thirty days of the transmittal of the manuscript, the report may be published. If at the end of that period any member of the manuscript committee withholds his approval, the President shall then notify each member of the Board, requesting approval or disapproval of publication, and thirty days additional shall be granted for this purpose. The manuscript shall then not be published unless at least a majority of the entire Board who shall have voted on the proposal within the time fixed or the receipt of votes shall have approved.

5. No manuscript may be published, though approved by each member of the special manuscript committee, until forty-five days have elapsed from the transmittal of the report in manuscript form. The interval is allowed for the receipt of any memorandum of dissent or reservation, together with a brief statement of his reasons, that any member may wish to express; and such memorandum of dissent or reservation shall be published with the manuscript if he so desires. Publication does not, however, imply that each member of the Board has read the manuscript, or that either members of the Board in general or the special committee have passed on its validity in every detail.

6. Publications of the National Bureau issued for informational purposes concerning the work of the Bureau and its staff, or issued to inform the public of activities of Bureau staff, and volumes issued as a result of various conferences involving the National Bureau shall contain a specific disclaimer noting that such publication has not passed through the normal review procedures required in this resolution. The Executive Committee of the Board is charged with review of all such publications from time to time to ensure that they do not take on the character of formal research reports of the National Bureau, requiring formal Board approval.

7. Unless otherwise determined by the Board or exempted by the terms of paragraph 6, a copy of this resolution shall be printed in each National Bureau publication.

(Resolution adopted October 25, 1926, as revised through September 30, 1974)

*To students and colleagues at the University of Chicago
and at Columbia University who contributed so
much to my human capital.*

Contents

Part Two: Empirical Analysis

Part Three: Economy-Wide Changes

Tables

Charts

Preface to the Third Edition

In the recent presidential campaign, both President Clinton and former President Bush emphasized the importance of improving the education and skills of American workers. They did not even shy away from using the term "investing in human capital" to describe the process of improving the quality of the labor force. A dozen years ago, this terminology would have been inconceivable in a presidential campaign. The President has proposed to implement his campaign pledge by spending more on investments in college education and on-the-job training.

The interest shown in human capital, not only in the academic literature but also in discussions of public policy, and the continuing attention paid to the second edition of this book, encouraged me to prepare a third one. As in the transition from the first to the second edition, I have not changed anything in the previous editions. I have added four essays written since the second edition was published in 1975.

One is the Ryerson Lecture at the University of Chicago in 1989 that revisits human capital and surveys the field in a nontechnical way. I recommend it especially for the noneconomists who want a brief statement of the contribution of human capital analysis to the understanding of economic and social behavior.

The other three essays included in this edition are more technical, and cover applications of human capital analysis to the understanding of income inequality and economic growth. They form a new Part 3 at the end of the book.

Obviously, I had no expectation when the first edition was published in 1964 that a third edition would be prepared thirty years later. I continue to be amazed by the way the human capital field has grown from being highly controversial to one that has gained acceptance not only in economics, but also in other disciplines and among the general public. This is a tribute to the foresight and influence of the pioneers in this field—especially T. W. Schultz, Milton Friedman, and Jacob Mincer—and to the fact that from the very beginning, the analysis of human capital combined theory with attention to major real-world problems and issues.

I am indebted to Geoffrey Huck of the University of Chicago Press for encouragement that there would be a market for another edition, to Shirley Kessel for preparing the index for this edition, to Myrna Hieke, my secretary of many years, for help in putting the new materials together, and to Becky Kilburn for her usual excellent research assistance. I am especially indebted to colleagues and students at the University of Chicago for a friendly but critical atmosphere that does not allow anyone to live off of past laurels and accomplishments. I have never encountered a better environment for conducting research and for the development of new ideas to help explain the world we live in.

Preface to the First Edition

The origin of this study can be traced both to the finding that a substantial growth in income in the United States remains after the growth in physical capital and labor has been accounted for and to the emphasis of some economists on the importance of education in promoting economic development. My original intention was to shed some exploratory light on these issues by bringing together readily available information from Census reports on the incomes of persons with different amounts of education and from the Office of Education on the costs of education. For if education were economically important, I reasoned, money rates of return on education ought to be significant.

A long time has elapsed between the start, back in 1957, and the appearance of this monograph presenting the full analysis. During that time interest in the economics of education has mushroomed throughout the world and stimulated a profusion of research and policy proposals. Estimates have been made of the amounts invested in and the rates of return on education in both rich and poor countries. Perhaps some of the expanding interest can be traced to preliminary reports on the National Bureau study.[1]

This interest and further reflection, in turn, encouraged me to transform the original aim into a more ambitious undertaking. I became interested in the general theory of investment in human capital with its ramifications for a variety of economic phenomena. The theoretical analysis in turn led to an empirical examination of several other effects of education, such as those centering around the shapes of age-earnings and age-wealth profiles. Finally, the discussion of rates of return covers a wider variety of evidence, groups, time periods, and implications than in other studies.

---

[1] The previously published reports consist of "Underinvestment in College Education?" in *American Economic Review*, May 1960, and "Investment in Human Capital: A Theoretical Analysis," *Investment in Human Beings*, NBER Special Conference 15, supplement to *Journal of Political Economy*, October 1962.

Support, assistance, and criticism were generously provided by many institutions and persons during the course of this study. Let me first thank the Carnegie Corporation of New York for their two grants to the National Bureau to explore work on the economic effects of education. Leave from teaching duties was provided by the Ford Professorship at Columbia University during the academic year 1960–1961, and a Ford Faculty Fellowship during 1963–1964.

The study would have been impossible without the aid of a series of unusually able and conscientious research assistants. Major contributions were made by Rosanne Cole, Linda Kee, and Eugenia Scandrett, with additional assistance from Mary Holman Faden, Shirley Johnson, and June Cohn.

T. W. Schultz, the major figure in the economics of education, has been liberal with encouragement and most helpful with criticism. I feel greatly indebted to him, and would like to record my appreciation here. Jacob Mincer has been exceedingly helpful in countless discussions and on numerous drafts with suggestions, criticisms, and that intangible asset—enthusiasm.

The National Bureau reading committee played an important role in improving the content. I am indebted to George J. Stigler, Richard Easterlin, Albert Fishlow, Milton Friedman, and Zvi Griliches. Many others commented on all or parts of various drafts. I would like to acknowledge the helpful contributions of M. Blaug, Arthur F. Burns, Edward F. Denison, Evsey Domar, Solomon Fabricant, Victor R. Fuchs, Leo Goodman, W. Lee Hansen, Hendrick Houthakker, C. Harry Kahn, James N. Morgan, Selma Mushkin, Alice Rivlin, and of various participants in the Labor Workshop at Columbia University. Members of the National Bureau Board of Directors who provided useful comments were V. W. Bladen, Marion B. Folsom, W. Allen Wallis, and Joseph H. Willits.

I am grateful to the editorial staff of the National Bureau, especially to Marie-Christine Culbert for her detailed and incisive comments. H. Irving Forman skillfully drew the charts.

Human Capital

CHAPTER I

Introduction to the Second Edition[1]

In the preface to the first edition, written about a decade ago, I remarked that in the preceding few years "interest in the economics of education has mushroomed throughout the world." The mushrooming has continued unabated; a bibliography on the economics of education prepared in 1957 would have contained less than 50 entries, whereas one issued in 1964 listed almost 450 entries and its second edition in 1970 listed over 1300 entries.[2] Moreover, this bibliography excludes the economic literature on health, migration, and other nonschooling investments in human capital, which has expanded even faster.[3]

[1] I am indebted for helpful suggestions to Robert Michael, Victor Fuchs, and William Landes.

[2] See M. Blaug, *Economics of Education*, 2nd ed., London, 1970.

[3] I do not attempt to summarize or survey this growing body of literature on investments in human capital. A number of surveys and collections of essays have been published recently and the interested reader is referred to these. See, for example, UNESCO, *Readings in the Economics of Education*, United Nations Educational, Scientific and Cultural Organization, Paris, France, 1968; M. Blaug, *Economics of Education*, Elmsford, N.Y., 1970; B. F. Kiker, *Investment in Human Capital*, Columbia, S.C., 1971. Within the National Bureau of Economic Research, there have been three recent surveys of certain aspects of this literature; see Jacob Mincer, "The Distribution of Labor Incomes: A Survey with Special Reference to the Human Capital Approach," *Journal of Economic Literature*, 8, 1, March 1970; Finis Welch, "The NBER Approach to Human Resources Problems," *NBER An-*

This sustained interest in human capital and the continuing attention shown to the first edition of this book has encouraged me to issue a second edition. Nothing in the first edition has been changed; even the errors remain, conspicuous as they are to me now.[4] I have, however, incorporated three additional papers written within the first few years after the publication of the first edition. One of these three additions has not previously been published and another has not been readily available.

Chapter II developed an analysis of postschool investment and used it to explain age-earnings profiles and to interpret data on earnings per hour. That chapter also introduced a distinction between specific and general training to explain the relation between job skills and labor turnover, and the "hoarding" of labor during cyclical swings in business. These concepts have spawned a large and important literature that has successfully explained many aspects of the labor market in the United States and elsewhere.[5]

Chapter III introduced an analysis of the accumulation of human capital over the life cycle to explain, among other things, the shape of age-earnings profiles, the concentration of investments at earlier ages, and the personal distribution of earnings. This chapter also helped stimulate a large and empirically relevant literature.[6]

---

nual Report, September 1971; and Theodore W. Schultz, "Human Capital: Policy Issues and Research Opportunities," in *Human Resources,* Fiftieth Anniversary Colloquium, Vol. VI, NBER, 1972.

[4] Let me mention only two here. In the adjustment (in Appendix A, section 1C) to determine what earnings would have been if nobody had been unemployed, I used the duration of unemployment; this was incorrect because I had, and used, information on the fraction unemployed. (I am indebted to Robert Solow for pointing out this error.) Fortunately, a correct adjustment gives only slightly different results from the incorrect one used. There is a more serious error in my discussion of the riskiness of investments in education (Chapter IV, section 4). I ignored the then developing literature on optimal portfolios, and did not derive my measure of marginal risk—the variance in the rate of return—from an analysis of utility maximization. (I am indebted to Lawrence Olson for pointing out these difficulties to me.)

[5] For a sampling of this literature, see Donald O. Parsons, "Specific Human Capital: An Application to Quit Rates and Layoff Rates," *Journal of Political Economy,* 80, 6, 1120–1143 (November-December 1972); Sherwin Rosen, "Learning and Experience in the Labor Market," *Journal of Human Resources,* 7, 3, Summer 1972, pp. 326–342; Lester Telser, *Competition, Collusion, and Game Theory,* Chicago, 1972; Masatoshi Kuratani, "A Theory of Training, Earnings, and Employment: An Application to Japan," Ph.D. dissertation, Columbia University, 1973; and L. Landes, "Male-Female Wage Differentials by Occupation," Ph.D. dissertation, Columbia University, 1973.

[6] See, for example, Jacob Mincer, "On-the-Job Training: Costs, Returns, and Some Implications," *Journal of Political Economy,* 70, 5, Part 2, October 1962, pp. 50–79; Yoram Ben-Porath, "The Production of Human Capital and the Life Cycle of Earnings," *Journal of Political Economy,* 75, 4, August 1967, Part I, pp. 352–

The personal distribution of earnings is partly determined by the distribution of, and the returns from, human capital. Mincer is responsible for the pioneering analysis that relates the distribution of earnings to human capital.[7] Section 3 of Chapter III extended his analysis by relating the distribution of earnings explicitly to rates of return and investment costs.

The additional material added in the second edition includes a portion of a paper, written jointly with Barry R. Chiswick,[8] which provides a convenient formulation for statistical estimation of the relation between the log of earnings, rates of return to human capital, and the time spent investing in human capital. Regression equations derived from this formulation are developed to estimate the contribution of schooling to earnings inequality in the United States, especially its contribution to the difference in earnings inequality between the South and the North. This line of empirical analysis has more recently been extended to include postschool investment in a major study by Mincer,[9] and in other studies as well.[10]

In the first edition, although Chapter III assumed that individuals maximize their well-being as they accumulate human capital over their lifetime, no explicit model of utility or wealth maximization was developed. Therefore, the factors determining the distribution of investments at different ages were not explicitly analyzed. In my Woytinsky Lecture, published in 1967 and reprinted here as an addendum to Chapter III (see p. 94), a model of wealth maximization is developed that explains the distribution of investments, in particular the decline in investments over time, by (a) the decline in benefits from additional capital as fewer years of life remain, and (b) the rise in

365; Michael Grossman, "On the Concept of Health Capital and the Demand for Health," *Journal of Political Economy*, 80, 2, March-April 1972, pp. 223–255; and Yoram Weiss, "Investment in Graduate Education," *American Economic Review*, 61, December 1971, pp. 833–852.

[7] See Jacob Mincer, "Investment in Human Capital and Personal Income Distribution," *Journal of Political Economy*, August 1958.

[8] Gary S. Becker and Barry R. Chiswick, "Education and the Distribution of Earnings," *American Economic Review*, May 1966.

[9] See his *Schooling, Experience, and Earnings*, NBER, 1974.

[10] See, for example, Barry R. Chiswick, *Income Inequality: Regional Analyses within a Human Capital Framework*, NBER, 1974; Thomas Johnson, "Returns from Investment in Human Capital," *American Economic Review*, 60, 4, September 1970, pp. 546–560; C. Michael Rahm, "The Occupational Wage Structure," Ph.D. dissertation, Columbia University, 1971; Jacob Mincer and Solomon Polachek, "Family Investments in Human Capital: Earnings of Women," *Journal of Political Economy*, 82, 2, March-April 1974; and Frank Stafford and G. Johnson, "The Earnings and Promotion of Women Faculty," Department of Economics, University of Michigan, mimeo, February 1973.

investment costs because foregone earnings rise as human capital is accumulated.[11]

Here the analysis goes behind the distribution of human capital and rates of return and examines the underlying distribution of opportunities and abilities. Since the observed distribution of earnings results from the interaction of these underlying distributions, the relative importance of opportunities and abilities is not easily "identified," although some tests are suggested. I have added a supplement to this discussion of "identifiability" that is motivated by many recent attempts to assess the independent effect of family background on earnings. It shows why these attempts understate the effect of background, and overstate the effect of human capital, on earnings, perhaps by substantial amounts.

The Woytinsky lecture also analyzes the effects on inequality and skewness in earnings of more equal opportunity, minimum schooling legislation, and "objective" selection of applicants to scarce places in schools. In it I attempt to explain, too, why earnings are more equally distributed and less skewed than incomes from nonhuman capital. Although the formulation has some unsolved analytical difficulties, I believe that this paper opens up a promising line of investigation that has received insufficient attention.[12]

The models of capital accumulation in the lecture—and in Ben-Porath's paper and several subsequent ones—have several limitations. Since the total hours supplied to the market sector are taken as given, these models do not consider the interaction between changes in wage rates over the life cycle resulting from the accumulation of human capital and the optimal allocation of time between the market and nonmarket sectors. Moreover, human capital is assumed to affect only earnings and the production of additional human capital, and to have no direct effect on utility or consumption.

These and some other restrictions are relaxed in the final essay added to this second edition. This paper, which I wrote and circulated in 1967 but never published, builds on the new approach to

---

[11] At about the same time, a similar but more rigorously formulated model was independently developed by Ben-Porath (*op. cit.*).

[12] However, see the discussions in Mincer, "The Distribution of Labor Incomes: A Survey with Special Reference to the Human Capital Approach," *Journal of Economic Literature*, 8, 1, March 1970, pp. 1–26; Barry Chiswick, "Minimum Schooling Legislation and the Cross-Sectional Distribution of Income," *Economic Journal*, 79, 3.5, September 1969, pp. 495–507; and Sherwin Rosen, "Income Generating Functions and Capital Accumulation," Harvard Institute of Economic Research, June 1973, unpublished.

household behavior. In this approach, households produce the commodities that enter their utility functions by combining market-purchased goods and services, their own time, and human capital and other environmental variables.[13] With this approach I consider the uses of an individual's time at different ages; in particular I focus on the allocation of time to three activities: the production of nonmarket commodities (nonmarket time); the production of human capital (investment time); and the production of earnings (labor market time). I am also able to treat systematically a direct effect of human capital on consumption by permitting it to affect the efficiency of household production.[14]

The empirical analysis from the first edition is left intact, even though a substantial body of additional evidence has been accumulated since then, because the major findings have stood up remarkably well to the additional evidence. These findings include:

1. The average money rate of return on a college education to white males is between 11 and 13 per cent, with higher rates on a high-school education, and still higher rates on an elementary-school education. This range for the rate of return on college education, as well as the decline in the rate with successive stages of schooling, has also been found in many subsequent studies.[15]

2. The higher earnings of, say, college graduates compared to high-school graduates are partly due to the college graduate's greater ability, ambition, health, and better educated and more successful parents. I concluded from an examination of several kinds of evidence that differences in these and related traits explain a relatively small part of the earnings differentials between college and high-school graduates (but a larger part of the differentials at lower education levels). Hence, rates of return to college graduates that are unadjusted for "selectivity" are not bad guides to the true rates. Subsequent studies have adjusted

---

[13] The approach is developed in my "A Theory of the Allocation of Time," *Economic Journal*, September 1965. A recent exposition can be found in Robert T. Michael and Gary S. Becker, "The New Approach to Consumer Behavior," *Swedish Journal of Economics*, 75, 4, 1973.

[14] A more extensive treatment of this subject, including some empirical work, can be found in Robert T. Michael, *The Effect of Education on Efficiency in Consumption*, NBER, 1972.

[15] See, for example, W. L. Hansen, "Total and Private Rates of Return to Investment in Schooling," *Journal of Political Economy*, 71, April 1963, pp. 128–140; G. Hanoch, "An Economic Analysis of Earnings and Schooling," *Journal of Human Resources*, 2, Summer 1967, pp. 310–329; and T. W. Schultz, *Investment in Human Capital*, New York, 1971.

for selectivity with a variety of data sources, and their conclusions usually have been quite similar to mine.[16]

Several papers in recent years have tried to formalize the rather old notion that education is largely a device to screen out abler persons for employers, and that, therefore, only a small part of earnings differentials by education can be attributed to the education per se.[17] *Even if schooling also works in this way, the significance of private rates of return to education is not affected at all.* Moreover, it should be noted that virtually no effort has been made to determine the empirical importance of screening. Furthermore, several major empirical issues must be resolved if screening is to be the primary explanation of earnings differentials. For example, college would be a horrendously expensive "employment agency": each year of college cost a typical individual in 1970 at least $6000 and cost society at least $1500 more than that. Surely, a year on the job or a systematic and intensive interview and applicant-testing program must be a much cheaper and more effective way to screen. My own opinion is that schooling-as-screening must occur in a world with imperfect information, but is a relatively minor influence in determining earnings differentials by education.

3. The evidence I examined indicated that rates of return on college and high-school education declined from about 1900 to 1940, but not after 1940, even though the relative number of college and high-school graduates also grew rapidly after 1940. I concluded that demand shifted more toward educated persons after 1940, partly due to the rapid growth of expenditures on R. and D., military technology, and services. The absence of any decline in rates of return after 1940

---

[16] For a sampling, see Orley Ashenfelter *et al.,* "Graduate Education, Ability, and Earnings," *Review of Economics and Statistics,* February 1968, pp. 78–86; Zvi Griliches and W. M. Mason, "Education, Income, and Ability," *Journal of Political Economy,* 80, May-June 1972, pp. S74–S103; W. L. Hansen, B. A. Weisbrod, and W. J. Scanlon, "Schooling and Earnings of Low Achievers," *American Economic Review,* 60, 3, June 1970, pp. 409–418; B. Weisbrod and P. Karpoff, "Monetary Returns to College Education, Student Ability and College Quality," *Review of Economics and Statistics,* November 1968; and A. Leibowitz, "Home Investments in Children," *Journal of Political Economy,* 82, 2, Supplement, March-April 1974, pp. S111–S131.

[17] See P. J. Taubman and T. J. Wales, "Higher Education, Mental Ability, and Screening," *Journal of Political Economy,* 8, 1, January-February 1973, pp. 28–55; M. Spence, "Market Signalling," Ph.D. dissertation, Department of Economics, Harvard University, 1972; J. E. Stiglitz, "The Theory of 'Screening,' Education, and the Distribution of Income," Cowles Foundation Discussion Paper #354, Yale University, March 1973; K. J. Arrow, "Higher Education as a Filter," in K. Lumsden, ed., *Efficiency in Universities,* New York, Elsevier, 1974.

has been confirmed in a few subsequent studies.[18] Perhaps the current (1973) weak market for highly skilled manpower is the beginning of a resumption of the earlier decline. Note, however, that the absence of any decline after 1940 is not unique in American history; skill differentials, and thus presumably rates of return on education, apparently did not decline from 1860 to 1890.[19]

4. Average money rates of return on education are not the same for all groups; they are higher on college education for urban white males than for black or rural males, and higher for black than for white women. The evidence I examined suggested that these differences in rates led to corresponding differences in the fraction of high-school graduates going on to college. This effect of rates of return on the incentive to acquire education has been found in other studies.[20] For example, a growth in the monetary return to blacks from a college education in the 1960s has apparently sizably increased their number going to college, as well as shifted their fields of specialization: out of professions that cater to segregated black markets, such as clergy and medicine, and into more integrated professions, such as business and engineering.[21]

5. In Chapter VII, I calculated age–human-wealth profiles for different education classes that show the relation between age and the present value of future earnings, and used them to understand, among other things, life-cycle variations in savings. Some studies have continued this analysis of the linkage between the accumulations of human and nonhuman wealth.[22] I also drew on evidence for slaves, the one example of an explicit market that trades and prices human capital stocks rather than simply the services yielded by these stocks. A major and insightful study has recently appeared that interprets the market

[18] See Z. Griliches, "Notes on the Role of Education in Production Functions and Growth Accounting," in *Education, Income and Human Capital*, W. L. Hansen, ed., NBER, 1970; and F. Welch, "Education in Production," *Journal of Political Economy*, 78, 1, January-February 1970.

[19] See C. Long, *Wages and Earnings in the United States*, 1860–1890, Princeton, 1960.

[20] See R. B. Freeman, *The Market for College-Trained Manpower*, Cambridge, 1971.

[21] See R. B. Freeman, "Changes in the Labor Market for Black Americans, 1948–1972," Brookings Papers on Economic Activity 1, Washington, D.C., 1973, pp. 67–120; and Finis Welch, "Education and Racial Discrimination," in O. Ashenfelter and A. Rees, eds., *Discrimination in Labor Markets*, Princeton, 1973.

[22] See G. Ghez and G. S. Becker, *The Allocation of Time and Goods over the Life Cycle*, NBER, 1974; and I. Ehrlich and U. Ben-Zion, "A Model of Productive Saving," mimeo, University of Chicago, 1972.

for slaves in the United States in terms of the theory of investment in human capital.[23]

The continuing vigor of the research in human capital is increasing testimony that this area of study is not one of the many fads that pass through the economics profession, but an important and lasting contribution. The major reason, in my judgment, is that the theoretical and empirical analyses have been closely integrated, with the theory often inspired by empirical findings.[24] The intimate relation of theory and observation has built a strong foundation for future work that cannot easily be torn down or ignored.

Therefore, I am confident that the analysis of human capital will continue to be a fruitful field of research. Although important studies of the effects of human capital in the market sector can be expected, I anticipate that the excitement will be generated by studies of its effects in the nonmarket sector. Major insights into the determinants of fertility, the production of health, the benefits from schooling to women who do not participate in the labor force, the productivity of marriage, and other topics will result from an integration of the theory of human capital with the allocation of time, household production functions, and the theory of choice.[25]

In short, the prospects for the analysis of human capital look almost as bright to me today as they did during its salad days.

---

[23] R. W. Fogel and S. Engerman, *Time on the Cross*, Boston, 1974.

[24] By contrast, in some other areas of research, such as research on economic growth, much of the theory seems to have developed quite independently of any empirical studies.

[25] For some beginnings, see Michael, *op. cit.*; Grossman, *op. cit.*; and the essays in T. W. Schultz, ed., *Economics of the Family: Marriage, Children, and Human Capital*, New York, NBER, 1975.

Introduction to the First Edition

Some activities primarily affect future well-being; the main impact of others is in the present. Some affect money income and others psychic income, that is, consumption. Sailing primarily affects consumption, on-the-job training primarily affects money income, and a college education could affect both. These effects may operate either through physical resources or through human resources. This study is concerned with activities that influence future monetary and psychic income by increasing the resources in people. These activities are called investments in human capital.

The many forms of such investments include schooling, on-the-job training, medical care, migration, and searching for information about prices and incomes. They differ in their effects on earnings and consumption, in the amounts typically invested, in the size of returns, and in the extent to which the connection between investment and return is perceived. But all these investments improve skills, knowledge, or health, and thereby raise money or psychic incomes.

Recent years have witnessed intensive concern with and research on investment in human capital, much of it contributed or stimulated by T. W. Schultz. The main motivating factor has probably been a realization that the growth of physical capital, at least as conventionally measured, explains a relatively small part of the growth of income in most countries. The search for better explanations has led to improved measures of physical capital and to an interest in less tangible entities, such as technological change and human capital. Also behind this concern is the strong dependence of modern military technology on education and skills, the rapid growth in expenditures on education and health, the age-old quest for an understanding of the personal distribution of income, the recent growth in unemployment in the United States, the Leontief scarce-factor paradox, and several other important economic problems.

The result has been the accumulation of a tremendous amount of circumstantial evidence testifying to the economic importance of human capital, especially of education. Probably the most impressive piece of evidence is that more highly educated and skilled persons almost always tend to earn more than others. This is true of developed countries as different as the United States and the Soviet Union, of underdeveloped countries as different as India and Cuba, and of the United States one hundred years ago as well as today. Moreover, few if any countries have achieved a sustained period of economic development without having invested substantial amounts in their labor force, and most studies that have attempted quantitative assessments of contributions to growth have assigned an important role to investment in human capital. Again, inequality in the distribution of earnings and income is generally positively related to inequality in education and other training. To take a final example, unemployment tends to be strongly related, usually inversely, to education.

Passions are easily aroused on this subject and even people who are generally in favor of education, medical care, and the like often dislike the phrase "human capital" and still more any emphasis on its economic effects. They are often the people who launch the most bitter attacks on research on human capital, partly because they fear that emphasis on the "material" effects of human capital detracts from its "cultural" effects, which to them are more important. Those denying the economic importance of education and other investments in human capital have attacked the circumstantial evidence in its favor. They argue that the correlation between earnings and investment in human capital is due to a correlation between ability and investment in human capital, or to the singling out of the most favorable groups, such as white male college graduates, and to the consequent neglect of women, dropouts, nonwhites, or high-school graduates. They consider the true correlation to be very weak, and, therefore, a poor guide and of little help to people investing in human capital. The association between education and economic development or between inequality in education and income is attributed to the effect of income on education, considering education as a consumption good, and hence of no greater causal significance than the association between automobile ownership and economic development or between the inequality in ownership and incomes.

This study hopes to contribute to knowledge in this area by going far beyond circumstantial evidence and analysis. Part One treats the theory of investment in human capital in detail and reveals its importance through the wide variety of economic phenomena that it encompasses. Chapter II derives a number of important effects of such investments on earnings and employment, while Chapter III shows how to estimate the total amount invested and how it changes when the anticipated gains change.

Part Two presents various empirical tests of the theoretical analysis. Chapters IV and V estimate the gains from college education in the United States in recent years. Costs as well as returns are considered, and estimates are presented not only for selected groups, such as white male college graduates, but also for typical college entrants (sections 1 and 3 of Chapter IV). Detailed attention is paid to the effect of the correlation between education and ability, and to the variation in the gain from college (sections 2 and 4 of Chapter IV). Social as well as private gains are estimated, and both are compared to corresponding estimates for physical capital (Chapter V).

Chapter VI briefly extends the discussion to high-school education, considering social as well as private costs and returns, and the effect of differential ability (section 1). This chapter also tries to discover the secular trend in the United States during the twentieth century in the economic effects of high-school and college education (section 2).

Chapter VII tests the implications of the theoretical analysis concerning the effect of human capital on the shape of age-earnings profiles (section 1). Also considered is the effect on the relation between age and the discounted value of subsequent earnings, which are called age-wealth profiles. These profiles are applied to the study of life-cycle variations in savings and consumption, and in a few other ways (section 2).

Perhaps it is best to conclude the introduction by emphasizing that the attention paid to the economic effects of education and other human capital in this study is not in any way meant to imply that other effects are unimportant, or less important than the economic ones. The advantages of a division of labor are no less real here than they are in research in general. I would like to urge simply that the economic effects are important and have been relatively neglected, at least until recently.

CHAPTER II

Human Capital Revisited[1]

1. Introduction

A Ryerson lecturer is supposed to tell the audience what he or she has been doing to earn a living from the University. Therefore it is an appropriate occasion for me to review what is known about human capital, especially the progress during the quarter-century since I published a book with that title. What has been called the human capital "revolution" began about three decades ago. Its pioneers include Ted Schultz, Jacob Mincer, Milton Friedman, Sherwin Rosen, and several others associated with the University of Chicago.

To most of you, capital means a bank account, one hundred shares of IBM, assembly lines, or steel plants in the Chicago area (especially during a Ryerson lecture). These are all forms of capital in the sense that they yield income and other useful outputs over long periods of time.

But I am going to talk about a different kind of capital. Schooling, a computer training course, expenditures on medical care, and lectures on the virtues of punctuality and honesty are capital too in the sense that they improve health, raise earnings, or add to a person's appreciation of

[1] I appreciate the helpful comments of Guity Nashat, Sherwin Rosen, and George Stigler and the assistance of David Meltzer.

15

literature over much of his or her lifetime. Consequently, it is fully in keeping with the capital concept as traditionally defined to say that expenditures on education, training, medical care, etc., are investments in capital. However, these produce human, not physical or financial, capital because you cannot separate a person from his or her knowledge, skills, health, or values the way it is possible to move financial and physical assets while the owner stays put. This embodiment of human capital in people is depressingly illustrated by the reactions of Hong Kong residents to the takeover of Hong Kong in 1997 by China. Many local people are busy protecting against China's policies by selling off some of their local financial and physical assets in order to invest in safer foreign securities and property. At the same time, however, computer experts, top management, and other skilled personnel are leaving Hong Kong in droves to seek citizenship elsewhere. They cannot reduce the risk to their human capital from China by investing only part of the human capital abroad; they must go where their capital goes.

It may seem odd now, but I hesitated a while before deciding to call my book *Human Capital*—and even hedged the risk by using a long subtitle. In the early days, many people were criticizing this term and the underlying analysis because they believed it treated people like slaves or machines. My, how the world has changed! The name and analysis are now readily accepted by most people not only in all the social sciences, but even in the media. I was surprised when a few months ago *Business Week* magazine had a cover story titled "Human Capital." And more amazing still, this has been their most popular cover story in several decades.

However, I should add that the concept of human capital remains suspect within academic circles that organize their thinking about social problems around a belief in the exploitation of labor by capital. It is easy to appreciate the problems created for this view by the human capital concept. For if capital exploits labor, does human capital exploit labor too—in other words, do some workers exploit other workers? And are skilled workers and unskilled workers pitted against each other in the alleged class conflict between labor and capital? If governments are to expropriate all capital to end such conflict, should they also expropriate human capital, so that governments would take over ownership of workers as well?

You can see why an idea developed to understand the economic and social world has been thrust into ideological discussions. Yet the concept of human capital has been popular in Communist countries. My book and those by Schultz and others on human capital are extensively used in the Soviet Union, Eastern Europe, and China. Even before the recent reforms, economists and planners there had no trouble with the concept of investing capital in people.

I will try to avoid technical analysis and jargon, and concentrate on showing how the analysis of investments in human capital helps in understanding a large and varied class of behavior not only in the Western world, but also in developing countries and countries with very different cultures. My discussion follows modern economics and assumes that these investments usually are rational responses to a calculus of expected costs and benefits.

2. Education and Training

Education and training are the most important investments in human capital. My book showed, and so have many other studies since then, that high school and college education in the United States greatly raise a person's income, even after netting out direct and indirect costs of schooling, and after adjusting for the better family backgrounds and greater abilities of more educated people. Similar evidence is now available for many points in time from over one hundred countries with different cultures and economic systems. The earnings of more educated people are almost always well above average, although the gains are generally larger in less-developed countries. Consider the differences in average earnings between college and high school graduates in the United States during the past fifty years. After being reasonably stable at between 40 and 50 percent until the early 1960s, they rose during that decade and then fell rather sharply. This fall during the 1970s led some economists and the media to worry about "overeducated Americans" (see Freeman, 1976). The concept of human capital itself fell into some disrepute.

But as Kevin Murphy and Finis Welch document in a recent study (1989), the monetary gains from a college education rose sharply during the 1980s to the highest level during these fifty years. The earnings advantage of high school graduates over high school dropouts also increased. Talk about overeducated Americans has vanished, and it has been replaced by concern once more about whether the United States provides adequate quality and quantity of education and other training.

These concerns are stimulated by tough economic competition from a renewed Europe, Japan, Korea, and other Asian countries, by sluggish rates of productivity advance in the United States during the past fifteen years, by a large drop in SAT scores, and by the dismal performance of American high school students on international tests in mathematics.

For those who prefer a monetary bottom line, trends in the earnings of young persons in the United States provide good reason for concern about the preparation they are receiving. The trend has been disastrous for the 15 percent of all students and much larger percentage of inner-city blacks who fail to complete high school. Their real wage rates have fallen by more than 30 percent since the early 1970s. Whether because of school problems, family instability, or other forces, young people without a college education are not being adequately prepared for work in modern economies.

A Labor Department commission on labor quality, of which I am a member, is considering what can be done to improve the quality of workers in the United States. The concerns that led to the creation of this commission have stimulated renewed academic interest in the analysis of human capital, which illustrates how research in social sciences responds, sometimes excessively, to public policy issues.

The fraction of high school graduates who entered college fell during the middle of the seventies when benefits from a college education dropped, and it rose again in the eighties when the benefits greatly increased. This caused an unexpected boom in college enrollments during the past few years, despite the relatively few people who are reaching college age. So, alas, the large rise in applications to our College in recent years is not due solely to more widespread appreciation of the superb education it provides. Many educators expected enrollments in the eighties to decline not only for demographic reasons, but also because college tuition was rising rapidly. They were wrong because they failed to appreciate that benefits from college rose even faster than costs, and that high school graduates respond to changes in both benefits and costs.

One might believe that enrollments in college would be easy to predict since the number of persons graduating from high school can be predicted quite closely. But demographic-based college enrollment forecasts have been wide of the mark during the past twenty years, as Steve Stigler and I, especially Steve, showed in a subcommittee report a few years ago to the Baker Commission. Such forecasts ignored the changing incentives to women, blacks, and older persons to enroll in college.

That human capital investments tend to respond rationally to benefits and costs is clearly indicated by changes in the education of women. Prior to the 1960s in the United States, women were more likely than men to graduate from high school but less likely to continue on to college. Women shunned math, sciences, economics, and law, and gravitated toward teaching, home economics, foreign languages, and literature. Since relatively few married women continued to work for pay, they rationally chose an education that helped in household production and no doubt also in the marriage market. All this has changed radically. The enormous increase in the participation of married women is the most important labor force change during the past twenty-five years. Many women now take little time off from their jobs even to have children. As a result, the value to women of market skills has increased enormously, and they are shunning traditional "women's fields" to enter accounting, law, medicine, engineering, and other subjects that pay well. Indeed, women now comprise one-third or so of enrollments in law, business, and medical schools, and many home economics departments have either shut down or are emphasizing the "new home economics," which is a true branch of economics.

The same trends in women's education are found in Great Britain, France, Scandinavia, Taiwan, Japan, Mexico, and other countries with large increases in the labor force participation of women, even when attitudes toward women differ greatly from those now prevalent in Europe and the United States. Whenever the labor force participation of married women has increased sharply, changes in the gains from work for pay have had a more powerful effect on the behavior of women than have traditional ideas about the proper role of women.

Job opportunities for women at first improved slowly as they started to move up in business and the professions during the past several decades. But the trend accelerated sharply after the late 1970s. The ratio of the earnings of full-time working women and men has increased more rapidly since 1979 than during any previous period in our history, and women are becoming much more prominent in many highly skilled jobs. Improvements in the economic position of black women have been especially rapid, and they now earn just about as much as white women.

Although the civil rights movement clearly contributed to greater job opportunities for women and other minorities, it is far from the whole story. This can be seen from the fact that women progressed most rapidly under the Reagan administration, which was opposed to affirmative action and did not have an active Civil Rights Commission. In my judgment, women advanced primarily because of their greater attachment to the labor force. This in turn was stimulated by a large decline in fertility, a rapid increase in divorce, and the growing importance of the service sector. Human capital analysis assumes that schooling raises earnings and productivity mainly by providing knowledge, skills, and a way of analyzing problems. An alternative view, however, denies that schooling does much to improve productivity, and instead it stresses "credentialism"—that degrees and education convey information about the underlying abilities, persistence, and other valuable traits of people.

According to extreme versions of this line of analysis, earnings of, for example, college graduates exceed those of high school graduates not because college education raises productivity, but because more productive students go on to college.

Credentialism obviously exists. But many kinds of evidence suggest that credentialism does not explain most of the positive association between earnings and schooling.

The main problem with credentialism is that companies do not want information on success at schoolwork, but on abilities and performance in the context of working life: the discipline imposed by factories, the need to please customers and get along with fellow employees, and so forth. Success in the flexible, individualistic, and rather undisciplined university atmosphere in most countries and in high schools in the United States does not convey much relevant information. I tell my classes that eccentrics and nuts can last much longer as students than as workers, and they respond that the same is true of professors.

A cheaper and more efficient way to provide information to employers is for teenagers to enter directly into the labor force, as they did prior to the industrial revolution. Far more would be learned about their work-related abilities and other characteristics after six years of work experience than after six additional years of schooling. High school and college education has spread extensively in modern economies because the additional knowledge and information acquired in school is so important in technologically advanced economies. I should add that advocates of the credentialism approach have become rather silent in recent years with the growing concerns about schools and labor quality in the United States.

Of course, learning and training also occur outside of schools, especially on jobs. Even college graduates are not well prepared for the labor market when they leave school, and they are fitted into their jobs through formal and informal training programs. The amount of on-the-job training ranges from an hour or so at simple jobs like dishwashing to several years at complicated tasks like engineering in an auto plant. The limited information available indicates that on-the-job training is an important source of the very large increase in earnings as workers gain greater experience at work. And recent bold estimates by Jacob Mincer suggest that the total investment in on-the-job training may be almost as large as the investment in education.

After a few years of frequent job changes, most workers settle down and remain with the same company for a long time. Workers and their employers get bonded together in large part because of the on-the-job learning and training. Therefore, it is not surprising that job changes are common among unskilled workers and uncommon among skilled workers. It also appears that job changes are much less frequent in Japan than in the United States mainly because on-the-job investments in workers are greater in Japan. My friends in the humanities like Dick Stern may complain that so far I have only mentioned "money," or they might say "mere money." Is there any place in human capital theory for education to appreciate literature, culture and the good life? Fortunately, nothing in the concept of human capital implies that monetary incentives need be more important than cultural and nonmonetary ones.

Obviously, it is much easier to quantify the monetary side, but, nevertheless, progress has been made on other aspects. Many studies show that education promotes health, reduces smoking, raises the propensity to vote, improves birth control knowledge, and stimulates the appreciation of classical music, literature, and even tennis. In an ingenious study that relies heavily on economic theory, Bob Michael (1972) quantifies some non-monetary benefits of education. His results and those of others indicate that such benefits of schooling are quite large, although for most people they are apparently smaller than monetary benefits.

3. Human Capital and the Family

No discussion of human capital can omit the influence of families on the knowledge, skills, values, and habits of their children. Parents who severely beat their children cause lasting damage, while at the other end of the spectrum, sympathetic and firm parents help motivate their children.

Large differences among young children grow over time with age and schooling because children learn more easily when they are better prepared. Therefore, even small differences among children in the preparation provided by their families are frequently multiplied over time into large differences when they are teenagers. This is why the labor market cannot do much for school dropouts who can hardly read and never developed good work habits, and why it is so difficult to devise policies to help these groups.

Parents have a large influence on the education, marital stability, and many other dimensions of their children's lives. The term "underclass" describes families in which low education, welfare dependence, early pregnancy, and marital instability pass from parents to children. In light of this, it is rather surprising that although earnings of parents and children are positively related, the relation is not strong. For example, if parents' earnings in the United States are 20 percent above the mean of their generation, the children's earnings tend to be less than 6 percent above the mean of their own generation. Earnings of parents and children appear to be a little more strongly related when parents are poorer.

It is easy to see why children's and parents' earnings may be closer in poorer families. Richer families can pay for the training of their children, including the earnings foregone when children spend time in training rather than at work. Many poorer parents would be willing to lend their children money to help them obtain further training if the parents could expect to get paid back later when they are old. But children may not carry out their part of the bargain, especially in highly mobile societies where children often live far from their parents.

One solution is for governments to lend money to students when their parents are unable or unwilling to finance the training. The federal government has developed an extensive loan program to help students finance college education. Unfortunately the program has serious flaws, including low caps on the maximum amounts that can be borrowed, misplaced and excessive subsidies, and shockingly high default rates. In addition to explicit loans, some direct subsidies to schools may, in effect, also be "loans" to students which they repay later with taxes that help finance support for the elderly. By combining publicly subsidized schooling with a social security system, countries may have found a very crude and indirect, but perhaps reasonably effective, way to provide loans to children that get repaid when the parents are old and collect retirement benefits (see Becker and Murphy, 1988).

Families divide their total spending on children between number of children and the amount spent per child. The number of children and spending per child tend to be negatively related. The reason is simple. An increased number of children raises the effective cost of adding to the spending on each child, because an additional dollar or hour of time spent on each child then means a larger total addition to spending. Similarly, an increase in the dollars or time spent on each child raises the cost of having an additional child. Consequently, even a modest tax on births can have a large negative effect on the number of children and a large positive effect on the amount spent on each child.

China imposed heavy, not modest, taxes and other penalties on large families during the past decade, especially in urban areas. It is revealing about the cross-cultural relevance of this analysis that sharp declines in urban fertility have been accompanied by discussions in the Chinese press of the "emperor child." This refers to only children who receive lavish toys and presents from their parents, and are pushed toward outstanding educational achievement.

This negative relation at the family level between number of children and spending per child implies a close and also usually negative relation at the aggregate level between population growth and investments in human capital. Differences among ethnic groups in the United States are fascinating. Groups with small families generally spend a lot on each child's education and training, while those with big families spend much less. The Japanese, Chinese, Jews, and Cubans have small families and the children become well educated, while Mexicans, Puerto Ricans, and blacks have big families and the education of children suffers. (I should add that the Mormons are an interesting exception, for they have both very large families and high levels of achievement). It should come as no surprise that children from the ethnic groups with small families and large investments in human capital typically rise faster and further in the United States' income-occupation hierarchy than do children from other groups.

Malthus' famous prediction that people marry earlier and birth rates rise when incomes increase was decisively contradicted by the industrial revolution, whose effects became evident only shortly after publication of the second edition of his book on population. This is a common paradox: a great book gets contradicted by events not long after publication. The contradiction to Malthus' theory is that fertility fell sharply, rather than rose, as per capita incomes grew in Great Britain, the United States, France, Germany, Sweden, and other Western countries. Rapid advances in education and other training accompanied the sharp declines in fertility. Parents did spend more on children when their incomes rose—as Malthus predicted—but they spent a lot more on each child and had fewer children, as human capital theory predicts.

Similar changes occur in other cultures when they experience rapid economic growth. Taiwan's birth rate was cut in half from 1960 to 1975, while the fraction of high school graduates doubled after Taiwan took off in the 1960s toward its remarkable economic growth. Mexico's birth rate did not fall much during its rapid economic growth in the 1950s and 1960s. But since 1975 birth rates have fallen by more than one-third, and school enrollments have expanded rapidly.

4. Human Capital and Economic Development

Economic analysis has no trouble explaining why, throughout history, few countries have experienced very long periods of persistent growth in income per person. For if per capita income growth is caused by the growth of land and physical capital per worker, diminishing returns from additional capital and land eventually eliminate further growth.

The puzzle, therefore, is not the lack of growth, but the fact that the United States, Japan, and many European countries have had continuing growth in per capita income during the past one hundred years and longer.

Presumably, the answer lies in the expansion of scientific and technical knowledge that raises the productivity of labor and other inputs in production. The systematic application of scientific knowledge to production of goods has greatly increased the value of education, technical schooling, and on-the-job training as the growth of knowledge has become embodied in people—in scientists, scholars, technicians, managers, and other contributors to output.

It is clear that all countries which have managed persistent growth in income have also had large increases in the education and training of their labor forces. First, elementary school education becomes universal, then high school education spreads rapidly, and finally children from middle income and poorer families begin going to college. A skeptic might respond that the expansion in education as countries get richer no more implies that education causes growth than does a larger number of dishwashers in richer countries imply that dishwashers are an engine of growth.

However, even economists know the difference between correlation and causation, and have developed rather straightforward methods for determining how much of income growth is caused by a growth in human capital. In an excellent study for the United States, Edward Denison (1985) finds that the increase in schooling of the average worker between 1929 and 1982 explains about one-fourth of the rise in per capita income during this period. He is unable to explain much of the remaining growth. I like to believe that this is mainly because he cannot measure the effects on earnings of improvements over time in health, on-the-job training, and other kinds of human capital.

The outstanding economic records of Japan, Taiwan, and other Asian economies in recent decades dramatically illustrate the importance of human capital to growth. Lacking natural resources—e.g., they import practically all their sources of energy—and facing discrimination from the West, these so-called Asian tigers grew rapidly by relying on a well-trained, educated, hard-working, and conscientious labor force. It surely is no accident, for example, that Japan's system of lifetime employment at large companies originated after World War II when they began to upgrade their technology rapidly partly by investing heavily in the training of employees. The lifetime system is not explained just by the traditional Japanese culture that emphasizes loyalty toward groups, for job changes in Japan were frequent during the first half of this century (see Hashimoto and Raisian, 1985).

Compelling evidence of the link between human capital and technology comes from agriculture. Education is of little use in traditional agriculture because farming methods and knowledge are then readily passed on from parents to children. Farmers in countries with traditional economies are among the least educated members of the labor force. By contrast, modern farmers must deal with hybrids, breeding methods, fertilizers, complicated equipment, and intricate futures markets for commodities. Education is of great value since it helps farmers adapt more quickly to new hybrids and other new technologies (see Welch, 1970). Therefore, it is no surprise that farmers are about as well educated as industrial workers in modern economies.

Education and training is also helpful in coping with changing technologies and advancing productivity in the manufacturing and service sectors. Recent studies show that more rapidly progressing industries do attract better-educated workers and provide greater training on the job (see Mincer and Higuchi, 1988; Gill, 1989).

5. Conclusions

We have reached the end of my visit. Perhaps I have succeeded in conveying the enormous energy devoted to the analysis of human capital during the past quarter-century and the impressive advances of analytical techniques and the accumulation of empirical regularities. Much is now known for many countries about the effects of education on earnings, occupation, employment, and unemployment of both men and women and various races and ethnic groups. Much too is known about the link between birth rates and investments in education and training, how families influence the human capital of their children, and the relation between investments in human capital and economic progress.

I indicated earlier that human capital analysis has been motivated partly by a desire to evaluate proposals to improve the quality of the work force through schooling, training, medical services, and child care. But its main purpose as far as I am concerned is to remove a little of the mystery from the economic and social world that we live in.

References

Becker, Gary S., and Kevin M. Murphy. "The Family and the State." *Journal of Law and Economics* 31 (1988): 1–18.

Denison, Edward F. *Trends in American Economic Growth, 1929–1982*. Washington, D.C.: The Brookings Institution, 1985.

Freeman, Richard. *The Overeducated American*. New York: Academic Press, 1976.

Gill, Indermit. "Technological Change, Education, and Obsolescence of Human Capital: Some Evidence for the U.S." University of Chicago, 1989.

Hashimoto, Masanori, and John Raisian. "Employment Tenure and Earnings Profiles in Japan and the United States." *American Economic Review* 75 (1985): 721–35.

Michael, Robert T. *The Effect of Education on Efficiency in Consumption.* New York: National Bureau of Economic Research, 1972.

Mincer, Jacob, and Yoshio Higuchi. "Wage Structures and Labor Turnover in the U.S. and Japan." *Journal of the Japanese and International Economies* (1988): 297–331.

Murphy, Kevin M., and Finis Welch. "Wage Premiums for College Graduates: Recent Growth and Possible Explanations." *Educational Researcher* 18 (1989): 17–27.

Welch, Finis. "Education in Production." *Journal of Political Economy* 78 (1970): 35–59.

Part One

Theoretical Analysis

"The most valuable of all capital is that invested in human beings."

Alfred Marshall, *Principles of Economics*

CHAPTER III

Investment in Human Capital: Effects on Earnings[1]

The original aim of this study was to estimate the money rate of return to college and high-school education in the United States. In order to set these estimates in the proper context, a brief formulation of the theory of investment in human capital was undertaken. It soon became clear to me, however, that more than a restatement was called for; while important and pioneering work had been done on the economic return to various occupations and education classes,[2] there had been few, if any, attempts to treat the process of investing in people from a general viewpoint or to work out a broad set of empirical implications. I began then to prepare a general analysis of investment in human capital.

---

[1] This chapter and the one that follows were published in somewhat different form in *Investment in Human Beings*, NBER Special Conference 15, supplement to *Journal of Political Economy*, October 1962, pp. 9–49.

[2] In addition to the earlier works of Smith, Mill, and Marshall, see the brilliant work (which greatly influenced my own thinking about occupational choice) by M. Friedman and S. Kuznets, *Income from Independent Professional Practice*, New York, NBER, 1945; see also H. Clark, *Life Earnings in Selected Occupations in the U.S.*, New York, Harper, 1937; J. R. Walsh, "Capital Concept Applied to Man," *Quarterly Journal of Economics*, February 1935; G. Stigler and D. Blank, *The Demand and Supply of Scientific Personnel*, New York, NBER, 1957. In recent years, of course, there has been considerable work, especially by T. W. Schultz; see, for example, his "Investment in Human Capital," *American Economic Review*, March 1961, pp. 1–17.

It eventually became apparent that this general analysis would do much more than fill a gap in formal economic theory: it offers a unified explanation of a wide range of empirical phenomena which have either been given ad hoc interpretations or have baffled investigators. Among these phenomena are the following: (1) Earnings typically increase with age at a decreasing rate. Both the rate of increase and the rate of retardation tend to be positively related to the level of skill. (2) Unemployment rates tend to be inversely related to the level of skill. (3) Firms in underdeveloped countries appear to be more "paternalistic" toward employees than those in developed countries. (4) Younger persons change jobs more frequently and receive more schooling and on-the-job training than older persons do. (5) The distribution of earnings is positively skewed, especially among professional and other skilled workers. (6) Abler persons receive more education and other kinds of training than others. (7) The division of labor is limited by the extent of the market. (8) The typical investor in human capital is more impetuous and thus more likely to err than is the typical investor in tangible capital.

What a diverse and even confusing array! Yet all these, as well as many other important empirical implications, can be derived from very simple theoretical arguments. The purpose here is to set out these arguments in general form, with the emphasis placed on empirical implications, although little empirical material is presented. Systematic empirical work appears in Part Two.

In this chapter a lengthy discussion of on-the-job training is presented and then, much more briefly, discussions of investment in schooling, information, and health. On-the-job training is dealt with so elaborately not because it is more important than other kinds of investment in human capital—although its importance is often underrated—but because it clearly illustrates the effect of human capital on earnings, employment, and other economic variables. For example, the close connection between indirect and direct costs and the effect of human capital on earnings at different ages are vividly brought out. The extended discussion of on-the-job training paves the way for much briefer discussions of other kinds of investment in human beings.

1. On-the-Job Training

Theories of firm behavior, no matter how they differ in other respects, almost invariably ignore the effect of the productive process itself on worker productivity. This is not to say that no one recognizes that productivity is affected by the job itself; but the recognition has not been formalized, incorporated into economic analysis, and its implications worked out. I now intend to do just that, placing special emphasis on the broader economic implications.

Many workers increase their productivity by learning new skills and perfecting old ones while on the job. Presumably, future productivity can be improved only at a cost, for otherwise there would be an unlimited demand for training. Included in cost are the value placed on the time and effort of trainees, the "teaching" provided by others, and the equipment and materials used. These are costs in the sense that they could have been used in producing current output if they had not been used in raising future output. The amount spent and the duration of the training period depend partly on the type of training since more is spent for a longer time on, say, an intern than a machine operator.

Consider explicitly now a firm that is hiring employees for a specified time period (in the limiting case this period approaches zero), and for the moment assume that both labor and product markets are perfectly competitive. If there were no on-the-job training, wage rates would be given to the firm and would be independent of its actions. A profit-maximizing firm would be in equilibrium when marginal products equaled wages, that is, when marginal receipts equaled marginal expenditures. In symbols

$$MP = W, \tag{1}$$

where W equals wages or expenditures and MP equals the marginal product or receipts. Firms would not worry too much about the relation between labor conditions in the present and future, partly because workers would only be hired for one period and partly because wages and marginal products in future periods would be independent of a firm's current behavior. It can therefore legitimately be assumed that workers have unique marginal products (for given amounts of other inputs) and wages in each period, which are, respectively, the maximum productivity in all possible uses and the market wage rate. A more complete set of equilibrium conditions would be the set

$$MP_t = W_t, \tag{2}$$

where t refers to the tth period. The equilibrium position for each period would depend only on the flows during that period.

These conditions are altered when account is taken of on-the-job training and the connection thereby created between present and future receipts and expenditures. Training might lower current receipts and raise current expenditures, yet firms could profitably provide this training if future receipts were sufficiently raised or future expenditures sufficiently lowered. Expenditures during each period need not equal wages, receipts need not equal the maximum possible marginal productivity, and expenditures and receipts during all periods would be interrelated. The set of equilibrium conditions summarized in equation (2) would be replaced by an equality between the *present values* of receipts and expenditures. If E_t and R_t represent expenditures and receipts during period t, and i the market discount rate, then the equilibrium condition can be written as

$$\sum_{t=0}^{n-1} \frac{R_t}{(1+i)^{t+1}} = \sum_{t=0}^{n-1} \frac{E_t}{(1+i)^{t+1}}, \qquad (3)$$

when n represents the number of periods, and R_t and E_t depend on all other receipts and expenditures. The equilibrium condition of equation (2) has been generalized, for if marginal product equals wages in each period, the present value of the marginal product stream would have to equal the present value of the wage stream. Obviously, however, the converse need not hold.

If training were given only during the initial period, expenditures during the initial period would equal wages plus the outlay on training, expenditures during other periods would equal wages alone, and receipts during all periods would equal marginal products. Equation (3) becomes

$$MP_0 + \sum_{t=1}^{n-1} \frac{MP_t}{(1+i)^t} = W_0 + k + \sum_{t=1}^{n-1} \frac{W_t}{(1+i)^t}, \qquad (4)$$

where k measures the outlay on training.

If a new term is defined,

$$G = \sum_{t=1}^{n-1} \frac{MP_t - W_t}{(1+i)^t}, \qquad (5)$$

equation (4) can be written as

$$MP_0 + G = W_0 + k. \qquad (6)$$

Since the term k measures only the actual outlay on training, it does not entirely measure training costs, for it excludes the time that a person spends on this training, time that could have been used to produce current output. The difference between what could have been produced, MP_0', and what is produced, MP_0, is the opportunity cost of the time spent in training. If C is defined as the sum of opportunity costs and outlays on training, (6) becomes

$$MP_0' + G = W_0 + C. \tag{7}$$

The term G, the excess of future receipts over future outlays, is a measure of the return to the firm from providing training; and, therefore, the difference between G and C measures the difference between the return from and the cost of training. Equation (7) shows that the marginal product would equal wages in the initial period only when the return equals costs, or G equals C; it would be greater or less than wages as the return was smaller or greater than costs. Those familiar with capital theory might argue that this generalization of the simple equality between marginal product and wages is spurious because a full equilibrium would require equality between the return from an investment—in this case, made on the job—and costs. If this implied that G equals C, marginal product would equal wages in the initial period. There is much to be said for the relevance of a condition equating the return from an investment with costs, but such a condition does not imply that G equals C or that marginal product equals wages. The following discussion demonstrates that great care is required in the application of this condition to on-the-job investment.

Our treatment of on-the-job training produced some general results —summarized in equations (3) and (7)—of wide applicability, but more concrete results require more specific assumptions. In the following sections two types of on-the-job training are discussed in turn: general and specific.

General Training

General training is useful in many firms besides those providing it; for example, a machinist trained in the army finds his skills of value in steel and aircraft firms, and a doctor trained (interned) at one hospital finds his skills useful at other hospitals. Most on-the-job training presumably increases the future marginal productivity of workers in the firms providing it; general training, however, also increases their

marginal product in many other firms as well. Since in a competitive labor market the wage rates paid by any firm are determined by marginal productivities in other firms, future wage rates as well as marginal products would increase in firms providing general training. These firms could capture some of the return from training only if their marginal product rose by more than their wages. "Perfectly general" training would be equally useful in many firms and marginal products would rise by the same extent in all of them. Consequently, wage rates would rise by exactly the same amount as the marginal product and the firms providing such training could not capture any of the return.

Why, then, would rational firms in competitive labor markets provide general training if it did not bring any return? The answer is that firms would provide general training only if they did not have to pay any of the costs. Persons receiving general training would be willing to pay these costs since training raises their future wages. Hence it is the trainees, not the firms, who would bear the cost of general training and profit from the return.[3]

These and other implications of general training can be more formally demonstrated in equation (7). Since wages and marginal products are raised by the same amount, MP_t must equal W_t for all $t = 1, \ldots n - 1$, and therefore

$$G = \sum_{t=1}^{n-1} \frac{MP_t - W_t}{(1 + i)^t} = 0. \tag{8}$$

Equation (7) is reduced to

$$MP_0' = W_0 + C, \tag{9}$$

or

$$W_0 = MP_0' - C. \tag{10}$$

In terms of actual marginal product

$$MP_0 = W_0 + k, \tag{9'}$$

---

[3] Some persons have asked why any general training is provided if firms do not collect any of the returns. The answer is simply that they have an incentive to do so wherever the demand price for training is at least as great as the supply price or cost of providing the training. Workers in turn would prefer to be trained on the job rather than in specialized firms (schools) if the training and work complemented each other (see the discussion in section 2 below).

or

$$W_0 = MP_0 - k. \qquad (10')$$

The wage of trainees would not equal their opportunity marginal product but would be less by the total cost of training. In other words, employees would pay for general training by receiving wages below their current (opportunity) productivity. Equation (10) has many other implications, and the rest of this section is devoted to developing the more important ones.

Some might argue that a really "net" definition of marginal product, obtained by subtracting training costs from "gross" marginal product, must equal wages even for trainees. Such an interpretation of net productivity could formally save the equality between marginal product and wages here, but not always, as shown later. Moreover, regardless of which interpretation is used, training costs would have to be included in any study of the relation between wages and productivity.

Employees pay for general on-the-job training by receiving wages below what they could receive elsewhere. "Earnings" during the training period would be the difference between an income or flow term (potential marginal product) and a capital or stock term (training costs), so that the capital and income accounts would be closely intermixed, with changes in either affecting wages. In other words, earnings of persons receiving on-the-job training would be net of investment costs and would correspond to the definition of *net* earnings used throughout this paper, which subtracts all investment costs from "gross" earnings. Therefore, our departure with this definition of earnings from the accounting conventions used for transactions in material goods—which separate income from capital accounts to prevent a transaction in capital from ipso facto[4] affecting the income side—is not capricious but is grounded in a fundamental difference between the way investment in material and human capital are "written off." The underlying cause of this difference undoubtedly is the widespread reluctance to treat people as capital and the accompanying tendency to treat all wage receipts as earnings.

Intermixing the capital and income accounts could make the reported "incomes" of trainees unusually low and perhaps negative, even though their long-run or lifetime incomes were well above average. Since a considerable fraction of young persons receive some

---

[4] Of course, a shift between assets with different productivities would affect the income account on material goods even with current accounting practices.

training, and since trainees tend to have lower current and higher subsequent earnings than other youth, the correlation of current consumption with the current earnings of young males[5] would not only be much weaker than the correlation with long-run earnings, but the signs of these correlations might even differ.[6]

Doubt has been cast on the frequent assertion that no allowance is made in the income accounts for depreciation on human capital.[7] A depreciation-type item is deducted, at least from the earnings due to on-the-job training, for the cost would be deducted during the training period. Depreciation on tangible capital does not bulk so large in any one period because it is usually "written off" or depreciated during a period of time designed to approximate its economic life. Hence human and tangible capital appear to differ more in the time pattern of depreciation than in its existence,[8] and the effect on wage income of a rapid "write-off" of human capital is what should be emphasized and studied.

This point can be demonstrated differently and more rigorously. The ideal depreciation on a capital asset during any period would equal its change in value during the period. In particular, if value rose, a negative depreciation term would have to be subtracted or a positive appreciation term added to the income from the asset. Since training costs would be deducted from earnings during the training period, the economic "value" of a trainee would at first increase rather than decrease with age, and only later begin to decrease. Therefore,

---

[5] The term "young males" rather than "young families" is used because, as J. Mincer has shown (in his "Labor Force Participation of Married Women," *Aspects of Labor Economics,* Princeton for NBER, 1962), the labor force participation of wives is positively correlated with the difference between a husband's long-run and current income. Participation of wives, therefore, makes the correlation between a family's current and a husband's long-run income greater than that between a husband's current and long-run income.

[6] A difference in signs is impossible in Friedman's analysis of consumer behavior because he assumes that, at least in the aggregate, transitory and long-run (that is, permanent) incomes are uncorrelated (see his *A Theory of the Consumption Function,* Princeton for NBER, 1957); I am suggesting that they may be *negatively* correlated for young persons.

[7] See C. Christ, "Patinkin on Money, Interest, and Prices," *Journal of Political Economy,* August 1957, p. 352; and W. Hamburger, "The Relation of Consumption to Wealth and the Wage Rate," *Econometrica,* January 1955.

[8] R. Goode has argued (see his "Educational Expenditures and the Income Tax," in Selma J. Mushkin, ed., *Economics of Higher Education,* Washington, 1962) that educated persons should be permitted to subtract from income a depreciation allowance on tuition payments. Such an allowance is apparently not required for on-the-job training costs or, as seen later, for the indirect costs of education; indeed, one might argue, on the contrary, that too much or too rapid depreciation is permitted on such investments.

a negative rather than a positive depreciation term would have to be subtracted initially.[9]

Training has an important effect on the relation between earnings and age. Suppose that untrained persons received the same earnings regardless of age, as shown by the horizontal line *UU* in Chart 1. Trained persons would receive lower earnings during the training period because training is paid for at that time, and higher earnings at later ages because the return is collected then. The combined effect of paying for and collecting the return from training in this way would be to make the age-earnings curve of trained persons, shown by *TT* in Chart 1, steeper than that of untrained persons, the difference

CHART 1

Relation of Earnings to Age

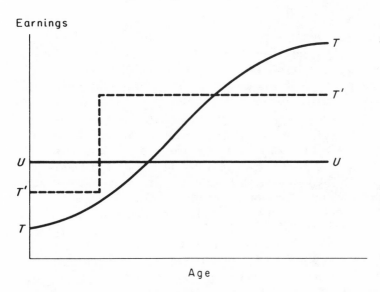

being greater the greater the cost of, and return from, the investment.

Not only does training make the curve steeper but, as indicated by Chart 1, also more concave; that is, the rate of increase in earnings is affected more at younger than at older ages. Suppose, to take an extreme case, that training raised the level of marginal productivity but had no effect on the slope, so that the marginal productivity of

[9] See Chapter VII, section 2, for some empirical estimates of "depreciation" on human capital.

trained persons was also independent of age. If earnings equaled marginal product, TT would merely be parallel to and higher than UU, showing neither slope nor concavity. Since, however, earnings of trained persons would be below marginal productivity during the training period and equal afterward, they would rise sharply at the end of the training period and then level off (as shown by the dashed line $T'T'$ in Chart 1), imparting a concave appearance to the curve as a whole. In this extreme case an extreme concavity appears (as in TT); in less extreme cases the principle would be the same and the concavity more continuous.

Foregone earnings are an important, although neglected, cost of much investment in human capital and should be treated in the same way as direct outlays. Indeed, *all* costs appear as foregone earnings to workers receiving on-the-job training; that is, all costs appear as lower earnings than could be received elsewhere, although direct outlays, C, may really be an important part of costs. The arbitrariness of the division between indirect and direct costs and the resulting advantage of treating total costs as a whole[10] can be further demonstrated by contrasting school and on-the-job training. Usually only the direct costs of school training are emphasized, even though opportunity costs are sometimes (as with college education) an important part of the total. A shift from school training to on-the-job training would, however, reverse the emphasis and make all costs appear as foregone earnings, even when direct outlays were important.

Income-maximizing firms in competitive labor markets would not pay the cost of general training and would pay trained persons the market wage. If, however, training costs were paid, many persons would seek training, few would quit during the training period, and labor costs would be relatively high. Firms that did not pay trained persons the market wage would have difficulty satisfying their skill requirements and would also tend to be less profitable than other firms. Firms that paid both for training and less than the market wage for trained persons would have the worst of both worlds, for they would attract too many trainees and too few trained persons.

These principles have been clearly demonstrated during the last few years in discussions of problems in recruiting military personnel.

10 The equivalence between indirect and direct costs applies to consumption as well as to investment decisions. In my paper *A Theory of the Allocation of Time,* IBM Research Paper RC 1149, March 20, 1964, an analysis incorporating both direct and indirect consumption costs is applied to the choice between work and nonwork, price and income elasticities of demand for goods, the economic function of queues, and several other areas. A shortened version was published with the same title in the *Economic Journal* of September 1965.

The military offers training in a wide variety of skills and many are very useful in the civilian sector. Training is provided during part or all of the first enlistment period and used during the remainder of the first period and hopefully during subsequent periods. This hope, however, is thwarted by the fact that reenlistment rates tend to be inversely related to the amount of civilian-type skills provided by the military.[11] Persons with these skills leave the military more readily because they can receive much higher wages in the civilian sector. Net military wages for those receiving training are higher relative to civilian wages during the first than during subsequent enlistment periods because training costs are largely paid by the military. Not surprisingly, therefore, first-term enlistments for skilled jobs are obtained much more easily than are reenlistments.

The military is a conspicuous example of an organization that both pays at least part of training costs and does not pay market wages to skilled personnel. It has had, in consequence, relatively easy access to "students" and heavy losses of "graduates." Indeed, its graduates make up the predominant part of the supply in several civilian occupations. For example, well over 90 per cent of United States commercial airline pilots received much of their training in the armed forces. The military, of course, is not a commercial organization judged by profits and losses and has had no difficulty surviving and even thriving.

What about the old argument that firms in competitive labor markets have no incentive to provide on-the-job training because trained workers would be bid away by other firms? Firms that train workers are supposed to impart external economies to other firms because the latter can use these workers free of any training charge. An analogy with research and development is often drawn since a firm developing a process that cannot be patented or kept secret would impart external economies to competitors. This argument and analogy would apply if firms were to pay training costs, for they would suffer a "capital loss" whenever trained workers were bid away by other firms. Firms can, however, shift training costs to trainees and have an incentive to do so when faced with competition for their services.[12]

[11] See *Manpower Management and Compensation,* report of the Cordiner Committee, Washington, D.C., 1957, Vol. I, Chart 3, and the accompanying discussion. The military not only wants to eliminate the inverse relation but apparently would like to create a positive relation because they have such a large investment in heavily trained personnel. For an excellent study, see Gorman C. Smith, "Differential Pay for Military Technicians," unpublished Ph.D. dissertation, Columbia University, 1964.

[12] Sometimes the alleged external economies from on-the-job training have been considered part of the "infant industry" argument for protection (see J. Black,

The difference between investment in training and in research and development can be put very simply. Without patents or secrecy, firms in competitive industries may have difficulty establishing property rights in innovations, and these innovations may become fair game for all comers. Patent systems try to establish these rights so that incentives can be provided to invest in research. Property rights in skills, on the other hand, are automatically vested, for a skill cannot be used without permission of the person possessing it. The property right of the worker in his skills is the source of his incentive to invest in training by accepting a reduced wage during the training period and explains why an analogy with unowned innovations is misleading.

Specific Training

Completely general training increases the marginal productivity of trainees by exactly the same amount in the firms providing the training as in other firms. Clearly some kinds of training increase productivity by different amounts in the firms providing the training and in other firms. Training that increases productivity more in firms providing it will be called specific training. Completely specific training can be defined as training that has no effect on the productivity of trainees that would be useful in other firms. Much on-the-job training is neither completely specific nor completely general but increases productivity more in the firms providing it and falls within the definition of specific training. The rest increases productivity by at least as much in other firms and falls within a definition of general training. A few illustrations of the scope of specific training are presented before a formal analysis is developed.

The military offers some forms of training that are extremely useful in the civilian sector, as already noted, and others that are only of minor use to civilians, i.e., astronauts, fighter pilots, and missile men. Such training falls within the scope of specific training because productivity is raised in the military but not (much) elsewhere.

"Arguments for Tariffs," *Oxford Economic Papers*, June 1959, pp. 205–206). Our analysis suggests, however, that the trouble tariffs are supposed to overcome must be traced back to difficulties that workers have in financing investment in themselves—in other words, to ignorance or capital market limitations that apply to expenditures on education and health, as well as on-the-job training. Protection would serve the same purpose as the creation of monopsonies domestically, namely, to convert general into specific capital so that firms can be given an incentive to pay for training (see the remarks on specific training below and in section 4 of this chapter). Presumably a much more efficient solution would be to improve the capital market directly through insurance of loans, subsidies, information, etc.

Resources are usually spent by firms in familiarizing new employees with their organization,[13] and the knowledge thus acquired is a form of specific training because productivity is raised more in the firms acquiring the knowledge than in other firms. Other kinds of hiring costs, such as employment agency fees, the expenses incurred by new employees in finding jobs, or the time employed in interviewing, testing, checking references, and in bookkeeping do not so obviously increase the knowledge of new employees, but they too are a form of specific investment in human capital, although not training. They are an investment because outlays over a short period create distributed effects on productivity; they are specific because productivity is raised primarily in the firms making the outlays; they are in human capital because they lose their value whenever employees leave. In the rest of this section reference is mostly to on-the-job specific training even though the analysis applies to all on-the-job specific investment.

Even after hiring costs are incurred, firms usually know only a limited amount about the ability and potential of new employees. They try to increase their knowledge in various ways—testing, rotation among departments, trial and error, etc.—for greater knowledge permits a more efficient utilization of manpower. Expenditures on acquiring knowledge of employee talents would be a specific investment if the knowledge could be kept from other firms, for then productivity would be raised more in the firms making the expenditures than elsewhere.

The effect of investment in employees on their productivity elsewhere depends on market conditions as well as on the nature of the investment. Very strong monopsonists might be completely insulated from competition by other firms, and practically all investments in their labor force would be specific. On the other hand, firms in extremely competitive labor markets would face a constant threat of raiding and would have fewer specific investments available.

These examples convey some of the surprisingly large variety of situations that come under the rubric of specific investment. This set is now treated abstractly in order to develop a general formal analysis. Empirical situations are brought in again after several major implications of the formal analysis have been developed.

If all training were completely specific, the wage that an employee could get elsewhere would be independent of the amount of training he had received. One might plausibly argue, then, that the wage paid

13 To judge from a sample of firms analyzed, formal orientation courses are quite common, at least in large firms (see H. F. Clark and H. S. Sloan, *Classrooms in the Factories*, New York, 1958, Chapter IV).

by firms would also be independent of training. If so, firms would have to pay training costs, for no rational employee would pay for training that did not benefit him. Firms would collect the return from such training in the form of larger profits resulting from higher productivity, and training would be provided whenever the return—discounted at an appropriate rate—was at least as large as the cost. Long-run competitive equilibrium requires that the present value of the return exactly equal costs.

These propositions can be stated more formally with the equations developed earlier. According to equations (5) and (7), the equilibrium of a firm providing training in competitive markets can be written as

$$MP_0' + G\left[= \sum_{t=1}^{n-1} \frac{MP_t - W_t}{(1 + i)^t}\right] = W_0 + C, \qquad (11)$$

where C is the cost of training given only in the initial period, MP_0' is the opportunity marginal product of trainees, W_0 is the wage paid to trainees, and W_t and MP_t are the wage and marginal product in period t. If the analysis of completely specific training given in the preceding paragraph is correct, W would always equal the wage that could be received elsewhere, $MP_t - W_t$ would be the full return in t from training given in 0, and G would be the present value of these returns. Since MP_0' measures the marginal product elsewhere and W_0 measures the wage elsewhere of trainees, MP_0' equals W_0. As a consequence G equals C, or, in full equilibrium, the return from training equals costs.

Before claiming that the usual equality between marginal product and wages holds when completely specific training is considered, the reader should bear in mind two points. The first is that the equality between wages and marginal product in the initial period involves opportunity, not actual marginal product. Wages would be greater than actual marginal product if some productivity were foregone as part of the training program. The second is that, even if wages equaled marginal product initially, they would be less in the future because the differences between future marginal products and wages constitute the return to training and are collected by the firm.

All of this follows from the assumption that firms pay all costs and collect all returns. But could not one equally well argue that workers pay all specific training costs by receiving appropriately lower wages initially and collect all returns by receiving wages equal to marginal product later? In terms of equation (11), W_t would equal MP_t, G would equal zero, and W_0 would equal $MP_0' - C$, just as with general training. Is it more plausible that firms rather than workers pay for and collect any return from training?

An answer can be found by reasoning along the following lines. If a firm had paid for the specific training of a worker who quit to take another job, its capital expenditure would be partly wasted, for no further return could be collected. Likewise, a worker fired after he had paid for specific training would be unable to collect any further return and would also suffer a capital loss. The willingness of workers or firms to pay for specific training should, therefore, closely depend on the likelihood of labor turnover.

To bring in turnover at this point may seem like introducing a *deus ex machina*, since turnover is almost always ignored in traditional theory. In the usual analysis of competitive firms, wages equal marginal product, and since wages and marginal product are assumed to be the same in many firms, no one suffers from turnover. It would not matter whether a firm's labor force always contained the same persons or a rapidly changing group. Any person leaving one firm could do equally well in other firms, and his employer could replace him without any change in profits. In other words, turnover is ignored in traditional theory because it plays no important role within the framework of the theory.

Turnover becomes important when costs are imposed on workers or firms, which are precisely the effects of specific training. Suppose a firm paid all the specific training costs of a worker who quit after completing the training. According to our earlier analysis, he would have been receiving the market wage and a new employee could be hired at the same wage. If the new employee were not given training, his marginal product would be less than that of the one who quit since presumably training raised the latter's productivity. Training could raise the new employee's productivity but would require additional expenditures by the firm. In other words, a firm is hurt by the departure of a trained employee because an equally profitable new employee could not be obtained. In the same way an employee who pays for specific training would suffer a loss from being laid off because he could not find an equally good job elsewhere. To bring turnover into the analysis of specific training is not, therefore, to introduce a *deus ex machina* but is made necessary by the important link between them.

Firms paying for specific training might take account of turnover merely by obtaining a sufficiently large return from those remaining to counterbalance the loss from those leaving. (The return on "successes"—those remaining—would, of course, overestimate the average return on all training expenditures.) Firms could do even better, however, by recognizing that the likelihood of a quit is not fixed but depends on wages. Instead of merely recouping on successes what is lost on failures, they might reduce the likelihood of failure itself by offering higher wages after training than could be received elsewhere. In effect, they would offer employees some of the return from training. Matters would be improved in some respects but worsened in others, for the higher wage would make the supply of trainees greater than the demand, and rationing would be required. The final step would be to shift some training costs as well as returns to employees, thereby bringing supply more in line with demand. When the final step is completed, firms no longer pay all training costs nor do they collect all the return but they share both with employees.[14] The shares of each depend on the relations between quit rates and wages, layoff rates and profits, and on other factors not discussed here, such as the cost of funds, attitudes toward risk, and desires for liquidity.[15]

If training were not completely specific, productivity would increase in other firms as well, and the wage that could be received elsewhere would also increase. Such training can be looked upon as the sum of two components, one completely general, the other completely specific; the former would be relatively larger, the greater the effect on wages in other firms relative to the firms providing the training. Since firms do not pay any of the completely general costs and only part of the completely specific costs, the fraction of costs paid by firms would be inversely related to the importance of the general component, or positively related to the specificity of the training.

Our conclusions can be stated formally in terms of the equations developed earlier. If G is the present value of the return from training collected by firms, the fundamental equation is

$$MP' + G = W + C. \qquad (12)$$

---

[14] A. Marshall (*Principles of Economics*, 8th ed., New York, 1949, p. 626) was clearly aware of specific talents and their effect on wages and productivity: "Thus the head clerk in a business has an acquaintance with men and things, the use of which he could in some cases sell at a high price to rival firms. But in other cases it is of a kind to be of no value save to the business in which he already is; and *then his departure would perhaps injure it by several times the value of his salary,* while probably he could not get half that *salary elsewhere.*" (My italics.) However, he overstressed the element of indeterminacy in these wages ("their earnings are determined . . . by a bargain between them and their employers, the terms of which are theoretically arbitrary") because he ignored the effect of wages on turnover (*ibid.*, fn. 2).

[15] The rate used to discount costs and returns is the sum of a (positive) rate measuring the cost of funds, a (positive or negative) risk premium, and a liquidity premium that is presumably positive since capital invested in specific training is very illiquid (see the discussion in section 2 of Chapter III).

If G' measures the return collected by employees, the total return, G'', would be the sum of G and G'. In full equilibrium the total return would equal total costs, or $G'' = C$. Let a represent the fraction of the total return collected by firms. Since $G = aG''$ and $G'' = C$, equation (12) can be written as

$$MP' + aC = W + C, \qquad (13)$$

or

$$W = MP' - (1 - a)C.^{16} \qquad (14)$$

Employees pay the same fraction of costs, $1 - a$, as they collect in returns, which generalizes the results obtained earlier. For if training were completely general, $a = 0$, and equation (14) reduces to equation (10); if firms collected all the return from training, $a = 1$, and (14) reduces to $MP_0' = W_0$; and if $0 < a < 1$, none of the earlier equations is satisfactory.

A few major implications of this analysis of specific training are now developed.

Rational firms pay generally trained employees the same wage and specifically trained employees a higher wage than they could get elsewhere. A reader might easily believe the contrary—namely, that general training would command a higher wage relative to alternatives than specific training does, since, after all, competition for persons with the latter is apt to be weaker than for those with the former. This view, however, overlooks the fact that general training raises the wages that could be received elsewhere while (completely) specific training does not, so a comparison with alternative wages gives a misleading impression of the *absolute* effect on wages of different types of training. Moreover, firms are not too concerned about the turnover of employees with general training and have no incentive to offer them a premium above wages elsewhere because the cost of such training is borne entirely by employees. Firms are concerned about the turnover of employees with specific training, and a premium is offered to reduce their turnover because firms pay part of their training costs.

The part of specific training paid by employees has effects similar

---

[16] If G'' did not equal C, these equations would be slightly more complicated. Suppose, for example, $G'' = G + G' = C + n$, $n \geq 0$, so that the present value of the total return would be greater than total costs. Then $G = aG'' = aC + an$, and

$$MP' + aC + an = W + C,$$

or

$$W = MP' - [(1 - a)C - an].$$

to those discussed earlier for general training: it is also paid by a reduction in wages during the training period, tends to make age-earnings profiles steeper and more concave, etc. The part paid by firms has none of these implications, since current or future wages would not be affected.

Specific, unlike general, training produces certain "external" effects, for quits prevent firms from capturing the full return on costs paid by them, and layoffs do the same to employees. These, however, are external *diseconomies* imposed on the employees or employers of firms providing the training, not external economies accruing to other firms.

Employees with specific training have less incentive to quit, and firms have less incentive to fire them, than employees with no training or general training, which implies that quit and layoff rates are inversely related to the amount of specific training. Turnover should be least for employees with extremely specific training and most for those receiving such general training that productivity is raised less in the firms providing the training than elsewhere (say, in schools). These propositions are as applicable to the large number of irregular quits and layoffs that continually occur as to the more regular cyclical and secular movements in turnover; in this section, however, only the more regular movements are discussed.

Consider a firm that experiences an unexpected decline in demand for its output, the rest of the economy being unaffected. The marginal product of employees without specific training—such as untrained or generally trained employees—presumably equaled wages initially, and their employment would now be reduced to prevent their marginal productivity from falling below wages. The marginal product of specifically trained employees initially would have been greater than wages. A decline in demand would reduce these marginal products too, but as long as they were reduced by less than the initial difference with wages, firms would have no incentive to lay off such employees. For sunk costs are sunk, and there is no incentive to lay off employees whose marginal product is greater than wages, no matter how unwise it was, in retrospect, to invest in their training. Thus workers with specific training seem less likely to be laid off as a consequence of a decline in demand than untrained or even generally trained workers.[17]

If the decline in demand were sufficiently great so that even the

[17] A very similar argument is developed by Walter Oi in "Labor as a Quasi-fixed Factor of Production," unpublished Ph.D dissertation, University of Chicago, 1961. Also, see his article with almost the same title in *Journal of Political Economy*, December 1962.

marginal product of specifically trained workers was pushed below wages, would the firm just proceed to lay them off until the marginal product was brought into equality with wages? To show the danger here, assume that all the cost of and return from specific training was paid and collected by the firm. Any worker laid off would try to find a new job, since nothing would bind him to the old one.[18] The firm might be hurt if he did find a new job, for the firm's investment in his training might be lost forever. If specifically trained workers were not laid off, the firm would lose now because marginal product would be less than wages but would gain in the future if the decline in demand proved temporary. There is an incentive, therefore, not to lay off workers with specific training when their marginal product is only temporarily below wages, and the larger a firm's investment the greater the incentive not to lay them off.

A worker collecting some of the return from specific training would have less incentive to find a new job when temporarily laid off than others would: he does not want to lose his investment. His behavior while laid off in turn affects his future chances of being laid off, for if it were known that he would not readily take another job, the firm could lay him off without much fear of losing its investment.

These conclusions can be briefly summarized. If one firm alone experienced an unexpected decline in demand, relatively few workers with specific training would be laid off, if only because their marginal product was initially greater than their wage. If the decline were permanent, all workers would be laid off when their marginal product became less than their wage and all those laid off would have to find jobs elsewhere. If the decline were temporary, specifically trained workers might not be laid off even though their marginal product was less than their wage because the firm would suffer if they took other jobs. The likelihood of their taking other jobs would be inversely related, and therefore the likelihood of their being laid off would be positively related, to the extent of their own investment in training.

The analysis can easily be extended to cover general declines in demand; suppose, for example, a general cyclical decline occurred. Assume that wages were sticky and remained at the initial level. If the decline in business activity were not sufficient to reduce the marginal product below the wage, workers with specific training would not be laid off even though others would be, just as before. If the decline reduced marginal product below wages, only one modification in the

18 Actually one need only assume that the quit rate of laid-off workers tends to be significantly greater than that of employed workers, if only because the opportunity cost of searching for another job is less for laid-off workers.

previous analysis is required. A firm would have a greater incentive to lay off specifically trained workers than when it alone experienced a decline because laid-off workers would be less likely to find other jobs when unemployment was widespread. In other respects, the implications of a general decline with wage rigidity are the same as those of a decline in one firm alone.

The discussion has concentrated on layoff rates, but the same kind of reasoning shows that a rise in wages elsewhere would cause fewer quits among specifically trained workers than among others. Specifically trained workers initially receive higher wages than are available elsewhere and the wage rise elsewhere would have to be greater than the initial difference before they would consider quitting. Thus both the quit and layoff rate of specifically trained workers would be relatively low and fluctuate relatively less during business cycles. These are important implications that can be tested with the data available.

Although quits and layoffs are influenced by considerations other than investment costs, some of these, such as pension plans, are more strongly related to investments than may appear at first blush. A pension plan with incomplete vesting privileges[19] penalizes employees who quit before retirement and thus provides an incentive—often an extremely powerful one—not to quit. At the same time pension plans "insure" firms against quits for they are given a lump sum—the non-vested portion of payments—whenever a worker quits. Insurance is needed for specifically trained employees because their turnover would impose capital losses on firms. Firms can discourage such quits by sharing training costs and the return with employees, but they would have less need to discourage them and would be more willing to pay for training costs if insurance were provided. The effects on the incentive to invest in one's employees may have been a major stimulus to the development of pension plans with incomplete vesting.[20]

An effective long-term contract would insure firms against quits, just as pensions do and also insure employees against layoffs. Firms would be more willing to pay for all kinds of training—assuming

---

[19] According to the National Bureau study of pensions, most plans have incomplete vesting. See R. F. Murray, *Economic Aspects of Pensions: A Summary Report*, New York, NBER, 1968.

[20] This economic function of incomplete vesting should caution one against conceding to the agitation for more liberal vesting privileges. Of course, in recent years pensions have also been an important tax-saving device, which certainly has been a crucial factor in their mushrooming growth.

future wages were set at an appropriate level—since a contract, in effect, converts all training into completely specific training. A casual reading of history suggests that long-term contracts have, indeed, been primarily a means of inducing firms to undertake large investments in employees. These contracts are seldom used today in the United States,[21] and while they have declined in importance over time, they were probably always the exception here largely because courts have considered them a form of involuntary servitude. Moreover, any enforceable contract could at best specify the hours required on a job, not the quality of performance. Since performance can vary widely, unhappy workers could usually "sabotage" operations to induce employers to release them from contracts.

Some training may be useful not in most firms nor in a single firm, but in a set of firms defined by product, type of work, or geographical location. For example, carpentry training would raise productivity primarily in the construction industry, and French legal training would not be very useful in the United States. Such training would tend to be paid by trainees, since a single firm could not readily collect the return,[22] and in this respect would be the same as general training. In one respect, however, it is similar to specific training. Workers with training "specific" to an industry, occupation, or country are less likely to leave that industry, occupation, or country than other workers, so their industrial, occupational, or country "turnover" would be less than average. The same result is obtained for specific training, except that a firm rather than an industry, occupation, or country is used as the unit of observation in measuring turnover. An analysis of specific training, therefore, is helpful also in understanding the effects of certain types of "general" training.

Although a discrepancy between marginal product and wages is frequently taken as evidence of imperfections in the competitive system, it would occur even in a perfectly competitive system where there is investment in specific training. The investment approach provides a very different interpretation of some common phenomena, as can be seen from the following examples.

A positive difference between marginal product and wages is usually said to be evidence of monopsony power; just as the ratio of product price to marginal cost has been suggested as a measure of

[21] The military and the entertainment industry are the major exceptions.

[22] Sometimes firms cooperate in paying training costs, especially when training apprentices (see R. F. Arnold, *A Look at Industrial Training in Mercer County, N.J.*, Washington, D.C., 1959, p. 3).

monopoly power, so has the ratio of marginal product to wages been suggested as a measure of monopsony power. But specific training would also make this ratio greater than one. Does the difference between the marginal product and the earnings of major-league baseball players, for example, measure monopsony power or the return on a team's investment? Since teams do spend a great deal on developing players, some and perhaps most of the difference must be considered a return on investment (even if there were no uncertainty about the abilities of different players).[23]

Earnings might differ greatly among firms, industries, and countries and yet there might be relatively little worker mobility. The usual explanation would be that workers were either irrational or faced with formidable obstacles in moving. However, if specific[24] training were important, differences in earnings would be a misleading estimate of what "migrants" could receive, and it might be perfectly rational not to move. For example, although French lawyers earn less than American lawyers, the average French lawyer could not earn the average American legal income simply by migrating to the United States, for he would have to invest in learning English and American law and procedures.[25]

In extreme types of monopsony, exemplified by an isolated company town, job alternatives for both trained and untrained workers are nil, and all training, no matter what its nature, would be specific to the firm. Monopsony combined with control of a product or an occupation (due, say, to antipirating agreements) converts training specific to that product or occupation into firm-specific training. These kinds of monopsony increase the importance of specific training and thus the incentive to invest in employees.[26] The effect on training of less extreme monopsony positions is more difficult to assess. Consider the monopsonist who pays his workers the best wage avail-

---

23 S. Rottenberg ("The Baseball Players' Labor Market," *Journal of Political Economy*, June 1956, p. 254) argues that the strong restrictions on entry of teams into the major leagues is prima-facie evidence that monopsony power is important, but the entry or threat of new *leagues,* such as have occurred in professional basketball and football, are a real possibility. And, of course, new teams have entered in recent years.

24 Specific, that is, to the firms, industries, or countries in question.

25 Of course, persons who have not yet invested in themselves would have an incentive to migrate, and this partly explains why young persons migrate more than older ones. For a further explanation, see the discussion in Chapter III; also see the paper by L. Sjaastad, "The Costs and Returns of Human Migration," *Investment in Human Beings,* pp. 80–93.

26 A relatively large difference between marginal product and wages in monopsonies might measure, therefore, the combined effect of economic power and a relatively large investment in employees.

able elsewhere. I see no reason why training should have a systematically different effect on the foregone earnings of his employees than
of those in competitive firms and, therefore, no reason why specific
training should be more (or less) important to him. But monopsony
power as a whole, including the more extreme manifestations, would
appear to increase the importance of specific training and the incentive for firms to invest in human capital.

2. Schooling

A school can be defined as an institution specializing in the production of training, as distinct from a firm that offers training in conjunction with the production of goods. Some schools, like those for
barbers, specialize in one skill, while others, like universities, offer a
large and diverse set. Schools and firms are often substitute sources of
particular skills. This substitution is evidenced by the shift over time,
for instance, in law from apprenticeships in law firms to law schools
and in engineering from on-the-job experience to engineering schools.[27]

Some types of knowledge can be mastered better if simultaneously
related to a practical problem; others require prolonged specialization. That is, there are complementary elements between learning
and work and between learning and time. Most training in the construction industry is apparently still best given on the job, while the
training of physicists requires a long period of specialized effort. The
development of certain skills requires both specialization and experience and can be had partly from firms and partly from schools.
Physicians receive apprenticeship training as interns and residents
after several years of concentrated instruction in medical schools. Or,
to take an example closer to home, a research economist spends not
only many years in school but also a rather extensive apprenticeship
in mastering the "art" of empirical and theoretical research. The
complementary elements between firms and schools depend in part
on the amount of formalized knowledge available: price theory can
be formally presented in a course, while a formal statement of the
principles used in gathering and handling empirical materials is
lacking. Training in a new industrial skill is usually first given on the
job, since firms tend to be the first to be aware of its value, but as
demand develops, some of the training shifts to schools.

[27] State occupational licensing requirements often permit on-the-job training to
be substituted for school training (see S. Rottenberg, "The Economics of Occupational Licensing," *Aspects of Labor Economics*, pp. 3–20).

A student does not work for pay while in school but may do so after or before school, or during vacations. His earnings are usually less than if he were not in school since he cannot work as much or as regularly. The difference between what could have been and what is earned (including any value placed on foregone leisure) is an important indirect cost of schooling. Tuition, fees, books, supplies, and unusual transportation and lodging expenses are other, more direct, costs. *Net* earnings can be defined as the difference between actual earnings and direct school costs. In symbols,

$$W = MP - k, \tag{15}$$

where MP is actual marginal product (assumed equal to earnings) and k is direct costs. If MP_0 is the marginal product that could have been received, equation (15) can be written as

$$W = MP_0 - (MP_0 - MP + k) = MP_0 - C, \tag{16}$$

where C is the sum of direct and indirect costs and where net earnings are the difference between potential earnings and total costs. These relations should be familiar since they are the same as those derived for general on-the-job training, which suggests that a sharp distinction between schools and firms is not always necessary: for some purposes schools can be treated as a special kind of firm and students as a special kind of trainee. Perhaps this is most apparent when a student works in an enterprise controlled by his school, which frequently occurs at many colleges.

Our definition of student net earnings may seem strange since tuition and other direct costs are not usually subtracted from "gross" earnings. Note, however, that indirect school costs are implicitly subtracted, for otherwise earnings would have to be defined as the sum of observed and foregone earnings, and foregone earnings are a major cost of high-school, college, and adult schooling. Moreover, earnings of on-the-job trainees would be net of *all* their costs, including direct "tuition" costs. Consistent accounting, which is particularly important when comparing earnings of persons trained in school and on the job, would require that earnings of students be defined in the same way.[28]

Regardless of whether all costs or merely indirect costs are sub-

---

[28] Students often have negative net earnings and in this respect differ from most on-the-job trainees, although at one time many apprentices also had negative earnings.

tracted from potential earnings, schooling would have the same kind of implications as general on-the-job training. Thus schooling would steepen the age-earnings profile, mix together the income and capital accounts, introduce a negative relation between the permanent and current earnings of young persons, and (implicitly) provide for depreciation on its capital. This supports my earlier assertion that an analysis of on-the-job training leads to general results that apply to other kinds of investment in human capital as well.

3. Other Knowledge

On-the-job and school training are not the only activities that raise real income primarily by increasing the knowledge at a person's command. Information about the prices charged by different sellers would enable a person to buy from the cheapest, thereby raising his command over resources; information about the wages offered by different firms would enable him to work for the firm paying the highest. In both examples, information about the economic system and about consumption and production possibilities is increased, as distinct from knowledge of a particular skill. Information about the political or social system—the effect of different parties or social arrangements—could also significantly raise real incomes.[29]

Let us consider in more detail investment in information about employment opportunities. A better job might be found by spending money on employment agencies and situation-wanted ads, by using one's time to examine want ads, by talking to friends and visiting firms, or in Stigler's language by "search."[30] When the new job requires geographical movement, additional time and resources would be spent in moving.[31] These expenditures constitute an investment in information about job opportunities that would yield a return in the form of higher earnings than would otherwise have been received. If workers paid the costs and collected the return, an investment in

[29] The role of political knowledge is systematically discussed in A. Downs, *An Economic Theory of Democracy*, New York, 1957, and more briefly in my "Competition and Democracy," *Journal of Law and Economics*, October 1958.

[30] See G. J. Stigler, "Information in the Labor Market," *Investment in Human Beings*, pp. 94–105.

[31] Studies of large geographical moves—those requiring both a change in employment and consumption—have tended to emphasize the job change more than the consumption change. Presumably money wages are considered to be more dispersed geographically than prices.

search would have the same implications about age-earnings profiles, depreciation, etc., as general on-the-job training and schooling, although it must be noted that the direct costs of search, like the direct costs of schooling, are usually added to consumption rather than deducted from earnings. If firms paid the costs and collected the return, search would have the same implications as on-the-job specific training.

Whether workers or firms pay for search depends on the effect of a job change on alternatives: the larger the number of alternatives made available by a change, the larger (not the smaller) is the fraction of costs that have to be paid by workers. Consider a few examples. Immigrants to the United States have usually found many firms that could use their talents, and these firms would have been reluctant to pay the high cost of transporting workers to the United States. In fact immigrants have almost always had to pay their own way. Even a system of contract labor, which was seen to be a means of protecting firms against turnover, was singularly unsuccessful in the United States and has been infrequently used.[32] Firms that are relatively insulated from competition in the labor market have an incentive to pay the costs of workers coming from elsewhere since they have little to worry about in the way of competing neighboring firms. In addition, firms would be willing partly to pay for search within a geographical area because some costs—such as an employment agency's fee—would be specific to the firm doing the hiring since they must be repeated at each job change.

4. Productive Wage Increases

One way to invest in human capital is to improve emotional and physical health. In Western countries today earnings are much more closely geared to knowledge than to strength, but in an earlier day, and elsewhere still today, strength had a significant influence on earnings. Moreover, emotional health increasingly is considered an important determinant of earnings in all parts of the world. Health, like knowledge, can be improved in many ways. A decline in the death rate at working ages may improve earning prospects by extending the period during which earnings are received; a better diet adds strength and stamina, and thus earning capacity; or an improvement

---

[32] For a careful discussion of the contract-labor system in the United States, see C. Erickson, *American Industry and the European Immigrant, 1860–1885*, Cambridge, Mass., 1957.

in working conditions—higher wages, coffee breaks, and so on—may affect morale and productivity.

Firms can invest in the health of employees through medical examinations, lunches, or avoidance of activities with high accident and death rates. An investment in health that increased productivity to the same extent in many firms would be a general investment and would have the same effect as general training, while an investment in health that increased productivity more in the firms making it would be a specific investment and would have the same effect as specific training. Of course, most investments in health in the United States are made outside firms, in households, hospitals, and medical offices. A full analysis of the effect on earnings of such "outside" investment in health is beyond the scope of this study, but I would like to discuss a relation between on-the-job and "outside" human investments that has received much attention in recent years.

When on-the-job investments are paid by reducing earnings during the investment period, less is available for investments outside the job in health, better diet, schooling, and other factors. If these "outside" investments were more productive, some on-the-job investments would not be undertaken even though they were very productive by "absolute" standards.

Before proceeding further, one point needs to be made. The amount invested outside the job would be related to current earnings only if the capital market was very imperfect, for otherwise any amount of "outside" investment could be financed with borrowed funds. The analysis assumes, therefore, that the capital market is extremely imperfect, earnings and other income being a major source of funds.[33]

A firm would be willing to pay for investment in human capital made by employees outside the firm if it could benefit from the resulting increase in productivity. The only way to pay, however, would be to offer higher wages during the investment period than would have been offered, since direct loans to employees are prohibited by assumption. When a firm gives a productive wage increase—that is, an increase that raises productivity—"outside" investments are, as it were, converted into on-the-job investments. Indeed, such a conversion is a natural way to circumvent imperfections in the capital market and the resultant dependence of the amount invested in human capital on the level of wages.

The discussion can be stated more formally. Let W represent wages

---

[33] Imperfections in the capital market with respect to investment in human capital are discussed in section 2 of Chapter III.

in the absence of any investment, and let a productive wage increase costing an amount C be the only on-the-job investment. Total costs to the firm would be $\pi = W + C$, and since the investment cost is received by employees as higher wages, π would also measure total wages. The cost of on-the-job training is not received as higher wages, so this formally distinguishes a productive wage increase from other on-the-job investments. The term MP can represent the marginal product of employees when wages equal W, and G the gain to firms from the investment in higher wages. In full equilibrium,

$$MP + G = W + C = \pi. \tag{17}$$

Investment would not occur if the firm's gain was nil $(G = 0)$, for then total wages (π) would equal the marginal product (MP) when there is no investment.

It has been shown that firms would benefit more from on-the-job investment the more specific the productivity effect, the greater their monopsony power, and the longer the labor contract; conversely, the benefit would be less the more general the productivity effect, the less their monopsony power, and the shorter the labor contract. For example, a wage increase spent on a better diet with an immediate impact on productivity might well be granted,[34] but not one spent on general education with a very delayed impact.[35]

The effect of a wage increase on productivity depends on the way it is spent, which in turn depends on tastes, knowledge, and opportunities. Firms might exert an influence on spending by exhorting

---

[34] The more rapid the impact, the more likely it is that it comes within the (formal or de facto) contract period. Leibenstein apparently initially assumed a rapid impact when discussing wage increases in underdeveloped countries (see his "The Theory of Underemployment in Backward Economies," *Journal of Political Economy*, April 1957). In a later comment he argued that the impact might be delayed ("Underemployment in Backward Economies: Some Additional Notes," *Journal of Political Economy*, June 1958).

[35] Marshall (*Principles of Economics*, p. 566) discusses delays of a generation or more and notes that profit-maximizing firms in competitive industries have no incentive to grant such wage increases.

"Again, in paying his workpeople high wages and in caring for their happiness and culture, the liberal employer confers benefits which do not end with his own generation. For the children of his workpeople share in them, and grow up stronger in body and in character than otherwise they would have done. The price which he has paid for labour will have borne the expenses of production of an increased supply of high industrial faculties in the next generation: but these faculties will be the property of others, who will have the right to hire them out for the best price they will fetch: neither he nor even his heirs can reckon on reaping much material reward for this part of the good that he has done."

employees to obtain good food, housing, and medical care, or even by requiring purchases of specified items in company stores. Indeed, the company store or truck system in nineteenth-century Great Britain has been interpreted as partly designed to prevent an excessive consumption of liquor and other debilitating commodities.[36] The prevalence of employer paternalism in underdeveloped countries has frequently been accepted as evidence of a difference in temperament between East and West. An alternative interpretation suggested by our study is that an increase in consumption has a greater effect on productivity in underdeveloped countries, and that a productivity advance raises profits more there either because firms have more monopsony power or because the advance is less delayed. In other words, "paternalism" may simply be a way of investing in the health and welfare of employees in underdeveloped countries.

An investment in human capital would usually steepen age-earnings profiles, lowering reported earnings during the investment period and raising them later on. But an investment in an increase in earnings may have precisely the opposite effect, raising reported earnings more during the investment period than later and thus flattening age-earning profiles. The cause of this difference is simply that reported earnings during the investment period tend to be net of the cost of general investments and gross of the cost of an increase in productive earnings.[37]

The productivity of employees depends not only on their ability and the amount invested in them both on and off the job but also on their motivation, or the intensity of their work. Economists have long recognized that motivation in turn partly depends on earnings because of the effect of an increase in earnings on morale and aspirations. Equation (17), which was developed to show the effect of investments outside the firm financed by an increase in earnings, can also show the effect of an increase in the intensity of work "financed" by an increase in earnings. Thus W and MP would show initial earnings and productivity, C the increase in earnings, and G the gain to firms from the increase in productivity caused by the "morale" effect of the increase in earnings. The incentive to grant a morale-boosting increase in earnings, therefore, would depend on the same factors as

---

[36] See G. W. Hilton, "The British Truck System in the Nineteenth Century," *Journal of Political Economy*, April 1957, pp. 246–247.

[37] If E represents reported earnings during the investment period and MP the marginal product when there is no investment, $E = MP - C$ with a general investment, $E = MP$ with a specific investment paid by the firm, and $E = MP + C$ with an increase in productive earnings.

does the incentive to grant an increase used for outside investments. Many discussions of wages in underdeveloped countries have stressed the latter,[38] while earlier discussions often stressed the former.[39]

[38] See Leibenstein, *Journal of Political Economy*, April 1957, and H. Oshima, "Underdevelopment in Backward Economies: An Empirical Comment," *Journal of Political Economy*, June 1958.

[39] For example, Marshall stressed the effect of an increase in earnings on the character and habits of working people (*Principles of Economics*, pp. 529–532, 566–569).

CHAPTER IV

Investment in Human Capital:
Rates of Return

The most important single determinant of the amount invested in human capital may well be its profitability or rate of return, but the effect on earnings of a change in the rate of return has been difficult to distinguish empirically from a change in the amount invested. For since investment in human capital usually extends over a long and variable period, the amount invested cannot be determined from a known "investment period." Moreover, the discussion of on-the-job training clearly indicated that the amount invested is often merged with gross earnings into a single net earnings concept (which is gross earnings minus the cost of or plus the return on investment).

1. Relation between Earnings, Costs, and Rates of Return

In this section, some important relations between earnings, investment costs, and rates of return are derived. They permit one to distinguish, among other things, a change in the return from a change in the amount invested. The discussion proceeds in stages from simple to complicated situations. First, investment is restricted to a single period and returns to all remaining periods; then investment is distributed over a known group of periods called the investment period. Finally, it is shown how the rate of return, the amount invested, and the investment period can all be derived from information on net earnings alone.

The discussion is from the viewpoint of workers and is, therefore, restricted to general investments; since the analysis of specific investments and firms is very similar, its discussion is omitted.

Let Y be an activity providing a person entering at a particular age, called age zero, with a real net earnings stream of Y_0 during the first period, Y_1 during the next period, and so on until Y_n during the last period. The general term "activity" rather than occupation or another more concrete term is used in order to indicate that any kind of investment in human capital is permitted, not just on-the-job training but also schooling, information, health, and morale. As in the previous chapter, "net" earnings mean "gross" earnings during any period minus tuition costs during the same period. "Real" earnings are the sum of monetary earnings and the monetary equivalent of psychic earnings. Since many persons appear to believe that the term "investment in human capital" must be restricted to monetary costs and returns, let me emphasize that essentially the whole analysis applies independently of the division of real earnings into monetary and psychic components. Thus the analysis applies to health, which has a large psychic component, as well as to on-the-job training, which has a large monetary component. When psychic components dominate, the language associated with consumer durable goods might be considered more appropriate than that associated with investment goods; to simplify the presentation, investment language is used throughout.

The present value of the net earnings stream in Y would be

$$V(Y) = \sum_{j=0}^{n} \frac{Y_j}{(1+i)^{j+1}}, \text{ [1]} \tag{18}$$

where i is the market discount rate, assumed for simplicity to be the same in each period. If X were another activity providing a net earning stream of $X_0, X_1, \ldots X_n$, with a present value of $V(X)$, the present value of the gain from choosing Y would be given by

$$d = V(Y) - V(X) = \sum_{j=0}^{n} \frac{Y_j - X_j}{(1+i)^{j+1}}. \tag{19}$$

---

[1] The discussion assumes discrete income flows and compounding, even though a mathematically more elegant formulation would have continuous variables, with sums replaced by integrals and discount rates by continuous compounding. The discrete approach is, however, easier to follow and yields the same kind of results. Extensions to the continuous case are straightforward.

Equation (19) can be reformulated to bring out explicitly the relation between costs and returns. The cost of investing in human capital equals the net earnings foregone by choosing to invest rather than choosing an activity requiring no investment. If activity Y requires an investment only in the initial period and if X does not require any, the cost of choosing Y rather than X is simply the difference between their net earnings in the initial period, and the total return would be the present value of the differences between net earnings in later periods. If $C = X_0 - Y_0$, $k_j = Y_j - X_j$, $j = 1, \ldots n$, and if R measures the total return, the gain from Y could be written as

$$d = \sum_{j=1}^{n} \frac{k_j}{(1 + i)^j} - C = R - C. \qquad (20)$$

The relation between costs and returns can be derived in a different and, for our purposes, preferable way by defining the internal rate of return,[2] which is simply a rate of discount equating the present value of returns to the present value of costs. In other words, the internal rate, r, is defined implicitly by the equation

$$C = \sum_{1}^{n} \frac{k_j}{(1 + r)^j}, \qquad (21)$$

which clearly implies

$$\sum_{j=0}^{n} \frac{Y_j}{(1 + r)^{j+1}} - \sum_{0}^{n} \frac{X_j}{(1 + r)^{j+1}} = d = 0, \qquad (22)$$

since $C = X_0 - Y_0$ and $k_j = Y_j - X_j$. So the internal rate is also a rate of discount equating the present values of net earnings. These equations would be considerably simplified if the return were the same in each period, or $Y_j = X_j + k$, $j = 1, \ldots n$. Thus equation (21) would become

$$C = \frac{k}{r} [1 - (1 + r)^{-n}], \qquad (23)$$

---

[2] A substantial literature has developed on the difference between the income gain and internal return approaches. See, for example, Friedrich and Vera Lutz, *The Theory of Investment of the Firm*, Princeton, 1951, Chapter ii, and the articles in *The Management of Corporate Capital*, Ezra Solomon, ed., Glencoe, 1959.

where $(1 + r)^{-n}$ is a correction for the finiteness of life that tends toward zero as people live longer.

If investment is restricted to a single known period, cost and rate of return are easily determined from information on net earnings alone. Since investment in human capital is distributed over many periods—formal schooling is usually more than ten years in the United States, and long periods of on-the-job training are also common—the analysis must, however, be generalized to cover distributed investment. The definition of an internal rate in terms of the present value of net earnings in different activities obviously applies regardless of the amount and duration of investment, but the definition in terms of costs and returns is not generalized so readily. If investment were known to occur in Y during each of the first m periods, a simple and superficially appealing approach would be to define the investment cost in each of these periods as the difference between net earnings in X and Y, total investment costs as the present value of these differences, and the internal rate would equate total costs and returns. In symbols,

$$C_j{}^1 = X_j - Y_j, \quad j = 0, \ldots m - 1,$$

$$C^1 = \sum_0^{m-1} C_j{}^1 (1 + r)^{-j},$$

and

$$C^1 = \frac{k}{r} \frac{[1 - (1 + r)^{m-1-n}]}{(1 + r)^{m-1}}. \tag{24}$$

If $m = 1$, this reduces to equation (23).

Two serious drawbacks mar this appealing straightforward approach. The estimate of total costs requires a priori knowledge and specification of the investment period. While the period covered by formal schooling is easily determined, the period covered by much on-the-job training and other investment is not, and a serious error might result from an incorrect specification: to take an extreme example, total costs would approach zero as the investment period is assumed to be longer and longer.[3]

[3] Since

$$C^1 = \sum_0^{m-1} (X_j - Y_j)(1 + r)^{-j}, \quad \lim_{m \to n} C^1 = \sum_0^{n-1} (X_j - Y_j)(1 + r)^{-j} = 0,$$

by definition of the internal rate.

A second difficulty is that the differences between net earnings in X and Y do not correctly measure the cost of investing in Y since they do not correctly measure earnings foregone. A person who invested in the initial period could receive more than X_1 in period 1 as long as the initial investment yielded a positive return.[4] The true cost of an investment in period 1 would be the total earnings foregone, or the difference between what could have been received and what is received. The difference between X_1 and Y_1 could greatly underestimate true costs; indeed, Y_1 might be greater than X_1 even though a large investment was made in period 1.[5] In general, therefore, the amount invested in any period would be determined not only from net earnings in the same period but also from net earnings in earlier periods.

If the cost of an investment is consistently defined as the earnings foregone, quite different estimates of total costs emerge. Although superficially a less natural and straightforward approach, the generalization from a single period to distributed investment is actually greatly simplified. Therefore, let C_j be the foregone earnings in the jth period, r_j the rate of return on C_j, and let the return per period on C_j be a constant k_j, with $k = \Sigma k_j$ being the total return on the whole investment. If the number of periods were indefinitely large, and if investment occurred only in the first m periods, the equation relating costs, returns, and internal rates would have the strikingly simple form of [6]

---

[4] If C_0 was the initial investment, r_0 its internal rate, and if the return were the same in all years, the amount

$$X_1^1 = X_1 + \frac{r_0 C_0}{1 - (1 + r_0)^{-n}}$$

could be received in period 1.

[5] Y_1 is greater than X_1 if

$$X_1 + \frac{r_0 C_0}{1 - (1 + r_0)^{-n}} - C_. > X_1, \quad \text{or if} \quad \frac{r_0 C_0}{1 - (1 + r_0)^{-n}} > C_1,$$

where C_1 is the investment in period 1.

[6] A proof is straightforward. An investment in period j would yield a return of the amount $k_j = r_j C_j$ in each succeeding period if the number of periods were infinite and the return were the same in each. Since the total return is the sum of individual returns,

$$k = \sum_0^{m-1} k_j = \sum_0^{m-1} r_j C_j = \mathcal{E} \sum_0^{m-1} \frac{r_j C_j}{C} = rC.$$

I am indebted to Helen Raffel for important suggestions which led to this simple proof.

$$C = \sum_0^{m-1} C_j = \frac{k}{\bar{r}}, \tag{25}$$

where

$$\bar{r} = \sum_0^{m-1} w_j r_j, \quad w_j = \frac{C_j}{C},$$

and

$$\sum_0^{m-1} w_j = 1. \tag{26}$$

Total cost, defined simply as the sum of costs during each period, would equal the capitalized value of returns, the rate of capitalization being a weighted average of the rates of return on the individual investments. Any sequence of internal rates or investment costs is permitted, no matter what the pattern of rises and declines, or the form of investments, be they a college education, an apprenticeship, ballet lessons, or a medical examination. Different investment programs would have the same ultimate effect on earnings whenever the average rate of return and the sum of investment costs were the same.[7]

Equation (25) could be given an interesting interpretation if all rates of return were the same. The term k/r would then be the value at the beginning of the mth period of all succeeding net earning differentials between Y and X discounted at the internal rate, r.[8] Total costs would equal the value also at the beginning of the mth period— which is the end of the investment period—of the first m differentials between X and Y.[9] The value of the first m differentials between X

[7] Note that the rate of return equating the present values of net earnings in X and Y is not necessarily equal to $\bar{r}$, for it would weight the rates of return on earlier investments more heavily than $\bar{r}$ does. For example, if rates were higher on investments in earlier than in later periods, the overall rate would be greater than $\bar{r}$, and vice versa if rates were higher in later periods. Sample calculations indicate, however, that the difference between the overall rate and $\bar{r}$ tends to be small as long as the investment period was not very long and the systematic difference between internal rates not very great.

[8] That is,

$$\sum_{j=m}^{\infty} (Y_j - X_j)(1 + r)^{m-1-j} = k \sum_m^{\infty} (1 + r)^{m-1-j} = \frac{k}{r}.$$

[9] Since, by definition,

$$X_0 - Y_0 = C_0, \quad X_1 - Y_1 = C_1 - rC_0,$$

and Y must equal the value of all succeeding differentials between Y and X, since r would be the rate of return equating the present values in X and Y.

The internal rate of return and the amount invested in each of the first m periods could be estimated from the net earnings streams in X and Y alone if the rate of return were the same on all investments. For the internal rate r could be determined from the condition that the present value of net earnings must be the same in X and Y, and the amount invested in each period seriatim from the relations[10]

$$C_0 = X_0 - Y_0, \quad C_1 = X_1 - Y_1 + rC_0$$

$$C_j = X_j - Y_j + r \sum_{k=0}^{j-1} C_k, \quad 0 \le j \le m - 1.^{[11]} \tag{27}$$

and more generally

$$X_j - Y_j = C_j - r \sum_{k=0}^{j-1} C_k, \quad 0 \le j < m,$$

then

$$\sum_{j=0}^{m-1} (X_j - Y_j)(1 + r)^{m-1-j} = \sum_{j=0}^{m-1} \left(C_j - r \sum_{0}^{j-1} C_k \right)(1 + r)^{m-1-j}$$

$$= \sum_{0}^{m-1} C_j \{ (1 + r)^{m-1-j} - r[1 + (1 + r) + \cdots + (1 + r)^{m-2-j}] \}$$

$$= \sum_{0}^{m-1} C_j = C.$$

The analytical difference between the naive definition of costs advanced earlier and one in terms of foregone earnings is that the former measures total costs by the value of earning differentials at the beginning of the investment period and the latter by the value at the end of the period. Therefore, $C^1 = C(1 + r)^{1-m}$, which follows from equation (24) when $n = \infty$.

[10] If the rate of return were not the same on all investments, there would be $2m$ unknowns—$C_0, \ldots C_{m-1}$, and $r_0, \ldots r_{m-1}$—and only $m + 1$ equations—the m cost definitions and the equation

$$k = \sum_{0}^{m-1} r_i C_i.$$

An additional $m - 1$ relation would be required to determine the $2m$ unknowns. The condition $r_0 = r_1 = \ldots r_{m-1}$ is only one form these $m - 1$ relations can take; another is that costs decrease at certain known rates. If the latter were assumed, all the r_i could be determined from the earnings data.

[11] In econometric terminology this set of equations forms a "causal chain" because of the natural time ordering provided by the aging process. Consequently, there is no identification or "simultaneity" problem.

Thus costs and the rate of return can be estimated from information on net earnings. This is fortunate since the return on human capital is never empirically separated from other earnings and the cost of such capital is only sometimes and incompletely separated.

The investment period of education can be measured by years of schooling, but the periods of on-the-job training, of the search for information, and of other investments are not readily available. Happily, one need not know the investment period to estimate costs and returns, since all three can be simultaneously estimated from information on net earnings. If activity X were known to have no investment (a zero investment period), the amount invested in Y during any period would be defined by

$$C_j = X_j - Y_j + r \sum_0^{j-1} C_k, \quad \text{all } j, \qquad (28)$$

and total costs by

$$C = \sum_0^\infty C_j. \qquad (29)$$

The internal rate could be determined in the usual way from the equality between present values in X and Y, costs in each period from equation (28), and total costs from equation (29).

The definition of costs presented here simply extends to all periods the definition advanced earlier for the investment period.[12] The

[12] Therefore, since the value of the first m earning differentials has been shown to equal

$$\sum_0^{m-1} C_j$$

at period m (see footnote 9), total costs could be estimated from the value of all differentials at the end of the earning period. That is,

$$C = \sum_0^\infty C_j = \sum_0^\infty (X_j - Y_j)^{\infty-1-j}.$$

Thus the value of all differentials would equal zero at the beginning of the earning period—by definition of the internal rate—and C at the end. The apparent paradox results from the infinite horizon, as can be seen from the following equation relating the value of the first f differentials at the beginning of the gth period to costs:

$$V(f, g) = \sum_{j=0}^{f-1} (X_j - Y_j)(1 + r)^{g-1-i} = \sum_{j=0}^{f-1} C_j (1 + r)^{g-f}.$$

When $f = \infty$ and $g = 0$, $V = 0$, but whenever $f = g$,

$$V = \sum_0^{f-1} C_j.$$

In particular, if $f = g = \infty$, $V = C$.

rationale for the general definition is the same: investment occurs in Y whenever earnings there are below the sum of those in X and the income accruing on prior investments. If costs were found to be greater than zero before some period m and equal to zero thereafter, the first m periods would be the empirically derived investment period. But costs and returns can be estimated from equation (28) even when there is no simple investment period.

A common objection to an earlier draft of this paper was that the general and rather formal definition of costs advanced here is all right when applied to on-the-job training, schooling, and other recognized investments, but goes too far by also including as investment costs many effects that should be treated otherwise.

Thus, so the protest might run, learning would automatically lead to a convex and relatively steep earnings profile not because of any associated investment in education or training, but because the well-known "learning curve" is usually convex and rather steep. Since the method presented here, however, depends only on the shape of age-earnings profiles, the effect of learning would be considered an effect of investment in human capital. I accept the argument fully; indeed, I believe that it points up the power rather than the weakness of my analysis and the implied concept of human capital.

To see this requires a fuller analysis of the effect of learning. Assume that Z permits learning and that another activity X does not and has a flat earnings profile: Z might have the profile labeled TT in Chart 1 (in Chapter II) and X that labeled UU. If TT were everywhere above UU—i.e., earnings in Z were greater than those in X at each age—there would be a clear incentive for some persons to leave X and enter Z. The result would be a lowering of TT and raising of UU; generally the process would continue until TT was no longer everywhere above UU, as in Chart 1. Earnings would now be lower in Z than in X at younger ages and higher only later on, and workers would have to decide whether the later higher earnings compensated for the lower initial earnings.

They presumably would decide by comparing the present value of earnings in Z and X, or, what is equivalent, by comparing the rate of return that equates these present values with rates that could be obtained elsewhere. They would choose Z if the present value were greater there, or if the equalizing rate were greater than those elsewhere. Therefore, they would choose Z only if the rate of return on their learning were sufficiently great, that is, only if the returns from learning—the higher earnings later on—offset the costs of learning—the lower earnings initially. Thus choosing between activities "with

a future" and "dead-end" activities involves exactly the same considerations as choosing between continuing one's education and entering
the labor force—whether returns in the form of higher subsequent
earnings sufficiently offset costs in the form of lower initial ones. Although learning cannot be avoided once in activities like Z, it can
be avoided beforehand because workers can enter activities like X that
provide little or no learning. They or society would choose learning
only if it were a sufficiently good investment in the same way that
they or society would choose on-the-job training if it were sufficiently
profitable.

Consequently, the conclusion must be that learning is a way to invest in human capital that is formally no different from education,
on-the-job training, or other recognized investments. So it is a virtue
rather than a defect of our formulation of costs and returns that
learning is treated symmetrically with other investments. And there is
no conflict between interpretations of the shape of earning profiles
based on learning theory[13] and those based on investment in human
capital because the former is a special case of the latter. Of course,
the fact that the physical and psychological factors associated with
learning theory[14] are capable of producing rather steep concave profiles, like TT and even $T'T'$ in Chart 1, should make one hesitate in
relating them to education and other conventional investments. The
converse is also true, however: the fact that many investments in
human capital in a market economy would produce "the learning
curve" should make one hesitate in relating it to the various factors
associated with learning theory.

Another frequent criticism is that many on-the-job investments are
really free in that earnings are not reduced at any age. Although this
would be formally consistent with my analysis since the rate of return
need only be considered infinite (in Chart 1, TT would be nowhere
below UU), I suspect that a closer examination of the alleged "facts"
would usually reveal a much more conventional situation. For example, if abler employees were put through executive training programs,
as is probable, they might earn no less than employees outside the
programs but they might earn less than if they had not been in training.[15] Again, the earnings of employees receiving specific training may

[13] See, for example, J. Mincer, "Investment in Human Capital and Personal Income Distribution," *Journal of Political Economy*, August 1958, pp. 287–288.

[14] See, for example, R. Bush and F. Mosteller, *Stochastic Models for Learning*,
New York, 1955.

[15] Some indirect evidence is cited by J. Mincer in "On-the-Job Training: Costs,
Returns, and Some Implications," *Investment in Human Beings*, NBER Special Conference 15, supplement to *Journal of Political Economy*, October 1962, p. 53.

not be reduced for the reasons presented in Chapter II. Finally, one must have a very poor opinion of the ability of firms to look out for their own interests to believe that infinite rates of return are of great importance.

So much in defense of the approach. To estimate costs empirically still requires a priori knowledge that nothing is invested in activity X. Without such knowledge, only the *difference* between the amounts invested in any two activities with known net earning streams could be estimated from the definitions in equation (28). Were this done for all available streams, the investment in any activity beyond that in the activity with the smallest investment could be determined.[16] The observed minimum investment would not be zero, however, if the rate of return on some initial investment were sufficiently high to attract everyone. A relevant question is, therefore: can the shape of the stream in an activity with zero investment be specified a priori so that the total investment in any activity can be determined?

The statement "nothing is invested in an activity" only means that nothing was invested after the age when information on earnings first became available; investment can have occurred before that age. If, for example, the data begin at age eighteen, some investment in schooling, health, or information surely must have occurred at younger ages. The earning stream of persons who do not invest after age eighteen would have to be considered, at least in part, as a return on the investment before eighteeen. Indeed, in the developmental approach to child rearing, most if not all of these earnings would be so considered.

The earning stream in an activity with no investment beyond the initial age (activity X) would be flat if the developmental approach were followed and earnings were said to result entirely from earlier investment.[17] The incorporation of learning into the concept of investment in human capital also suggests that earnings profiles would be flat were there no (additional) investment. Finally, the empirical evidence, for what it is worth (see comments in Chapter VII), suggests that earnings profiles in unskilled occupations are quite flat. If the earnings profile in X were flat, the unobserved investment could easily be determined in the usual way once an assumption were made about its rate of return.

[16] The technique has been applied and developed further by Mincer (*ibid.*).

[17] If C measured the cost of investment before the initial age and r its rate of return, $k = rC$ would measure the return per period. If earnings were attributed entirely to this investment, $X_i = k = rC$, where X_i represents earnings at the ith period past the initial age.

The assumption that lifetimes are infinite, although descriptively unrealistic, often yields results that are a close approximation to the truth. For example, I show later (see Chapter VI, section 2) that the average rate of return on college education in the United States would be only slightly raised if people remained in the labor force indefinitely. A finite earning period has, however, a greater effect on the rate of return of investments made at later ages, say, after forty; indeed, it helps explain why schooling and other investments are primarily made at younger ages.

An analysis of finite earning streams can be approached in two ways. One simply applies the concepts developed for infinite streams and says there is disinvestment in human capital when net earnings are above the amount that could be maintained indefinitely. Investment at younger ages would give way to disinvestment at older ages until no human capital remained at death (or retirement). This approach has several important applications and is used in parts of the study (see especially Chapter VII). An alternative that is more useful for some purposes lets the earning period itself influence the definitions of accrued income and cost. The income resulting from an investment during period j would be defined as

$$k_j = \frac{r_j C_j}{1 - (1 + r_j)^{j-n}}, \tag{30}$$

where $n + 1$ is the earning period, and the amount invested during j would be defined by

$$C_j = X_j - Y_j + \sum_{k=0}^{k=j-1} \frac{r_k C_k}{1 - (1 + r_k)^{k-n}}. \tag{31}$$

Addendum: The Allocation of Time and Goods over Time

Basic Model

This section discusses the allocation of time and goods over a lifetime among three main sectors: consumption, investment in human capital, and labor force participation. It uses the framework developed in my "A Theory of the Allocation of Time," *Economic Journal*, September 1965. That paper, however, considered the allocation only at a moment of time among various kinds of consumption and time utilizations; this discussion generalizes the analysis to decisions over time and to investment in human capital.

Assume that a person is certain that he will live n periods. His economic welfare depends on his consumption over time of objects of choice called commodities, as in

$$U = U(C_i, \ldots C_n), \tag{32}$$

where C_i is the amount of the commodity consumed during period i. As assumed in the paper cited above, C_i is in turn produced "at home" with inputs of his market goods and his own time. Let the (composite) market goods used in period i be x_i, and the (composite) amount of time combined with x_i be t_{c_i}. Then

$$C_i = {_i}f(x_i, t_{c_i}), \quad i = 1, \ldots n \tag{33}$$

where ${_i}f$ is the production function in period i. If initially it is assumed that time can be allocated only between consumption and labor force participation (called "work"), the following identity holds in each period

$$t_{c_i} + t_{w_i} = t, \quad i = 1, \ldots n \tag{34}$$

where t_{w_i} is the amount of work in i, and t, the total time available during i, is independent of i if all periods are equally long.

The "endowment" in each period is not simply a fixed amount of "income" since that is affected by the hours spent at work, which is a decision variable. Instead it is the vector (w_i, v_i), where v_i is the amount of property income and w_i is the wage rate available in the ith period.

Suppose that there is a perfect capital market with an interest rate, r, the same in each period. Then a constraint on goods that complements the constraints on time given by (34) is that the present value of expenditures on goods must equal the present value of incomes:[18]

$$\sum_{i=1}^{n} \frac{p_i x_i}{(1 + r)^{i-1}} = \sum_{i=1}^{n} \frac{w_i t_{w_i} + v_i}{(1 + r)^{i-1}}. \tag{35}$$

---

[18] Savings in period i is defined as

$$S_i = w_i t_{w_i} + v_i - p_i x_i.$$

Our formulation is implicitly assuming that the savings process itself takes no time; a somewhat weaker assumption, say that savings is less time-intensive than consumption, would not result in greatly different conclusions. I. Ehrlich and U. Ben-Zion have since analyzed the effect of time on savings in "A Theory of Productive Savings," University of Chicago, 1972.

Substitution for t_{w_i} from equation (34) into (35) gives the set of constraints

$$\sum_{i=1}^{n} \frac{p_i x_i + w_i t_{c_i}}{(1 + r)^{i-1}} = \sum_{i=1}^{n} \frac{w_i t + v_i}{(1 + r)^{i-1}}, \qquad (36)$$

and

$$0 \leq t_{c_i} \leq t, \quad x_i \geq 0. \qquad\qquad i = 1, \ldots n \quad (37)$$

The term on the right equals "full wealth," which is an extension of the definition of "full income" given in my earlier article. The term on the left shows how this full wealth is "spent": either on goods or on the foregone earnings associated with the use of time in consumption. Each person (or family) is assumed to maximize his utility function given by equation (32) subject to the constraints given by (36) and (37), and the production functions given by (33). The decision variables are the t_{c_i} and x_i, $2n$ variables. If the optimal values of these variables are assumed to be in the interior of the regions given by (37), and if the wage rates w_i are independent of x_i and t_{c_i}, the first order optimality conditions are simply

$$U_i \cdot {}_i f_x = \frac{\lambda p_i}{(1 + r)^{i-1}} \qquad\qquad i = 1, \ldots, n \quad (38)$$

$$U_i \cdot {}_i f_t = \frac{\lambda w_i}{(1 + r)^{i-1}} \qquad\qquad i = 1, \ldots, n \quad (39)$$

where

$${}_i f_x = \frac{\partial_i f}{\partial x_i}, \quad {}_i f_t = \frac{\partial_i f}{\partial t_{c_i}}, \quad U_i = \frac{\partial U}{\partial C_i}$$

and λ is a Lagrangian multiplier equal to the marginal utility of wealth.

Dividing equation (39) by (38) gives

$$\frac{{}_i f_t}{{}_i f_x} = \frac{w_i}{p_i}, \qquad\qquad i = 1, \ldots, n \quad (40)$$

or in each period the marginal product of consumption time relative to goods equals the real wage rate in the same period, and is independent of the interest rate. In other words, consumption time should have a relatively high marginal product when the real wage rate is relatively high.

To understand the implications of equation (40) somewhat better, assume that all $_jf$ are homogeneous of the first degree, which is a fairly innocuous assumption in the present context. Let us also temporarily assume that the productivity of goods and consumption time do not vary with age, so that f's are the same. Since the marginal productivities of linear homogeneous production functions depend only on factor proportions, equation (40) implies, if marginal products are declining, with these additional assumptions that the production of commodities is relatively time-intensive when real wages are relatively low, and relatively goods-intensive when real wages are relatively high.

Note that this last result is a "substitution" effect and is unambiguous: it is not offset by any "income" effect that operates in the opposite direction. There is no offsetting income or wealth effect because "full" wealth is *fixed*, by the right-hand side of equation (36), and is *completely* independent of the allocation of time and goods over time or at a moment in time. Note, however, that this "substitution" effect is in terms of the *relative* time or goods intensities in different periods, and *not* in terms of the *absolute* amount of consumption time (sometimes called "leisure") in different periods. The latter cannot be determined from equation (40) alone, and depends on the allocation of commodities over time. Only if the consumption of commodities were the same at all periods would relative and absolute intensities necessarily move in the same direction.

To see what happens to commodity consumption over time, consider an alternative form of equation (38):

$$\frac{U_i}{U_j} = \frac{p_i f_{x_i}}{p_j f_{x_i}} (1 + r)^{(j-i)}. \qquad i, j = 1, \ldots n \quad (41)$$

If prices are assumed to be stable, $p_i = p_j = 1$ and equation (41) becomes

$$\frac{U_i}{U_j} = \frac{f_{x_i}}{f_{x_i}} (1 + r)^{(j-i)}. \qquad (42)$$

It has been shown that $t_{c_i}/x_i > t_{c_j}/x_j$ if $w_j > w_i$. It follows from the assumptions of homogeneity and diminishing returns that $f_{x_i} > f_{x_j}$. Hence from (42)

$$\frac{U_i}{U_j} \lesseqgtr (1 + r)^{(j-i)} \quad \text{as} \quad w_i \lesseqgtr w_j. \qquad (43)$$

Note that equality of the left- and right-hand sides, which is undoubtedly the most famous equilibrium condition in the allocation of consumption over time,[19] holds if, and only if, the wage rates are the same in the ith and j^{th} periods.

Consider the implications of (43) for the optimal consumption path over time. I assume neutral time preference in the weak sense that all the U_i would be the same if all the C_i were the same. Then if equality held in (43), all the C_i would be the same if $r = 0$, and would tend to rise over time (ignoring differential wealth effects) if $r > 0$. Equality holds, however, only if the w_i were the same in all periods. But actual wage rates tend to rise with age until the mid-forties, fifties, or sixties, and then begin to decline. With that pattern for the w_i, (43) implies that if $r = 0$, the C_i would not be stationary, but would tend to decline with age until the peak w_i was reached, and then would tend to rise as the w_i fell (see Chart 2).[20]

The rate of fall and then rise of the C_i depends, of course, on the elasticities of substitution in consumption. In addition, the initial decline in C_i would be shorter and less steep and the subsequent rise would be longer, the larger r was (see Chart 2); for sufficiently large r, C_i might rise throughout.

Since $\frac{t_c}{x}$, the ratio of consumption time to goods, would fall as the wage rate rose, and rise as it fell (see Chart 3), if C_i were constant, the absolute value of t_c would have the same pattern as this ratio. A fortiori, if $r = 0$, and if C_i declined as w_i rose and rose as w_i fell (see Chart 2), t_c would fall as w_i rose and rise as it fell (see Chart 3). If $r > 0$, C_i declines more briefly and less rapidly than when $r = 0$, and consequently, so would t_c; in particular, t_c would reach a minimum before w_i reached a maximum. Put differently, hours of work, t_w, would reach a maximum before the wage rate did. The difference between the peaks in t_w and w would be positively related to the size of r, and the elasticities of substitution between different C_i and C_j. Households faced with high interest rates, for example, should hit their peak hours of work earlier than otherwise similar households with low interest rates.

[19] Its derivation is presumably due to I. Fisher (see *The Theory of Interest*, New York, 1965, Chapters XII and XIII); it is also used in countless other studies: see, for example, J. Henderson and R. Quandt, *Microeconomics: A Mathematical Approach*, New York, 1971.

[20] I say "tend to" because of possible differential degrees of substitution between consumption in different periods. For example, high consumption in period l might so raise the marginal utility of consumption in period k as to cause the equilibrium value of C_k to exceed C_j, even though $w_j < w_k$. If the utility function is fully separable, this cannot occur.

CHART 2

Relations between Age, Wage Rates, and Commodity Consumption
Indexes

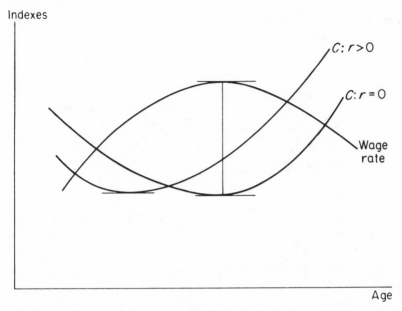

It may appear that the Fisherian equality has simply been hidden
and not replaced by the concentration on C instead of x. Indeed, equation (42) does imply a kind of Fisherian equality if the f terms are
transposed to the left side to yield

$$\frac{MU_{x_i}}{MU_{x_i}} = \frac{U_i f_{x_i}}{U_j f_{x_i}} = (1 + r)^{j-i}. \qquad (44)$$

The term $U_i f_{x_i}$ is the marginal utility of an additional unit of x_i,
and similarly for the j term. Equation (44) would seem to imply a horizontal path of the x_i if $r = 0$ and if time preference were neutral, the
Fisherian result.

However plausible, this conclusion does not follow, and the Fisherian
result cannot be saved. This is partly because the utility function depends directly on C and only indirectly on x, and partly because the
path of x is also dependent on the production function f. If $r = 0$ and
U implied neutral time preference with respect to the C, then the
movement in C would tend to be inversely, and that in x/t_c directly,

CHART 3

Relations between Age, Wage Rates, and Time Spent in Consumption

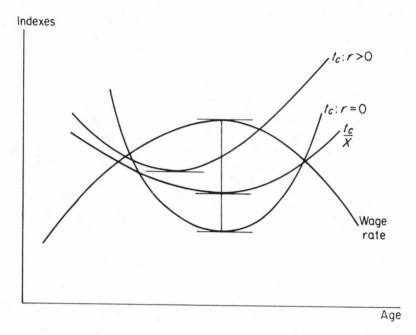

related to the movement in w. The size of these respective movements depends on the elasticities of substitution between the C in U, and between x and t_c in f. The movement in C tends to make x inversely related to the movement in w, whereas that in x/t_c makes it directly related.

The actual movement in x, therefore, is determined by the relative strength of these opposing forces, that is, by the relative size of the elasticities of substitution in consumption and in production. The larger the latter elasticity, the more likely that x is directly related to w. Only if the elasticities were identical would the two substitutions offset each other, and would x be stationary with $r = 0$.[21] Of course, x (and C) are more likely to rise over time the higher r is.

Note that a rise in the consumption of goods with age, which is

[21] For further developments, see G. Ghez, *A Theory of Life Cycle Consumption*, Ph.D. dissertation, Columbia University, 1970, and G. Ghez and G. Becker, *The Allocation of Time and Goods over the Life Cycle*, New York, NBER, 1975.

frequently observed at least until age forty-five, can be explained without recourse to assumptions about time preference for the future, elastic responses to interest rate changes, or underestimation of future incomes. Neutral time preference, negligible interest rate responses, and perfect anticipation of the future could all be assumed if there were sufficiently easy substitution between time and goods in the production of commodities. The time path of goods consumption is not, however, a reliable guide to the path of true consumption (that is, of commodities) since the latter could well be inversely correlated with the former.

Investment in Human Capital

Instead of assuming that time can be allocated only between market labor force activity and nonmarket consumption activity, I now introduce a third category, investment in human capital. For the present an increased amount of human capital, measured by E, is assumed to affect only wage rates. Each person produces his own human capital by using some of his time and goods to attend "school," receive on-the-job training, etc. The rate of change in his capital equals the difference between his rate of production and the rate of depreciation on his stock.[22]

In symbols,

$$\phi_i = \psi_i(t_{e_i}, x_{e_i}),\tag{45}$$

where ϕ_i is the output of human capital in the ith period, and t_{e_i} and x_{e_i} are the time and goods inputs, respectively. Then

$$E_{i+1} = E_i + \phi_i - dE_i,\tag{46}$$

where E_{i+1} is the stock at the beginning of the $i + 1$ period, and d is the rate of depreciation during a period. Each household maximizes the utility function in (32), subject to the production constraints in

[22] This model of human capital accumulation is very similar to and much influenced by that found in Y. Ben-Porath, "The Production of Human Capital and the Life Cycle of Earnings," *Journal of Political Economy*, August 1967, or in the addendum to this volume "Human Capital and the Personal Distribution of Income: An Analytical Approach," pp. 94–144.

(33), (45), and (46), and to the following time and goods "budget" constraints

$$t_{c_i} + t_{w_i} + t_{e_i} = t, \qquad i = 1, \ldots n \quad (47)$$

$$\sum_{i=1}^{n} \frac{x_i + x_{e_i}}{(1 + r)^i} = \sum_{i=1}^{n} \frac{\alpha_i E_i t_{w_i} + v_i}{(1 + r)^i}, \qquad (48)$$

where $w_i = \alpha_i E_i$ and α_i is the payment per unit of human capital in period i. If, for simplicity, one assumes that ϕ_i depends only on t_{e_i} and that ψ_i is the same in all periods, and if the optimal solution has nonzero values of x_i, t_{c_i}, t_{w_i}, and t_{e_i}, the first order optimality conditions are

$$U_i f_{x_i} = \lambda \frac{1}{(1 + r)^i} \qquad i = 1, \ldots n \quad (49)$$

$$U_i f_{t_i} = \lambda \frac{\alpha_i E_i}{(1 + r)^i} \qquad i = 1, \ldots n \quad (50)$$

$$0 = \lambda \left[\frac{\alpha_i E_i}{(1 + r)^i} - \sum_{j=i+1}^{n} \frac{\alpha_j t_{w_j}}{(1 + r)^j} \frac{\partial E_j}{\partial t_{e_i}} \right]. \qquad (51)$$

Equations (49) and (50) are essentially the same as (38) and (39). Therefore, investment in human capital, under the present assumptions, does not basically change the implications derived so far. For example, the time spent in consuming, t_c, would still tend to decline with age, reach a trough before the peak wage rate age, and then increase, and the time path of goods would still depend on the interest rate, and the elasticities of substitution in consumption and production. Two significant differences are, first, that the path of the wage rate is no longer given, but is determined by the path of the endogenous variable E_i. The wage rate would reach a peak before, at, or after the peak in α_i as E_i peaked before, at, or after α_i. Second, the behavior of t_w is no longer simply the complement of the behavior of t_c, since t_w also depends on t_e, which is determined by equation (51).

Equation (51) expresses the well-known equilibrium condition that the present value of the marginal cost of investing in human capital equals the present value of future returns. This equation clearly shows that the amount of time spent investing in human capital would tend to decline with age for two reasons. One is that the number of remaining periods, and thus the present value of future returns, would decline with age. The other is that the cost of investment would tend to rise with age as E_i rose because foregone earnings would rise.

Several interesting consequences follow from the tendency for t_{e_i} to fall as i increases. One is that hours of work, t_w, would be lower at younger ages and rise more rapidly than if there were no investment in human capital. Consequently, as long as t_{e_i} was positive, the peak in t_w would tend to come after the trough in t_c, and might even also come after the peak in w_i. However, since t_e declines with age, if it became sufficiently small by some age p before n, then for $i > p$, the behavior of t_w would be approximately the complement of the behavior of t_c.

If so much time at younger ages were put into investment in human capital that no time remained to allocate to work ($t_w = 0$), t_c and t_e would be complements at these ages. Marginal investment costs would not be measured by foregone earnings, but by the marginal value of time used in consumption, which would exceed foregone earnings (otherwise $t_w > 0$).

If $t_{w_i} = 0$, $i = 1, \ldots q$, instead of equations (49) to (51), the first order optimality condition for $i = 1, \ldots q$ would be

$$U_i f_{x_i} = \lambda \frac{1}{(1 + r)^i} \qquad\qquad i = 1, \ldots q \quad (52)$$

$$U_i f_{t_i} = s_i \qquad\qquad i = 1, \ldots q \quad (53)$$

$$s_i = \lambda \sum_{j=i+1}^{n} \frac{\alpha_j t_{w_j}}{(1 + r)^i} \frac{\partial E_j}{\partial t_{e_i}} \qquad i = 1, \ldots q \quad (54)$$

where s_i is the marginal utility of an additional hour of time spent at consumption in the ith period. If $U_i f_{t_i}$ is substituted for s_i in equation (54),

$$\frac{U_i f_{t_i}}{\lambda} = \sum_{j=i+1}^{n} \frac{\alpha_j t_{w_j}}{(1 + r)^i} \frac{\partial E_j}{\partial t_{e_i}}, \qquad i = 1 \ldots q \quad (55)$$

or the present value of the returns from an additional hour spent investing would equal not foregone earnings but the money equivalent of the marginal utility from an additional hour spent in consumption.

When equation (53) is divided by (52), and a substitution for s_i is made from (54), one has

$$\frac{f_{t_i}}{f_{x_i}} = \sum_{j=i+1}^{n} \frac{\alpha_j t_{w_j}}{(1 + r)^{j-i}} \frac{\partial E_j}{\partial t_{e_i}}; \qquad i = 1 \ldots q \quad (56)$$

the ratio of the marginal products of time and goods is not equated to the wage rate since no time is spent working, but to the monetary value of the marginal productivity of time used in investing. Even if w_i for $i < q$ were small, therefore, the production of commodities would be goods-intensive if the return to investment time were high.

Age and the Production Functions

By assuming that the production functions for commodities and human capital are the same at all ages, I have been able to analyze the different time and goods combinations at different ages in terms of differences in real wage rates and returns alone. Yet presumably as a person gains (or loses) experience, knowledge, and strength with age, the production possibilities available to him also change. This section analyzes the consequences of such changes for the optimal allocation of goods and time.

Let us concentrate on changes in the production functions for commodities, and assume that productive efficiency rises with age until a peak efficiency is reached, and then declines until age n. If the changes in efficiency were factor neutral, the production functions could be written as

$$_i f = g_j f(t_{c_i}, x_j), \qquad (57)$$

where the g_j are coefficients that rise at first and then decline. Equation (49) would become

$$U_i \,_i f_{x_i} \equiv g_i U_i f_{x_i} = \lambda \frac{1}{(1 + r)^i}, \qquad (58)$$

equation (50) would become

$$U_i \,_i f_{t_i} = g_i U_i f_{t_i} = \lambda \frac{\alpha_i E_i}{(1 + r)^i}, \qquad (59)$$

while equation (51) would be unaffected.

If equation (58) is divided by (59), the efficiency coefficients g_i drop out, and the optimal combination of time and goods depends, as before, only on the shape of f and $\alpha_i E_i$. Therefore, goods intensity rises until a peak is reached at the peak wage age, and then falls, and does not at all depend on the path of the s_i.

If $r = 0$ and w were rising with age, the decline in C with age would be greater than when production functions did not change if productive efficiency (measured by g) were falling with age because the marginal cost of producing C would rise faster with age; conversely if g were rising with age. The effect on the x and t_c is less definite and depends also on the elasticity of substitution in consumption because changes in the efficiency of producing C—the use of x and t_c per unit of C—can offset the change in C. If this elasticity exceeded unity, changes in efficiency would change x and t_c in the same direction as it changes C.

If changes in efficiency were not factor neutral but, say, changed the marginal product of consumption time more than that of goods ("goods-saving" change), there would be less incentive to substitute goods for time as wages rose if efficiency also rose. Therefore, production would not become as goods-intensive when wages and efficiency were rising, or as time-intensive when they were both falling. The converse would hold, of course, if changes in efficiency changed the marginal product of goods more than time.

Human Capital and Consumption

So far I have assumed that an increase in human capital directly only changes the productivity of time in the marketplace. Human capital might, however, also change the productivity of time and goods used in producing household consumption or in producing additional human capital itself.

Studies of investment in education and other human capital have been repeatedly criticized for ignoring the consumption aspects, although critics have been no more successful than others in treating these aspects in a meaningful way. One approach is to permit human capital to enter utility functions, but given the difficulties in measuring, quantifying, and comparing utilities, this does not seem too promising. An alternative is to assume that human capital "shifts" household production functions,[23] as in

$$C_i = {}_if(x_i, t_{c_i}; E_i). \tag{60}$$

The marginal effect* of human capital on consumption in the ith period can be defined as the marginal product or "shift" of C_i with respect to E_i:

$$MP_{e_i} = \frac{\partial C_i}{\partial E_i} = \frac{\partial_i f}{\partial E_i} = {}_if_{e_i}. \tag{61}$$

[23] This approach is treated in considerable detail, both theoretically and empirically, by R. Michael, *The Effect of Education on Efficiency in Consumption*, New York, NBER, 1972, an outgrowth of a 1969 Ph.D. dissertation at Columbia.

The optimal allocation of time and goods can still be found by differentiating the utility function subject to the production functions and budget constraints. Equilibrium conditions (49) and (50) or (52) and (53) would be formally unaffected by the inclusion of E in the production of commodities. The equilibrium conditions with respect to t_e, the time spent investing in human capital, would, however, change from equation (51) to

$$\sum_{j=i+1}^{n} U_j f_{e_i} \frac{\partial E_j}{\partial t_{e_i}} = \lambda \left(\frac{\alpha_i E_i}{(1+r)^i} - \sum_{j=i+1}^{n} \frac{\alpha_j t_{w_j}}{(1+r)^i} \frac{\partial E_j}{\partial t_{e_i}} \right) \qquad (62)$$

or

$$\frac{\alpha_i E_i}{(1+r)^i} = \sum_{j=i+1}^{n} \frac{U_j}{\lambda} f_{e_i} \frac{\partial E_j}{\partial t_{e_i}} + \sum_{j=i+1}^{n} \frac{\alpha_j t_{w_j}}{(1+r)^i} \frac{\partial E_j}{\partial t_{e_i}}. \qquad (63)$$

A similar change would be produced in equation (54).

The term on the left-hand side of equation (63) is the present value of foregone earnings in period i—the cost of using more time in period i to produce human capital—and the terms on the right give the present value of the benefits. The second term on the right is the familiar present value of monetary returns, and gives the increase in wealth resulting from an additional investment in human capital in period i. The first term on the right is less familiar and measures the effect of additional investment on consumption. It essentially measures the present value of the reduction in goods and time required to produce a given basket of commodities resulting from increased investment in period i.[24]

---

[24] Since f is homogeneous of the first degree in x and t_c,

$$C_i \equiv f_{x_i} x_i + f_{t_i} t_{c_i}, \qquad (1')$$

then

$$\frac{\partial C_i}{\partial E_i} \equiv f_{e_i} \equiv \frac{\partial f_{x_i}}{\partial E_i} x_i + \frac{\partial f_{t_i}}{\partial E_i} t_{c_i}. \qquad (2')$$

Define

$$\tilde{f}_{x_i} \equiv \frac{\partial f_{x_i}}{\partial E_i} \Big/ f_{x_i} \quad \text{and} \quad \tilde{f}_{t_i} \equiv \frac{\partial f_{t_i}}{\partial E_i} \Big/ f_{t_i}. \qquad (3')$$

Then

$$f_{e_i} \equiv \tilde{f}_{x_i}(f_{x_i} x_i) + \tilde{f}_{t_i}(f_{t_i} t_{c_i}). \qquad (4')$$

Substituting from the equilibrium conditions (49) and (50) for f_{x_i} and f_{t_i} yields

$$f_{e_i} = \frac{\lambda}{U_i} \left(\tilde{f}_{x_i} \frac{x_i}{(1+r)^i} + \tilde{f}_{t_i} \frac{\alpha_i E_i t_{c_i}}{(1+r)^i} \right), \qquad (5')$$

Treated in this way, the effect of human capital on consumption becomes symmetrical to its effect on investment: the latter gives the monetary value of the stream of increased incomes, whereas the former gives the monetary value of the stream of reduced costs.

A few implications of the inclusion of the consumption effects of human capital can be noted briefly. Since they clearly raise the total benefits from investment, more time at each age would be spent investing than if these effects were nil. This in turn implies a greater likelihood of "corner" solutions, especially at younger ages, with the equilibrium conditions given by equations (52), (53), and an extension of (54)[25] being relevant. Moreover, there would now be justification for an assumption that efficiency in consumption and wage rates rise and fall together, because they would be the joint results of changes in the stock of human capital.

Some Extensions of the Analysis

It is neither realistic nor necessary to assume that wage rates are given, aside from the effects of human capital. The average wage rate and the number of hours a person works are generally related because of fatigue, differences between part-time and full-time opportunities,

---

and thus

$$\frac{U_i}{\lambda} f_{e_i} = \widetilde{f}_{x_i} \frac{x_i}{(1+r)^i} + \widetilde{f}_{t_i} \frac{\alpha_i E_i l_{c_i}}{(1+r)^i}. \tag{6'}$$

The terms $\widetilde{f}_{x_i}$ and $\widetilde{f}_{t_i}$ equal the percentage reductions in goods and time respectively in period i required to produce a given C_i resulting from the "shift" in f caused by a unit increase in E_i. Hence, the full term on the right-hand side of (6') gives the present value of the savings in goods and time in period i required to achieve a given amount of C_i. Consequently,

$$\sum_{j=i+1}^{n} \frac{U_j}{\lambda} f_{e_j} \frac{\partial E_j}{\partial t_{e_i}} = \sum_{j=i+1}^{n} \frac{\widetilde{f}_{x_j} x_j}{(1+r)^j} + \frac{\widetilde{f}_{t_j} \alpha_j E_j l_{c_j}}{(1+r)^j} \frac{\partial E_j}{\partial t_{e_i}} \tag{7'}$$

gives the full present value of the savings in goods and time resulting from additional investment in human capital in period i.

25 With consumption effects, equation (54) is replaced by

$$\sum_{j=i+1}^{n} U_j \frac{\partial E_j}{\partial t_{e_i}} - s_i + \lambda \sum_{j=i+1}^{n} \frac{\alpha_j l_{w_j}}{(1+r)^j} \frac{\partial E_j}{\partial t_{e_i}} = 0,$$

or

$$\frac{s_i}{\lambda} = \sum_{j=i+1}^{n} \frac{U_j}{\lambda} f_{e_j} \frac{\partial E_j}{\partial t_{e_i}} + \sum_{j=i+1}^{n} \frac{\alpha_j l_{w_j}}{(1+r)^j} \frac{\partial E_j}{\partial t_{e_i}}. \tag{54'}$$

fixed costs of working, overtime provisions, and so forth. Our analysis can easily incorporate an effect of t_w on w, as in

$$w_i = w_i(t_{w_i}), \qquad (64)$$

or even more generally in

$$w_i = w_i(t_{w_i}, t_{w_{i-1}}, \ldots t_{w_1}) \qquad (65)$$

if on-the-job learning is to be analyzed separately from other human capital. Marginal, not average, wage rates are the relevant measures of the cost of time and would enter the equilibrium conditions.[26]

It would also be more realistic to consider several commodities at any moment in time, each having its own production function and goods and time inputs. This could easily be done by introducing the utility function

$$U = U(C_{1l}, \ldots C_{1n}, C_{2l}, \ldots C_{2n}, \ldots C_{ml}, \ldots C_{mn}), \qquad (66)$$

where C_j is the amount of the jth commodity consumed in the ith period. This function would be maximized subject to separate production functions for each commodity (and perhaps in each period) and to the budget constraints. One of the main implications is that when wage rates are relatively high, not only is the production of each commodity relatively goods-intensive, but consumption shifts toward relatively goods-intensive commodities and away from time-intensive commodities. The latter (such as children or grandchildren) would be consumed more at younger and older ages if wage rates or more generally the cost of time rose at younger ages and fell eventually; conversely, goods-intensive commodities would be consumed more at middle ages. These age patterns in the consumption of time and goods-intensive commodities strengthen the tendency for consumption time to fall initially and for goods to rise initially with age.

The accumulation of human capital might also "shift" the production function used to produce human capital itself since investors with much human capital might well be more productive than those with little. This has been discussed elsewhere,[27] and I only mention here

---

[26] For example, if equation (64) is the wage rate function, equation (65) would be replaced by

$$U_i f_{t_i} = \lambda \left(\frac{\alpha_i E_i}{(1+r)^i} + \frac{\partial \alpha_i}{\partial t_{w_i}} \frac{t_{w_i} E_i}{(1+r)^i} \right). \qquad (65')$$

[27] See Ben-Porath, *op. cit.*, and addendum to this volume "Human Capital and the Personal Distribution of Income: An Analytical Approach," pp. 94–144.

one implication. The tendency for the amount invested to decline with age would be somewhat retarded because investment would be encouraged as capital was accumulated, since time would become more productive and this would offset the effect of its becoming more costly.

The allocation over a lifetime should be put in a family context, with the decisions of husbands, wives, and possibly also children interacting with each other. For example, if wives' wage rates are more stationary than their husbands', the analysis in this paper predicts that the labor force participation of married women would be relatively high at younger and older ages, and relatively low at middle ages, precisely what is observed. A similar result would follow if the productivity in consumption of married women's time is higher at middle ages because child rearing is time-intensive. The analysis developed here seems capable of throwing considerable light on the differential labor force participation patterns by age of husbands and wives.[28]

Empirical Analysis

Some implications of this model have been tested by the author with data from the 1960 Census 1/1000 sample giving earnings, hours, and weeks worked, cross-classified by age, sex, race, and education.[29]

2. The Incentive to Invest

Number of Periods

Economists have long believed that the incentive to expand and improve physical resources depends on the rate of return expected. They have been very reluctant, however, to interpret improvements in the effectiveness and amount of human resources in the same way, namely, as systematic responses or "investments" resulting in good part from the returns expected. In this section and the next one, I try to show that an investment approach to human resources is a powerful and simple tool capable of explaining a wide range of phenomena, in-

---

28 This has been confirmed in several studies since this was written; see A. Leibowitz, "Women's Allocation of Time to Market and Non-Market Activities," Ph.D. dissertation, Columbia University, 1972; or H. Ofek, "Allocation of Goods and Time in a Family Context," Ph.D. dissertation, Columbia University, 1971; or J. Smith, "A Life Cycle Family Model, NBER Working Paper 5, 1973.

29 The results are published in Ghez and Becker, *op. cit.*, Chapter 3.

cluding much that has been either ignored or given ad hoc interpretations. The discussion covers many topics, starting with the life span of activities and ending with a theory of the distribution of earnings. [An increase in the life span of an activity would, other things being equal, increase the rate of return on the investment made in any period. The influence of life span on the rate of return and thus on the incentive to invest is important and takes many forms, a few of which will now be discussed.

The number of periods is clearly affected by mortality and morbidity rates; the lower they are, the longer is the expected life span and the larger is the fraction of a lifetime that can be spent at any activity. The major secular decline of these rates in the United States and elsewhere probably increased the rates of return on investment in human capital,[30] thereby encouraging such investment.[31] This conclusion is independent of whether the secular improvement in health itself resulted from investment; if so, the secular increase in rates of return would be part of the return to the investment in health.

A relatively large fraction of younger persons are in school or on-the-job training, change jobs and locations, and add to their knowledge of economic, political, and social opportunities. The main explanation may not be that the young are relatively more interested in learning, able to absorb new ideas, less tied down by family responsibilities, more easily supported by parents, or more flexible about changing their routine and place of living. One need not rely only on life-cycle effects on capabilities, responsibilities, or attitudes as soon as one recognizes that schooling, training, mobility, and the like are ways to invest in human capital and that younger people have a greater incentive to invest because they can collect the return over more years. Indeed, there would be a greater incentive even if age had no effect on capabilities, responsibilities, and attitudes.

The ability to collect returns over more years would give young

---

[30] I say *probably* because rates of return are adversely affected (via the effects on marginal productivity) by the increase in labor force that would result from a decline in death and sickness. If the adverse effect were sufficiently great, their decline would reduce rates of return on human capital. I am indebted to my wife for emphasizing this point.

[31] The relation between investment in training and length of life is apparently even found in the training of animals, as evidenced by this statement from a book I read to my children: "Working elephants go through a long period of schooling. Training requires about ten years and costs nearly five thousand dollars. In view of the animal's long life of usefulness [they usually live more than sixty years], this is not considered too great an investment" (M. H. Wilson, *Animals of the World*, New York, 1960).

persons a much greater incentive to invest even if the internal rate of return did not decline much with age. The internal rate can be seriously misleading here, as the following example indicates. If $100 invested at any age yielded $10 a year additional income forever, the rate of return would be 10 per cent at every age, and there would be no special incentive to invest at younger ages if only the rate of return were taken into account. Consider, however, a cohort of persons aged eighteen deciding when to invest. If the rate of return elsewhere were 5 per cent and if they invested immediately, the present value of the gain would be $100. If they waited five years, the present value of the gain, i.e., as of age eighteen, would only be about $78, or 22 per cent less; if they waited ten years, the present value of the gain would be under $50, or less than half. Accordingly, a considerable incentive would exist for everyone to invest immediately rather than waiting. In less extreme examples some persons might wait until older ages, but the number investing would tend to decline rapidly with age even if the rate of return did not.[32]

Although the unification of these different kinds of behavior by the investment approach is important evidence in its favor, other evidence is needed. A powerful test can be developed along the following lines.[33] Suppose that investment in human capital raised earnings for p periods only, where p varied between 0 and n. The size of p would be affected by many factors, including the rate of obsolescence since the more rapidly an investment became obsolete the smaller p would be. The advantage in being young would be less the smaller p was, since the effect of age on the rate of return would be positively related to p. For example, if p equaled two years, the rate would be the same at all ages except the two nearest the "retirement" age. If the investment approach were correct, the difference between the amount

32 One clear application of these considerations can be found in studies of migration, where some writers have rejected the importance of the period of returns because migration rates decline strongly with age, at least initially, while rates of return (or some equivalent) decline slowly (see the otherwise fine paper by L. Sjaastad, "The Costs and Returns of Human Migration," *Investment in Human Beings*, pp. 89–90). My analysis suggests, however, that persons with a clear gain from migration have a strong incentive to migrate early and not wait even a few years. Since the persons remaining presumably have either no incentive or little incentive to migrate, it is not surprising that their migration rates should be much lower than that of all persons.

33 This test was suggested by George Stigler's discussion of the effect of different autocorrelation patterns on the incentive to invest in information (see "The Economics of Information," *Journal of Political Economy*, June 1961, and "Information in the Labor Market," *Investment in Human Beings*, pp. 94–105).

invested at different ages would be positively correlated with p, which is not surprising since an expenditure with a small p would be less of an "investment" than one with a large p, and arguments based on an investment framework would be less applicable. None of the life-cycle arguments seem to imply any correlation with p, so this provides a powerful test of the importance of the investment approach.

The time spent in any one activity is determined not only by age, mortality, and morbidity but also by the amount of switching between activities. Women spend less time in the labor force than men and, therefore, have less incentive to invest in market skills; tourists spend little time in any one area and have less incentive than residents of the area to invest in knowledge of specific consumption opportunities;[34] temporary migrants to urban areas have less incentive to invest in urban skills than permanent residents; and, as a final example, draftees have less incentive than professional soldiers to invest in purely military skills.

Women, tourists, and the like have to find investments that increase productivity in several activities. A woman wants her investment to be useful both in her roles as a housewife and as a participant in the labor force, or a frequent traveler wants to be knowledgeable in many environments. Such investments would be less readily available than more specialized ones—after all, an investment increasing productivity in two activities also increases it in either one alone, extreme complementarity aside, while the converse does not hold; specialists, therefore, have greater incentive to invest in themselves than others do.

Specialization in an activity would be discouraged if the market were very limited; thus the incentive to specialize and to invest in oneself would increase as the extent of the market increased. Workers would be more skilled the larger the market, not only because "practice makes perfect," which is so often stressed in discussions of the division of labor,[35] but also because a larger market would *induce* a greater investment in skills.[36] Put differently, the usual analysis of the division of labor stresses that efficiency, and thus wage rates, would be

---

[34] This example is from Stigler, "The Economics of Information," *Journal of Political Economy*, June 1961.

[35] See, for example, A. Marshall, *Principles of Economics*, New York, 1949, Book IV, Chapter ix.

[36] If "practice makes perfect" means that age-earnings profiles slope upward, then according to my approach it must be treated along with other kinds of learning as a way of investing in human capital. The above distinction between the effect of an increase in the market on practice and on the incentive to invest would then simply be that the incentive to invest in human capital is increased even aside from the effect of practice on earnings.

greater the larger the market, and ignores the potential earnings period in any activity, while mine stresses that this period, and thus the incentive to *become* more "efficient," would be directly related to market size. Surprisingly little attention has been paid to the latter, that is, to the influence of market size on the incentive to invest in skills.

Wage Differentials and Secular Changes

According to equation (30), the internal rate of return depends on the ratio of the return per unit of time to investment costs. A change in the return and costs by the same percentage would not change the internal rate, while a greater percentage change in the return would change the internal rate in the same direction. The return is measured by the absolute income gain, or by the absolute income difference between persons differing only in the amount of their investment. Note that absolute, not relative, income differences determine the return and the internal rate.

Occupational and educational wage differentials are sometimes measured by relative, sometimes by absolute, wage differences,[37] although no one has adequately discussed their relative merits. Since marginal productivity analysis relates the derived demand for any class of workers to the ratio of their wages to those of other inputs,[38] wage ratios are more appropriate in understanding forces determining demand. They are not, however, the best measure of forces determining supply, for the return on investment in skills and other knowledge is determined by absolute wage differences. Therefore neither wage ratios nor wage differences are uniformly the best measure, ratios being more appropriate in demand studies and differences in supply studies.

The importance of distinguishing between wage ratios and differences, and the confusion resulting from the practice of using ratios

[37] See A. M. Ross and W. Goldner, "Forces Affecting the Interindustry Wage Structure," *Quarterly Journal of Economics*, May 1950; P. H. Bell, "Cyclical Variations and Trend in Occupational Wage Differentials in American Industry since 1914," *Review of Economics and Statistics*, November 1951; F. Meyers and R. L. Bowlby, "The Interindustry Wage Structure and Productivity," *Industrial and Labor Relations Review*, October 1953; G. Stigler and D. Blank, *The Demand and Supply of Scientific Personnel*, New York, NBER, 1957, Table 11; P. Keat, "Long-Run Changes in Occupational Wage Structure, 1900–1956," *Journal of Political Economy*, December 1960.

[38] Thus the elasticity of substitution is usually defined as the percentage change in the ratio of quantities employed per 1 per cent change in the ratio of wages.

to measure supply as well as demand forces, can be illustrated by considering the effects of technological progress. If progress were uniform in all industries and neutral with respect to all factors, and if there were constant costs, initially all wages would rise by the same proportion and the prices of all goods, including the output of industries supplying the investment in human capital,[39] would be unchanged. Since wage ratios would be unchanged, firms would have no incentive initially to alter their factor proportions. Wage differences, on the other hand, would rise at the same rate. as wages, and since investment costs would be unchanged, there would be an incentive to invest more in human capital, and thus to increase the relative supply of skilled persons. The increased supply would in turn reduce the rate of increase of wage differences and produce an absolute narrowing of wage ratios.

In the United States during much of the last eighty years, a narrowing of wage ratios has gone hand in hand with an increasing relative supply of skill, an association that is usually said to result from the effect of an autonomous increase in the supply of skills—brought about by the spread of free education or the rise in incomes—on the return to skill, as measured by wage ratios. An alternative interpretation suggested by the analysis here is that the spread of education and the increased investment in other kinds of human capital were in large part *induced* by technological progress (and perhaps other changes) through the effect on the rate of return, as measured by wage differences and costs. Clearly a secular decline in wage ratios would not be inconsistent with a secular increase in real wage differences if average wages were rising, and, indeed, one important body of data on wages shows a decline in ratios and an even stronger rise in differences.[40]

The interpretation based on autonomous supply shifts has been favored partly because a decline in wage ratios has erroneously been taken as evidence of a decline in the return to skill. While a decision ultimately can be based only on a detailed reexamination of the evi-

---

[39] Some persons have argued that only direct investment costs would be unchanged, indirect costs or foregone earnings rising along with wages. Neutral progress implies, however, the same increase in the productivity of a student's time as in his teacher's time or in the use of raw materials, so even foregone earnings would not change.

[40] Keat's data for 1906 and 1953 in the United States show both an average annual decline of 0.8 per cent in the coefficient of variation of wages and an average annual rise of 1.2 per cent in the real standard deviation. The decline in the coefficient of variation was shown in his study (*ibid.*); I computed the change in the real standard deviation from data made available to me by Keat.

dence,[41] the induced approach can be made more plausible by considering trends in physical capital. Economists have been aware that the rate of return on capital could be rising or at least not falling while the ratio of the "rental" price of capital to wages was falling. Consequently, although the rental price of capital declined relative to wages over time, the large secular increase in the amount of physical capital per man-hour is not usually considered autonomous, but rather induced by technological and other developments that, at least temporarily, raised the return. A common explanation based on the effects of economic progress may, then, account for the increase in both human and physical capital.[42]

Risk and Liquidity

An informed, rational person would invest only if the expected rate of return were greater than the sum of the interest rate on riskless assets and the liquidity and risk premiums associated with the investment. Not much need be said about the "pure" interest rate, but a few words are in order on risk and liquidity. Since human capital is a very illiquid asset—it cannot be sold and is rather poor collateral on loans—a positive liquidity premium, perhaps a sizable one, would be associated with such capital.

The actual return on human capital varies around the expected return because of uncertainty about several factors. There has always been considerable uncertainty about the length of life, one important determinant of the return. People are also uncertain about their ability, especially younger persons who do most of the investing. In addition, there is uncertainty about the return to a person of given age and ability because of numerous events that are not predictable. The long time required to collect the return on an investment in human capital reduces the knowledge available, for knowledge re-

[41] For those believing that the qualitative evidence overwhelmingly indicates a continuous secular decline in rates of return on human capital, I reproduce Adam Smith's statement on earnings in some professions. "The lottery of the law, therefore, is very far from being a perfectly fair lottery; and that, as well as many other liberal and honourable professions, is, in point of pecuniary gain, evidently under-recompensed" (*The Wealth of Nations*, Modern Library edition, New York, 1937, p. 106). Since economists tend to believe that law and most other liberal professions are now overcompensated relative to nonprofessional work "in point of pecuniary gain," the return to professional work could not have declined continuously if Smith's observations were accurate.

[42] Some quantitative evidence for the United States is discussed in Chapter VI, section 2.

quired is about the environment when the return is to be received, and the longer the average period between investment and return, the less such knowledge is available.

Informed observation as well as calculations I have made suggest that there is much uncertainty about the return to human capital.[43] The response to uncertainty is determined by its amount and nature and by tastes or attitudes. Many have argued that attitudes of investors in human capital are very different from those of investors in physical capital because the former tend to be younger,[44] and young persons are supposed to be especially prone to overestimate their ability and chance of good fortune.[45] Were this view correct, a human investment that promised a large return to exceptionally able or lucky persons would be more attractive than a similar physical investment. However, a "life-cycle" explanation of attitudes toward risk may be no more valid or necessary than life-cycle explanations of why investors in human capital are relatively young (discussed above). Indeed, an alternative explanation of reactions to large gains has already appeared.[46]

Capital Markets and Knowledge

If investment decisions responded only to earning prospects, adjusted for risk and liquidity, the adjusted marginal rate of return would be the same on all investments. The rate of return on education, training, migration, health, and other human capital is supposed to be higher than on nonhuman capital, however, because of financing diffi-

---

[43] For example, Marshall said: "Not much less than a generation elapses between the choice by parents of a skilled trade for one of their children, and his reaping the full results of their choice. And meanwhile the character of the trade may have been almost revolutionized by changes, on which some probably threw long shadows before them, but others were such as could not have been foreseen even by the shrewdest persons and those best acquainted with the circumstances of the trade" and "the circumstances by which the earnings are determined are less capable of being foreseen [than those for machinery]" (*Principles of Economics*, p. 571). In section 4 of Chapter IV some quantitative estimates of the uncertainty in the return to education are presented.

[44] Note that our argument above implied that investors in human capital would be younger.

[45] Smith said: "The contempt of risk and the presumptuous hope of success are in no period of life more active than at the age at which young people choose their professions" (*Wealth of Nations*, p. 109). Marshall said that "young men of an adventurous disposition are more attracted by the prospects of a great success than they are deterred by the fear of failure" (*Principles of Economics*, p. 554).

[46] See M. Friedman and L. J. Savage, "The Utility Analysis of Choices Involving Risks," reprinted in *Readings in Price Theory*, G. J. Stigler and K. Boulding, eds., Chicago, 1952.

culties and inadequate knowledge of opportunities. These will now be discussed briefly.

Economists have long emphasized that it is difficult to borrow funds to invest in human capital because such capital cannot be offered as collateral, and courts have frowned on contracts that even indirectly suggest involuntary servitude. This argument has been explicitly used to explain the "apparent" underinvestment in education and training and also, although somewhat less explicitly, underinvestment in health, migration, and other human capital. The importance attached to capital market difficulties can be determined not only from the discussions of investment but also from the discussions of consumption. Young persons would consume relatively little, productivity and wages might be related, and some other consumption patterns would follow only if it were difficult to capitalize future earning power. Indeed, unless capital limitations applied to consumption as well as investment, the latter could be indirectly financed with "consumption" loans.[47]

Some other implications of capital market difficulties can also be mentioned:

1. Since large expenditures would be more difficult to finance, investment in, say, a college education would be more affected than in, say, short-term migration.

2. Internal financing would be common, and consequently wealthier families would tend to invest more than poorer ones.

3. Since employees' specific skills are part of the intangible assets or good will of firms and can be offered as collateral along with tangible assets, capital would be more readily available for specific than for general investments.

4. Some persons have argued that opportunity costs (foregone earnings) are more readily financed than direct costs because they require only to do "without," while the latter require outlays. Although superficially plausible, this view can easily be shown to be wrong: opportunity and direct costs can be financed equally readily, given the state of the capital market. If total investment costs were $800, potential earnings $1000, and if all costs were foregone earnings, investors would have $200 of earnings to spend; if all were direct costs, they would initially have $1000 to spend, but just $200 would remain after

---

[47] A person with an income of X and investment costs of Y ($Y < X$) could either use X for consumption and receive an *investment loan* of Y, or use $X - Y$ for consumption, Y for investment, and receive a *consumption loan* of Y. He ends up with the same consumption and investment in both cases, the only difference being in the names attached to the loans.

paying "tuition," so their *net* position would be exactly the same as before. The example can be readily generalized and the obvious inference is that indirect and direct investment costs are equivalent in imperfect as well as perfect capital markets.

While it is undeniably difficult to use the capital market to finance investments in human capital, there is some reason to doubt whether otherwise equivalent investments in physical capital can be financed much more easily. Consider an eighteen-year-old who wants to invest a given amount in equipment for a firm he is starting rather than in a college education. What is his chance of borrowing the whole amount at a "moderate" interest rate? Very slight, I believe, since he would be untried and have a high debt-equity ratio; moreover, the collateral provided by his equipment would probably be very imperfect. He, too, would either have to borrow at high interest rates or self-finance. Although the difficulties of financing investments in human capital have usually been related to special properties of human capital, in large measure they also seem to beset comparable investments in physical capital.

A recurring theme is that young persons are especially prone to be ignorant of their abilities and of the investment opportunities available. If so, investors in human capital, being younger, would be less aware of opportunities and thus more likely to err than investors in tangible capital. I suggested earlier that investors in human capital are younger partly because of the cost in postponing their investment to older ages. The desire to acquire additional knowledge about the return and about alternatives provides an incentive to postpone any risky investment, but since an investment in human capital is more costly to postpone, it would be made earlier and presumably with less knowledge than comparable nonhuman investments. Therefore, investors in human capital may not have less knowledge *because* of their age; rather both might be a *joint* product of the incentive not to delay investing.

The eighteen-year-old in our example who could not finance a purchase of machinery might, without too much cost, postpone the investment for a number of years until his reputation and equity were sufficient to provide the "personal" collateral required to borrow funds. Financing may prove a more formidable obstacle to investors in human capital because they cannot postpone their investment so readily. Perhaps this accounts for the tendency of economists to stress capital market imperfections when discussing investments in human capital.

3. Some Effects of Human Capital

Examples

Differences in earnings among persons, areas, or time periods are usually said to result from differences in physical capital, technological knowledge, ability, or institutions (such as unionization or socialized production). The previous discussion indicates, however, that investment in human capital also has an important effect on observed earnings because earnings tend to be net of investment costs and gross of investment returns. Indeed, an appreciation of the direct and indirect importance of human capital appears to resolve many otherwise puzzling empirical findings about earnings. Consider the following examples:

1. Almost all studies show that age-earnings profiles tend to be steeper among more skilled and educated persons. I argued earlier (Chapter II, section 1) that on-the-job training would steepen age-earnings profiles, and the analysis of section 1 of this chapter generalizes the argument to all human capital. For since observed earnings are gross of returns and net of costs, investment in human capital at younger ages would reduce observed earnings then and raise them at older ages, thus steepening the age-earnings profile.[48] Likewise, investment in human capital would make the profile more concave.[49]

[48] According to equation (28), earnings at age j can be approximated by

$$Y_j = X_j + \sum_{k=0}^{k=j-1} r_k C_k - C_j,$$

where X_j are earnings at j of persons who have not invested in themselves, C_k is the investment at age k, and r_k is its rate of return. The rate of increase in earnings would be at least as steep in Y as in X at each age and not only from "younger" to "older" ages if and only if

$$\frac{\Delta Y_j}{\Delta j} \geq \frac{\Delta X_j}{\Delta j},$$

or

$$r_j C_j \geq \frac{\Delta C_j}{\Delta j}.$$

This condition is usually satisfied since $r_j C_j \geq 0$ and the amount invested tends to decline with age.

[49] Following the notation of the previous footnote, Y would be more concave than X if and only if

$$\Delta \left(\frac{\Delta Y_j}{\Delta j} \right) - \Delta \left(\frac{\Delta X_j}{\Delta j} \right) = \Delta \left(\frac{r_j C_j}{\Delta j} \right) - \Delta \left(\frac{\Delta C_j}{\Delta j} \right) < 0.$$

The first term on the right is certain to be negative, at least eventually, because

2. In recent years students of international trade theory have been somewhat shaken by findings that the United States, said to have a relative scarcity of labor and an abundance of capital, apparently exports relatively labor-intensive commodities and imports relatively capital-intensive commodities. For example, one study found that export industries pay higher wages than import-competing ones.[50]

An interpretation consistent with the Ohlin-Heckscher emphasis on the relative abundance of different factors argues that the United States has an even more (relatively) abundant supply of human than of physical capital. An increase in human capital would, however, show up as an apparent increase in labor intensity since earnings are gross of the return on such capital. Thus export industries might pay higher wages than import-competing ones primarily because they employ more skilled or healthier workers.[51]

3. Several studies have tried to estimate empirically the elasticity of substitution between capital and labor. Usually a ratio of the input of physical capital (or output) to the input of labor is regressed on the wage rate in different areas or time periods, the regression coefficient being an estimate of the elasticity of substitution.[52] Countries, states, or time periods that have relatively high wages and inputs of physical capital also tend to have much human capital. Just as a correlation between wages, physical capital, and human capital seems to obscure the relationship between relative factor supplies and commodity prices, so it obscures the relationship between relative factor supplies and factor prices. For if wages were high primarily because of human capital, a regression of the relative amount of physical capital on wages

---

both r_j and C_j would eventually decline, while the second term would be positive because C_j would eventually decline at a decreasing rate. Consequently, the inequality would tend to hold and the earnings profile in Y would be more concave than that in X.

[50] See I. Kravis, "Wages and Foreign Trade," *Review of Economics and Statistics,* February 1956.

[51] This kind of interpretation has been put forward by many writers; see, for example, the discussion in W. Leontief, "Factor Proportions and the Structure of American Trade: Further Theoretical and Empirical Analysis," *Review of Economics and Statistics,* November 1956.

[52] Interstate estimates for several industries can be found in J. Minasian, "Elasticities of Substitution and Constant-Output Demand Curves for Labor," *Journal of Political Economy,* June 1961, pp. 261–270; intercountry estimates in Kenneth Arrow, Hollis B. Chenery, Bagicha Minhas, and Robert M. Solow, "Capital-Labor Substitution and Economic Efficiency," *Review of Economics and Statistics,* August 1961.

could give a seriously biased picture of the effect on wages of factor proportions.[53]

4. A secular increase in average earnings has usually been said to result from increases in technological knowledge and physical capital per earner. The average earner, in effect, is supposed to benefit indirectly from activities by entrepreneurs, investors, and others. Another explanation put forward in recent years argues that earnings can rise because of direct investment in earners.[54] Instead of only benefiting from activities by others, the average earner is made a prime mover of development through the investment in himself.[55]

Ability and the Distribution of Earnings

An emphasis on human capital not only helps explain differences in earnings over time and among areas but also among persons or families within an area. This application will be discussed in greater detail than the others because a link is provided between earnings, ability, and the incentive to invest in human capital.

Economists have long been aware that conventional measures of ability—intelligence tests or aptitude scores, school grades, and personality tests—while undoubtedly relevant at times, do not reliably measure the talents required to succeed in the economic sphere. The latter consists of particular kinds of personality, persistence, and intelligence. Accordingly, some writers have gone to the opposite extreme and argued that the only relevant way to measure economic talent is by

53 Minasian's argument (in his article cited above, p. 264) that interstate variations in skill level necessarily bias his estimates toward unity is actually correct only if skill is a perfect substitute for "labor." (In correspondence Minasian stated that he intended to make this condition explicit.) If, on the other hand, human and physical capital were perfect substitutes, I have shown (in an unpublished memorandum) that the estimates would always have a downward bias, regardless of the true substitution between labor and capital. Perhaps the most reasonable assumption would be that physical capital is more complementary with human capital than with labor; I have not, however, been able generally to determine the direction of bias in this case.

54 The major figure here is T. W. Schultz. Of his many articles, see especially "Education and Economic Growth," in Social Forces Influencing American Education, Sixtieth Yearbook of the National Society for the Study of Education, Chicago, 1961, Part II, Chapter 3.

55 One caveat is called for, however. Since observed earnings are not only gross of the return from investments in human capital but also are net of some costs, an increased investment in human capital would both raise and reduce earnings. Although average earnings would tend to increase as long as the rate of return was positive, the increase would be less than if the cost of human capital, like that of physical capital, was not deducted from national income.

results, or by earnings themselves.[56] Persons with higher earnings would simply have more ability than others, and a skewed distribution of earnings would imply a skewed distribution of abilities. This approach goes too far, however, in the opposite direction. The main reason for relating ability to earning is to distinguish its effects from differences in education, training, health, and other such factors, and a definition equating ability and earnings ipso facto precludes such a distinction. Nevertheless, results are relevant and should not be ignored.

A compromise might be reached through defining ability by earnings only when several variables have been held constant. Since the public is very concerned about separating ability from education, on-the-job training, health, and other human capital, the amount invested in such capital would have to be held constant. Although a full analysis would also hold discrimination, nepotism, luck, and several other factors constant, a reasonable first approximation would say that if two persons have the same investment in human capital, the one who earns more is demonstrating greater economic talent.

Since observed earnings are gross of the return on human capital, they are affected by changes in the amount and rate of return. Indeed, it has been shown that, after the investment period, earnings (Y) can be simply approximated by

$$Y = X + rC, \tag{67}$$

where C measures total investment costs, r the average-rate of return, and X earnings when there is no investment in human capital. If the distribution of X is ignored for now, Y would depend only on r when C was held constant, so "ability" would be measured by the average rate of return on human capital.[57]

In most capital markets the amount invested is not the same for everyone nor rigidly fixed for any given person, but depends in part on the rate of return. Persons receiving a high marginal rate of return would have an incentive to invest more than others.[58] Since marginal

---

[56] Let me state again that the word "earnings" stands for real earnings, or the sum of monetary earnings and the monetary equivalent of psychic earnings.

[57] Since r is a function of C, Y would indirectly as well as directly depend on C, and therefore the distribution of ability would depend on the amount of human capital. Some persons might rank high in earnings and thus high in ability if everyone were unskilled, and quite low if education and other training were widespread.

[58] In addition, they would find it easier to invest if the marginal return and the resources of parents and other relatives were positively correlated.

and average rates are presumably positively correlated [59] and since ability is measured by the average rate, one can say that abler persons would invest more than others. The end result would be a positive correlation between ability and the investment in human capital,[60] a correlation with several important implications.

One is that the tendency for abler persons to migrate, continue their education,[61] and generally invest more in themselves can be explained without recourse to an assumption that noneconomic forces or demand conditions favor them at higher investment levels. A second implication is that the separation of "nature from nurture," or ability from education and other environmental factors, is apt to be difficult, for high earnings would tend to signify both more ability and a better environment. Thus the earnings differential between college and high-school graduates does not measure the effect of college alone since college graduates are abler and would earn more even without the additional education. Or reliable estimates of the income elasticity of demand for children have been difficult to obtain because higher-income families also invest more in contraceptive knowledge.[62]

The main implication, however, is in personal income distribution. At least ever since the time of Pigou economists have tried to reconcile the strong skewness in the distribution of earnings and other income with a presumed symmetrical distribution of abilities.[63] Pigou's main suggestion—that property income is not symmetrically distributed—does not directly help explain the skewness in earnings. Subsequent attempts have largely concentrated on developing ad hoc random and other probabilistic mechanisms that have little relation to the main-

[59] According to a well-known formula,

$$r_m = r_a \left(1 + \frac{1}{e_a} \right),$$

where r_m is the marginal rate of return, r_a the average rate, and e_a the elasticity of the average rate with respect to the amount invested. The rates r_m and r_a would be positively correlated unless r_a and $1/e_a$ were sufficiently negatively correlated.

[60] This kind of argument is not new; Marshall argued that business ability and the ownership of physical capital would be positively correlated: "[economic] forces . . . bring about the result that there is a far more close correspondence between the ability of business men and the size of the businesses which they own than at first sight would appear probable" (*Principles of Economics*, p. 312).

[61] The first is frequently alleged (see, for example, *ibid.*, p. 199). Evidence on the second is discussed in Chapter IV, section 2.

[62] See my "An Economic Analysis of Fertility," in *Demographic and Economic Change in Developed Countries*, Special Conference 11, Princeton for NBER, 1960.

[63] See A. C. Pigou, *The Economics of Welfare*, 4th ed., London, 1950, Part IV, Chapter ii.

stream of economic thought.[64] The approach presented here, however, offers an explanation that is not only consistent with economic analysis but actually relies on one of its fundamental tenets, namely, that the amount invested is a function of the rate of return expected. In conjunction with the effect of human capital on earnings, this tenet can explain several well-known properties of earnings distributions.

By definition, the distribution of earnings would be exactly the same as the distribution of ability if everyone invested the same amount in human capital; in particular, if ability were symmetrically distributed, earnings would also be. Equation (67) shows that the distribution of earnings would be exactly the same as the distribution of investment if all persons were equally able; again, if investment were symmetrically distributed, earnings would also be.[65] If ability and investment both varied, earnings would tend to be skewed even when ability and investment were not, but the skewness would be small as long as the amount invested were statistically independent of ability.[66]

---

[64] A sophisticated example can be found in B. Mandelbrot, "The Pareto-Lévy Law and the Distribution of Income," *International Economic Review*, May 1960. In a later paper, however, Mandelbrot brought in maximizing behavior (see "Paretian Distributions and Income Maximization," *Quarterly Journal of Economics*, February 1962).

[65] J. Mincer ("Investment in Human Capital and Personal Income Distribution," *Journal of Political Economy*, August 1958) concluded that a symmetrical distribution of investment in education implies a skewed distribution of earnings because he defines educational investment by school years rather than costs. If Mincer is followed in assuming that everyone was equally able, that schooling was the only investment, and that the cost of the nth year of schooling equaled the earnings of persons with $n-1$ years of schooling, then, say, a normal distribution of schooling can be shown to imply a log-normal distribution of school costs and thus a log-normal distribution of earnings.

The difference between the earnings of persons with $n-1$ and n years of schooling would be $k_n = Y_n - Y_{n-1} = r_n C_n$. Since r_n is assumed to equal r for all n, and $C_n = Y_{n-1}$, this equation becomes $Y_n = (1+r) Y_{n-1}$, and therefore

$$C_1 = Y_0$$
$$C_2 = Y_1 = Y_0(1+r)$$
$$C_3 = Y_2 = Y_1(1+r) = Y_0(1+r)^2$$
$$C_n = Y_{n-1} = \cdots = Y_0(1+r)^{n-1},$$

or the cost of each additional year of schooling increases at a constant *rate*. Since total costs have the same distribution as $(1+r)^n$, a symmetrical, say, a normal, distribution of school years, n, implies a log-normal distribution of costs and hence by equation (32) a log-normal distribution of earnings. I am indebted to Mincer for a helpful discussion of the comparison and especially for the stimulation provided by his pioneering work. Incidentally, his article and the dissertation on which it is based cover a much broader area than has been indicated here.

[66] For example, C. C. Craig has shown that the product of two independent normal distributions is only slightly skewed (see his "On the Frequency Function of XY," *Annals of Mathematical Statistics*, March 1936, p. 3).

It has been shown, however, that abler persons would tend to invest more than others, so ability and investment would be positively correlated, perhaps quite strongly. Now the product of two symmetrical distributions is more positively skewed the higher the positive correlation between them, and might be quite skewed.[67] The economic incentive given abler persons to invest relatively large amounts in themselves does seem capable, therefore, of reconciling a strong positive skewness in earnings with a presumed symmetrical distribution of abilities.

Variations in X help explain an important difference among skill categories in the degree of skewness. The smaller the fraction of total earnings resulting from investment in human capital—the smaller rC relative to X—the more the distribution of earnings would be dominated by the distribution of X. Higher-skill categories have a greater average investment in human capital and thus presumably a larger rC relative to X. The distribution of "unskilled ability," X, would, therefore, tend to dominate the distribution of earnings in relatively unskilled categories while the distribution of a product of ability and the amount invested, rC, would dominate in skilled categories. Hence if abilities were symmetrically distributed, earnings would tend to be more symmetrically distributed among the unskilled than among the skilled.[68]

Equation (67) holds only when investment costs are small, which tends to be true at later ages, say, after age thirty-five. Net earnings at earlier ages would be given by

$$Y_j = X_j + \sum_0^{j-1} r_i C_i + (-C_j), \qquad (68)$$

where j refers to the current year and i to previous years, C_i measures the investment cost of age i, C_j current costs, and r_i the rate of return on C_j. The distribution of $-C_j$ would be an important determinant

[67] Craig (*ibid.*, pp. 9–10) showed that the product of two normal distributions would be more positively skewed the higher the positive correlation between them, and that the skewness would be considerable with high correlations.

[68] As noted earlier, X does not really represent earnings when there is no investment in human capital, but only earnings when there is no investment after the initial age (be it 14, 25, or 6). Indeed, the developmental approach to child rearing argues that earnings would be close to zero if there were no investment at all in human capital. The distribution of X, therefore, would be at least partly determined by the distribution of investment before the initial age, and if it and ability were positively correlated, X might be positively skewed, even though ability was not.

of the distribution of Y_j since investment is large at these ages. Hence the analysis would predict a smaller (positive) skewness at younger than at older ages partly because X would be more important relative to $\Sigma r_i C_i$ at younger ages and partly because the presumed negative correlation between $-C_j$ and $\sum_0^{j-1} r_i C_i$ would counteract the positive correlation between r_i and C_i.

A simple analysis of the incentive to invest in human capital seems capable of explaining, therefore, not only why the overall distribution of earnings is more skewed than the distribution of abilities, but also why earnings are more skewed among older and skilled persons than among younger and less skilled ones. The renewed interest in investment in human capital may provide the means of bringing the theory of personal income distribution back into economics.

Addendum: Education and the Distribution of Earnings: A Statistical Formulation[69]

A Statistical Formulation

The contribution of human capital to the distribution of earnings could be easily calculated empirically if the rates of return and investments in equation (1) were known.[70] Although information on investment in human capital has grown significantly during the last few years, it is still limited to aggregate relations for a small number of countries. Much more is known about one component of these investments; namely, the period of time spent investing, as given, for example, by years of schooling.

To utilize this information we have reformulated the analysis to bring out explicitly the relation between earnings and the investment period. The principal device used is to write the cost of the jth "year" of investment to the ith person as the fraction k_{ij} of the earnings that would be received if no investment was made during that year. If for

---

[69] Reprinted from pp. 363–369 of an article by G. S. Becker and B. R. Chiswick in *American Economic Review*, May 1966.

[70] Equation (1):

$$E_i = X_i + \sum_{j=1}^{m} r_{ij} C_{ij},$$

where C_{ij} is the amount spent by the ith person on the jth investment, r_{ij} is his rate of return on this investment, and X_i is the effects of the original capital.

convenience r_{ij} in equation (1) is replaced by $\bar{r}_j + r_{ij}{}^*$, where $\bar{r}_j$ is the average rate of return on the jth investment and $r_{ij}{}^*$ is the (positive or negative) premium to the ith person resulting from his (superior or inferior) personal characteristics, then it can be shown that equation (1) could be rewritten as

$$E_i = X_i[1 + k_{i1}(\bar{r}_1 + r_{i1}{}^*)][1 + k_{i2}(\bar{r}_2 + r_{i2}{}^*)] \cdots$$
$$[1 + k_{in_i}(\bar{r}_{n_i} + r_{in_i}{}^*)] \quad (69)$$

where n_i is the total investment period of the ith person.[71] If the effect of luck and other such factors on earnings is now incorporated within a multiplicative term e^{u_i}, the log transform of equation (69) is

$$\log E_i = \log X_i + \sum_{j=1}^{n_i} \log [1 + k_{ij}(\bar{r}_j + r_{ij}{}^*)] + u_i. \quad (70)$$

By defining $X_i = \overline{X}(1 + \alpha_i)$, where α_i measures the "unskilled" personal characteristics of the ith person, and $k_{ij} = \bar{k}_j + t_{ij}$, where $\bar{k}_j$ is the average fraction for the jth investment, and by using the relation

$$\log [1 + k_{ij}(\bar{r}_j + r_{ij}{}^*)] \cong k_{ij}(\bar{r}_j + r_{ij}{}^*), \quad (71)$$

equation (70) could be written as

$$\log E_i \cong a + \sum_{j=1}^{n_i} \bar{r}_j' + v_i, \quad (72)$$

where $a = \log \overline{X}$, $\bar{r}_j' = \bar{k}_j \bar{r}_j$, and

$$v_i = \log (1 + \alpha_i) + \sum_j k_{ij} r_{ij}{}^* + \sum_j t_{ij} \bar{r}_j + u_i. \quad (73)$$

The term v_i largely shows the combined effect on earnings of luck and ability. If the $\bar{r}_j'$ was the same for each period of investment, the equation for earnings is simply

$$\log E_i \cong a + \bar{r}'n_i + v_i. \quad (74)$$

If $\bar{r}'$, the average rate of return adjusted for the average fraction of earnings foregone, and the investment period n_i were known, equation

[71] The interested reader can find a proof for a somewhat special case in footnote 65 above.

(74) could be used to compute their contribution to the distribution of earnings. For example, they would jointly "explain" the fraction

$$R^2 = (\bar{r}')^2 \frac{\sigma^2(n)}{\sigma^2(\log E)} \tag{75}$$

of the total inequality in earnings, where $\sigma^2(n)$ is the variance of investment periods, and $\sigma^2(\log E)$ is the variance of the log of earnings, the measure of inequality in earnings.[72] Ability and luck together would "explain" the fraction $\sigma^2(v)/\sigma^2(\log E)$, and the (perhaps negative) remainder of the inequality in earnings would be "explained" by the covariance between ability, luck, and the investment period.

Even equations (72) and (74), simplified versions of (69), make excessive demands on the available data. For one thing, although the period of formal schooling is now known with tolerable accuracy for the populations of many countries, only bits and pieces are known about the periods of formal and informal on-the-job training, and still less about other kinds of human capital. Unfortunately, the only recourse at present is to simplify further: by separating formal schooling from other human capital, equation (72) becomes

$$\log E_i = a + \sum_{j=1}^{q_i} \bar{r}'_j S_j + v'_i, \tag{76}$$

where $\bar{r}'_1$ is the adjusted average rate of return on each of the first S_1 years of formal schooling, $\bar{r}'_2$ is a similar rate on each of the succeeding S_2 years of formal schooling, etc.;

$S_i = \sum_1^{q_i} S_j$ is then the total formal schooling years of the ith person, and

$$v'_i = v_i + \sum \bar{r}'_k T_k \tag{77}$$

includes the effect of other human capital.

A second difficulty is that although an almost bewildering array of rates of return have been estimated in recent years, our empirical analysis requires many more. Additional estimates could be developed by making equation (76) do double duty: first it could be used to estimate the adjusted rates and only then to show the contribution of

---

[72] Note that this measure, one of the most commonly used measures of income inequality, is not just arbitrarily introduced but is derived from the theory itself.

schooling, including these rates, to the distribution of earnings. If the S_j and v' were uncorrelated, an ordinary least squares regression of log E on the S_j would give unbiased estimates on these rates, and, therefore, of the contribution of schooling. If, however, the S_j and v' were positively or negatively correlated, the estimated rates would be biased upward or downward, and so would the estimated direct contribution of schooling.

Some components of v' are probably positively and others are negatively correlated with years of schooling, and the net bias, therefore, is not clear a priori. It is not unreasonable to assume that α_i and u_i in equation (73) are only slightly correlated with the S_j. The $r_{ij}{}^*$ term in (73), on the other hand, would be positively correlated with the S_j[73] since the theory developed earlier suggests that persons of superior ability and other personal characteristics would invest more in themselves. Some empirical evidence indicates a positive correlation between years of schooling and the amount invested in other human capital.[74] The term v' depends, however, on the correlation between years of schooling and years invested in other human capital, a correlation which might well be negative. Certainly persons leaving school early begin their on-the-job learning early, and possibly continue for a relatively long time period (see fn. 75). Finally, one should note that random errors in measuring the period of schooling would produce a negative correlation between the measured period and v'. Although the correlations between the S_j and these components of v' go in both directions and thus to some extent must offset each other, a sizable error probably remains in estimating the adjusted rates and the contribution of schooling to the distribution of earnings.

Empirical Analysis

The sharpest regional difference in the United States in opportunities and other characteristics is between the South and non-South, and Table 1 presents some results of regressing the log of earnings on years of schooling separately in each region for white males at least age twenty-five. Adjusted average rates of return have been estimated by these regressions separately for low, medium, and high education levels. As columns 1, 2, 6, 7, and 8 indicate, the adjusted rates at each of these school levels and the variances in the log of earnings and in years of

---

[73] That is, unless a negative correlation between k_{ij} and $r_{ij}{}^*$ was sufficiently strong.

[74] See p. 167.

TABLE 1

Results of Regressing Natural Log of Earnings on Education for 1959 Earnings of White Males Aged 25 to 64 in the South and Non-South

	Variance of Natural Log of Earnings (1)	Variance of Education (2)	Average Natural Log of Earnings[c] (3)	Average Education (4)	Intercepts[c] (5)	Adjusted Rates of Return[a] (standard errors)[b]			Adjusted Coefficient of Determination (R²)	Unadjusted R² (9)	Residual Variance in Natural Log of Earnings (10)
						Low Education (6)	Medium Education (7)	High Education (8)			
Non-South	.42	11.28	1.66	10.78	1.09	.05	.06	.08	.07	.11	.39
					(.67)	(.09)	(.06)	(.06)			
South	.55	15.23	1.43	9.96	.66	.07	.09	.09	.16	.20	.46
					(.50)	(.08)	(.07)	(.06)			

Source: *United States Census of Population: 1960, Subject Reports-Occupation by Earnings and Education*, Bureau of the Census, Washington, D.C., 1963, Tables 2 and 3.

[a] "Low" education is defined as 0–8 years of school completed, "medium" as 8–12 years, and "high" as more than 12 years.

[b] In calculating the standard errors and the adjusted coefficients of determination, the number of degrees of freedom was assumed to equal the number of cells minus the number of parameters estimated. The true number is clearly somewhat greater than this.

[c] Earnings measured in thousands of dollars.

schooling are all a fair amount larger in the South. Moreover, these differences in schooling and rates exceed the difference in earnings, for as column 9 shows, the coefficient of determination, or the fraction of the variance in the log of earnings "explained" by schooling, is considerably higher in the South. The regional difference in earnings does not entirely result from schooling, however, for column 10 shows that the "residual" inequality in earnings is also larger in the South.

These results can be given an interesting interpretation within the framework of the theory presented in the addendum "Human Capital and the Personal Distribution of Income: An Analytical Approach." The greater inequality in the distribution of schooling in the South is presumably a consequence of the less equal opportunity even for whites there and would only be strengthened by considering the differences in schooling between whites and nonwhites. The higher adjusted rates of return in the South[75] are probably related to the lower education levels there, shown in column 4, which in turn might be the result of fewer educational opportunities.

The residual v' is heavily influenced by the distributions of luck and ability, which usually do not vary much between large regions. Therefore, greater rates of return and inequality in the distribution of schooling would go hand in hand not only with a greater absolute but also with a greater relative contribution of schooling to the inequality in earnings. The residual is also influenced, however, by investment in other human capital. Since the rates of return to and distribution of these investments would be influenced by the same forces influencing schooling, the absolute, but not relative, contribution of the residual to the inequality in earnings would tend to be greater when the absolute contribution of schooling was greater. Consequently, our theory can explain why both the coefficient of determination and the residual variance in earnings are greater in the South.

In order to determine whether these relations hold not only for the most extreme regional difference in the United States but also for

[75] Higher rates of return to whites in the South have been found when estimated by the "present value" method from data giving earnings classified by age, education, and other variables (see G. Hanoch, "An Economic Analysis of Earnings and Schooling," *Journal of Human Resources*, 2, Summer 1967, pp. 310–329). Although estimates based on the present value method are also biased upward by a positive correlation between ability and schooling and downward by errors in measuring school years, they are less sensitive to the omission of other human capital (see this volume, pp. 167-168). Consequently, the fact that Hanoch's estimates are almost uniformly higher than ours (after adjustment for the k_i) suggests, if anything, a negative correlation between school years and the years invested in other human capital. This could also explain why Hanoch's rates tend to decline with increases in years of schooling while ours tend to rise.

more moderate differences, similar regressions were calculated for all fifty states. To avoid going into details at this time let us simply report that the results strongly confirm those found at the extremes: there is a very sizable positive correlation across states between inequality in adult male incomes, adjusted rates of return, inequality in schooling, coefficients of determination, and residual inequality in incomes, while they are all negatively related to the average level of schooling and income. Whereas only about 18 per cent of the inequality in income within a state is explained, on the average, by schooling, the remaining 82 per cent explained by the residual, about one-third of the differences in inequality between states is directly explained by schooling, one-third directly by the residual, and the remaining one-third by both together through the positive correlation between them.

Similar calculations have also been made for several countries having readily available data: United States, Canada, Mexico, Israel, and Puerto Rico (treated as a country). Again there is a strong tendency for areas with greater income inequality to have higher rates of return, greater schooling inequality, higher coefficients of determination, and greater residual inequality. While there is also a tendency for poorer countries to have lower average years of schooling, greater inequality in income, etc., there are a couple of notable exceptions. For example, Israel, for reasons rather clearly related to the immigration of educated Europeans during the 1920s and 1930s, had unusually high schooling levels and low inequality in earnings until the immigration of uneducated Africans and Asians after 1948 began to lower average education levels and raise the inequality in earnings.

Addendum: Human Capital and the Personal Distribution of Income: An Analytical Approach*

1. Introduction

Interest among economists in the distribution of income has as long a history as modern economics itself. Smith, Mill, Ricardo, and others recognized that many problems of considerable economic importance partly turned on various aspects of income distribution. Although they defined poverty, for example, in absolute terms, they also recognized that each generation's "poor" are mainly those significantly below the average income level. In addition to poverty, the degree of opportu-

* Originally published as Woytinsky Lecture, University of Michigan, 1967.

nity, aggregate savings, and investment, the distribution of family sizes and the concentration of private economic power were believed to be related to income distribution.

How does one explain then that in spite of the rapid accumulation of empirical information and the persisting and even increasing interest in some of these questions, such as poverty, economists have somewhat neglected the study of personal income distribution during the past generation? In my judgment the fundamental reason is the absence, despite ingenious and valiant efforts, of a theory that both articulates with general economic theory and is useful in explaining actual differences among regions, countries, and time periods. By emphasizing investment in human capital one can develop a theory of income distribution that satisfies both desiderata. This essay focuses on the relation between investment in human capital and the distribution of earnings and other income. The discussion is theoretical and no systematic effort is made to test the theory empirically. I expect to report on some quantitative tests in a future publication.

The next section sets out the basic theory determining the amount invested in human capital by a "representative" person, and shows the relation between earnings, investments, and rates of return. Essentially all that is involved is the application to human capital of a framework traditionally used to analyze investment in other capital, although several modifications are introduced. Section 3 of the essay shifts the attention from a single person to differences among persons, and shows how the distribution of earnings and investments are determined by the distributions of ability, tastes, subsidies, wealth, and other variables.

Section 4 uses the framework developed in sections 2 and 3 to analyze the effects on the distribution of earnings of an increase in the equality of opportunity, of a more efficient market for human capital, of the use of tests and other "objective" criteria to ration investments in human capital, and of legislation requiring a minimum investment in human capital. Section 5 extends the discussion to the distribution of property income, and suggests why such income, both inherited and self-accumulated, is more unequally distributed than earnings. Section 6 summarizes the discussion and adds a few conclusions, and 7 is a mathematical appendix.

2. Optimal Investment in Human Capital

a. The model. I have shown elsewhere that what I call the "net" earnings of a person at any age t (E_t) approximately equals the earnings he would have at t if no human capital had been invested in him (X_t) plus the total returns to him at t on investments made in him earlier (k_t) minus the cost to him of investments at t (C_t), as in

$$E_t = X_t + k_t - C_t. \tag{78}$$

Total returns depend on the amounts invested and their rates of return; for example, if returns on each investment were the same at all ages during the labor force period,[76] total returns would be the sum of the products of the amounts invested and their rates of return, adjusted for the finiteness of the labor force period. Equation (78) could then be written as

$$E_t = X_t + \sum_{j=1}^{n} r_{t-j} f_{t-j} C_{t-j} - C_t, \tag{79}$$

where r_{t-j} is the rate of return on capital invested at $t - j$ and f_{t-j} is the finite life adjustment. I applied this analysis to various problems, including the shapes of age-earnings and age-wealth profiles, the relation between unemployment and on-the-job training, the so-called Leontief paradox, and several others.[77]

I suggested that differences in the total amounts invested by different persons are related to differences in the rates of return obtainable, a suggestion that can explain why white urban males with high IQs acquire more education than others, or why the division of labor is limited by the extent of the market.[78] I did not, however, systematically develop a framework to explain why rates of return and investments differ so greatly among persons. This essay tries to develop such a framework. This not only provides a rigorous justification for these suggestions in *Human Capital*, but also begins to provide an explanation of the personal distribution of earnings.

The term X_t in equations (78) and (79) represents the earnings of a person that are unrelated to human capital invested in him, and are presumably, therefore, largely independent of his current choices. Particularly in developed economies but perhaps in most, there is sufficient investment in education, training, informal learning, health, and just plain child rearing that the earnings unrelated to investment in human capital are a small part of the total. Indeed, in the develop-

---

[76] This is the "one-hoss shay" assumption applied to human capital.

[77] See this volume, Chapters II–III.

[78] See pp. 74–75, 157–166, 169–181.

mental approaches to child rearing, all the earnings of a person are ultimately attributed to different kinds of investments made in him.[79] Consequently, there is considerable justification for the assumption that X_t is small and can be neglected, an assumption we make in this paper. In any case a significant X_t only slightly complicates the analysis and can be readily incorporated.

Another assumption made throughout most of the paper is that human capital is homogeneous in the sense that all units are perfect substitutes in production for each other and thus add the same amount to earnings. Of course, this assumption does not deny that some units may have been produced at considerably greater costs than others. The assumption of homogeneous human capital clearly differs in detail rather drastically from the usual emphasis on qualitative differences in education, training, and skills. I hope to demonstrate that these differences, while descriptively realistic and useful, are not required to understand the basic forces determining the distribution of earnings; indeed, they sometimes even distract attention from these determinants. Section 3g does, however, generalize the analysis to cover many kinds of human capital.

Chart 4 plots along the horizontal axis the amount invested in human capital measured for convenience by its cost rather than in physical units. Equal distances along the axis, therefore, do not necessarily measure equal numbers of physical units.

The curve D shows the marginal benefit, for simplicity measured by the rate of return, to a particular person on each additional dollar of investment, and is supposed to represent his demand curve for human capital. The curve S shows the effective marginal financing cost to him, measured for simplicity by the rate of interest, of each additional dollar invested, and represents in essence his supply curve of capital. If D exceeded S, the marginal rate of return would exceed the marginal rate of interest, and income would be increased by additional investment, while the opposite would be true if S exceeded D. Consequently, income is maximized by investing up to the point where $D = S$, given by p in the figure, and implying a total capital investment of OC_o.

b. *Demand curves.* The marginal rate of return depends on the time series of marginal returns and the marginal production cost of investment: if returns are constant for a long labor force period, it essentially equals the ratio of returns to these costs. Since all human

[79] See S. J. Mushkin, "Health as an Investment," *Journal of Political Economy*, 70, Special Supplement, October 1962, pp. 149–151.

CHART 4

Supply and Demand Curves for Investment in Human Capital

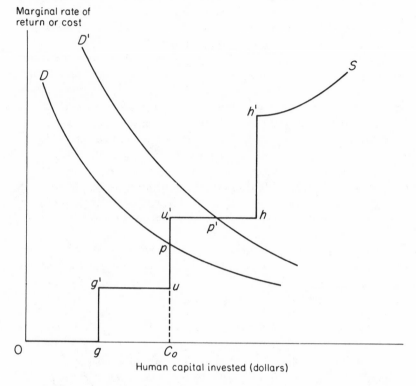

Human capital invested (dollars)

capital is assumed to be homogeneous, even an extremely large percentage change in the capital invested by any one person would have a negligible effect on the total quantity of capital available. Consequently, in order to explain why the demand curves for human capital in Chart 4 are negatively inclined and not horizontal, other effects of capital accumulation must be analyzed.

The principal characteristic that distinguishes human from other kinds of capital is that, by definition, the former is embedded or embodied in the person investing. This embodiment of human capital is the most important reason why marginal benefits decline as additional capital is accumulated. One obvious implication of embodiment is that since the memory capacity, physical size, etc. of each investor is limited, eventually diminishing returns set in from producing additional capital.[80] The result is increasing marginal costs of producing a dollar of returns.

Closely dependent on the embodiment of human capital is the importance of an investor's own time in the production of his own human capital.[81] Own time is so important that an increase in the amount invested in good part corresponds to an increase in the time spent investing:[82] in fact the only commonly used measures of schooling and training are years of schooling and training, measures entirely based on the input of own time. The cost of this time has been measured for several kinds of human capital, shown to be generally important, and given the name "foregone earnings." [83]

If the elasticities of substitution between own time and teachers, books, and other inputs were infinite, the use of own time and the deferral of investments could be avoided, without cost, aside from the limitations imposed by B, by an accumulation of all the desired capital instantaneously through complete substitution of other inputs for own time. If substitution were significantly imperfect (which is the more likely situation), the elimination of own time would cause the marginal costs of producing human capital to be higher and rise faster as capital was accumulated than if it was combined optimally with other inputs. In the latter case, however, the accumulation of capital is necessarily spread out over a period of calendar time called the

[80] If

$$h = f(I, B),$$

where h is the number of units of capital produced by a person per unit time, f is his production function, I is his capital investment in dollars per unit time, and B represents his physical and mental powers, then eventually

$$\frac{\partial^2 h}{\partial I^2} < 0.$$

[81] The production function in the previous footnote can be expanded to

$$h = f(R, T, B),$$

where R is the rate of input of other resources, and T is the rate of input of the investor's time per unit calendar time.

[82] If the horizontal axis in Chart 4 were replaced by one measuring investment time, the chart would be almost identical to those used in the "Austrian" theory of capital to explain optimal aging of trees or wine. Indeed, the main relevance of the Austrian approach in modern economics is to the study of investment in human capital!

[83] See T. W. Schultz, "Capital Formation by Education," *Journal of Political Economy*, 68, 1960, pp. 571–583.

"investment period." Presumably there are optimal combinations of inputs over an optimal investment period that maximizes the present value of benefits from a given capital investment. The spreading out of capital accumulation forced by the importance of own time can, however, only reduce but not eliminate the decline in marginal benefits as more is accumulated.[84]

In the first place, with finite lifetimes, later investments cannot produce returns for as long as earlier ones and, therefore, usually have smaller total benefits. This effect is important in societies with heavy adult mortality, but probably is not in the low mortality environment of modern Western societies. For unless fewer than approximately twenty years of working life remained, a reduction of, say, a year in the number of years remaining does not have much effect on the present value of benefits.[85] In the second place, later investments are less profitable than earlier ones because the present value of net benefits (or profits) is reduced merely by postponing them (and the reduction can be sizable, even for postponements of a few years).[86]

A third consideration is probably of great importance, although one cannot yet measure its quantitative significance. Since nobody can use his time at any activity without taking with him all of his human capital, the latter enters as an input along with his time in the production of additional capital. Initially, at young ages, the value of the time is small and probably even negative because parents or other baby-sitting services must be employed if he is not in school, or otherwise investing.[87] As he continues to invest, however, the capital accumulated becomes increasingly valuable, and so does his time.

Other things being the same, an increase in the value of time raises the marginal cost of later investments compared to earlier ones since the former use more expensive time. For any given rate of increase in its value as he ages, the costs of later investments are relatively greater, the larger the share of foregone earnings in costs and the smaller the

---

[84] The fact that a person's optimal stock of human capital is not immediately reached is often used in explaining the shape of his demand curve for human capital. On the problems in explaining why his optimal stock of nonhuman capital is not immediately reached, see D. W. Jorgenson, "The Theory of Investment Behavior," in *Determinants of Investment Behavior*, Universities-National Bureau Conference Series No. 18, Columbia University Press for NBER, 1967.

[85] For a demonstration of this, see pp. 47–48.

[86] See *ibid.*, pp. 72–73.

[87] For an attempt to measure the value of such services provided by elementary schools, see B. Weisbrod, "Education and Investment in Human Capital," *Journal of Political Economy*, 70, Special Supplement, October 1962, pp. 116–117.

elasticity of substitution between own time and other inputs.[88] One other thing that may not remain the same is the productivity of time: just as a greater amount of human capital is more productive than a lesser amount of capital in the rest of the economy, so too it may be more productive when used to produce additional human capital itself.[89] Marginal costs of later investments would not be greater if the increased productivity of own time was at least as great as its increased value. Because own human capital is carried along with own time, more productive or not, I am inclined to believe that its effect on productivity would be less, at least eventually, than its effect on the cost of own time. If so, the accumulation of human capital would on balance eventually increase later investment costs,[90] and thus decrease the present value of later benefits.

To digress a moment, the presumption that the marginal costs of typical firms are rising[91] is usually rationalized in terms of a limited "entrepreneurial capacity," an input that can only be imperfectly replaced by managers and other hired inputs. "Entrepreneurial capacity" is a construct developed to reconcile competition, linear homogeneous production functions, and determinate firm sizes, and most writers agree that there are no obvious empirical counterparts.[92] Indeed, the extremely large size achieved by many firms suggests that, frequently at least, entrepreneurial capacity is not very limiting. Per-

---

[88] This elasticity is relevant because investors may try to economize on their more costly time by substituting other inputs for time. Rough evidence of such substitution in education is found in the tendency for more valuable resources to be used per hour of the time of more advanced than less advanced students. The elasticity probably does not exceed unity, however, since the share of foregone earnings in total costs appears to rise with the level of education (see Schultz, *op. cit.*).

[89] If H measures the stock of human capital embodied in an investor, then the production function in footnote 81 can be expanded to include H, as in

$$h = f(R, T, H, B).$$

The productivity of greater human capital means a positive sign to $\partial h / \partial H$.

[90] Even if the effect on productivity continued to exceed that on the cost of own time, diminishing returns would cause the decrease in investment costs to become smaller and smaller over time. (For an illustration of this in a model that is quite similar to, although more rigorously developed than, the one presented here, see Y. Ben-Porath, "The Production of Human Capital and the Life Cycle of Earnings," *Journal of Political Economy*, August 1967). On the other hand, the decrease in the present value of benefits that results from a decrease in the number of years remaining would become larger and larger over time.

[91] This presumption can be justified by the observation that usually only firms producing a limited share of the output of an industry manage to survive.

[92] See M. Friedman, *Price Theory*, Chicago, 1962.

sons investing in human capital can be considered "firms" that combine such capital perhaps with other resources to produce earning power. Since "entrepreneurial" time is required to produce human capital, and since the latter is embodied in the entrepreneur, teachers, managers, and other hired resources can only imperfectly substitute for him. Therefore, in this case, "entrepreneurial capacity" is a definite concept, has a clear empirical counterpart, and, as has been indicated, can lead to significantly rising costs, which in turn limits the size of these "firms."

It is the sum of monetary benefits and the monetary equivalent of psychic benefits (which may be negative) from human capital, not just the former alone, that determines the demand curve for capital investment. If one makes the usual assumption of diminishing monetary equivalents, marginal psychic as well as monetary benefits would decline as capital is accumulated. The considerable uncertainty about future benefits also contributes to a negatively inclined demand curve if there is increasing marginal aversion to risk as more capital is accumulated.

c. Supply curves. The supply curves in Chart 4 show the marginal cost of financing, as opposed to producing, an additional unit of capital. The marginal cost of financing can be measured, for simplicity, by the rate of interest that must be paid to finance an additional dollar of capital. If the annual repayment required on a "loan" was constant for the remaining period of labor force participation, the marginal rate of interest would simply equal the annual repayment on an additional dollar of funds, adjusted upward for the finiteness of the labor force period.

If the capital market were homogeneous, with no segmentation due to special subsidies or taxes, transaction costs, legal restrictions on lending or borrowing, etc., and if risk were constant, even a large change in the amount of capital used by any person would have a negligible effect on his marginal cost of funds since it would have a negligible effect on the funds available to others. In the actual world, however, the market for human capital is extremely segmented: there are local subsidies to public elementary and high schools, state and federal subsidies to certain undergraduate and graduate students, transaction costs that often make own funds considerably cheaper than borrowed funds, and significant legal limitations on the kind of borrowing that is permitted. The result is that although certain sources of funds are cheaper than others, the amounts available to any person from the cheaper sources are usually rationed since the total demand for the funds tends to exceed their supply. This means that a person accumulating capital must shift from the cheapest to the second cheapest and on eventually to expensive sources. This shift from less to more expensive sources is primarily responsible for the positive inclination of the supply curve of funds even to one person. The rate of increase in each curve tends to be greater the greater the segmentation, since there is then greater diversity in the cost of different sources, with smaller amounts available from each.

The cheapest sources usually are gifts from parents, relatives, foundations, and governments that can be used only for investment in human capital. Their cost to investors is nil, and is represented in Chart 4 by the Og segment of the supply curve S that lies along the horizontal axis.[93]

Highly subsidized but not free loans from governments and universities, for example, that also can be used only for investment in human capital are somewhat more expensive: they are represented by the $g'u$ segment of S. Then come the resources of investors themselves, including inheritances and other outright gifts, that could be used elsewhere. Their cost is measured by the foregone opportunities represented by the $u'h$ segment of S. After these funds are exhausted, investors must turn either to commercial loans in the marketplace or to reductions in their own consumption during the investment period. These funds are usually available only at considerably higher, and somewhat rapidly rising costs: they are represented by the upward sloped segment $h'S$.

As emphasized earlier, the accumulation of human capital is not instantaneous, but is usually spread over a lengthy investment period. The rate of increase in financing costs, like that in production costs, would generally be less, the more slowly capital is accumulated because, for example, the accumulation of own resources could reduce the need to rely on more expensive sources.[94] The rate of increase in

___

[93] Conceptual separation of production costs from financial conditions suggests that direct government and private subsidies to educational institutions and other "firms" producing human capital might be included in the Og segment. When so separated, demand curves incorporate all production costs, not only those borne by investors themselves, supply curves incorporate all subsidies, and the rates of return relate "private" returns to "social" costs (for definitions of "private" and "social" see this volume, Chapter V).

[94] Superficially, there are many actual examples of the cost of funds depending on the period or stage of accumulation, such as the special subsidies to students of medicine or advanced physics. Many of these are best treated, however, as examples of a segmented capital market for different kinds of human capital, and are more appropriately discussed in section 3g, where the interaction among different kinds is analyzed.

each supply curve also depends, therefore, on the accumulation pattern that is chosen.

d. *Equilibrium.* Since both the stream of benefits and of financing costs depend on the path of capital accumulation, the latter cannot be chosen with respect to either alone. The rational decision is to select a path that maximizes the present value of "profits"; that is, the present value of the difference between these benefits and costs. With a model as general as the one presented so far, the supply and demand curves shown in Chart 4 would not be uniquely determined nor independent of each other. In order to justify, therefore, uniqueness and independence and to permit a relatively simple analysis of income distribution, it is sufficient to assume that own time and hired inputs are used in fixed proportions to produce human capital, that a unit of hired inputs is available at a given price, and that a unit of own time is also available at a given price (foregone earnings) up to a certain maximum amount, beyond which no time is available at any price. If the analysis of income distribution presented in this essay turns out to be useful, the implications of more general assumptions about the production of human capital should be explored.[95]

With these assumptions, the value of benefits is given by the area under the unique demand curve shown in Chart 4, the value of financing costs by that under the unique supply curve,[96] and the maximum difference is found by investing up to their point of intersection. At that point, marginal benefits equal marginal financing costs, which can be taken to mean that the marginal rate of return equals the marginal rate of interest.

Corresponding to the optimal accumulation path is an optimal investment period. If both the returns on each dollar invested and the repayments on each dollar borrowed were constant for the remaining labor force period, the current value of total profits, which is the difference between total returns and total repayments, would rise throughout the optimal investment period. A peak would be reached at the end, remain constant at that level throughout the labor force period, and then drop to zero.

[95] A start is made by Ben-Porath, *op. cit.,* section 4.

[96] For simplicity, the figures in this essay plot along the vertical axis marginal rates of return and interest on each additional dollar of investment rather than the present or current values of marginal benefits and financing costs. If returns and repayment costs were constant for indefinitely long periods, marginal rates of return and interest would exactly equal the current values of the flow of benefits and financing costs respectively on an additional dollar of investment.

The earnings actually measured in national income accounts do not purport to represent the profits on human capital. For one thing, the costs of funds are not deducted from returns, regardless of whether they consist of direct interest payments, foregone income, or undesired reductions in consumption. During the investment period, moreover, some and often all the costs of producing human capital are implicitly deducted before reporting earnings.[97] Consequently, measured earnings after the investment period only represent total returns, while during the period it is a hybrid of returns and production costs. I discuss first and most extensively the factors determining the distribution of measured earnings after the investment period, and only briefly consider the distribution of profits or of measured earnings during this period.

A major assumption of the remainder of this essay is that actual accumulation paths are always the same as optimal paths. Sufficient conditions for this assumption are that all persons are rational [98] and that neither uncertainty nor ignorance prevents them from achieving their aims. Of course, these are strong conditions, and a fuller model would make room for irrationality, uncertainty, discrepancies between actual and "desired" capital stocks, etc. Given, however, our rudimentary knowledge of the forces generating income distributions, it is instructive to determine how far even a simple model takes us. What impresses me about this model are the many insights it appears to provide into the forces generating inequality and skewness in the distribution of earnings and other income. In any case, it can be easily generalized to incorporate many of the considerations neglected, such as uncertainty, or discrepancies between actual and "desired" capital stocks.

3. The Distribution of Earnings

This model implies that the total amount invested in human capital differs among persons because of differences in either demand or supply conditions: those with higher demand or lower supply curves

---

[97] This intermingling of stocks and flows has many implications for age-earnings and age-wealth profiles that have been discussed elsewhere (see this volume, Chapters II, III, and VII).

[98] Since all persons are very young during much of their investment period, it may seem highly unrealistic to assume that their decisions are rational. Children have their decisions guided, however, as well as partly financed, by their parents, and as long as parents receive some monetary or psychic benefits from an increase in their children's economic well-being, parents have an incentive to help children make wise decisions.

invest more than others. There is some evidence that in the United States, persons with urban employment or high IQ and grades tend to invest more in formal education than those with rural employment or low IQ and grades partly because the former receive higher rates of return.[99] If the model is empirically correct, as assumed in the remainder of the essay, the sizable observed differences in education,[100] on-the-job training, and other kinds of human capital would suggest sizable differences in either one or both sets of curves.

Persons who invest relatively large amounts in themselves tend to receive relatively high profits and measured earnings after the investment period. If they invest more because of higher demand curves, as D' is higher than D in Chart 4, both the area under the demand curve and the difference between it and the area under a given supply curve is greater (compare point p' with p). If they invest more because of lower supply curves, the area under the supply curve for a given capital investment is smaller, and the difference between it and the area under a given demand curve, therefore, is greater.

a. "Egalitarian" approach. Instead of starting immediately with variations in both supply and demand conditions, I first treat a couple of important special cases. One of them assumes that demand conditions are the same for everyone, and that the only cause of inequality is differences in supply conditions. This can be considered an approximate representation of the "egalitarian" approach to the distributions of investments in human capital and earnings, which assumes that everyone more or less has the same capacity to benefit from investment in human capital. Investment and earnings differ because of differences in the environment; in luck, family wealth, subsidies, etc. which give some the opportunity to invest than others. Eliminating environmental differences would eliminate these differences in opportunities, and thereby eliminate the important differences in earnings and investments.

Adam Smith took this view in his *The Wealth of Nations* when he said "The difference between the most dissimilar characters, between a philosopher and a common street porter, for example, seems to arise not so much from nature, as from habit, custom, and education." [101]

---

[99] See pp. 157–181.

[100] For example, the standard deviation of years of schooling exceeds three years in more countries.

[101] Modern Library edition, New York, 1937, p. 15. E. Cannan, ed., remarks that Smith was following David Hume, who said "consider how nearly equal all men are in their bodily force, and even in their mental powers and faculties, ere cultivated by education" (quoted *ibid.*).

Currently, many persons in the United States argue that most persons are intrinsically equally capable of benefiting from a college education; only poverty, ignorance, and prejudice prevent some from acquiring one.

Generally, the most important cause of differences in opportunities is differences in the availability of funds.[102] These in turn are derived from the same segmentation in the capital market which implies that cheaper funds are rationed, and that supply curves of funds are positively inclined even to individual investors. For a variety of reasons cheaper funds are more accessible to some persons than to others, and the former then have more favorable supply conditions. Some may live in areas providing liberal government and other subsidies to investment in human capital, or receive special scholarships because of luck or political contacts. Others may be born into wealthy families, have generous parents, borrow on favorable terms, or willingly forego consumption while investing. For all these reasons and more, supply curves of funds could differ considerably, and Chart 5 shows a few that differ in level or elasticity. For simplicity they are assumed to rise more continuously than the supply curve depicted in Chart 4.

If supply conditions alone varied, the equilibrium positions of different persons would be given by the intersections of the common demand curve with the different supply curves; the points p_1, p_2, p_3, and p_4 in Chart 5 represent a few such positions. Full knowledge of these positions, of the marginal rate of return associated with each amount of capital investment, would permit the common demand curve to be "identified." Moreover, the marginal rates could themselves be "identified" from the earnings received by persons with different capital investments.[103]

Persons with favorable supply conditions would invest relatively large amounts in themselves: the equilibrium positions in Chart 5 are further to the right, the lower the supply curves are. The distribution of the total capital invested obviously would be more unequal and skewed, the more unequal and skewed was the distribution of supply curves.

---

[102] Of course, it is not the only cause; for example, discrimination and nepotism are often important, and yet usually affect the benefits from rather than the financial costs of investing in human capital.

[103] Using the assumption that white males have the same demand curve for formal education, G. Hanoch first estimated the marginal rates of return to education from earning differentials between persons at different education levels, and then "identified" their common demand curve. See his *Personal Earnings and Investment in Schooling*, Ph.D. dissertation, University of Chicago, 1965, Chapter II.

CHART 5

Equilibrium Levels of Investment in Human Capital Resulting
from Differences in "Opportunities"

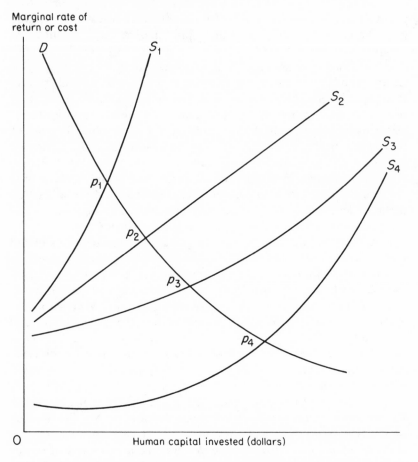

If the labor force period was long, earnings would be related to the
amount of capital invested by

$$E = \bar{r}C, \tag{80}$$

where E is earnings, C the total capital invested, and $\bar{r}$ the average
rate of return on C. The distribution of E clearly depends on the distribution of C; indeed, if the demand curve for capital was completely
elastic, $\bar{r}$ would be the same for everyone, and the distributions of

earnings and investments would be identical except for a difference in units ($\bar{r}$) that depended on the aggregate supply of and demand for human capital. Since it is shown above that C is more unequally distributed and skewed the more unequal and skewed is the distribution of supply curves, the same applies to the distribution of E.

As we have seen, the demand curve for capital investment is usually negatively inclined rather than infinitely elastic primarily because human capital is embodied in investors. E will, therefore, usually be more equally distributed than C because a given percentage change in C will change E by a smaller percentage since $\bar{r}$ will decline as C increases and increase as C declines. Moreover, both E and C will be more unequally distributed and skewed the more elastic the demand curve is; for the greater the latter, the more that persons with favorable supply conditions would be encouraged to invest still more by a higher $\bar{r}$; and the more that those with unfavorable supply conditions would be encouraged to invest still less by a lower $\bar{r}$.

Similarly, an increase in the elasticities of supply curves that held constant their locations at the average value of C would also increase the inequality and skewness in E and C. Persons with unfavorable supply conditions would be encouraged to cut back their investments at the same time that those with favorable conditions were encouraged to expand theirs.

In the Mathematical Appendix exact relations between the distributions of E and C and the parameters of supply and demand curves are derived under the special assumption that all supply curves have the same constant elasticity, and that the demand curve also has a constant elasticity. Among the results of this more special model is that earnings are likely to be less unequally distributed and less skewed than supply curves (that is, than opportunities).[104]

b. *"Elite" approach.* At the other end of the spectrum is the assumption that supply conditions are identical and that demand conditions alone vary among persons. This can be considered an approximate representation of the "elite" approach to the distributions of investment in human capital and earnings, which assumes that everyone more or less has effectively equal opportunities. Actual investments and earnings differ primarily because of differences in the capacity to benefit from investment in human capital: some persons are abler and form an elite. In spite of the position taken by Smith and Hume, educational policy in England and some other parts of Europe has

[104] See section 6 of the Appendix.

been predicated on a version of the elite view: "There is a tendency of long historical standing in English educational thought (it is not nearly so visible in some other countries) to concentrate too much on the interests of the abler persons in any group that is being considered and to forget about the rest." [105]

Just as opportunities have been measured primarily by supply curves, so capacities are measured primarily by demand curves.[106] For a given (dollar) amount invested, persons with higher demand curves receive higher rates of return than others; or looked at differently, they have to invest more than others to lower the marginal rate to a given level. Since all human capital is assumed to be identical, demand curves can be higher only if more units of capital are produced by a given expenditure. It is natural to say that persons who produce more human capital from a given expenditure have more capacity or "ability." [107]

Since a higher demand curve means greater earnings from a given investment, in effect, ability is being measured indirectly; namely, by the earnings received when the investment in human capital is held constant.[108] This approach is an appealing compromise between defi-

---

[105] *Fifteen to Eighteen,* a report of the Central Advisory Council for Education, Geoffrey Crowther, Chairman, 1959, p. 87. In addition, many formal models of income distribution developed by economists are largely based on an underlying distribution of abilities. See, for example, A. D. Roy, "The Distribution of Earnings and of Individual Output," *Economic Journal,* 60, 1950, pp. 489–505, and B. Mandelbrot, "Paretian Distributions and Income Maximization," *Quarterly Journal of Economics,* 76, 1962, pp. 57–85.

[106] Let me repeat, however, that some differences in opportunities, such as those resulting from discrimination and nepotism, affect demand curves. Similarly, some differences in capacities affect supply curves.

[107] If the production function notation of footnote 81 is used, the ith and jth persons have the functions

$$h_i = f_i(R_i, T_i, B_i)$$
$$h_j = f_j(R_j, T_j, B_j).$$

The ith person has more ability if $f_i > f_j$ when R and T, the inputs of market resources and own time, respectively, are held constant. If sometimes $f_i > f_j$ and sometimes $f_j > f_i$, there is no unique ranking of their abilities.

Note, however, that since demand curves incorporate psychic benefits and costs from human capital as well as monetary ones, i could have a higher demand curve than j, and thus be considered to have more capacity, simply because he receives more psychic benefits than j does.

[108] Note the similar definition by R. H. Tawney: "In so far as the individuals between whom comparison is made belong to a homogeneous group, whose members have equal opportunities of health and education, of entering remunerative occupations, and of obtaining access to profitable financial knowledge, it is plausible, no doubt, if all questions of chance and fortune are excluded, to treat the varying positions which they ultimately occupy as the expression of differences in their personal qualities" (*Equality,* Capricorn Books edition, New York, 1961, p. 121).

nitions of ability in terms of scores on IQ, personality, or motivation tests without regard to the effect on earnings, and definitions in terms of earnings without regard to opportunities.[109] The former pay excessive attention to form and not enough to results, while the latter hopelessly confound "nature" and "nurture," or ability and environment. Our approach directly relates ability to results, and at the same time recognizes the impact that environment has on results.[110]

If demand curves alone varied, the capital investments and marginal rates of return of different persons would be found at the intersections of the different demand curves with the common supply curve. In Chart 6 there clearly is a positive relation between the height of a demand curve, the amount of capital invested and the marginal rate. Knowledge of the latter two quantities for many different persons would permit an "identification" of the common supply curve, just as such information earlier permitted an "identification" of a common demand curve.

An important difference, however, is that the marginal rates themselves could not now be "identified" from information on the earnings and investments of different persons alone. In Chart 6 the marginal rate of return to investing OC_3 rather than OC_2 would be proportional to the area $p_2C_2C_3q_2$ for persons with the demand D_2 and to the larger area $q_3C_2C_3p_3$ for those with D_3. If a marginal rate was simply estimated from the difference in earnings between persons investing OC_2 and OC_3, the estimate would be proportional to $D_2p_2C_2C_3p_3D_3$, which clearly greatly exceeds both true rates. To arrive at correct estimates, either the earnings of persons investing OC_2 would be adjusted upward by the area $D_3D_2p_2q_3$, or the earnings of those investing OC_3 adjusted downward by the area $D_3D_2q_2p_3$.[111] Note, incidentally, that those arguing that most of the differences in earnings between persons at different levels of education or training result from differences in ability are essentially assuming a common supply curve and steeply inclined demand curves.

Aside from chance, Tawney mainly stresses the importance of holding constant health, education, and financial knowledge, which are simply different kinds of human capital.

[109] For a review of these definitions in the context of analyzing income distributions, see H. Staehle, "Ability, Wages, and Income," *The Review of Economics and Statistics,* 25, 1943, pp. 77–87.

[110] I have not tried to explain why some people are "abler" than others; this might ultimately be traced back to differences in numerous basic ability "factors." For a model of this kind, see Mandelbrot, *op. cit.*

[111] Some adjustments along these lines to estimated rates of return on formal education can be found in this volume, pp. 202–204.

CHART 6

Equilibrium Levels of Investment in Human Capital Resulting
from Differences in "Abilities"

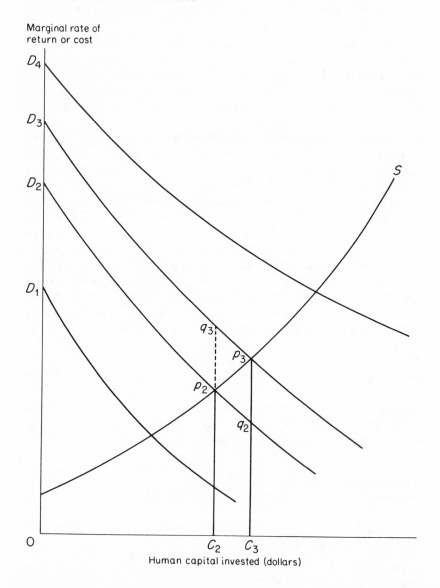

Marginal rate of
return or cost

Earnings and capital investments are clearly more unequally distributed and skewed the more unequally distributed and skewed are demand curves. The same kind of arguments as those used in the previous section should make it apparent that both distributions are also more unequal and skewed, the greater the elasticities of the supply and demand curves. If the supply curve was positively inclined, the average rate of return would tend to be greater, the larger the amount invested. Therefore, earnings would tend to be more unequally distributed and skewed than investments.

In the Mathematical Appendix exact relations between the distributions of earnings and capital investment and the parameters of the supply and demand curves are derived under the special assumption that all demand curves have the same constant elasticity, and that the supply curve also has a constant elasticity. One of the more interesting results is that earnings and investments would *necessarily* be more unequally distributed and skewed than demand curves.[112] If, for example, demand curves (i.e., capacities) were symmetrically distributed, both earnings and investments would be skewed to the right.

c. A comparison of these approaches. Before moving on to the general case that incorporates variations in both supply and demand conditions, it is illuminating to contrast the more important implications of these special cases. For under the guise of the "egalitarian" and "elite" approaches, they are frequently explicitly advanced and are still more widely implicitly assumed.

The "egalitarian" approach implies that the marginal rate of return is lower, the larger the amount invested in human capital, while the "elite" approach implies the opposite relation. Marginal rates of return appear[113] to decline in the United States as years of schooling increase, which supports the "egalitarian" approach. However, in Canada, a country in many economic respects quite similar to the United States, estimated marginal rates do not decline consistently as schooling increases.[114]

---

112 See section 4 of the mathematical appendix on p. 138.

113 I say "appear" because these rates have not been fully corrected for differences in the average level of "ability" at different education levels; such a correction might eliminate the apparent decline (see Hanoch, *op. cit.*, or this volume, p. 202).

114 See J. R. Podoluk, *Earnings and Education*, Dominion Bureau of Statistics, 1965. Note that since different years of schooling are not perfect substitutes, the pattern of rates are also affected by the relative demand for and supply of different years. Thus the relatively small number of college-educated persons in Canada might explain the relatively high rates of return to college education there.

The inequality in earnings tends to be less than that in supply conditions in the "egalitarian" approach, and greater than that in demand conditions in the "elite" approach because the former implies a negative, and the latter a positive, correlation between rates of return and amounts invested. Put differently and perhaps more interestingly, to understand the observed inequality in earnings, the "egalitarian" approach has to presume greater inequality in opportunities than the "elite" one has to presume about capacities. Inequality in earnings is a more serious problem to the former, therefore, in the sense that a given observed amount implies greater underlying "inequities" or "noncompeting groups" [115] than it does to the latter.

For a similar reason, the positive skewness in earnings is probably less than that in opportunities under the "egalitarian" approach and greater than that in capacities under the "elite" approach. Indeed, as pointed out in the last section, it is shown in the Mathematical Appendix using the assumptions of constant and identical elasticities of demand, and a constant elasticity of supply, that a symmetrical distribution of capacities *necessarily* results in a positively skewed distribution of earnings. Therefore, an age-old problem of economists —how to reconcile a skewed distribution of income with a presumed symmetrical normal distribution of abilities[116]—turns out to be no problem at all.[117] In the "egalitarian" approach, on the other hand, observed skewness is more difficult to explain because it implies still greater skewness in the distribution of opportunities, a skewness that may be associated with a skewed distribution of gifts and inheritance, etc.[118]

---

[115] The interpretation of income inequality in terms of noncompeting groups was popular among nineteenth and early twentieth century writers. For a review see H. Dalton, *Some Aspects of the Inequality of Incomes in Modern Communities,* London, 1920, Part II. "Groups" may be noncompeting either because of differences in opportunities, as assumed in the "egalitarian" approach, or because of differences in capacities, as assumed in the "elite" approach.

[116] For example, A. C. Pigou said "Now, on the face of things, we should expect that, if as there is reason to think, people's capacities are distributed on a plan of this kind [i.e., according to a symmetrical normal distribution], their incomes will be distributed in the same way. Why is not this expectation realized?" *The Economics of Welfare,* 4th edition, New York, 1950, p. 650. See also P. A. Samuelson, *Economics,* 6th edition, New York, 1964, pp. 120–121.

[117] It is not possible, however, to reconcile extremely large skewness in earnings with a symmetrical distribution of capacities.

[118] Pigou's principal answer to the question he sets out in footnote 116 is largely based on a presumed skewed distribution of inheritances, which affects, among other things, the distribution of investments in training (*ibid.,* pp. 651–654). Or, as Allyn Young said, "The worst thing in the present situation is undoubtedly the

d. A more general approach. If either all demand or all supply curves were identical, the supply and demand curves of persons investing the same amount would also be identical if different demand or different supply curves did not touch in the relevant region. This, in turn, means that all persons investing the same amount would have identical earnings. Yet if the amount invested is measured by years of schooling, there is abundant evidence of considerable variability in the earnings of persons with the same investment.[119] Possibly improved measures of investment or the introduction of transitory earnings would eliminate most of the variability; I suspect, however, that a significant portion would remain. If so, neither special case—that is neither variations in demand nor in supply curves alone—is sufficient, although one set of curves might vary much more than the other.

If both supply and demand curves varied, different persons could invest the same amount, and yet some could earn more than others because they had higher demand (*and* supply) curves; in Chart 7, the same amount would be invested by persons with D_3 and S_1, D_2 and S_2, and D_1 and S_3. As this example indicates, knowledge of the various equilibrium marginal rates of return and investments would no longer be sufficient to identify either a supply or a demand curve because the equilibrium positions would be on different curves. Moreover, again the marginal rates themselves could not be identified from information on earnings and investments alone because persons with different investments would generally have different demand curves.

The distributions of earnings and investments would partly depend on the same parameters already discussed: both would be more unequal and skewed, the greater the elasticities of supply and demand curves, and the more unequal and skewed their distributions. The distributions of earnings and investments also depend, how-

---

extreme skewness of the income frequency curve . . . reflecting as it undoubtedly does the presence of a high degree of inequality in the distribution of opportunity" ("Do the Statistics of the Concentration of Wealth in the United States Mean What they are Commonly Assumed to Mean?," *Journal of the American Statistical Association,* 15, 1917, pp. 481–482). One should point out, however, that even "a high degree of inequality in the distribution of opportunity" is not sufficient to produce skewness in earnings, and that skewed distribution of opportunities is necessary, at least in the "egalitarian" approach.

119 For example, the coefficient of variation in the incomes of white males aged 35–44 in 1949 was 0.60 for high school graduates and 0.75 for college graduates (see this volume, Table 9, p. 182). Or in 1959, years of schooling explained less than 20 per cent of the variance in the earnings of white males aged 25–64 in both the South and non-South (see Table 1, p. 92).

CHART 7

Equilibrium Levels of Investment in Human Capital Resulting
from Differences in "Abilities" and "Opportunities"

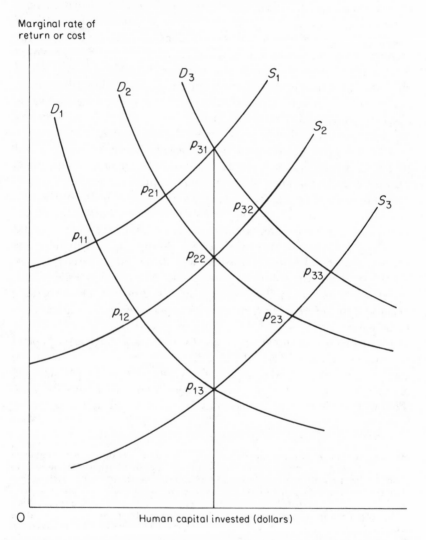

ever, on a new parameter: namely, the correlation between different
curves.

There are several reasons why supply conditions do not vary independently of demand conditions. Abler persons are more likely

to receive public and private scholarships, and thus have their supply curves shifted downward. Or children from higher-income families probably, on the average, are more intelligent and receive greater psychic benefits from human capital. On the other hand, private and public "wars" on poverty can significantly lower the supply curves of some poor persons. Since the first two considerations have, unquestionably, been stronger than the third, it is reasonable to presume a positive[120] correlation between supply and demand conditions, perhaps a sizable one.

If supply and demand curves were uncorrelated, one might have the equilibrium positions given by p_{31}, p_{32}, and p_{33} in Chart 7; if they were negatively correlated, by p_{31}, p_{22}, and p_{13}; and if they were positively correlated, by p_{11}, p_{22}, and p_{33}. The chart clearly shows that a positive correlation increases the inequality in both investments and earnings; it also increases skewness by increasing the earnings and investments of persons who would have relatively high earnings and investments anyway.

An impression of a negative correlation between supply and demand conditions—that is, between opportunities and capacities—is sometimes obtained from persons investing the same amount. As the curves D_3 and S_1, D_2 and S_2, and D_1 and S_3 in Chart 7 clearly show, however, the supply and demand curves of persons investing the same amount must be negatively correlated, regardless of the true overall correlation between them. Valid evidence of this latter correlation is provided by information on the amount of variation in earnings "explained" (in the analysis of variance sense) by the variation in investments. For example, if the correlation between supply and demand curves was perfect and positive, all the variation in earnings would be "explained" by investments. Moreover, the smaller the algebraic value of this correlation, the less the variation in earnings is "explained" by investments, and the more that earnings vary among persons making the same investment.

Supplement: Estimating the Effect
of Family Background on Earnings[121]

One important implication of the above analysis on the interaction between opportunities and capacities (i.e., supply and demand condi-

---

120 By "positive" is meant that more favorable demand conditions are associated with more favorable supply conditions.

121 The issues considered in this addendum were already briefly considered by J. Mincer in "The Distribution of Labor Incomes: A Survey," *Journal of Economic Literature*, March 1970, p. 20.

tions) was mentioned but not sufficiently stressed—namely, that opportunities and capacities would be negatively correlated for persons investing the same amount, regardless of the overall correlation between them. For example, if, as many studies suggest, investment opportunities are less favorable to children in large families, ability and number of siblings would be *positively* correlated for persons investing the same amount, even if they were negatively correlated in the population as a whole.[122]

I want to stress, however, its importance in separating the effect of family background on earnings from the effect of schooling. In recent years, many studies have tried to separate these effects by running multiple regressions of earnings on years of schooling and background variables (and often other variables as well), and using the schooling regression coefficients as a measure of the independent effect of schooling, and the background coefficient as a measure of the independent effect of background.[123] Yet if years of schooling result not from random behavior but from optimizing behavior, these studies may be seriously understating the contribution of background to earnings and overstating that of schooling.

To show this in a dramatic fashion, assume that family background only has an effect on opportunities, capacities being independent of background, and that background is the only variable affecting opportunities. A series of equilibrium positions are shown in Chart 8: b_1, b_2, b_3, and b_4 are supply curves of particular persons with different background (b_4 is a more favorable background than b_3, etcetera), and d_1, d_2, d_3, and d_4 are their corresponding demand curves (or capacities). The optimal accumulation of capital by each person is given by the intersection of his supply and demand curve, or by the points e_1, e_2, e_3, and e_4.

If the independent effect of background on earnings were estimated from differences in earnings between persons with the same accumulation of human capital but different backgrounds, point e_2 would be compared to e_1 or point e_4 to e_3. In both comparisons, persons with

---

[122] This implication was derived and tested many years ago by R. A. Fisher. See his *The Genetical Theory of Natural Selection*, 2nd ed., New York, 1958, Chapter 11.

[123] See, for example, S. Bowles, "Schooling and Inequality from Generation to Generation," *Journal of Political Economy*, 80, 3, Supplement, May–June, 1972; A. Leibowitz, "Home Investments in Children," *Journal of Political Economy*, 82, 2, Supplement, March–April, 1974; J. Coleman and P. Rossi, "Processes of Change in Occupation and Income," mimeograph, 1974; or Louis Levy-Garboua, "Does Schooling Pay?," *Entroit de Consommation*, 3, 1973.

CHART 8

The Effect of Background and Ability on Earnings
and the Accumulation of Human Capital

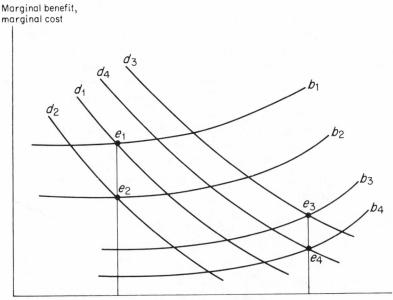

Human capital accumulated

higher backgrounds have *lower* earnings,[124] yet in this example a
better background certainly does not lower earning capacity. Of
course, the reason for this erroneous result is that persons with superior
backgrounds (i.e., superior opportunitities) would accumulate the same
amount of human capital as those with inferior backgrounds (i.e.,
inferior opportunities) only if the former have inferior earning
capacities.

A similar argument shows that the effect of human capital on earnings is overstated when estimated from differences in earnings between
persons with the same background but different accumulations of
human capital. For they choose to invest different amounts only be-

---

124 Leibowitz, *op. cit.,* Tables 4–6, does find a negative effect of mother's education on earnings when own years of schooling are held constant. (However, she
also finds a positive coefficient for parent's income.)

cause they differ in earning capacity.[125] In other words, the effect of human capital on earnings would be more accurately estimated if background were omitted as a separate variable than if held constant.

The argument holds, more generally, when background affects earning capacity as well as opportunities, and other variables affect opportunities as well as capacities, if background is a major determinant of opportunities, which is surely true, and other variables are a major determinant of capacities, which is also true. A multiple regression of earnings on background and human capital would then always understate the effect of background and overstate that of human capital.

In principle, the appropriate statistical procedure is a simultaneous equations model that would "identify" the opportunities and capacities functions, including the effects on both functions of background and human capital accumulation. In practice, however, a good specification is not easily obtained because information on variables that can "shift" these functions is limited. Some progress can be made, however, by starting with simple models. For example, the model depicted in Chart 8 can be written as

$$r_d = a + bH + u$$
$$r_s = \alpha + \partial H + \gamma B + v$$
$$r_d = r_s,$$

where r_d is the marginal rate of return on, and r_s is the marginal cost of, financing, the human capital accumulation H, u, and v represent disturbance terms that are uncorrelated with each other and with the exogenous background variable B, and $b < 0$, $\partial > 0$, and $\gamma < 0$. Then the demand function can be identified—i.e., b can be estimated—by using the reduced form equations: r regressed on B and H regressed on B. The supply function is not identifiable in this system but would be also if there were information on exogenous "ability" variables that only entered the demand function.

e. The effects of age. A common method of explaining the rise in the inequality of earnings with age is to introduce random influences and let their effects partly accumulate over time.[126] An alternative method suggested by our analysis is to introduce earnings during the investment period. It has already been stressed that investing in hu-

---

[125] Again, Leibowitz finds that controlling for background tends to *raise* the estimated effect of schooling.

[126] See, for example, J. Aitchison and J. A. C. Brown, *The Lognormal Distribution,* London, 1957, pp. 108–111.

man capital takes time primarily because an investor's own time is an important input into the investment process. Persons who invest relatively little tend also to cease investing at relatively early ages; for example, dropouts from elementary school generally cease investing before college graduates do. If, therefore, persons with higher demand or lower supply curves tend to have longer investment periods as well as larger investments,[127] the accrued earnings (that is, the area under demand curves) of persons with high earnings would increase for longer periods than would those of others. The effect would be greater inequality in the distribution of accrued earnings at older ages as long as an appreciable number of persons are still investing. In other words, inequality could rise with age because it takes abler persons and those with favorable opportunities longer to reach their full earning power.

Measured earnings differ, however, from accrued earnings during investment periods partly because the income and capital accounts are confounded: measured are derived from accrued earnings only after some investment costs are deducted. Since the amounts deducted are large and variable, measured earnings during investment periods may be only weakly positively or even negatively correlated with earnings afterwards.[128] The effect of mixing earnings and investment costs on the inequality in earnings is less clear-cut. On the one hand, inequality is decreased because high earners invest larger amounts and for longer periods; on the other hand, the inequality is increased by the variation among persons in the amounts deducted.

f. Profits on human capital. The profits on investments in human capital are not measured by earnings or returns alone, but rather by the difference between returns and repayment costs. Geometrically, they do not equal the area under a demand curve alone, but the difference between the areas under a demand and supply curve. Although profits are obviously less than earnings, the former are not necessarily distributed either less or more unequally than the latter. Indeed, a very useful theorem proved in the Appendix states that if all demand curves had the same constant elasticity, and if supply curves also did, the percentage difference between earnings and profits would be the same for everyone, and thus the distribution of profits would be exactly

---

[127] They necessarily have larger investments if supply and demand curves are not negatively correlated.

[128] For one piece of evidence indicating virtually no correlation, see J. Mincer, "On-the-Job Training: Costs, Returns, and Some Implications," *Journal of Political Economy*, 70, Special Supplement, October 1962, p. 53.

the same, aside from scale, as the distribution of earnings.[129] If constant and identical elasticities can be taken as a rough first approximation to the truth, there is no need to dwell on the distribution of profits, for it would depend on exactly the same variables already discussed in detail for earnings. To summarize and apply those results: profits would be more unequally distributed and skewed, the more unequally distributed and skewed were the supply and demand curves, the greater the positive correlation between these curves, and the greater their elasticities.

g. Heterogeneous human capital. A major assumption has been that all human capital is homogeneous, an assumption that conflicts with obvious qualitative differences in types of education, on-the-job training, informal learning, etc. in the same way that the frequently used assumption of homogeneous physical capital conflicts with myriad observed differences in plant, equipment, etc. The advantage of these assumptions is that by sweeping away qualitative detail—detail that, incidentally, has received excessive attention in the literature on human capital—one can concentrate on more fundamental relationships.

For those unable to accept, even tentatively, an assumption of homogeneous human capital, let me hasten to stress that different kinds can rather easily be incorporated into the analysis. For example, with two kinds of capital, each person would have two sets of demand and supply curves, and in equilibrium, marginal benefits and financing costs would be equal for each set. The distribution of earnings would still depend in the same way on the distributions and elasticities of the supply and demand curves. The only significant new parameters introduced are those giving the correlations between the different supply and also between the different demand curves for the two kinds of capital. These correlations measure the extent to which people are relatively able or have access to funds on relatively favorable terms for both kinds. These correlations are presumably positive, but by no means perfect, because both ability and access to funds carry over to some extent, but not perfectly, from one kind of capital to another. It should be intuitively clear that positive correlations tend to make both earnings and investments more unequally distributed and skewed, for then persons who invest much (or little) in and earn much (or little) from one kind of capital also tend to invest and earn much (or little) from the other.

---

[129] See section 8 of the Mathematical Appendix for a proof (pp. 143–145).

4. Some Applications

The supply and demand curves for investment in human capital that affect the distribution of earnings are not immutable, but are partly determined by aspirations, private generosity, and public policy. Although in a long run perspective all may be subject to change, the variables influencing opportunities are more easily and immediately influenced than are those influencing capacities. It is not surprising, therefore, that the various institutions discussed in this section all influence the distribution of earnings through their impact on the distribution of opportunities. The institutions covered are rather diverse: more "equal" opportunity, admission to education and other training institutions on the basis of "objective" testing, compulsory minimum schooling and other investments, and improvements in the capital market. Their diversity and importance demonstrates the value of our analysis in relating the distribution of earnings to private and public actions.

a. Equality of opportunity. An avowed goal of many countries, especially the United States, has been to achieve "equality of opportunity," yet the meaning and implications of this term have not been carefully explored.[130] A natural statement within our framework is: equality of opportunity implies that all supply curves are identical, with opportunity being more unequal, the greater their dispersion. A full definition might also include elimination of public and private discrimination and nepotism, which would limit the dispersion in demand curves as well. The implications of this statement can be easily derived by building on the analysis developed in the last section.

For example, if supply curves were identical and discrimination and nepotism eliminated, earnings and investments would differ essentially because of differences in capacities, a major goal of those advocating equal opportunity.[131] Therefore, the "egalitarian" ap-

---

[130] One of the better statements is by Tawney: "[Equality of opportunity] obtains in so far as, and only in so far as, each member of a community, whatever his birth, or occupation, or social position, possesses in fact, and not merely in form, equal chances of using to the full his natural endowments of physique, of character, and of intelligence" (*Equality, op. cit.*, p. 106). Tawney does not, however, relate this definition to any analysis of income inequality.

[131] Tawney said: "The inequality which they [and Tawney] deplore is not inequality of personal gifts, but of the social and economic environment" (*Ibid.*, p. 38). Inequality in position in Michael Young's "meritocracy" is entirely related to inequality in ability. See his *The Rise of the Meritocracy 1870–2033*, New York, 1959.

proach to distribution implies that equalizing opportunity would essentially eliminate all the inequality in earnings and investments, while the "elite" approach denies that it would make any essential difference.

The effect of equal opportunity on the inequality in earnings and investments is also clear-cut. If supply and demand curves were not negatively correlated, and if equal opportunity did not raise the algebraic value of this correlation or the absolute values of the supply and demand elasticities, then it must reduce the inequality in earnings. The reason is simply that one of the basic determinants of inequality, the dispersion in supply curves (and partly also in demand curves), is eliminated while the others are not affected "perversely." Unless the correlation between supply and demand curves was positive and sizable, the reduction in the inequality of earnings would be less than that in investments, however, because the elimination of inequality in supply curves would raise the correlation between investments and rates of return, which would partly offset the reduction in the inequality of investments.

Identical supply curves can be achieved in many ways: subsidies to institutions providing investments, such as through the public schools; scholarships to investors, especially poorer ones; government-financed or insured loans to investors; "head start" programs for poorer children; and so on. Probably the most desirable system is to subsidize the external or "neighborhood" cultural, political, and economic benefits of investments, and develop loan programs to finance the direct or private benefits.[132] Only if external benefits completely dominated, which is not true even for education,[133] would this lead to "free" investments.

b. Objective selection. Often confused with policies that equalize opportunities are those that ration entrance into highly subsidized schools and other investment institutions not by "favoritism," but by "objective" standards, such as scores on special examinations, grades or class standing in prior training, etc. Of the many examples throughout

---

[132] The first and most discussed proposal along these lines can be found in M. Friedman, "The Role of Government in Education," in *Economics and the Public Interest*, Robert A. Solow, ed., New Brunswick, N.J., 1955, pp. 123–144. For a variant of the Friedman proposal see W. Vickrey, "A Proposal for Student Loans," in *Economics of Higher Education*, S. J. Mushkin, ed., Washington, D.C., 1962, pp. 268–280.

[133] See pp. 196–198.

the world, one can mention the examinations at the end of middle schooling in Japan that have sharply limited the number going on to public higher schools,[134] the "eleven plus" examinations in Great Britain that have determined entrance into grammar schools,[135] or the high-school records that help determine admission to the University of California, Harvard University, and many other universities in the United States.

"Objective" selection is an illusion in the "egalitarian" approach to distribution because if differences in capacities are unimportant, selection cannot be "objective" and must be subjective. This explains why there is continuous pressure on public universities in the United States to admit essentially all applicants meeting minimum qualifications. There is greater justification within the "elite" approach; not surprisingly, therefore, "objective" selection has been prominent in countries like Great Britain and Japan. If differences in capacities are obvious and substantial, tests administered even as early as ages eleven or fifteen can select the more promising students.

Generally, persons failing examinations or other standards are not prevented from continuing their investments; only the cost of funds to them is greater. Objective standards clearly do not, therefore, equalize opportunity because persons selected obtain funds under relatively favorable conditions. Since a system of objective standards, if used successfully, also tends to increase the positive correlation between supply and demand conditions, the resulting inequality in earnings and investments would exceed that under equality of opportunity.[136] Indeed, the resulting inequality would even tend to exceed that under a system selecting applicants at random because objective standards encourage abler persons, who probably earn and invest more than others anyway, to earn and invest still more because they are heavily subsidized.[137]

---

[134] The pressure felt by parents and pupils has been known as "the examination hell." See H. Passin, *Society and Education in Japan*, Teachers College, Columbia University, 1965, pp. 104–108.

[135] About four-fifths of the eleven- and twelve-year-olds are not admitted to grammar schools. See Crowther, *op. cit.*, p. 87. Although the others generally can continue their education in "all age" or "secondary modern" schools, their chances of continuing beyond age fifteen are considerably reduced because many of these schools do not provide fifth and higher years of secondary schooling (*ibid.*).

[136] Assuming, of course, that the elasticities of supply and demand curves and the distribution of the latter are the same in both situations.

[137] In the quote from the Crowther report in section 3b above there is an implied criticism of the system of objective selection in Great Britain.

c. Compulsory minimum investments. Virtually every country has laws requiring a minimum investment in human capital. Usually only a minimum number of school years is required,[138] although sometimes apprenticeship programs and other on-the-job training can be substituted. Since differences in the generosity or wealth of parents are a major cause of inequality in the "egalitarian" approach to income distribution, minimum investment legislation would make sense under that approach. For by imposing minimum standards, poorer and less generous parents are forced to spend more on their children, which improves the latter's opportunities and earnings. Since differences in capacities are the major cause of inequality in the "elite" approach, there would not be much interest in these standards under that approach.[139]

In Chart 9 let D be the demand curve and S the supply curve of a particular person in the absence of minimum standards, and OC_s be his equilibrium capital investment. If legislation is passed requiring at least OC_m, his supply curve would be shifted to the curve C_mS because his parents are forced to become more "generous," and his equilibrium investment would be increased to OC_m. The distribution of investments would be truncated at OC_m, with everyone who would have invested less being brought up to that point.[140]

Truncating the distribution of investments reduces the inequality in investments and through that in earnings as well. In effect, the inequality of opportunity is reduced by bringing supply curves closer together;[141] indeed, by setting the minimum standard at least equal

---

[138] For example, the British in practice require only attendance through age fifteen. The Act of 1944 also required part-time education for those leaving before age sixteen, but it has not been put into effect (see Crowther, *op. cit.*, p. 105); for the first half of this century the Dutch simply required seven consecutive years of schooling. See M. M. Loren, *Education in the Netherlands,* Netherlands Information Bureau, New York, 1942, p. 12.

[139] Except, of course, to the extent that investment in human capital produces significant external benefits.

[140] In 1900 the Dutch passed a law providing for at least seven years of schooling; by 1960 virtually no one in the male labor force had less and almost 60 per cent were about at that level. Similarly, in 1951 about two-thirds of the persons in the labor force in Great Britain had nine years of schooling, the minimum amount required, and only one in ten had less. See B. R. Chiswick, *Human Capital and the Distribution of Personal Income,* Ph.D. dissertation, Columbia University, 1967. Educational distributions are not so truncated in the United States because different states passed laws at different times and heavy internal migration and immigration from abroad moved people from their educational origins.

[141] If minimum standards, apply only to one kind of human capital, such as schooling, some parental funds may simply be drawn away from other kinds, such as on-the-job training, which would increase the dispersion in the supply of funds to these kinds.

CHART 9

The Effect of a Compulsory Investment Law on the Amount Invested

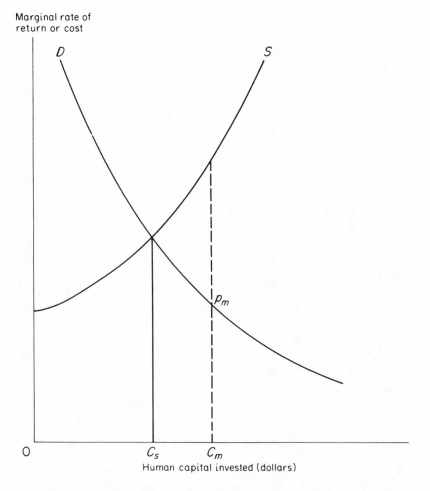

Marginal rate of
return or cost

D

S

p_m

O

C_s C_m

Human capital invested (dollars)

to the maximum amount anyone would have invested, identical investments and full equality of opportunity could be obtained. Moreover, opportunity is equalized at the same time that the elasticities of supply are drastically reduced (compare S with C_mS in Chart 9), which also contributes to a reduction in the inequality of earnings and investments. As section 4e shows, however, greater equality is obtained only at the expense of a less efficient allocation of the total investment in human capital.

Since the purpose of minimum standards is to offset the effects of poverty and niggardliness, appropriate subsidies could in principle achieve the same result without compulsion. The effectiveness of voluntary investment in human capital is often underrated [142] because subsidies to human capital usually cover, at best, only a portion of the earnings foregone. If they covered all costs, including those foregone, almost all children, I am confident, would continue in school through the age desired.

d. *Improvements in the capital market.* It was emphasized earlier that the major cause of both the rise in the cost of funds as a person's investments increased and the differences in the cost to different persons is the rationing of cheaper sources of funds due to a segmentation of the capital market. Government funds are generally the cheapest because of subsidies, own funds are usually cheaper than those borrowed commercially because of transaction costs and the difficulty of using human capital as collateral, and so forth. Less segmentation— due, for example, to a reduction in subsidies or transaction costs— would narrow the spread among different sources, and thus both increase the elasticities of supply curves and reduce the dispersion among them.[143]

An improvement in the capital market would, therefore, have somewhat conflicting effects on the distributions of earnings and of investments. A narrower dispersion of supply conditions reduces the inequality, while increased elasticities of supply increase both the inequality and skewness in earnings and investment. Apparently, skewness would tend to increase, but inequality could go in either direction.

e. *Equality and efficiency.* The discussion of capital market improvements, minimum investment legislation, and other changes in opportunities has emphasized inequality and skewness and ignored efficiency. Yet the trade off and conflict between equity and efficiency have occupied as much time of social commentators as any other economic issue. One important advantage of the analytical framework developed in this study is, therefore, that efficiency can be as easily and

---

[142] "Voluntary staying-on seems both too haphazard and too precarious to be depended on as the basis of a national system" (Crowther, *op. cit.*, p. 107).

[143] The reduced segmentation would contribute, therefore, to greater equality of opportunity.

systematically handled as distribution. This is now illustrated with some examples previously discussed. It is shown, in particular, that, while equality and efficiency are sometimes affected differently, they also sometimes change in the same direction.

If subjective attitudes toward risk are ignored, the criterion for an efficient allocation of the total investment in human capital is well known; namely, that the marginal social rate of return be the same for all persons. If one assumes that the ratio of social to private rates is identical for everyone, this criterion simply requires equality between all marginal private rates, while inefficiency can be measured quantitatively essentially by the inequality in these rates. Efficient allocation of investment between human and other capital requires that the marginal rates on each type of capital be equal to each other, but this aspect of efficiency is not discussed here.

If all supply curves have infinite elasticities, equalizing opportunities not only reduces the inequality in earnings and investments, but also reduces the inequality in marginal rates, which means that the total investment in human capital is allocated more efficiently. A reduction in the segmentation of the capital market that increases the elasticities and reduces the dispersion of supply curves may or may not reduce the inequality in earnings and investments, but does tend to reduce the inequality in marginal rates, and thus improve efficiency. On the other hand, compulsory minimum standards reduce the inequality in earnings and investments, but by lowering supply elasticities widen the inequality in marginal rates, and thereby reduce efficiency.

Rising supply curves that are due to a segmented capital market create an inefficient allocation of the total investment in human capital by penalizing abler persons, who tend to invest more than others. If the market could not be made less segmented, efficiency could be increased by other, "second best," policies that favor the abler. The use of objective standards to select applicants for admission to subsidized investment institutions does favor abler persons, and could, therefore, offset the higher marginal cost of funds to them. Consequently, although objective selection may result in large inequality in earnings and investments, it could help allocate efficiently the total investment in human capital.[144]

Even severe critics of the distribution of incomes have generally protested only against unequal opportunities, and have treated in-

[144] See section 9 of the mathematical appendix for a formal proof (p. 143).

equality resulting from differences in ability with indulgence, if not positive affirmation.[145] Possibly this simply reflects a basic philosophical distinction; I suspect, however, that partly reflected also is an implicit judgment about the interaction between equality and efficiency. By increasing the elasticities of and reducing the differences among supply curves, improved capital markets, scholarships to the needy, compensatory education, and the like reduce the inequality in earnings and at the same time generally improve the allocation of the total investment in human capital. The elasticities of and differences among demand curves, on the other hand, are less related to man-made factors, and more to the embodiment of capital in human beings, differences in intelligence, and other basic forces that are less easily corrected.[146]

5. The Distribution of Property Income

The discussion now shifts from the distribution of human capital and earnings to physical (that is, all nonhuman) capital and property income. Although earnings constitute 75 to 80 per cent of total incomes in the United States and are a major determinant of its distribution as well as level, property income should not be neglected in a serious study of income distribution. For one thing, most of the Anglo-Saxon literature on income distribution has stressed inheritance and property income even more than earnings.[147] Moreover, since property income is considerably more unequally distributed and skewed than earnings, its contribution to income distribution greatly exceeds that to income levels. Fortunately, the analysis developed in the previous sections seems capable of explaining why property incomes

[145] "Rightly interpreted, equality meant, not the absence of violent contrasts of income and condition, but equal opportunities of becoming unequal" (Tawney, op. cit., p. 105); "But the greater the approach towards equality of opportunity, the more reasonable the contention that a distribution according to the value of work done is just" (Dalton, op. cit., pp. 22–23); and in the meritocracy, "stratification has been in accord with a principle of merit, generally accepted at all levels of society" (Young, op. cit., p. 99).

[146] Of course, even these forces could be offset by a system of taxes and subsidies, as, say, through a progressive tax on earnings. Since a progressive tax reduces inequality by redistributing earnings from the top earners, it discourages their investment in human capital more than others, and thereby tends to allocate the total investment in human capital less efficiently.

[147] For example, H. Dalton's classic study of inequality (op. cit.) devotes one chapter to incomes from work and seven to property income and inheritance.

are so unequal and skewed, and even why only a small fraction of the population appears to receive any inheritance.

The property income of any person can be divided into his "original" income and that due to his own capital accumulations. "Original" property income presumably comes from an inheritance and cannot be neglected as readily as "original" earnings were; it is discussed shortly. "Own" property income depends on the amounts invested and their rates of return, and assuming rational behavior once again, these two determinants in turn depend on the supply and demand curves for physical capital. The distributions of own property income and earnings differ, therefore, if and only if the distributions and elasticities of the supply and demand curves for physical and human capital differ.

There are no obvious reasons why the distribution of demand curves for physical and human capital differ significantly in any particular direction, but the other determinants are another story. Although the difference is sometimes exaggerated,[148] undoubtedly the market for physical capital is less segmented than is that for human capital. It was argued in section 4d that, while the net effect on inequality of greater segmentation is not clear a priori, it does cause lesser skewness.

Probably the major difference, however, is in the elasticities of demand. Section 2 argued that the marginal rate of return to an investor in human capital declines with increases in the amount he invests primarily because his human capital is embodied in himself and, therefore, his time is a crucial input into the investment process. Physical capital, on the other hand, is not embodied in people and generally the amount owned is not a major input into additional investments;[149] consequently, there is less reason to expect significant declines in the rate of return to any investor in physical capital as the amount invested increases.

Since demand curves for physical capital can be expected, therefore, to be more elastic than those for human capital, abler investors can be expected to specialize more in physical capital, that is, to invest considerably more than the less able investors.[150] As shown earlier, greater specialization causes the distributions of investments and in-

[148] See my remarks on pp. 78–80.

[149] The important exceptions are the examples beloved by the Austrians in their approach to capital theory: the aging of trees, wines, etc.

[150] This partly explains why some accumulations of physical capital dwarf any accumulations of human capital.

comes to be more unequally distributed and skewed. Primarily, therefore, because of differences in demand elasticities,[151] although aided
somewhat by differences in supply elasticities, our analysis implies that
investments in physical capital and property income are more unequally distributed and skewed than are investments in human capital
and earnings.

A person leaving an inheritance must decide how to distribute it
between human and physical capital: a rational aim is to select that
combination yielding maximum benefits. Since at least relatively small
investments in human capital apparently generally yield considerably
higher payoffs than those in physical capital,[152] one would expect the
preponderant part of small inheritances to be placed in human capital,
say in the form discussed earlier of gifts to children to finance their
education, training, and health.[153] Since statistics and discussions of
inheritance usually only include physical (that is, nonhuman) capital,
probably most small inheritances are overlooked entirely!

As the amount inherited by any person increased significantly, his
marginal rate of return on investments in human capital would decline significantly, and at some point would be brought into line with
that obtainable on physical capital. The fraction going into the latter
would then increase. As his inheritance increased still further, the
marginal rates would decline on both forms of capital, but especially
on human capital because its demand curves are less elastic. A larger
and larger fraction would be placed in physical capital until, for extremely large inheritances, the preponderant part would be placed not
in human but in physical capital.

To summarize, the analysis developed in this paper can predict a
wide variety of facts about physical capital. Among them are why
large accumulations of physical capital dwarf any of human capital,

---

[151] I pointed out earlier that investments in human capital yield declining rates
of return partly because the time remaining to collect returns becomes smaller and
smaller (if lifetimes are finite). The result is that human capital is accumulated over
a much shorter period of time than the length of a working lifetime. There is no
such time limitation on physical capital, and it can be and is accumulated throughout
a lifetime. Accordingly, the argument that property income is more unequally distributed and skewed than earnings because physical capital is accumulated for longer
periods of time than human capital is partly a special case of our argument in terms
of greater elasticities of demand.

[152] See pp. 191–193.

[153] Just as these inheritances were assumed to affect the supply curves of funds for
own investment in human capital, so inheritances in physical capital could be
assumed to affect the supply curves of funds for own investments in such capital. The
supply of funds might then be more unequally distributed for physical than human
capital because, as shown in the following, inheritances invested in the former are
more unequally distributed than are those in the latter.

why own property income is more unequally distributed and skewed than earnings, why only a small and select part of the population appears to receive any inheritance, and why inheritances used for investments in human capital are less unequally distributed than those used for physical capital.

6. Summary and Conclusions

The main purpose of this essay has been to develop a theory of the distribution of earnings and to some extent of other income as well. Earnings are made dependent on the amounts invested in human capital, and the latter are assumed to be determined by a rational comparison of benefits and costs. In other words, each person is assumed to have a negatively inclined demand curve showing the marginal benefit and a positively inclined supply curve showing the marginal financing cost from an additional dollar of capital invested: the optimal capital investment occurs where these two functions intersect. The supply curve to an individual investor is positively inclined because the segmentation in the market for human capital forces him to tap more costly funds as he expands his capital investment. His demand curve is negatively inclined because the embodiment of human capital in investors makes their own time a major input into the investment process. The rise in the value of this time as capital is accumulated over calendar time, combined with the finiteness of working lives, eventually forces marginal benefits to decline as more capital is accumulated.

The distributions of earnings and investments would then depend on the distributions and shapes of these supply and demand curves. The "egalitarian" approach to income distribution, which neglects differences in demand and relates differences in supply to man-made differences in opportunities, implies that earnings are probably more equally distributed and less skewed than opportunities. The "elite" approach, on the other hand, neglects differences in supply and relates differences in demand to more intrinsic differences in capacities. It implies that earnings are more unequally distributed and skewed than capacities. A more general approach combines both differences in supply and demand—that is, in opportunities and capacities—and implies that earnings and investments are more unequally distributed and skewed the more elastic are the supply and demand curves, the more these curves are unequally distributed and skewed, and the greater the positive correlation between them.

The effects of various changes in opportunities on the distribution

of earnings and on the efficiency of the allocation of the total investment in human capital were analyzed. Greater "equality of opportunity" not only tends to reduce the inequality in earnings, but also
to increase the efficiency of the allocation. A less segmented capital
market also tends to improve the allocation, but it increases the
skewness and possibly also the inequality in the distribution of earnings. The use of "objective" criteria to select applicants for admisson to
subsidized schools and other investment institutions could result in
considerable inequality in earnings. "Objective" selection, by its favor-
ing of abler investors, could, however, lead to a more efficient allocation since it could offset the penalty to abler investors from the positively sloped supply curves associated with a segmented capital market.

The analysis was also briefly applied to the distributions of physical
(that is, all nonhuman) capital and the property income yielded. Since
human capital is and physical capital is not embodied in investors,
the demand curves for investment in the former tend to be less elastic
than those for the latter. This can explain the observed greater inequality and skewness in the distributions of physical capital and
property income than human capital and earnings. Inheritances appear to be received by only a small and select part of the population
because small inheritances are invested in human capital and therefore are not reported in inheritance statistics. As the amount inherited
by any person increased, a larger and larger fraction would be invested in physical capital. This can explain the sizable inequality in
reported inheritances and can contribute to the large inequality in
physical capital and property income.

The model developed in this essay can be looked upon as a special
case of a more general model that includes uncertainty,[154] discrepancies
between actual and desired capital stocks and investment rates,
random shocks, and so forth. Although I believe that the special model
is extremely useful in understanding actual income distributions, I
have not tried to defend this view with any systematic empirical tests.
Other empirical studies[155] do offer strong support for the relevance and
significance of the theory developed in this essay.

[154] Reactions to uncertainty form the basis of the theory developed by M. Friedman in "Choice, Chance, and the Personal Distribution of Income," *Journal of
Political Economy*, 71, 1953, pp. 277–290.

[155] See J. Mincer, *Schooling, Experience, and Earnings*, New York, NBER, 1974;
B. R. Chiswick, *Income Inequality: Regional Analyses within a Human Capital
Framework*, New York, NBER, 1974, and "The Average Level of Schooling and the
Intra-Regional Inequality of Income: A Clarification," *American Economic Review*,
58, 3, June 1968, pp. 495–500; and Becker and Chiswick, "Education and the Distri-
bution of Earnings," *American Economic Review*, 56, 2, May 1966, pp. 358–369.

An important attraction of this theory is that it relies fundamentally on maximizing behavior, the basic assumption of general economic theory. Moreover, at the same time, various "institutional" factors are incorporated: inheritance of property income, distribution of abilities, subsidies to education and other human capital, unequal opportunities, and other factors all have important parts in the discussion. The body of economic analysis rather desperately needs a reliable theory of the distribution of incomes. Whether or not this approach is ultimately judged to be satisfactory, it should demonstrate that such a theory need not be a patchwork of Pareto distributions, ability vectors, and ad hoc probability mechanisms, but can rely on the basic economic principles that have so often proven their worth elsewhere.

7. Mathematical Appendix

1. If the returns on each investment in human capital were constant for the whole remaining working lifetime, earnings of the jth person at some age p after the investment period was completed would be

$$E_{jp} = X_{jp} + \int_0^{C_i} r_j(C) f_j \, dC, \tag{81}$$

where X_{jp} are the earnings at age p if there was no investment in human capital, $r_j(C)$ is the rate of return on the Cth dollar invested, f_j is a correction for the finiteness of working lives, and C_j is the total capital investment. If X_{jp} is small enough to be neglected, if working lives are long enough so that $f_j \cong 1$, and if the average rate of return is defined as

$$\bar{r} = \frac{1}{C} \int_0^C r(C) dC, \tag{82}$$

equation (81) can be approximated by

$$E_j = \bar{r}_j C_j, \quad \text{all } p. \tag{83}$$

The distribution of earnings would be related to the distributions of average rates of return and total capital investment, and to the interaction between them. Although some useful insights can be obtained from this relation,[156] the number is limited by the fact that average

[156] See pp. 83–88.

rates and capital investments are themselves both derived from more basic determinants of choice.

2. These determinants can easily be analyzed if investments are assumed to be carried to the point where the marginal rates of return just equal the marginal rates of cost. The function

$$\bar{r}_j = D_j(C_j) \qquad (84)$$

gives the average rate of return to the jth person, where

$$\frac{d\bar{r}_j}{dC_j} \leq 0. \qquad (85)$$

By a well-known formula the marginal rate would then be

$$r_j \equiv \frac{d(\bar{r}_j C_j)}{dC_j} = \bar{r}_j \left(1 + \frac{1}{e_j}\right),$$

with

$$e_j \equiv \frac{dC_j}{d\bar{r}_j} \cdot \frac{\bar{r}_j}{C_j}. \qquad (86)$$

Similarly the function

$$\bar{i} = S(C_j) \qquad (87)$$

gives the average rate of repayment financing costs to the jth person, where

$$\frac{d\bar{i}_j}{dC_j} \geq 0. \qquad (88)$$

By the same formula the marginal rate of cost is

$$i_j \equiv \frac{d(\bar{i}_j C_j)}{dC_j} = \bar{i}_j \left(1 + \frac{1}{\epsilon_j}\right),$$

with

$$\epsilon_j \equiv \frac{dC_j}{d\bar{i}_j} \cdot \frac{\bar{i}_j}{C_j}. \qquad (89)$$

Equilibrium requires equality between these marginal rates, or

$$i_j \equiv S_j \left(1 + \frac{1}{\epsilon_j}\right) = r_j \equiv D_j \left(1 + \frac{1}{e_j}\right), \quad \text{all } j. \qquad (90)$$

Each of these j equations is a function of a single variable alone, C_j, and could, therefore, be solved for the set of optimal capital investments. Equation (84) would then give the set of optimal rates of return and (83) the set of earnings. Clearly the distribution of earnings would depend solely on the supply and demand curves, the D_j and S_j.

3. This dependency can be made explicit by assuming particular functional forms for these curves; a simple form that is also a first approximation to more general forms is the well-known constant elasticity function:

$$\bar{r}_j = D_j(C_j) = a_j C_j^{-1/b_j}$$

$$\bar{i}_j = S_j(C_j) = \frac{1}{\alpha_j} C_j^{1/\beta_j}, \tag{91}$$

where α_j and a_j are constants and > 0, and b_j and β_j are constants defined by

$$b_j = -e_j = \frac{-dC_j}{d\bar{r}_j} \cdot \frac{\dot{\bar{r}}_j}{C_j} > 0$$

$$\beta_j = \epsilon_j = \frac{dC_j}{d\bar{i}_j} \cdot \frac{\bar{i}_j}{C_j} > 0. \tag{92}$$

Equations (86) or (89) obviously imply that the marginal function has the same constant elasticity as the average one.

Substituting equation (91) into (90) gives

$$\frac{1}{\alpha_j}\left(1 + \frac{1}{\beta_j}\right) C_j^{1/\beta_i} = a_j\left(1 - \frac{1}{b_j}\right) C_j^{-1/b_i}, \tag{93}$$

or

$$C_j = \left(\frac{1 - \dfrac{1}{b_j}}{1 + \dfrac{1}{\beta_j}}\right)^{\frac{b_i\beta_i}{b_i + \beta_i}} (a_j\alpha_j)^{\frac{b_i\beta_i}{b_i + \beta_i}}, \quad \text{all } j. \tag{94}$$

Therefore, by equations (83) and (91)

$$E_j = \left(\frac{1 - \dfrac{1}{b_j}}{1 + \dfrac{1}{\beta_j}}\right)^{\left(\frac{b_i\beta_i}{b_i + \beta_i}\left(1 - \frac{1}{b_i}\right)\right)} \cdot (a_j\alpha_j)^{\left(\frac{b_i\beta_i}{b_i + \beta_i}\left(1 - \frac{1}{b_i}\right)\right)} \cdot a_j. \tag{95}$$

Note that for positive earnings $b_j > 1$, an important restriction on the elasticities that is used later on. The distribution of earnings would depend on the joint distribution of the four parameters b_j, β_j, a_j, and α_j.

To simplify the analysis still further assume that the elasticities of supply and demand are the same for everyone:

$$
\begin{aligned}
b_j &= b \\
\beta_j &= \beta.
\end{aligned}
\tag{96}
$$

Then by using the notation

$$
k(b, \beta) \equiv \left(\frac{1 - \dfrac{1}{b}}{1 + \dfrac{1}{\beta}} \right)^{\frac{\beta(b - 1)}{b + \beta}},
\tag{97}
$$

equation (95) can be written more simply as

$$
E_j = k\alpha_j^{\frac{\beta(b - 1)}{b + \beta}} a_j^{\frac{b(\beta + 1)}{b + \beta}}
\tag{98}
$$

4. Before discussing the general case given by equation (98), a few special cases are considered. If all supply curves were identical and had an infinite elasticity: $\alpha_j = \alpha$ and $\beta = \infty$, (98) becomes

$$
E_j = k' a_j^b,
\tag{99}
$$

while (94) becomes

$$
C_j = k^* a_j^b.
\tag{100}
$$

The distributions of earnings and investments differ only by a constant.

A log transform of (99) gives

$$
\ln E_j = \ln k' + b \ln a_j,
\tag{101}
$$

and

$$
\sigma(\ln E) = b\sigma(\ln a),
\tag{102}
$$

where σ is the standard deviation. Thus, the standard deviation of the log of earnings, a common measure of inequality, would be positively related to the elasticity of demand and to the standard deviation of the location of the demand curves. The shape of the distribution of E would also depend on b and on the distribution of a. For example, if a had a log normal distribution, so would E, and its skewness would be positively related to the size of b and the skewness of a. Indeed, since $b > 1$, both the skewness and inequality in E would exceed that in a.[157]

Moreover, the distribution of E could be positively skewed even if a was not, the more so the larger b. For example, if a was symmetric, the values of a both below and above its mean would be increased by the E transform (neglecting the new units k' and except, of course, for $a \leq 1$), but those above would be increased by greater absolute and percentage amounts. The result would be a stretching out of the larger values into an elongated tail, and the stretching would be greater, the larger b was.

To show this more explicitly, let $f(a)$ be the density distribution of a and $f'(E)$ be the corresponding distribution of E. Then by a well-known formula[158]

$$f'(E) = \frac{da}{dE} f(a) \tag{103}$$

$$= {}'k \frac{1}{b} E^{1/b-1} f(a). \tag{104}$$

If $\hat{a}$ and $\hat{E}$ are the modes of a and E respectively,

$$\hat{E} < k' \hat{a}^b, \tag{105}$$

which is evidence of the elongation of the right tail. The mode of E is found by differentiating equation (104) and setting it equal to zero. If a derivative is denoted by a dot $(\cdot)$ over the function differentiated, one has

$$\dot{f}'(E) = \left(\frac{'k}{b}\right)^2 (E^{1/b-1})^2 f(a) + \dot{f}(a) \frac{'k}{b} \left(\frac{1}{b} - 1\right) E^{1/b-2} = 0, \tag{106}$$

or

$$\hat{E}^{1/b} = \frac{b-1}{'k} \frac{f(a')}{\dot{f}(a)}, \tag{107}$$

where a' is the value of a that transforms into $\hat{E}$. Since $\hat{E}^{1/b}$, $'k$, $b-1$, and $f(a')$ must all be positive, so must $\dot{f}(a')$. But if a were a unimodal

---

157 The simplest proof is to note that both the skewness and variance of a log normal distribution depend only on the variance of the normal distribution obtained by a log transformation (see J. Aitchison and J. A. C. Brown, *op. cit.*, pp. 8–9).

158 See M. G. Kendall, *The Advanced Theory of Statistics*, London, 1945, Vol. I, pp. 16–18.

distribution, $\dot{f}(a')$ would be positive only if $a' < \hat{a}$, for $\dot{f}(\hat{a}) = 0$ by definition.

The discussion can be made more concrete by considering a couple of well-known distributions. If a was uniformly distributed, its density distribution would be

$$f(a) = \frac{1}{N_2 - N_1},\tag{108}$$

and, therefore, from equation (104)

$$f(E) = \frac{'k}{b(N_2 - N_1)} E^{1/b-1}.\tag{109}$$

A uniform distribution is transformed into a monotonically declining distribution, the rate of decline being faster, the higher b. This long-tailed distribution has exactly the same shape as the Pareto distribution, except that the exponent in the latter is < -2, while $1/b - 1 > -1$; it is even closer to the distributions discussed by Zipf and Yule.[159]

If a was approximately normally distributed, the mode of E would be found from the relation[160]

$$a' = \frac{u + \sqrt{u^2 - 4(b-1)\sigma^2}}{2},\tag{110}$$

where u is the mean and σ the standard deviation of a. If $b - 1 > \left(\dfrac{u}{2\sigma}\right)^2$, the mode of E would be at the origin and E would be another long-tailed distribution. For smaller b, E would rise to a peak[161] at a value for a' between $u/2$ and u, and then decline in a long tail.

---

159 For a comparison of several long-tailed distributions see H. Simon, "On a Class of Skew Distribution Functions," *Models of Man*, New York, 1957, Chapter 9.

160 A proof is based on noting that for a normal distribution

$$\frac{f(a)}{\dot{f}(a)} = \frac{-\sigma^2}{a - u}.$$

Then from equation (107)

$$a' = \frac{-\sigma^2(b-1)}{a' - u}.$$

161 Since the density of a is not zero when $a = 0$, the density of E would approach infinity as $E \to 0$ and would decline to a local minimum at a value of a equal to

$$a' = \frac{u - \sqrt{u^2 - 4(b-1)\sigma^2}}{2}.$$

5. If β was finite, equation (98) becomes

$$E_j = k'' a_j^{\frac{b(\beta + 1)}{b + \beta}}, \tag{111}$$

while (94) becomes

$$\hat{C}_j = k^{*\prime} a^{\frac{b(\beta + 1)}{b + \beta}} \tag{112}$$

The distributions of earnings and investments still differ only by a constant. Since

$$1 < \frac{b(\beta + 1)}{b + \beta} < b, \tag{113}$$

the distribution of E and C would still be more unequal and skewed than a, but the differences would be smaller than when $\beta = \infty$. As $b \to \infty$, the exponent in (111) and (112) would approach $\beta + 1$.

6. If all demand curves were identical so that $a_j = a$, all j, earnings would be

$$E_j = k_i \alpha_j^{\frac{\beta(b - 1)}{b + \beta}}, \tag{114}$$

while the amount invested would equal

$$C_j = k_* \alpha_j^{\frac{b\beta}{b + \beta}}. \tag{115}$$

These distributions are the same, aside from scale, only when $\beta = 0$ or $b = \infty$. Otherwise, since $b\beta > \beta(b - 1)$, C would be more unequally distributed and skewed. Moreover, since $\beta(b - 1) < b + \beta$ unless $b > 2$ and $\beta > b/b - 2$, E would very likely be less skewed and more equally distributed than α. A comparison of equations (111) and (112) with (114) and (115) shows that E and C would be more unequal and skewed for a given distribution of a_j, the demand curves, than for the same distribution of α_j, the supply curves.

7. If both a_j and α_j varied, E_j would be given by equation (98), and the variance of the log of E would be

$$\sigma^2(\log E) = \frac{\beta^2(b - 1)^2}{(b + \beta)^2} \sigma^2(\log \alpha) + \frac{b^2(\beta + 1)^2}{(b + \beta)^2} \sigma^2(\log a)$$

$$+ \frac{2b\beta(b - 1)(\beta + 1)}{(b + \beta)^2} R(\log \alpha, \log a)\sigma(\log \alpha)\sigma(\log a), \tag{116}$$

where R is the correlation coefficient between log α and log a. The inequality in E would be positively related not only to b and β and to the variation in a and α, but also to the correlation between the latter pair. The variance in log E would exceed that in either log α or log a unless $\sigma^2(\log \alpha)$ was much less than $\sigma^2(\log a)$, R was very negative, and b and β were rather small.

Note that the distribution of E (and of C) would be unaffected, aside from scale, by equal percentage changes in all a_j or α_j. Thus economy-wide changes in the cost of funds or the productivity of human capital that change all average rates of return or all average repayment costs by the same percentage could significantly affect average earnings and capital investments, but have no effect on the distributions around the averages. Therefore, the usual emphasis on skill differentials in discussions of the distribution of earnings is completely beside the point, in our model, if these differentials are measured by average rates of return.

The skewness in E would be greater, the greater the skewness in α and a, the larger b and β, and the larger R. For example, if a and α were log normally distributed, E would also be, with a skewness positively related to the variance of its log, which by equation (116) is positively related to R. Again, if log a and log α were perfectly positively correlated, they would be related by the constant elasticity formula

$$\alpha_j = ga_j{}^d, \quad g, d > 0, \tag{117}$$

and E_j could be written as

$$E_j = ka_j{}^s, \tag{118}$$

with

$$s = \frac{b(\beta + 1)}{b + \beta} + \frac{d\beta(b - 1)}{b + \beta}.$$

For a given distribution of a_j, equation (118) has the same shape as (111): if a_j was uniformly distributed, both are monotonically declining distributions of the Yule-Zipf class, while if a_j was normally distributed, both are skewed distributions with modes given by equation (110). The inequality and skewness in (118) however, always exceeds that in (111), the difference being greater the larger d, the elasticity of α with respect to a.

8. The contribution of investment in human capital to "profits" is

not measured by total returns alone, but by the difference between them and total repayment costs:

$$P_j = \bar{r}_j C_j - \bar{i}_j C_j. \tag{119}$$

The distributions of P and E are exactly the same, however, aside from scale, so that all the results in the previous sections apply to P as well as E. For a proof, simply first substitute the definitions in equation (91) into (119), and get

$$P_j = a_j C_j^{1-1/b} - \frac{1}{\alpha_j} C_j^{1+1/\beta}; \tag{120}$$

then substitute the optimal value of C_j, and have

$$P_J = n^{1 - \frac{1}{b}} \alpha_j^{\frac{\beta(b-1)}{b+\beta}} a_j^{1 + \frac{\beta(b-1)}{b+\beta}} - n^{\left(1 + \frac{1}{\beta}\right)} \alpha_j^{\left(-1 + \frac{b(\beta+1)}{b+\beta}\right)} a_j^{\frac{b(\beta+1)}{b+\beta}}, \tag{121}$$

or

$$P_j = n' \alpha_j^{\frac{\beta(b-1)}{b+\beta}} a_j^{\frac{b(\beta+1)}{b+\beta}} \tag{122}$$

Thus, aside from a difference in scale, P_j in equation (122) is exactly the same as E_j in equation (98).

9. To maximize total earnings from a given total capital investment, one

$$\text{Max } E = \Sigma E_j = \Sigma r_j C_j, \tag{123}$$

subject to $\qquad\qquad\qquad \Sigma C_j = C_o$

which gives as a necessary condition

$$\frac{\partial E_j}{\partial C_j} = \lambda, \quad \text{all } j, \tag{124}$$

where λ is the marginal rate of return; that is,

$$\frac{\partial E_j}{\partial C_j} \equiv r_j \equiv \bar{r}_j + C_j \frac{\partial \bar{r}_j}{\partial C_j} = \lambda, \quad \text{all } j. \tag{125}$$

Equation (125) can be expressed in terms of the underlying parameters as

$$'k\alpha_j^{\frac{-\beta}{b+\beta}} a_j^{\frac{b}{b+\beta}} = \lambda. \tag{126}$$

Equation (126) necessarily holds if either $\alpha_j = \alpha$, for all j and $\beta = \infty$, or $a_j = a$, for all j and $b = \infty$. If b and β are both positive and finite, and a_j and α_j both variable, then (126) can only hold if $\log a$ and $\log \alpha$ are perfectly correlated, and related by the linear equation

$$\log \alpha_j = d + \frac{b}{\beta} \log a_j; \tag{127}$$

otherwise the equilibrium marginal rates of return, the left-hand side of (126), differ. One easily shows that the variance of the log of these marginal rates is smaller, the smaller the variances of $\log a$ and $\log \alpha$, and the larger the positive correlation between them.

Part Two

Empirical Analysis

"An investment in knowledge pays the best interest."

Benjamin Franklin, *Poor Richard's Almanack*

CHAPTER V

Rates of Return from College Education

Virtually all the implications developed in Part One, from income distributions to unemployment, are based on the effect of investment in human capital on earnings and productivity. Consequently, the significance of that analysis can be determined most directly through an empirical examination of the relation between earnings or productivity and human capital. This will be done in the next three chapters for a number of time periods and demographic groups in the United States.

Although an investigation of many kinds of human capital would be illuminating, the absence of readily available data makes it necessary to concentrate primarily on formal education. Fortunately, education is of considerable interest in its own right and a matter of much current concern: laymen, policy-makers, and researchers are all worrying about the role of education in promoting economic and cultural progress, and about ways to improve the educational process. Quantitative evidence on the economic effects of education would add an important dimension to these discussions because all too often they have been based on grossly inaccurate economic notions.

This chapter and the following one estimate rates of return on college education in the United States during recent years, and Chapter VI covers high-school education and earlier years. Rates of return provide the most convenient and complete summary of the economic effects of education and, therefore, can be used to answer a variety of questions, such as the following:

1. Do relatively few female, nonwhite, and rural high-school graduates attend college primarily because of relatively low rates of return, or because of financial difficulties, discrimination, and still other factors?

2. Are private rates of return higher on education than on physical capital and, if so, is the explanation to be found in risk, ignorance of effects, nonpecuniary factors, or imperfections in the capital market? Has the large subsidy to education reduced its social rate of return below that on other capital, or has the subsidy been an inadequate response to a very large discrepancy between social and private returns from education?

3. Do more intelligent persons receive higher rates of return from education than others?

4. Has the large secular growth in education caused a decline in returns from education, or has the growth itself been induced by an increase in returns?

The materials analyzed in these chapters shed appreciable light on these and other questions, although, of course, definitive answers are not provided.

This chapter presents estimates of rates of return to urban white males who graduated from college after 1939, estimates for college dropouts, and estimates for college-educated women, nonwhites, and rural persons. Considerable attention is paid to determining the dispersion in rates of return on college education.

1. Money Rates of Return to White Male College Graduates

Returns in 1939

The effect of education on income could easily be determined if information were available on the income of units differing only in education, for then differences in income could be attributed solely to differences in education. These could be geographical units, as countries or states; time units, as the United States today and, say, fifty years ago; or individuals, as college and high-school graduates in the United States. Unfortunately, units differing in education also tend to differ in other factors that influence incomes. For example, higher-income geographical units also tend to have more physical capital per person, while college graduates tend to be abler than high-school graduates. In other words, the raw information has to be standardized for other factors in order to isolate the effect of education. A few attempts have been made to standardize the information on geographical units, and although interesting qualitative results have emerged, only a limited quantitative analysis has been possible.[1] I decided to exploit the extensive data available for the United States since the 1930s on the earnings and incomes of persons with different amounts of education because they seemed most capable of yielding quantitative, although admittedly rough, estimates of rates of return on education.

The national data on the incomes of persons at different educational levels provided by the 1940 and 1950 Censuses can be supplemented during the 1950s with smaller surveys. Table 2 shows absolute and percentage differences in mean earnings during 1939 at various age classes between urban, native white, male college and high school graduates. Average earnings computed from the 1940 Census were uniformly adjusted upward by 10 per cent because of the underestimation of wages and salaries in the Census data. They were also corrected for the abnormally large unemployment in 1939 so that the data could reflect a more normal economic situation.[2] The adjustment for underestimation raises absolute earning differentials but not percentage ones, while the adjustment for unemployment lowers percentage differentials but does not change absolute ones very much. Since only persons with at least $1 of wages or salaries and less than $50 of other income are covered in the 1940 Census, independent professionals and many other persons were excluded. In order to expand the coverage, the earnings of college graduates were considered to be a weighted average at each age of the earnings of college graduates given by the Census and of independent doctors, lawyers, and dentists given elsewhere, the weights being the number of persons in each group. Both the absolute and percentage differences in columns 2 and 1 of Table 2 are substantial and rise with age, averaging about $1100 (in 1939 dollars) and 45 per cent, respectively, and rising from $450 and 30 per cent at about age 27 to $1700 and 60 per cent at about age 50.

Since Table 2 gives the income gains of surviving members of different cohorts, one way to relate costs and returns would be to compare these gains with the college costs of the different cohorts. Another,

[1] One exception is a study by Zvi Griliches of the effect of education on agricultural output using counties as the unit of analysis (see his "The Sources of Measured Productivity Growth: United States Agriculture, 1940–60," *Journal of Political Economy*, August 1963, pp. 331–336).

[2] A detailed discussion of these and other adjustments can be found in Appendix A.

TABLE 2

Actual Earning Differentials
between Urban, Native White, Male
College and High School Graduates in 1939
at Various Ages

Age	Percentage (1)	Absolute (2)
23–24	4	51
25–29	29	455
30–34	47	949
35–44	56	1449
45–54	59	1684
55–64	53	1386
18–19	−108	−557
20–21	−95	−805
22	−46	−487

Source: Basic data from *1940 Census of Population, Educational Attainment by Economic Characteristics and Marital Status*, Bureau of the Census, Washington, D.C., 1947, Table 29, p. 148. M. Zeman estimated mean incomes at various age and education classes from the Census data (see his "A Quantitative Analysis of White–Non-White Income Differentials in the United States in 1939," unpublished Ph.D. dissertation, University of Chicago, 1955). These data were adjusted for the underreporting of professional earnings (see my Table A-6), the underreporting of wages and salaries (see Table A-4), and unemployment (see Table A-5). Cost estimates in the last three rows of the table were obtained by the methods discussed in Appendix A.

and for my purposes easier, way would be to compare the costs and returns of a given cohort as it ages over time. Since these data are not directly available, the returns to different cohorts as of the moment in time have to be converted into returns to a given cohort aging over time.

The average earnings of a cohort at any age is a weighted average of the earnings of survivors and of those dying earlier. Obviously the latter earn nothing after they die, so the weighted average can be computed simply by multiplying the earnings of survivors by the fraction surviving. Accordingly, the average earnings in 1939 of different cohorts were multiplied by life table survivorship rates[3] to help convert them into earnings at different ages of a single cohort. Since the same rates were used for high school and college graduates (although a slightly higher rate should have been used for the latter), percentage earnings differentials were unaffected while absolute ones were lowered, especially at older ages.

The secular growth in real earnings per capita would usually enable the cohort of persons graduating from high school or college in any year to earn more at each age than was earned in that year by persons who had graduated earlier. Earnings received in 1939 have to be adjusted upward, therefore, if they are to represent the earnings of cohorts graduating in 1939. Only part of the substantial rate of growth since 1939 in earnings per capita can be used in the adjustment, however, because much of the growth in earnings resulted from the increase in education itself. Moreover, earnings did not grow at the same rate in all age and education categories. Not being able to make an exhaustive study, I simply assumed that if $d(t)$ were the differential observed in 1939 between cohorts graduating from college and high school t years earlier, the differential t years later for cohorts who had graduated in 1939 would be $d(t)(1 + g)^t$, where g is the annual rate of growth in the differential. The most plausible value for g seems to be about .0125, although results are also presented for $g = 0$ and $g = .02$.[4]

Cross-sectional and cohort earnings also differ in several other respects. For example, the former are much more affected by business cycles, and, consequently, as already mentioned, the 1939 data had to be adjusted for the depressed economic conditions at that time. An interesting difference can be found in the adjustment for income tax payments required to convert before-tax returns into private returns. In 1939 tax rates were low and so only a minor adjustment need be made to incomes received at that time. A much more substantial adjustment, however, has to be made to the incomes of cohorts gradu-

---

[3] They should also be multiplied by labor force participation rates because the 1940 Census only includes persons with at least $1 of earnings in 1939. Experiments on the 1950 Census data indicate, however, that this adjustment has only a slight effect on the results.

[4] According to E. Denison, national income per capita has grown at a rate of 1.7 per cent per annum from 1929 to 1957 and about 25 per cent of this was due to the growth in years of education (see his *Sources of Economic Growth in the United States*, Committee for Economic Development, Washington, 1962). His Table 33 fixes the contribution of education at more than 40 per cent, but it is clear from his derivation that half of that was due to the increase in the number of days of attendance in each school year, which should *not* be excluded from our adjustment.

ating in 1939 because they received the bulk of their incomes in the 1940s and later, and taxes have risen substantially during these years. Accordingly, two alternative adjustments have been made: one is simply based on the 1939 tax rates, while the other utilizes the much higher rates prevailing in 1919 to approximate the effects of the different tax rates in the 1940s, 1950s, and 1960s.

Costs in 1939

Total private costs of attending college can be considered the sum of private direct and indirect costs. The former includes tuition, fees, outlays on books and supplies, and any living expenses beyond what would be incurred when not in college. Average tuition and fees per college student in 1939 and other years can be estimated without too much trouble from data collected by the Office of Education. Books and unusual living expenses can be estimated from other surveys, notably a large national sample taken by the Education Office in the 1950s. Private direct costs per student averaged about $173 in 1939, of which 65 per cent or $112 were tuition and fees.

Since students earn less than if they were participating full time in the labor force, the earnings foregone are an indirect cost of schooling. The amount foregone depends both on the number of hours spent at schoolwork and the opportunities for part-time (after school) and seasonal (summer) work. The latter determinant is quite sensitive to business conditions and the age, race, sex, etc., of students, so indirect costs vary more over time and among demographic groups than direct costs do.[5]

---

[5] For the purpose of estimating rates of return, it is only necessary to recognize— as everyone must—that students earn less than if they were participating in the labor force. This difference in earnings need not be called a cost of education nor related to direct costs. However, foregone earnings are treated as a cost here and throughout the book, because such a treatment adds to the understanding of the economic effects of education (and other human capital). Moreover, the arguments advanced against doing so cannot withstand close scrutiny. To take one prominent example, John Vaizey, who has written extensively on the economic effects of education, in arguing against the inclusion of foregone earnings, said: "for young people there is no alternative; the law forbids them to work," or "if income foregone is added to education costs it must also be added to other sectors of the economy (notably housewives, mothers, unpaid sitters-in, voluntary work of all sorts)" and "Analytically, too, it would be necessary to adjust the costs by some notional estimate of benefits incurred while being educated" (see his *The Economics of Education,* Glencoe, 1962, pp. 42–43). Now if foregone earnings are excluded because schooling is compulsory, surely direct costs have to be excluded also. If the foregone earnings of other activities are important, then, of course, they should be treated as costs too

Indirect costs were estimated by assuming that the typical person attends college from the age of eighteen to twenty-two and one-half and earns one-quarter of what he could have earned. Four and a half years of college are assumed because the Census group with "sixteen +" years of schooling appears to have that much undergraduate and postgraduate training.[6] The one-quarter assumption is based on the notion that college attendance is a full-time occupation for three-quarters of a year—vacations occupying the remaining quarter—for which notion there is direct evidence provided by several studies.[7] In principle, the potential earnings of first-year college students should be measured by the actual earnings of otherwise equivalent persons who entered the full-time labor force after completing high school, the potential earnings of second-year students by the actual earnings of otherwise equivalent persons who entered the labor force after completing one year of college, and so on. Limitations of data necessitated the use of a simpler, but not too inaccurate, method. The potential earnings of students during the first four years of college were measured by the actual earnings of "equivalent" high school graduates of the same age, and potential earnings during the last half year of study by the earnings of college dropouts of the same age.

The last three rows of Table 2 show absolute and percentage differentials from ages eighteen to twenty-two between the net earnings of college students and high-school graduates. "Net" earnings means that direct college costs have been subtracted from the earnings of college students. The total private cost of attending college for the average urban native white male in 1939 is roughly measured by the series of absolute differentials. Foregone earnings account for about 74 per cent of the total, tuition and fees for only about 17 per cent, and other direct costs for the remaining 9 per cent. Therefore, if tuition and fees alone were eliminated—if colleges were made "free" in the usual meaning of this term—only a relatively small part of the private burden of attending college would be eliminated. That is to say, even at the private level "free" colleges are not really very free after all!

(and are in my paper *A Theory of the Allocation of Time,* IBM Research Paper RC-1149, March 20, 1964, a shorter version of which was published as "A Theory of the Allocation of Time" in the *Economic Journal* of September 1965). Finally, that benefits are incurred while being educated is no more an argument against the inclusion of indirect costs than against the inclusion of direct costs.

[6] See P. C. Glick and H. P. Miller, "Education Level and Potential Income," *American Sociological Review,* June 1956, p. 311.

[7] See Appendix A, section 2a.

Rates of Return in 1939

The monetary gain from attending college can be determined from a comparison of returns and costs. A person deciding whether or not college "pays" should discount both the streams of returns and costs in order to incorporate the basic economic fact that $1000 promised in ten years is worth less than $1000 available today. Discounting of future income is incorporated into the internal rate of return, which is simply a rate of discount that makes the series of absolute earnings differentials between college and high-school graduates sum to zero.[8] One could also compute the present value of the monetary gain, which is the sum of all absolute differentials *after* they have been discounted at appropriate market interest rates (see Chapter III). Both methods are used in this chapter, although greater attention is paid to the internal rate.

Since the concern is with the gain achieved by cohorts, the data in Table 2 have to be adjusted for mortality, growth, and taxation. Note that both measures of monetary gain use absolute, not percentage, earning differentials, so any adjustment changing the former would change the estimated gain, even if the latter were not changed. Thus the adjustments for mortality and growth do not change percentage differentials, but, as shall be seen, they do significantly alter the estimated gain. Note further that the rate of return to a cohort can be computed either from the stream of total (cohort) absolute differentials or from the mean (that is, per capita) differentials. Likewise, the present value of the gain can be computed either from total differentials or on a per member basis from mean differentials. There has been considerable controversy over whether mean or median differentials are the more appropriate measure of the central tendency of returns (and presumably also of costs) to education. Means are clearly more appropriate when calculating *cohort* gains; perhaps medians are better for other purposes.[9]

Table 3 presents several alternative estimates of the private rate of return to the cohort of urban native white males graduating from college in 1939. The estimates increase a little over 1 percentage point for each percentage point of increase in the secular growth in earn-

---

[8] The internal rate does not, however, necessarily equate the present values of returns and costs (see the discussion in Chapter III).

[9] Edward Renshaw prefers the median to the mean for reasons I find largely unconvincing. See his "Estimating the Returns to Education," *Review of Economics and Statistics*, August 1960, p. 322.

TABLE 3

Alternative Estimates of Rates of Return to 1939
Cohort of Native White Male College Graduates
(per cent)

Secular Rate of Growth in Earnings (per cent)	Straight 4 Per Cent Tax Rate (1)	1949 Actual Tax Rates (2)
2	16.8	15.3
1	15.6	14.1
0	14.4	13.0

ings, and are about 1.5 percentage points lower when the tax rates prevailing in 1949 are used in place of those in 1939. A figure of slightly over 14.5 per cent is probably the best single estimate of the rate. This figure and indeed *all* the estimates indicate a very substantial private gain to white male college graduates.

The dominance of foregone earnings and the relative unimportance of tuition can be vividly demonstrated with rate of return calculations. The gain from attending college would, of course, increase if any component of cost decreased. But while the complete elimination of tuition would increase the rate of return to these college graduates only by a little over 1 percentage point, the elimination of foregone earnings would almost double it. Thus, good economic reasons, as well as lack of information and motivation, may prevent poorer high school graduates from attending even tuition-free colleges. The elimination of foregone earnings, which incidentally has never been tried on a large scale in the United States, should have a much greater effect on their incentive to go to college.

Rates of Return in 1949

Independent estimates of the rate of return to college graduates can be based on data collected by the 1950 Census. Table 4 presents absolute and percentage differentials between the net incomes of college and high school graduates in 1949, where net income means that direct costs have been subtracted from the earnings of college graduates at ages 18 to 22½. I tried to approximate the returns and costs of the cohort of persons graduating from college about 1949 by adjusting these figures for mortality, growth, and taxation. The mortality adjustment was based on rates prevailing in 1949, and income differen-

TABLE 4

Earning Differentials between White Male
College and High School Graduates in 1949
at Various Ages

Age	Percentage (1)	Absolute (2)
23–24	−16	−372
25–29	+8	+230
30–34	42	1440
35–44	86	3419
45–54	100	4759
55–64	85	4068
18–19	−111	−1073
20–21	−95	−1647
22	−59	−1324

Source: *United States Census of Population: 1950,
Special Reports—Education*, Bureau of the Census,
Washington, 1953, Vol. IV, Part 5, Chapter B,
Table 12. Cost estimates used in the last three
rows of the table were obtained by the methods
discussed in Appendix A.

tials were again assumed to grow at a little over 1 per cent per annum.
The tax adjustment was based on the incidence of the personal income
tax in 1949, although a somewhat greater adjustment would be more
appropriate as taxes have risen a little since 1949. No adjustment for
unemployment is necessary since 1949 was a rather normal economic
year.

The private rate of return to the 1949 cohort would be 12.7 per
cent if income differentials grew at 1 per cent per annum, and about
1 percentage point higher or lower if they grew at 2 per cent or not
at all. Probably the best single estimate is close to 13 per cent, somewhat lower than the 14.5 per cent estimate based on the 1940 Census
data. Their general agreement increases the confidence that can be
placed in the statistical (as opposed to conceptual) reliability of our
calculations.

Is the slight decline between 1939 and 1949 indicative of a general
secular decline in the monetary gain from education? Secular changes
are discussed in Chapter VI, so now I shall only consider whether the
apparent decline is spurious owing to a shift in the statistical base.

The 1949 data refer to the total incomes of all whites, while the 1939 data refer only to the earnings of urban native whites. For obvious reasons, the inclusion of property income raises the estimated return in 1949, although probably not by very much (see Appendix A). While the direction and, a fortiori, the magnitude of the effect of the other differences is more difficult to determine,[10] they probably cannot fully explain the apparent decline during the 1940s.

2. Some Conceptual Difficulties

Correlation between "Ability" and Education

Although the similarity between the estimates derived from the 1940 and 1950 Censuses should increase one's confidence in the statistical foundations of the analysis, it does not make the conceptual foundations any firmer. And the technique of estimating the private rate of return on education from income differentials between persons differing in education has been repeatedly and strongly attacked. Simply worded, the argument is that the true rate of return on education is grossly overestimated because persons differing in education also differ in many characteristics that cause their incomes to differ systematically. By explicitly considering the variation in earnings with age and by restricting the analysis to persons of a given sex, race, and in 1939 urban-rural and nativity status, I have already managed to eliminate the more important demographic sources of bias.

Unquestionably the most serious remaining difficulty results from the presumed positive correlation between education and "ability," which has been argued with fervor by intelligent persons in the United States and many other countries. Moreover, the theory developed earlier implies that abler persons invest more in themselves, at least when "ability" is defined in an economic sense (see Chapter III, section 3). Finally, the available quantitative materials definitely show a positive relation between education and several measures of ability. Table 5 summarizes some evidence on the abilities of high-school and college persons in the United States in the 1950s. In columns 1 and 2 "intelligence" is measured by the average IQ (intelligence quotient) and the fraction with high IQs; in column 3 a combination of intel-

---

[10] For example, rural and foreign-born whites generally have less education, lower incomes at each education level, and a lower return from additional education than urban native whites do. The first two factors would increase, the third decrease, the rate of return estimated for 1949.

TABLE 5

Several Measures of Ability at Different Educational Levels
in the 1950s

Education	Average IQ[a] (1)	Percentage with IQ Over 120[a] (2)	Average Rank in High School Graduating Class[b] (percentile) (3)	Percentage with Fathers in Professional, Semiprofessional, or Managerial Occupations[c] (4)
High school graduate	106.8	20.8	44	22
College graduate	120.5	50.0	68	45
College dropout	106.2	16.3	48	44

Source: Dael Wolfle, *America's Resources of Specialized Talent*, New York, 1954. Columns 1–3 computed from Table G.2, p. 314, and Table H.1, p. 316; column 4 from Table VI.6, p. 160, and Table VI.7, p. 162.

[a] The IQ estimates, based on the Army General Classification Test, are for 1953 and were based partly on special studies conducted by the Commission on Human Resources and partly on estimates made by others. Among the latter is the study by V. Benson, "The Intelligence and Later Scholastic Success of Sixth Grade Pupils," *School and Society*, February 1942. Her data are especially interesting because the subsequent education of children receiving IQ tests in the sixth grade was determined. Therefore, the positive relation between IQ and education in her study—which shows differences similar to those given above—cannot be considered a consequence of the education itself.

[b] These data on grades are national estimates prepared by the Commission for 1953. Almost identical results are given in the Bureau of the Census study *Factors Related to College Attendance of Farm and Nonfarm High School Graduates: 1960*, Series Census-ERS (P-27) No. 32, Washington, 1962, Table 8.

[c] The distributions by father's occupation omit children with fathers in farm occupations and are rough estimates prepared by the Commission from the 1950 Census. Similar differences by father's education and income are given in *School Enrollment and Education of Young Adults and Their Fathers: October 1960*, Bureau of the Census, Washington, 1961, Tables 9–10.

ligence, interest in schooling, and perseverance is measured by the average rank in high school; and in column 4 a combination of "contacts," tastes, and knowledge about better-paying occupations is measured by the fraction with fathers in professional, semiprofessional, and managerial occupations. All suggest significantly greater ability among college than high-school graduates: an average IQ about 13 per cent higher, over twice the rate of IQs above 120, a 50 per cent higher class ranking in high school, and a 100 per cent larger number with fathers in the top occupations.

Although general observation, theoretical analysis, and quantitative evidence suggest a strong correlation between ability and education, what can be said about the magnitude of the bias in rate of return estimates based on the income differential approach used in the last section? In particular, is most of the apparently large return to college graduates due to their greater ability, or only, say, 10 per cent? Neither general observation nor theoretical analysis has much to suggest about this, so considerable reliance has to be placed on the limited quantitative evidence, derived from five main independent methods presented below. The evidence suggests that this correlation explains only a small part of the apparently large return. Let me point out, however, that the discussion in Chapter VI concludes (see section 1) that much of the large apparent return to primary and secondary school education does result from differential ability.

1. It would be desirable to recalculate the rates of return presented earlier after the data had been fully standardized for ability. Either the incomes of college graduates could be standardized for the distribution of ability among high-school graduates, or the incomes of the latter could be standardized for the ability of the former. The first method would determine the rate of return to a typical high-school graduate who decided to enter college, while the second would indicate the rate actually received by a typical college graduate. The latter would be greater if college graduates were abler and if abler persons benefit more from college.

Table 5 indicates that rank in class is strongly related to extent of education, so its effects are considered first. A good source of information on the relation between rank and earnings is the study of college graduates employed by the Bell Telephone Company. Rank in college did not affect starting salaries much, but after fifteen years the employees who had been in the top two-fifths of their college class earned about 20 per cent more than those in the bottom two-fifths, and in later years the differences were still greater.[11] The differences after fifteen years seem to be a good measure of the average relation between college rank and earnings.[12]

According to column 3 of Table 5, the typical person who did not

[11] See Donald S. Bridgman, "Success in College and Business," *The Personnel Journal*, June 1930. A more recent and comprehensive study, as yet unpublished, appears to give very similar results.
[12] If earnings of abler graduates rise more rapidly with age partly because of greater investment on the job and in other human capital (see Chapter II, section 1), the extent of the relation between rank and earnings would be underestimated by the differentials at younger ages and overestimated by those at older ages. Differentials after fifteen years of employment tend to avoid the extremes of either bias.

go to college after finishing high school ranked much lower in high school than persons who completed college. Presumably, the former would also have ranked much lower in college if he had gone on. Consequently, according to the Bell data, he would also have earned less, perhaps a good deal less, than college graduates actually do. To be concrete, he would have earned about 7 per cent less if the Bell data accurately measure the relation between college rank and earnings, and if high-school and college graduates would have had the same relative ranking in college as they had in high school.[13]

Income differentials between college and high-school graduates would, therefore, significantly overstate the gain to a typical high-school graduate from completing college, for at ages 35 to 44 (roughly fifteen years after completing college) 7 per cent of college graduates' incomes equals almost 20 per cent of the apparent gain from college.[14] The rate of return estimates would be reduced by a smaller percentage. The best estimate of the private rate would be reduced from about 14.5 to a little over 12.5 per cent for the 1939 cohort and from 13 to about 11.5 per cent for the 1949 cohort, or an average reduction of about 12 per cent.[15]

2. An adjusted rate of return to a typical college graduate could be computed if the relation between rank and the earnings of high-school graduates were known. Unfortunately, the Bell study did not collect information on the earnings of high-school graduates. But this as well

[13] If E_i is the average earnings of college graduates who were at the ith rank level in college, and if d_{ih} and d_{ic} give the proportion of college and high school graduates who would have been at this level, the ratio of their earnings after college would be

$$p = \frac{\Sigma E_i d_{ih}}{\Sigma E_i d_{ic}}.$$

If E_1 covers the top two-fifths, E_2 the third fifth, and E_3 the bottom two-fifths, then, according to the Bell Telephone study, $E_1 = 1.18E_3$ and $E_2 = 1.02E_3$. Data from the Commission on Human Resources indicate that 68 per cent of persons graduating from college were in the top two-fifths of their high-school class, 17 per cent in the third fifth, and 14 per cent in the bottom two-fifths, while only 32 per cent of high-school graduates not going on to college were in the top two-fifths, 20 per cent were in the third fifth, and 48 per cent in the bottom two-fifths (see Wolfle, *America's Resources*, Appendix H, Table 1). Substituting these figures into the equation gives $p = .93$.

[14] It is about 19 per cent of the apparent gain to the 1939 cohort of college graduates and 16 per cent of that to the 1949 cohort.

[15] The adjusted rates probably should be slightly lower because the direct college costs of a typical high-school graduate were assumed to equal the actual average direct costs of college graduates, even though the former's tuition would probably be somewhat higher since colleges engage in "price discrimination" against persons with lower high-school ranks. Since the assumption that college students earn one-quarter of the amount earned by high-school graduates of the same age already incorporates a correction for the differential ability of college students (see Appendix A, section 2a), no adjustment of indirect costs would be necessary.

as other useful information can be found in a study of Wolfle and Smith.[16] They obtained annual salaries some fifteen to twenty years later of about 2800 male graduates of high schools in Illinois, Minnesota, and Rochester, N.Y., in the middle and late 1930s. Most of the persons included from Illinois and Minnesota were in the upper 60 per cent, either in class standing or IQ, while the Rochester sample (which was smaller) was limited to persons in the top 20 per cent on either measure.

The top panel of Table 6 presents the relation between percentile rank in high school, median earnings, and education for the whole sample. The Bell study gives the relation of college rank, this one (in column 3) the relation of high-school rank, to the earnings of college graduates. Those at the top earn significantly more than those at the bottom of their high-school class, where the bottom 1–60 percentile class actually is largely restricted to persons in the 40–60 percentile class. Indeed, the relation of rank and the earnings of college graduates given here is almost exactly the same as that given in the Bell study. Fifteen years after graduation, persons who had been in the top two-fifths of their class were earning 16 per cent more than those in the third fifth, according to the latter study, and averaged about $6600, compared to the $5700 earned by those in the third fifth, according to the former study. Thus, rank-adjusted rates of return to typical high-school graduates computed from these data would be essentially the same as those computed earlier from the Bell study.

The stub entries in Table 6 provide the data necessary to compute rank-adjusted returns to typical college graduates. However, since there was little systematic relationship[17] between rank and the earnings of high-school graduates, no adjustment is required. The typical college graduate apparently receives a higher rate of return from college than would a typical high-school graduate, because the former has a higher class rank, and the payoff from college is greater for those with higher ranks. Indeed, this greater payoff is presumably an important reason why persons with higher class ranks go to college much more frequently than others do.[18]

[16] See D. Wolfle and J. Smith, "The Occupational Value of Education for Superior High School Graduates," *Journal of Higher Education*, April 1956, pp. 201–213.

[17] At least within the top sixtieth percentile, which is essentially all that is relevant to the typical college graduate.

[18] Almost 50 per cent in the top two-fifths of their high-school class go to college, while only 22 per cent in the bottom two-fifths go (see Wolfle, *America's Resources*, Table VI-2, p. 150). For similar results, see *Factors Related to College Attendance*, Table 9. Some studies indicate, moreover, that rank increases the likelihood of attending college even when the parents' economic position is held constant. See *ibid.*, Tables 14–16; also see some references in C. C. Cole, *Encouraging Scientific Talent*, New York, 1956, pp. 57 ff.

TABLE 6

Median Salaries of Illinois, Minnesota, and Rochester Men, by Rank
in High School Graduating Class and by Intelligence Test Score
(dollars)

	Education		
Ability Measure	High School (1)	Some College (2)	One College Degree or More (3)
Percentile rank in high school class[a]			
91–100	4880	5600	7100
81– 90	4780	5400	6300
71– 80	4720	5300	6500
61– 70	4810	5700	5700
1– 60	4655	5300	5700
Intelligence test, percentile in sample[b]			
Highest 20	4000	5300	6300
Next 35	4500	5200	6100
Bottom 45	4300	4100	5200
Intelligence quotient[c]			
Over 120	5500	6100	7600
Under 120	5000	5700	7400

Source: Dael Wolfle and Joseph Smith, "The Occupation Value of Education
for Superior High School Graduates," *Journal of Higher Education*, April 1956,
pp. 201–213, Tables II, IV, and V.

[a] Illinois, Minnesota, and Rochester men.

[b] Minnesota men.

[c] Rochester men.

The bottom two panels of Table 6 give the effect of IQ on earnings.
The Rochester data are derived from a small and highly restrictive
sample. The Minnesota data are more interesting since they cover
persons with IQs mostly above the top sixtieth percentile of all high-
school students. This sample indicates that an increase in IQ has the
same kind of effect on earnings as an increase in rank: a negligible
effect among high school graduates[19] and a 15 to 20 per cent effect

[19] One should point out, however, that high school graduates with high IQs and
high grades may not go to college precisely because they rank low in other kinds of
ability. This may explain why they do not earn much more than other high school
graduates.

among college graduates. So an adjustment for IQ alone would reduce the apparent gain from college by about the same amount as the adjustment for rank did. These effects cannot, however, be added together to get the effect of simultaneously adjusting for rank and IQ since they are very highly correlated.[20] Therefore, adding an IQ adjustment to the rank adjustment would lower the rate of return to a typical high-school graduate probably by less than 0.5 of a percentage point: from 12.5 to 12.0 per cent for the 1939 cohort and from 11.5+ to 11+ per cent for the 1949 cohort. The rate of return to an average college graduate would hardly be reduced at all, and would remain near 14.5 and 13 per cent for the 1939 and 1949 cohorts, respectively.

The Wolfle-Smith study also contains useful information on the relation between father's occupation, education, and earnings. Once again the effect is much greater at the college level. College graduates with fathers in professional or managerial occupations earned about 16 per cent more than those with fathers in unskilled or service occupations, while high-school graduates with fathers in top occupations earned only about 4 per cent more. Therefore, an adjustment for father's occupation alone would hardly reduce the gain to a typical college graduate and would reduce the gain from college to a typical high-school graduate by about 7 per cent.[21] Again, the high correlation between rank, IQ, and father's occupation implies that the effect of adjusting for father's occupation, in addition to adjusting for rank and IQ, would be much less than if it were the sole adjustment.

This discussion of the data provided by the Committee on Human Resources can now be summarized. Even if rank in high school, IQ, and father's occupation are adjusted for separately, the rate of return from college to a typical college graduate would hardly be affected, while that to a typical high-school graduate would be reduced by about 35 per cent. College education itself would be the major determinant of the apparently high return associated with education. Moreover, the sum of the separate effects grossly overstates the combined effect, since rank, IQ, and father's occupation are quite closely correlated. Thus, the fraction of the unadjusted return attributable to college education itself would be very high.

[20] See Wolfle, *America's Resources*, Appendix H, Table 1.

[21] The effect on income can be found from the formula in footnote 13 above where the index i would now refer to father's occupation rather than school rank. The distribution of high-school and college graduates by father's occupation can be found in Wolfle, *America's Resources*, Tables VI.6 and VI.7, pp. 160 and 162. Substituting these weights and the data on earnings given by Wolfle and Smith (*Journal of Higher Education*, April 1956) into the formula gives $p = .963$. The adjusted rate of return would then be estimated at a little more than 13.5 and 12 per cent instead of 14.5 and 13 per cent for the 1939 and 1949 cohorts.

3. J. Morgan and M. H. David published an interesting attempt to isolate the effect of education on earnings through standardization by multiple regression for other influences.[22] In one set of regressions, they adjusted the family earnings of white male heads of nonfarm households in the labor force for measures of religion, personality, father's education, labor market conditions, mobility, and supervisory responsibilities. The share of the unadjusted earnings differential between college and high-school graduates explained by these factors was about 40 per cent at ages 18 to 34 and 12 per cent at ages 35 to 74.[23] In other regressions, measures of rank in school and ability to understand and answer questions were of negligible importance.[24] Hence, in their sample, too, college education itself is the major cause of differentials between college and high-school graduates, especially when one recognizes—as Morgan and David do—that supervisory responsibility and mobility are primarily simply means through which the economic effects of education operate.[25]

4. A very different way to eliminate the influence of several dimensions of ability is to consider the earnings of college dropouts. Table

[22] See their "Education and Income," *Quarterly Journal of Economics,* August 1963, pp. 423–437. The data were collected by the Survey Research Center from a national sample of approximately 3000 heads of spending units.

[23] See *ibid.,* Table III. These results refer to college graduates with a bachelor's degree only and high-school graduates without any nonacademic (presumably formal) training. The results for persons with advanced degrees and nonacademic training are about the same. However, differentials between all college and all high-school graduates could not be computed because the number of cases in each group was not given.

[24] *Ibid.,* pp. 428–429. For an earlier and in some ways more complete discussion, see J. Morgan, M. H. David, W. J. Cohen, and H. E. Brazer, *Income and Welfare in the United States,* New York, 1962, Chapter 5.

[25] In general, when standardizing by multiple regression or some other technique to obtain the effect of education on earnings, one must be careful not to go too far. For education has little direct effect on earnings; it operates primarily indirectly through the effect on knowledge and skills. Consequently, by standardizing for enough measures of knowledge and skill, such as occupation or ability to communicate, one can eliminate the entire true effect of education on earnings.

This comment is relevant not only to the Morgan-David study, but also to several others, such as an interesting dissertation by Shane Hunt (see "Income Determinants for College Graduates and the Return to Educational Investment," unpublished Ph.D. dissertation, Yale University, 1963). He utilizes a survey in 1947 by *Time* magazine of the incomes of college graduates and finds that graduates of relatively expensive colleges received about a 12 per cent crude rate of return on their additional costs, i.e., those not incurred by graduates of relatively cheap colleges. After standardization for several variables, he cuts the rate substantially. Among those held constant, however, are variables, like occupational category, which clearly partly measure the way in which education affects earnings. Nevertheless, even after all his adjustments, higher-quality college education still yields a significant gain, which is about half the crude gain.

4 indicates that college entrants who drop out before completing four years do not have higher IQs or grades than high-school graduates. True, the same table indicates that the former came from higher social and economic backgrounds, but they were unable to finish an activity that they had started,[26] and so their advantage may be counterbalanced by lack of sustained effort. College dropouts, therefore, do not seem to have much, if any, greater "ability" than high-school graduates (see the discussion in section 3 below). If so, unadjusted rates of return to dropouts would in effect already standardize for ability and would not overestimate the true payoff to some college.

In section 3 below unadjusted rates of return to the 1939 and 1949 cohorts of college dropouts are estimated at about 9.5 and 8 per cent, respectively. Even if these are used to measure the adjusted gain to college graduates, almost two-thirds[27] of the apparent gain from college can be attributed to the education itself. Moreover, the adjusted gain to graduates is probably still larger because the gain from the third, fourth, and later college years is somewhat greater than that from earlier years (see section 3 below).

5. A study during the late 1920s adjusted for ability in a rather unique way, namely, by considering the incomes of brothers with different amounts of education.[28] Since brothers come from the same economic and social background, and presumably differ less in native ability than typical elementary, high-school, and college persons, many kinds of ability often considered important in explaining earning differentials would be held constant. On the other hand, some brothers may become relatively well-educated precisely because of unusual ambition and other kinds of ability rather than because of interest, "luck," and other factors uncorrelated with earnings. Therefore, the study probably does not entirely correct for differences in ability.

Tables 17 and 18 in Chapter VI indicate that the effect of education on income was substantial among these brothers: for example, those averaging 15.5 years of schooling earned about $834 more than those averaging 10.8 years, or about $175 per school year. Lacking reliable income data for the 1920s, this gain will be compared with the unadjusted gain in 1939. One difficulty here is that the Census data are known to understate earnings and to omit the foreign-born,

26 Of course, some persons discontinuing school after graduation from junior college, because of marriage, etc., may not have planned to finish four years of college.

27 That is, $9.5 \div 14.5 = .65$ and $8 \div 13 = .62$.

28 See Donald E. Gorseline, *The Effect of Schooling Upon Income*, Bloomington, 1932.

the self-employed, and some other categories of whites, while the biases in the data on the brothers are not known. So the brothers' differentials will be compared with both raw and corrected Census differentials. In 1939 prices the brothers' gain at ages thirty to thirty-four would be 67 per cent of the gain per school year to college graduates based on 1940 Census data corrected for underreporting of earnings and independent professionals, and 81 per cent of the uncorrected gain. So these data also indicate that college education itself explains most of the apparent gain to college graduates.[29]

Five independent adjustments for differential ability—adjustments that cover such diverse influences as rank in class, IQ, father's education and occupation, personality, ability to communicate, motivation, and family upbringing—all suggest that college education itself explains most of the unadjusted earnings differential between college and high-school graduates. Although any one study is subject to many qualifications, the evidence provided by all taken together has to be given considerable weight. Consequently, it may be concluded that, even after adjustment for differential ability, the private rate of return to a typical white male college graduate would be considerable, say, certainly more than 10 per cent.

A reader might well wonder how this conclusion squares with the evidence, from general observations and theory, advanced earlier that ability and education are quite highly correlated. These observations may have been based primarily on relations below the college level,[30] and as already pointed out, the discussion later on (in Chapter VI) indicates that differential ability has a greater impact there. The theory developed in Part One suggests a positive correlation between ability and education, in that high-school graduates who go to college would receive a higher rate of return from college than graduates who do not go. The limited evidence available supports this suggestion, for data from the Commission on Human Resources do indicate that a typical college graduate gains more from college than would a typical person dropping out after completing high school. Even the latter, however, would receive a high rate of return.

---

[29] Since these brothers were on the average only about thirty years old, perhaps their gain should be compared to that received by the Census category aged 25 to 29. Such a comparison would increase the fraction of the Census differentials attributable to college education itself. On the other hand, brothers with more education were about two years older on the average than those with less education, so the apparent effect of more education is in part an effect of older age.

[30] A more cynical explanation would be that vocal observers are themselves primarily successful college graduates and, therefore, naturally biased toward the view that ability is a major cause of the high earnings received by college graduates.

Correlation between Education
and Other Human Capital

A correlation between the amount invested in education and in on-the-job and vocational training, health, and other human capital would also affect the earning differentials between education classes. The effect of education itself could be isolated only if the amount of other human capital as well as ability were held constant. This section considers the effect on the apparent gain from education of adjusting for the relation between education and other capital.

The empirical evidence available here is even more limited than that available on differential ability. More than half of all high-school graduates in the sample from three states compiled by the Commission on Human Resources had some technical school training.[31] Although the Commission presented no evidence on this, such training is probably less common among college graduates. Other studies indicate that on-the-job training and expenditures on health, adult education, and migration are greater among college than among high-school graduates.[32] College graduates seem, therefore, also to invest more in other human capital than high-school graduates, although the opposite is clearly true for some kinds of capital, and a fuller treatment would have to incorporate these differences.

However, the net effect of even a positive correlation between education and other human capital on the earning differentials between college and high-school graduates may contradict the reader's intuitive presumption. Consider college graduates who received on-the-job training from, say, the age of 24 to 30; after that age they would earn more than if they had had no training, but they would earn less during the training period because training costs are then paid by a reduction in reported earnings (see Chapter II, section 1). Training, and more generally all other investments in human capital, would therefore increase observed differentials at older ages and reduce them at

31 See Wolfle and Smith, *Journal of Higher Education*, April 1956.
32 Indirect estimates of the relation between on-the-job training and education were prepared by J. Mincer in "On-the-Job Training: Costs, Returns, and Some Implications," *Investment in Human Beings*, NBER Special Conference 15, Supplement to *Journal of Political Economy*, October 1962, Tables 1 and 2. Evidence on the relation between health and education is cited by S. Mushkin (*ibid.*, p. 131). Evidence indicating a strong positive correlation between adult education and formal education can be found in J. W. C. Johnstone, *Volunteers for Learning*, National Opinion Research Center, Report No. 89, Chicago, 1963. Tabulations from the 1950 Census indicate that more educated persons have higher migration rates (computed by June Cohn for the Labor Workshop at Columbia University).

younger ones, the net effect depending on the relation between deducted costs and returns from the investments, and the rate at which future earnings are discounted. Deducted costs may be less than actual costs because the direct costs of health, migration, and certain other investments are not deducted from earnings. This consideration is not too important, since foregone earnings are usually the main component of costs.

If the rate of return on other investments was the same as the rate on education, the rate computed from the education-earnings differentials would equal the true rate on education, and thus would *not* be biased. This rate would make the present value of the gross differentials equal to zero because it makes both the present value of the differentials due to other investments and those due to education equal to zero. If the rates of return on other investments were smaller than the rate on education, the rate computed from the gross differentials would also be smaller than the true rate on education, still assuming that education and other investments were positively correlated. For the rate on education would make the present value of the differentials due to other investments negative. Conversely, if the rates of return on other investments were larger, the rate computed from the gross differentials would also be larger than the true rate on education. The opposite conclusions hold if education and other investments are negatively correlated.

Thus, rates of return computed from gross differentials could be seriously biased estimates of the true rates on education only if the rates of return on education and other human capital differed considerably. Moreover, even if education and other capital were very positively correlated, computed rates could *understate* the true rates on education, and would do so whenever the latter were greater than the rates on other capital.

A priori arguments are ambiguous and do not indicate whether rates on education are higher or lower than those on other human capital.[33] Unfortunately, moreover, few empirical studies of rates of return on other human capital have been made; some preliminary estimates by Mincer suggest higher rates on college education than on other capital.[34] If so, rates computed from differentials between college and high-school graduates would be biased *downward* if the former also invested more in other kinds of human capital.

[33] See Mincer in *Investment in Human Beings*, pp. 63–64.
[34] *Ibid.*, pp. 64–65.

3. Rates of Return to Other College Persons

White male college graduates make up less than a third of all persons who receive some college education; about half of those starting college drop out before completing four years, and more than a third of all graduates are female or nonwhite.[35] Therefore, the average gain from college would be seriously overstated by estimates based on white male graduates if, as is often alleged, they gain much more from college than dropouts, nonwhites, or females.[36] This section discusses the gains to dropouts, nonwhites, women, and rural persons, and concludes that they are smaller than the gain to urban white male graduates, although the differences are less than is often alleged. Also considered are discrimination against nonwhites, the relationship between marriage and education, some historical testimony on the importance of foregone earnings, and an indirect method of assessing relative gains.

College Dropouts

If college graduates were more successful than the average person with some college, concentration on graduates alone would overestimate the gain to all persons with some college, in the same way that concentration on long-running plays alone would overestimate the gain from investing in Broadway plays. As already mentioned, a bias here could be important since almost half of all males starting college drop out before completing four years, and some writers have implied that the gain to dropouts is substantially less than that to graduates. To

---

35 See R. E. Ibbert, *Retention and Withdrawal of College Students*, U.S. Office of Education, Washington, 1957, Table 8, p. 18, and *Population Characteristics, Educational Attainment: March 1957*, Current Population Reports of the Bureau of the Census, Series P-20, No. 77, Tables B-C, 2, 3, and 4.

36 "Furthermore, the statistics show that graduation at any level yields a bonus amounting to about twice the investment realized by the average man who starts a given type of school (elementary school, high school or college) but does not finish" (Glick and Miller, *American Sociological Review*, June 1956, p. 309). Or, as H. Houthakker said, "Hence it may not be true, in the case of higher learning, that it is better to have loved and lost than never to have loved at all" ("Education and Income," *Review of Economics and Statistics*, February 1959, p. 27). For views on the relative gains to Negroes and women, see Morgan and David, *Quarterly Journal of Economics*, August 1963, p. 437, and H. Schaffer, "Investment in Human Capital: Comment," *American Economic Review*, December 1961, pp. 1031-1032.

take an extreme case, if the rate of return to dropouts were zero,[37] the rate to all persons entering college would be about two-thirds that of graduates,[38] or less than 10 per cent for the 1939 and 1949 cohorts. Consequently, if college were of no economic value to dropouts, the rate of return on college would begin to seem rather modest.

Dropouts earn relatively little more than high-school graduates, which explains why their gain is quite often considered small. In 1949, for example, the average income of white male high-school graduates aged 35 to 44 was about 60 per cent of that of college graduates and 80 per cent of that of college dropouts the same age. However, one must not forget that costs are also less for dropouts since they average only about two years of college,[39] while graduates average about four and a half years. The rate of return would be lower for dropouts only if the difference in returns were greater than the difference in costs. Depending on the adjustment for growth and taxation, the private

[37] This is not the most extreme case, since the rate could be negative, and would be if the sum of returns were less than the sum of costs.

[38] The rate of return can be approximated by $r = k/C$, where r is the rate for the cohort, k the average return per period, and C is the sum of costs (see Chapter III, section 1). Let the subscripts g, d, and a refer to graduates, dropouts, and all entrants, respectively; since by assumption $r_d = 0$, then $k_d = 0$. If dropouts attend college for two years on the average and are equal in number to graduates, then

$$k_a = 0 + k_g, \quad \text{and} \quad C_a = C_g + \tfrac{4}{9}C_g = \tfrac{13}{9}C_g.$$

Therefore,

$$r_a = k_a/C_a = k_g/\tfrac{13}{9}C_g = \tfrac{9}{13}k_g/C_g = \tfrac{9}{13}r_g.$$

[39] The Office of Education followed a sample of students entering college in 1950 for four years (see *Retention and Withdrawal of College Students*). Persons dropping out of their institution of first registration averaged about 1.4 years of school (estimated from *ibid.*, Table 8). This underestimates the average college education of the Census category 13–15 years of schooling for two major reasons. The Office of Education study refers only to dropouts from the institution of first registration, yet 17 per cent of these were known to have transferred to other institutions before the fall of 1954 (*ibid.*, p. 81). In addition, the Census category is supposed to include only persons who have completed at least thirteen years and less than sixteen years of schooling. If persons dropping out before *completing* the first year were omitted from the special study, dropouts would average about 2.4 years of college. Some other biases, however, work in the opposite direction. For example, transferees eventually completing college presumably average more years of college initially than other dropouts. More importantly, the special study only includes colleges offering a four-year program. Graduates and dropouts from junior colleges have no more than two years of schooling from their institution of first registration. I decided to split the difference between 1.4 and 2.4 and take two years as the average college education of persons reporting 13–15 years of schooling.

Some supporting evidence is given in a tabulation of the number of persons completing 13, 14, or 15 years of schooling. If all persons in this category dropped out just after completing a year, the 13–15 category would average about 13.8 years; if they dropped out in midyear, they would average 14.3 (computed from *Population Characteristics, Educational Attainment: March 1957*, Table D).

rate of return would range from 8.2 to 11.6 per cent for the 1939 cohort of urban, native white, male college dropouts and from 6.6 to 8.7 per cent for the 1949 cohort of white male dropouts, with the best single estimates at about 9.5 and 8 per cent, respectively (see the discussion in section 1 above). These rates are far from negligible and indicate that some college is by no means an economic waste. At the same time they are decidedly less than the corresponding rates of 14.5 and 13 per cent for college graduates, and suggest that the difference in costs does not completely offset the difference in returns. According to these estimates the last two and a half years of college would yield about 18 per cent,[40] while the rate for all entrants would be some 1.5 percentage points less than that for graduates.[41]

As already mentioned, these unadjusted rates of return to college dropouts may not be biased upward since dropouts have about the same IQ and class rank as high-school graduates (see Table 5), and while dropouts come from higher socioeconomic backgrounds, they have demonstrated a certain lack of persistence. This view receives support from the study by Morgan and David referred to in section 2 above: differentials between college dropouts and high-school graduates after adjustment for a measure of socioeconomic background and other variables are almost as large as or perhaps even larger than the unadjusted differentials.[42] On the other hand, the discussion in section 2 indicates that the crude rates of return to college graduates are somewhat biased upward. One set of adjustments for class rank and IQ reduced the gain from college to a typical high-school graduate from about 13.5 per cent to slightly under 11.5 per cent, which eliminates almost half of the crude difference in rates between graduates and dropouts. Adjustments performed by Morgan and David also reduce but do not eliminate the differential between graduates and dropouts.[43] Consequently, much, although not all, of the very large

[40] The rate on all four and a half years is approximately a simple average of those for each year (see Chapter III, section 1, especially footnote 7).

[41] Using the notation and assumptions of footnote 38 gives $C_a = C_g + C_d$, $k_a = k_g + k_d$, and, therefore,

$$r_a = \frac{k_a}{C_a} = \frac{k_g + k_d}{C_g + C_d} = r_g \frac{C_g}{C_g + C_d} + r_d \frac{C_d}{C_g + C_d} = wr_g + (1 - w)r_d.$$

If $r_g = 13.5$ per cent and $r_d = 8.5$ per cent, r_a is approximately 12 per cent since w is about 9/13.

[42] The ratio of unadjusted to adjusted differentials is 87 per cent at ages 18 to 34 and 113 per cent at older ages (see *Quarterly Journal of Economics*, August 1963, Table III). Moreover, in some ways the unadjusted differentials were overadjusted (see my comments on their study in section 2).

[43] *Ibid.* They were reduced by 65 and 14 per cent at ages 18 to 34 and 35 to 74, respectively.

apparent bonus for college graduation would seem to result from the differential ability of college graduates. The remaining bonus may indicate some "increasing returns" to the third, fourth, and later years of college study.

Nonwhites

Absolute income differentials between college and high-school graduates are substantially less for nonwhites than for whites: for example, in 1939 nonwhite male college graduates aged 35 to 44 earned about $700 more in the South and $500 more in the North than nonwhite high-school graduates, about one-third of the $2000 differential for whites. Nonwhites do not necessarily gain less from college, however, since both their direct and indirect college costs are much lower. Indirect costs are lower because nonwhite high-school graduates earn less than white graduates, and direct costs are lower because nonwhites attend cheaper (and "lower-quality") colleges.[44] Again the relevant question is whether the difference in costs is sufficient to compensate for the difference in returns. Depending on the adjustments for taxes and growth, the 1939 cohort of urban, nonwhite, male college graduates received rates of return ranging from 10.6 to 14 per cent in the South, and from 6.6 to 10 per cent in the North, with the best estimates at about 12.3 and 8.3 per cent.[45] Both are less than the 14.5 per cent rate for urban native white males.[46] This evidence indicates that nonwhite male high-school graduates have less incentive than white graduates, but not much less, to go to college.

[44] Most nonwhites are Negroes and about 85 per cent of Negro college students in 1947 were enrolled in Negro colleges (see *Higher Education for American Democracy*, A Report of the President's Commission on Higher Education, Washington, 1947, Vol. II, p. 31). In 1940 the average expenditure per student in Negro colleges was only about 70 per cent of that in white colleges. For white costs, see *Current Operating Expenditures and Income of Higher Education in the United States, 1930, 1940 and 1950*, Commission on Financing Higher Education, New York, 1952, Tables 58 and 3; for Negro costs, see "Statistics of Higher Education, 1939–40," *Biennial Survey of Education in the U.S., 1938–40*, Washington, 1944, Vol. II, Chapter IV, Tables 18 and 19. For some complaints about the low quality of Negro colleges, see the article by F. M. Hechinger in *The New York Times*, Sept. 22, 1963.

[45] All nonwhite graduates are assumed to go to Negro colleges, which was nearly true of nonwhites in the South and largely true of those in the North. If northern nonwhites went to white colleges, their rate of return would only be about 7.3 per cent.

[46] None of these rates have been adjusted for differential ability because the relevant data are not available for nonwhites. Their *differential* ability is probably greater than that for whites because only the more ambitious and otherwise able nonwhites can overcome their very low socioeconomic background and go on to college. If so, adjusted rates would be relatively lower for nonwhites.

One way to check such a conclusion, as well as to provide indirect evidence on rates of return when direct evidence is not available, is to look at actual behavior. Each group of high-school graduates can be said to have a curve relating the fraction going to college to the gain expected from college. Presumably these curves are positively inclined, and their location and elasticity are determined, respectively, by the average level and the dispersion around the average in ability, availability of financing, tastes, and attitudes toward risk. If two groups had identical supply curves, the gain expected by one would be larger if, and only if, the fraction going to college were also larger.

Now if white and nonwhite males had identical supply curves, the modestly higher rate of return estimated for whites would imply—if the elasticity was of medium size—that a modestly larger fraction of whites would go to college.[47] Many readers may be surprised to learn that almost as many nonwhite high-school graduates go to college as white: in 1957, about one-third of all nonwhite male high-school graduates over twenty-five had some college, while a little over two-fifths of all white male graduates did.[48] Of course, the fact that fewer nonwhites go to college cannot be considered impressive support of the evidence indicating that nonwhites gain less. For their supply curve has probably been to the left of that of whites,[49] and thus fewer nonwhites would go to college even if the gains were the same. But the relatively small difference in the fractions going to college is impressive support of the evidence indicating that the difference in gains is not very great. For *many fewer* nonwhites would go to college if their supply curve were much to the left *and* if they gained much less from college.[50]

[47] Of course, the quantity supplied would be a function of the expected real gain, not merely the monetary gain. In relating relative supplies to relative monetary gains, I am implicitly assuming that any differences in psychic gains can be ignored. See Chapter V for a further discussion of psychic gains and their relation to actual behavior.

[48] See *Population Characteristics, Educational Attainment: March 1957*, Tables 1 and 3.

[49] Nonwhites typically have less resources, and experience greater difficulty in gaining admission to certain colleges.

[50] Moreover, there is some evidence that fewer nonwhite male graduates generally go to college even when father's education and several other variables are held constant (see *School Enrollment, and Education of Young Adults and Their Fathers: October 1960*, Current Population Reports, Washington, 1961, Table 9; and *Factors Related to College Attendance of Farm and Nonfarm High School Graduates: 1960*, U.S. Bureau of the Census, Washington, 1962, Table 16). In general, nonwhites have been found to have less education even when many other factors are held constant (see M. H. David, H. Brazer, J. Morgan, and W. Cohen, *Educational Achievement—Its Causes and Effects*, Ann Arbor, 1961, Tables 1–10).

Discrimination against nonwhites.[51] It may be surprising that the rate of return to nonwhite college graduates appears lower in the North than in the South and only slightly lower than the rate of return to whites, since discrimination is clearly much greater in the South and increases in both regions with the education of nonwhites.[52] In this section, rate of return estimates are related to the analysis of discrimination, thus reconciling the findings here with my earlier work on discrimination. The main result of this reconciliation is to support the implications of the rate of return estimates; namely, discrimination against nonwhite college graduates may have been less in the South than in the North and relatively modest, especially in the South.

The market discrimination coefficient (MDC) between two groups has been defined as[53]

$$MDC = \frac{\pi_w}{\pi_n} - \frac{\pi_w^0}{\pi_n^0}, \tag{128}$$

where π_w and π_n are actual earnings and π_w^0 and π_n^0 are what they would be in the absence of market discrimination. If these groups were equally productive, $\pi_n^0 = \pi_w^0$, and

$$MDC = \frac{\pi_w}{\pi_n} - 1. \tag{129}$$

If several sets of these groups can be distinguished by an ordered characteristic, such as occupation, education, age, or income, the MDC can be said to measure average discrimination, and a marginal MDC measuring the additional discrimination encountered as a result of moving to a higher level can be defined in terms of the change in earnings between levels, as:

$$MDC_{ij} = \frac{\pi_w^j - \pi_w^i}{\pi_n^j - \pi_n^i} - \frac{\pi_w^{0j} - \pi_w^{0i}}{\pi_n^{0j} - \pi_n^{0i}}, \tag{130}$$

where j and i are different levels of the characteristic in question. Equal productivity between W and N would give the simpler relation

$$MDC_{ij} = \frac{\pi_w^j - \pi_w^i}{\pi_n^j - \pi_n^i} - 1. \tag{131}$$

[51] This section deviates from the main line of argument and can be skipped by persons not especially concerned with discrimination against nonwhites.
[52] See my *Economics of Discrimination,* Chicago, 1957, Chapters 7 and 8.
[53] See *ibid.,* Chapter 2.

Well-known relations between marginal and average functions imply that the marginal *MDC* would be above, equal to, or less than the average *MDC* depending on whether the latter was increasing, constant, or decreasing.

TABLE 7

Average and Marginal Market Discrimination against Nonwhites for Various Age and Education Classes, by Region, 1939

	Average MDC by Years of Education			Marginal MDC by Years of Education		Adjusted Marginal MDC by Years of Education	
Age	*16+* (1)	*12* (2)	*7 & 8* (3)	*16+* (4)	*12* (5)	*16+* (6)	*12* (7)
			SOUTH				
25–29	.82	1.08	.69	.35	4.35	.37	3.57
30–34	1.27	1.23	.89	1.33	2.97	.43	2.65
35–44	1.50	1.68	1.12	1.23	4.49	.61	3.66
45–54	1.57	1.62	1.27	1.49	2.85	.69	2.57
55–64	1.56	1.55	1.08	1.62	3.61	.72	3.07
			NORTH				
25–29	.47	.50	.37	.37	1.23	.71	1.52
30–34	.78	.72	.45	.89	2.82	.99	2.61
35–44	1.17	.96	.64	1.75	2.70	1.44	2.53
45–54	1.37	.85	.73	3.92	1.17	2.58	1.48
55–64	1.23	.70	.63	5.11	.86	3.20	1.27

Source: Basic data from *16th Census of the United States: 1940, Population, Educational Attainment by Economic Characteristics and Marital Status*, Bureau of the Census, Washington, 1947, Tables 29, 31, 33, 35. Zeman (in his unpublished Ph.D. dissertation, "A Quantitative Analysis of White–Non-White Income Differentials") computed mean incomes from these data for whites and nonwhites by region, age, and education class. The average, marginal, and adjusted *MDC*s are all defined and discussed in the text.

Columns 1, 2, and 3 of Table 7 measure the average and columns 4 and 5 the marginal *MDC* at various ages in 1939 between white and nonwhite elementary, high-school, and college graduates, assuming that nonwhites and whites are really equally productive. In the North both marginals tend to be above the corresponding averages, while in the South they are somewhat below at the college level.

These marginal *MDC*s measure the ratio of the returns from additional schooling to whites and nonwhites,[54] and are greater, equal to, or less than zero as the return to whites is greater, equal to, or less than that to nonwhites. The previous discussion indicated that the return from college is lower for nonwhites partly because both their costs and their incremental benefits are lower. To the extent that returns differ because of cost differences, they do not measure market discrimination alone; rather they measure the combined effects of market and nonmarket discrimination.

The more general definition in equation (130) tries to correct for these influences by subtracting from the observed differentials those differences that would exist were there no marginal market discrimination. The empirical implementation of such a correction is always difficult;[55] a simple approach is to assume that if there were no marginal market discrimination, whites and nonwhites would receive the same rate of return on their additional schooling. Their respective costs are taken as given, although in reality they may differ because of nonmarket discrimination and other factors.[56] With this approach, the marginal MDC becomes proportional to the percentage difference in rates of return, the factor of proportionality being the ratio of costs.[57] So the rate of return and market discrimination approaches

[54] According to equation (131), the marginal MDC at a particular age would be

$$MDC_{ij} = \frac{\pi_{wj} - \pi_{wi}}{\pi_{nj} - \pi_{ni}} - 1,$$

$$= \frac{\Delta\pi_{wij}}{\Delta\pi_{nij}} - 1,$$

where π_{wi} and π_{wj} are the incomes of whites at two schooling levels, and π_{ni} and π_{nj} are the incomes of nonwhites. But $\Delta\pi_{wij}$ and $\Delta\pi_{nij}$ are simply the returns to whites and nonwhites, respectively, from going from the ith to the jth school level.

[55] See *ibid.*, pp. 93–95 and 130–131.

[56] One such factor is market discrimination at lower age and educational levels since the lower foregone earnings of nonwhite college students results partly from market discrimination against nonwhite elementary and high-school graduates. Consequently, this approach implies that market discrimination at lower levels reduces the earnings that nonwhite college graduates would receive even if there were no discrimination against nonwhite *college graduates*. This implication may or may not be considered reasonable, but for my purposes it is not necessary to use a more sophisticated method.

[57] The marginal discrimination coefficient can be written as

$$MDC_{ij} = \frac{\Delta\pi_w}{\Delta\pi_n} - \frac{\Delta\pi_w{}^0}{\Delta\pi_n{}^0}.$$

To a first approximation

$$\Delta\pi_w = r_w C_w \quad \text{and} \quad \Delta\pi_n = r_n C_n,$$

come more or less to the same thing when a distinction is drawn between marginal and average discrimination.

Consequently, since the rate of return to nonwhite college graduates is much higher in the South than in the North, the adjusted marginal MDC should be much lower there.[58] Moreover, the rather small difference between the rate of return to whites and to southern nonwhites implies that the adjusted MDC in the South should be quite small, certainly much smaller than the average and the unadjusted marginal $MDCs$ against college graduates. Column 6 (of Table 7), which assumes that nonwhite college graduates would have received the same rate of return as white graduates were there no market discrimination against them, supports these implications: the adjusted marginal MDC is only about .6 in the South compared to 1.4 in the North and to average and unadjusted marginal $MDCs$ in the South of 1.5 and 1.2, respectively.

Market discrimination against southern nonwhite college graduates is apparently relatively small, even though market discrimination against nonwhites is generally quite large in the South.[59] One possible line of explanation emphasizes that nonwhite college graduates partially avoid white discrimination by catering to their own market, where the discrimination against them is presumably less severe. A relatively large fraction of nonwhite college graduates were, indeed, in occupations that cater to a segregated market: in 1940 about 50 per cent of nonwhite graduates were doctors, dentists, clergymen,

---

where r_w and r_n are the rates of return and C_w and C_n are the costs of moving from the ith to the jth educational level. By assumption,

$$\Delta\pi_w{}^0 = rC_w \quad \text{and} \quad \Delta\pi_n{}^0 = rC_n.$$

Therefore, the first equation in the footnote can be written as

$$MDC_{ij} = \frac{r_w C_w}{r_n C_n} - \frac{rC_w}{rC_n}$$

$$= \frac{C_w}{C_n}\left(\frac{r_w - r_n}{r_n}\right).$$

[58] This conclusion presupposes that the rate of return to white college graduates is also not much higher in the South. The available evidence suggests that the rate of return to whites is somewhat higher in the South.

[59] The 1950 Census also shows larger earning differentials between college and high-school nonwhites in the South than North (see C. A. Anderson, "Regional and Racial Differences in Relations between Income and Education," *The School Review*, January 1955, pp. 38–46). The 1950 Census data, however, did not separate rural from urban persons, and many more southern than northern nonwhites live in rural areas, especially at lower educational levels. Perhaps this explains why the 1950 Census, unlike the 1940 Census, also shows larger differentials in the South between nonwhites with high-school and elementary school educations.

teachers, or lawyers, while only 35 per cent of white graduates were.[60] The opportunities to cater to a segregated market were probably more available to southern graduates since the nonwhite market is both larger (relative to supply) and more segregated there.[61] Fewer opportunities to avoid discrimination are available to nonwhite high-school graduates: the same fraction of whites and nonwhites were in occupations not catering to segregated markets.[62] This would explain why column 7 of Table 7, which presents adjusted marginal *MDC*s against nonwhite high-school graduates, shows substantially greater discrimination in the South.

Let me emphasize, however, in concluding this section, that a much more intensive examination of the evidence, especially of that collected in the 1960 Census, is necessary before these findings can be fully accepted.

Women

Absolute income differentials are much smaller for female than male college graduates, but the rate of return may not be smaller because direct costs are somewhat lower and opportunity costs are much lower for women. One reason why a smaller money—not necessarily real—rate of return would be expected is the much lower labor force participation of women. In fact, the difference in costs does not seem to compensate fully for the difference in returns. Both Mincer and Renshaw find that the rate of return received by white women college graduates is several percentage points lower than that received by white men.[63] Actual behavior is consistent with the evidence on gains: about 30 per cent of women high-school graduates go to college, while 40 per cent of the men do.[64] Although this difference can also be explained by other factors, such as a prejudice against higher education for women, the fact that a larger fraction of nonwhite than

[60] See *1940 Census of Population, Occupational Characteristics* (sample statistics), Bureau of the Census, Washington, 1943, Table 3.

[61] For a discussion of evidence on income distributions that led to the same interpretation, see M. Friedman, *A Theory of the Consumption Function*, Princeton for NBER, 1957, pp. 84–85.

[62] For example, in 1940 about 37 per cent of both white and nonwhite high-school graduates were craftsmen, operators, or laborers, occupational groups that do not sell their services to segregated markets. (See *1940 Census of Population, Occupational Characteristics*, Table 3.)

[63] See Mincer in *Investment in Human Beings*, p. 68, and Renshaw in *Review of Economics and Statistics*, August 1960.

[64] See *Population Characteristics, Educational Attainment: March 1957*, Tables B and 2, for data referring to 1950 and 1957.

white women high-school graduates have gone to college[65] cannot be so easily explained by these factors since nonwhite women have less resources, are discriminated against even more by certain colleges, etc. Yet nonwhite women might have gained more from college if only because they participate more in the labor force. Indeed, Renshaw does find a high rate of return to nonwhite women college graduates.[66]

Many women drop out of college after marriage, and college women are more likely to marry educated and wealthy men. These well-known facts suggest that women go to college partly to increase the probability of marrying a more desirable man. If the marriage factor were important, the gain to women from additional schooling should be determined by *family* earnings classified by the wife's education rather than by personal earnings so classified,[67] and the full money gain to women may be much higher than previous estimates have indicated.

Table 8 presents data from a survey of subscribers to Consumers' Union that classified family income by the education of both spouses.[68] Women college graduates tend to have slightly higher family incomes than men with the same education, while women high-school graduates have much higher family incomes than men high-school graduates.[69] Thus differentials between the family incomes of college and high-school graduates are also much less for women than men. Accordingly, even when the gain from a more lucrative marriage is included, the money rate of return from college seems less for women, a conclusion that is, as already mentioned, consistent with actual behavior. Table 8 suggests that the gain from postgraduate study is also less for women, a

---

[65] *Ibid.*, Tables C, 2, and 3.

[66] *Review of Economics and Statistics*, August 1960, p. 322.

[67] Presumably the differential in their wives' earnings should be included as part of the gain to men from additional schooling, but double counting would occur if the earnings of both spouses were fully included as gains of both. Probably the ideal way to avoid duplication would be to define returns as

$$R_m = W_1 r_{mm} + W_2 r_{mw}$$
$$R_w = W_1' r_{wm} + W_2' r_{ww},$$

where R is the full return, the W's are weights, r_{mm} is the differential earnings of men from additional schooling, r_{mw} is the differential earnings of their wives, and r_{wm} and r_{ww} are similar concepts applied to women (very likely $W_1 > W_2$ and $W_2' > W_1'$).

[68] The survey was conducted by the Workshop in Expectational Economics at Columbia University and I am indebted to Albert Hart and Marshall Kolin for making the data available to me.

[69] Presumably the main reason is that they tend to marry men of higher education, although the high-school figures may also be biased because the relatively small number of male subscribers who never completed high school are included with the male high-school graduates.

result consistent with crude evidence on actual behavior,[70] but perhaps not with evidence restricted to unmarried college graduates.

TABLE 8

Family Incomes of Married Men and Women in 1960,
by Education and Years after First Job
(dollars)

Years after First Job	Years of Education and Sex					
	16+ Men (1)	16+ Women (2)	16 Men (3)	16 Women (4)	12 Men (5)	12 Women (6)
7–8	10,140	9,718	8,310	9,190	5,850	7,980
9–10	10,210	10,784	8,920	9,380	6,630	7,410
19–20	11,330	11,018	10,000	10,980	7,470	9,200

Source: May 1960 survey of subscribers to Consumers' Union sponsored by the Workshop in Expectational Economics of Columbia University.

Rural Persons

Income differentials between college and high-school graduates are apparently much less for rural than for urban persons,[71] but indirect costs are also less[72] because rural high-school graduates earn less than urban ones. They may also be less because rural persons earn relatively more while in college, for they can help with farm chores during summer vacations.[73]

[70] See Population Characteristics, Educational Attainment: March 1957, Table D.

[71] See Income of Families and Persons in the United States for 1956 and 1958, Current Population Report, Series P-60, Nos. 27 and 33, U.S. Bureau of the Census, Washington, 1958 and 1960, and other calculations from Census data included in an unpublished manuscript by Z. Griliches.

[72] It is not clear whether direct costs are less. On the one hand, tuition is less because rural persons more frequently attend heavily subsidized state colleges; on the other hand, transportation and other direct costs are higher because they attend colleges further from their homes than urban persons do.

[73] In October 1960 students aged 18 to 24 worked a slightly smaller number of hours relative to nonstudents of the same age when employed in agriculture than when employed elsewhere. (See The Employment of Students, October 1960, Bureau of Labor Statistics, Special Labor Force Report, No. 16, Washington, 1961, Tables E and F.) I suspect, however, that summer employment is much greater for rural college students, so that on balance they forego relatively less earnings. This has certainly been true at the high-school level, where rural students work more than

Instead of trying to determine directly whether the differences in returns exceed those in costs, the evidence provided by actual behavior is utilized. A much smaller fraction of the graduates of rural than of urban high schools go to college; indeed, a smaller fraction of rural males go than urban females or urban males with fathers who are manual or service workers. Relatively few rural graduates go to college even when family income, IQ, type of high-school curriculum, scholastic standing, and several other variables are held constant.[74] The difference in returns is apparently more important than the difference in costs.

4. Variation in Rates of Return

The private rate of return to cohorts of white male college graduates seems considerable even after adjustment for differential ability. Rates to cohorts of college dropouts, nonwhites, women, and rural persons, although smaller, are also far from negligible. Evidence such as this has encouraged various public bodies and interested citizens to exhort young persons in their own interest to go to college and to succeed in graduating. Now results for cohorts can be applied to individuals only if different members of a cohort are affected more or less to the same extent; if, however, they are affected very differently, they may well be justified in largely ignoring the cohort results.

The gain from college has been shown to vary by sex, race, urban or rural, and graduate or dropout status, and (see section 2) even within a given demographic group, according to ability. This section indicates that the variation in gain within a group like white male college graduates is much greater than can even be explained by the variation in ability alone. So great is it that an individual can be only loosely

---

urban ones during the school year (see, e.g., *ibid.*), and even attend school many fewer days.

Indeed, the much heralded increase in the length of the school year since the turn of the century has been entirely the result of the spread to rural areas of patterns already established sixty years ago in New York, Chicago, and other large cities (see E. Denison "The Residual Factor and Economic Growth," paper prepared for a May 1963 meeting of the OECD). One might even claim that the development of trimester and quarterly systems at many colleges and a few high schools is a reaction to the secular growth of foregone earnings and the spread of urbanization. Since urban communities do not experience the summer increase in demand for labor that rural ones do, the summer holiday is an anachronism and an expensive luxury in a high-wage urban community.

74 See *Factors Related to College Attendance of Farm and Nonfarm High School Graduates: 1960*, Tables 11, 12, 15, and 16.

guided by the gain of his cohort, and has to place considerable weight on his own situation and hope for the best.

TABLE 9

Coefficients of Variation in After-Tax Income of White Males, by Age and Years of Education, 1939 and 1949

	1949		1939	
Age	12 (1)	16+ (2)	12 (3)	16+ (4)
25–29	.44	.75	.55	.73
30–34	.47	.59	.69	.75
35–44	.60	.75	.79	.66
45–54	.83	1.01	.75	.66
55–64	1.05	.92	.77	.68

Source: Computed from *1940 Census of Population, Education*, and *1950 Census of Population, Education*. The 1949 incomes apply to all white males, while those for 1939 apply only to urban native white males. The adjustments for personal income taxes are described in Appendix A.

Table 9 presents, for several age classes and high-school and college graduates, coefficients of variation in the incomes of native white urban males in 1939 and white males in 1949.[75] The variation is certainly not negligible since these coefficients average more than two-thirds. There is some tendency, especially in 1949, for the variation to increase with age,[76] while there is little systematic difference by educational level.

These coefficients do not fully measure the variation in income among all members of a given educational cohort because only the

[75] Similar measures for 1949 can be found in H. Houthakker, *Review of Economics and Statistics*, February 1959, Table 1. I shall only consider the dispersion among white males, although it would be of some interest to compare different races and sexes.

[76] Some of the increase is spurious because the two youngest age classes cover only five years while the three oldest cover ten. The variation is generally larger, the larger the number of years covered by an age class because earnings tend either to rise or decline systematically with age.

The 16+ category in 1939 failed to show a rise with age almost certainly because independent professionals were not included in these calculations. Their dispersion definitely rises with age and they would be more important at older ages. The inclusion of property income in 1949 and the exclusion of self-employed persons in 1939 explains why the variation seems to be lower in 1939, especially at older ages and among college graduates.

incomes of survivors are included and, therefore, the dispersion in length of life is ignored. The latter is still considerable, although it has declined over time along with the decline in mortality.[77]

Columns 1 and 2 of Table 10 present coefficients of variation in survivorship from eighteen to selected ages.[78] These are larger at older ages and smaller in 1949 than in 1939.

A more complete measure of variation within a cohort would take account of both survivorship and the incomes of survivors, and such measures are shown in the rest of Table 10.[79] At younger ages the full variation is not much greater than that in incomes alone because the probability of surviving to these ages is close to unity. But at older

[77] In the United States the expected lifespan (ignoring years after age sixty-five) of eighteen-year-old males increased from thirty-two years in 1900 to thirty-eight years in 1950, while the coefficient of variation changed even more, from 0.74 to 0.54. (For 1900, see *United States Life Tables 1890, 1901, 1910 and 1901–1910*, Bureau of the Census, Washington, 1921, Table 3. For 1950, see *United States Life Tables 1949–51*, Vital Statistics-Special Reports, National Office of Vital Statistics, Vol. 41, No. 1, Washington 1954, Table 2.)

A revealing comment on the dispersion in length of life in the past was made by Adam Smith: "The work which he learns to perform . . . will replace to him the whole expense of his education, with at least the ordinary profits of any equally valuable capital. It must do this too in a reasonable time, *regard being had to the very uncertain duration of human life, in the same manner as to the more certain duration of the machine*" (*Wealth of Nations*, New York, 1937, Book I, Chapter X, my italics).

[78] If a random variable S_x takes on the value of 1 when a person survives from age eighteen to age x, and the value of 0 when he dies before x, the square of the coefficient of variation of S_x equals

$$G(S_x) = \frac{1 - P_x}{P_x},$$

where P_x is the probability of surviving to age x and, therefore, also the expected value of S_x. Columns 1 and 2 list different values of $[G(S_x)]^{1/2}$.

[79] The problem is to find the coefficient of variation in $S_x I_x$, where S_x is defined in the previous footnote and I_x measures incomes at age x. Since S_x takes on the value of 1 for survivors and 0 for others, the relevant income variable is that of survivors. If I_x is so defined, the variance of SI is

$$\sigma^2(SI) = (1 - P)P^2(EI)^2 + P[EI^2 - 2P(EI)^2 + P^2(EI)^2]$$
$$= P[EI^2 - P(EI)^2]$$
$$= P[\sigma^2(I) + (EI)^2(1 - P)]$$
$$= P\sigma^2(I) + \sigma^2(S)(EI)^2$$

and

$$G(SI) = \frac{\sigma^2(SI)}{(ESI)^2} = \frac{G(I)}{P} + G(S).$$

These equations also follow as special cases of theorems on the variation of products if the distribution of I defined over all values of S was independent of the distribution of S. (See L. A. Goodman, "On the Exact Variance of Products," *Journal of the American Statistical Association*, December 1960.) In other words, the distribution of I among survivors would be the same as the full distribution of I.

TABLE 10

Coefficients of Variation in Mortality and Cohort Incomes for
College and High School Graduates, by Age, 1939 and 1949

| | Coefficient of Variation in Mortality | | Coefficient of Variation in Income by Years of Education | | | |
| | | | 1939 | | 1949 | |
Age	1939 (1)	1949 (2)	12 (3)	16+ (4)	12 (5)	16+ (6)
25–29	.14	.12	.57	.75	.46	.77
30–34	.18	.16	.72	.79	.50	.62
35–44	.26	.22	.85	.72	.65	.79
45–54	.39	.34	.89	.81	.94	1.12
55–64	.61	.55	1.09	1.01	1.31	1.18

Source: Columns 1 and 2 computed from *State and Regional Life Tables 1939–41*,
and *United States Life Tables 1949–51*; columns 3 through 6 computed from
columns 1 and 2 and from Table 8, using the formula in footnote 80.

ages it is significantly greater—more than a third greater at ages 55
to 64—because the variation in survivorship becomes quite large then.
The substantial increase in the variation of survivorship with age
makes the full variation increase rather sharply with age, generally
being more than 50 per cent larger at ages 55 to 64 than at 25 to 29.
There is still no appreciable relation with education, although the
variation among college graduates is usually greater in 1949.

Although these adjusted coefficients are interesting and relevant,
they would be the appropriate measures of the variation within cohorts only if different educational levels were mutually exclusive
alternatives, as working in New York or San Francisco are. A college
graduate is, however, usually also a high-school and elementary-school
graduate. Therefore, a person deciding whether to go to college wants
to know how much *additional* variation is caused by going, in the
same way that nonwhites want to know how much additional discrimination results from moving to a higher educational level. In
other words, the additional or marginal variation caused by a college
education should be measured, just as the marginal discrimination
against nonwhite college graduates was measured (see section 3).

If the gain from college is measured by the rate of return, marginal
variation should be measured by the variation in this rate. According

to the analysis in Chapter III, if returns were the same in each year
and lasted forever, the rate of return could be written as

$$r = k/C,$$

where r is the rate, k is the return in any year, and C is the cost of
college. The variation in r would be larger, the larger the variation
in k and C and the smaller the correlation between them.[80] If returns
were not the same in different years, the simple formula in equation
(38) would not hold, but it is apparent that the variation in r would
be smaller, the smaller the serial correlation among returns.

Therefore, the variation in the rate of return among members of a
given cohort depends on four basic parameters: the variation in costs,
the variation in returns, the correlation between returns and costs,
and the correlation between returns in different periods.[81] Unfortunately, little is known about some of these, so the effect of college on
income variation cannot yet be fully ascertained. But I shall try to
determine what the effect appears to be by briefly discussing what is
known about each parameter.

Least is known about the correlation between costs and returns. The
significant differences between the incomes of graduates from Negro
and other cheaper colleges and those from Ivy League and other
expensive ones[82] certainly indicate that the correlation is positive.
The fact, however, that graduates of the same college receive very
different incomes suggests that although the correlation may be positive
and significant, it is also very far from perfect.[83]

The variation in costs among college graduates is apparently con-

[80] If σ^2 stands for the variance and E for the expected value,

$$\sigma^2(r) = E^2(k)\sigma^2\left(\frac{1}{C}\right) + E^2\left(\frac{1}{C}\right)\sigma^2(k) + \sigma(k)\sigma\left(\frac{1}{C}\right),$$

when the correlation between k and $\frac{1}{C}$ equals zero. A more complicated formula
applies when it differs from zero (see *ibid.*).

[81] Both these correlations are special cases of the more general correlation between
income differentials (either costs or returns) in different periods.

[82] Some evidence on the incomes of graduates from different schools can be found
in E. Havemann and P. S. West, *They Went to College*, New York, 1952. Their book
is based on the survey of incomes in 1947 by *Time* magazine. As mentioned in section 2, Hunt ("Income Determinants for College Graduates") used the same data
and found a positive relation between the incomes of alumni and estimates of the
amount spent on students by different colleges.

[83] Thus the partial regression coefficient that Hunt finds between incomes and
expenditures, although sizable, is just barely statistically significant.

siderable. For in 1940 the coefficient of variation in expenditures per student in one state alone—New York—was .9 among private colleges and .3 among public ones,[84] and the variation in the whole country was surely greater. Moreover, I have already shown that foregone earnings can vary widely, certainly among demographic groups, and probably also within groups, because of differences in ability, local labor market conditions, and so forth.

There is no direct evidence on the serial correlation of returns to college graduates, but it probably can be closely approximated by a weighted average of the serial correlation between the incomes of college graduates and of high-school graduates.[85] The correlation be-

[84] Computed from "Statistics of Higher Education, 1939–40," Chapter IV, Tables 18 and 19.

[85] If $k_1 = Y_{c1} - Y_{h1}$ and $k_0 = Y_{c0} - Y_{h0}$ were the returns in years 1 and 0, respectively, the correlation coefficient between returns would be

$$R(k_0, k_1) = \frac{\text{Cov } (k_0, k_1)}{\sigma(k_0)\sigma(k_1)}.$$

If Y_c and Y_h were always uncorrelated, and if small y's represent deviations from means,

$$\text{Cov } (k_0, k_1) = E(y_{c1} - y_{h1})(y_{c0} - y_{h0})$$
$$= E(y_{c1}y_{c0}) + E(y_{h1}y_{h0}),$$

and

$$\sigma^2(k) = E(y_c - y_h)^2 = \sigma^2(y_c) + \sigma^2(y_h).$$

Then

$$R(k_0, k_1) = \frac{E(y_{c1}, y_{c0}) + E(y_{h1}, y_{h0})}{[\sigma^2(y_{c1}) + \sigma^2(y_{h1})][\sigma^2(y_{c0}) + \sigma^2(y_{h0})]}.$$

If it is assumed for simplicity that

$$\sigma^2(y_{c1}) = \sigma^2(y_{c0}) = \sigma^2(y_c), \quad \text{and} \quad \sigma^2(y_{h1}) = \sigma^2(y_{h0}) = \sigma^2(y_h),$$

then

$$R(k_0, k_1) = R(y_{c1}, y_{c0}) \frac{\sigma^2(y_c)}{\sigma^2(y_c) + \sigma^2(y_h)} + R(y_{h1}, y_{h0}) \frac{\sigma^2(y_h)}{\sigma^2(y_c) + \sigma^2(y_h)}$$

$$= wR(y_{c1}, y_{c0}) + (1 - w)R(y_{h1}, y_{h0}).$$

The major assumption is that Y_c and Y_h are uncorrelated, but the result would not be very different if they were positively correlated. For the correlation between returns would be greater, equal to, or less than that given in the last equation as

$$R(y_{ct'}, y_{ht'}) \gtreqless R(y_{ct}, y_{ht})R(y_{et}, y_{et'}),$$

where the left term is the average correlation coefficient between the incomes of college graduates in year t and otherwise equivalent high-school graduates in t'; the first term on the right is the average correlation coefficient between their incomes in the same year; and the second term on the right is the average correlation coefficient between the incomes in t and t' of persons with the same education. If the forces determining $R(Y_{ct'}, Y_{ht})$ were independent of those determining $R(y_{et}, y_{et'})$, as is probably approximately true, equality would hold, and the correlation between returns would be given by the equation above.

tween the adjacent incomes of persons with a given education is very high and even those between incomes separated by a few years remain high.[86] While the correlation between incomes separated by many years is probably much less, one explanation may be that these intermingle a positive correlation between returns in different periods and a positive correlation between returns and costs.[87]

Remaining is the variation in returns during any period, which depends on the variation in the earnings of college graduates (given for white males in Table 10), the variation in their earnings if they had not gone on to college, and the correlation between these two. The variation in the earnings of college graduates if they had not gone to college may differ from the actual variation among high-school graduates because of the differences in "ability" between college and high-school graduates discussed in section 2. As pointed out there, however, three important measures of "ability"—rank in class, IQ, and father's occupation—although they have significant effects on the earnings of college graduates, apparently have little effect on those of high-school graduates. If they are representative of the effects of other differences, the actual variation in high-school earnings could be used to estimate the hypothetical variation among college graduates. The same argument suggests that the correlation between these earnings would not be very high, for the factors making earnings high among college graduates are apparently quite different from those making them high among high-school graduates.

Table 11 presents estimates of the coefficient of variation in the return to college graduates. These assume that the variation in the income of college graduates if they had not gone to college can be measured by the actual variation among high-school graduates. Two estimates are presented at each age class: one assuming no correlation between the incomes of college and high-school graduates aside from a common mortality experience,[88] and the other assuming a perfect

---

[86] Some correlations for independent professionals, whose earnings are presumably less stable than those of the typical college graduate, averaged about .85 between adjacent earnings and .75 between those separated by two years (see Friedman, *Consumption Function,* Table 18; for other evidence, see I. Kravis, *The Structure of Income,* Philadelphia, 1962, Chapter VIII).

[87] See Mincer in *Investment in Human Beings,* p. 53, especially footnote 8.

[88] The correlation coefficient between the incomes of college and high-school graduates at a particular age x equals

$$r = \frac{E[(S_{cx}I_{cx} - ES_{cx}EI_{cx})(S_{hx}I_{hx} - ES_{hx}EI_{hx})]}{E(S_{cx}I_{cx})E(S_{hx}I_{hx})\sqrt{G(S_{cx}I_{cx})G(S_{hx}I_{hx})}},$$

where S, G, etc., are defined in previous footnotes. Now if $S_c = S_h = S_x$ and if I_c and

TABLE 11

Coefficients of Variation in the Returns
to College Graduates, by Age,
1939 and 1949[a]

Age	1939 (1)	1949 (2)
25–29	3.35	8.73
	1.28	3.57
30–34	2.74	1.72
	.91	.94
35–44	2.56	2.00
	.47	1.00
45–54	2.59	2.55
	.65	1.33
55–64	3.09	2.98
	.84	.99

Source: Table 9 and the formula

$$\sigma^2(R) = \sigma^2(c) + \sigma^2(h) - 2r_{ch}\sigma(c)\sigma(h),$$

where R is the return, and c and h represent
the earnings of college and high-school graduates, and σ^2 represents a variance.

[a] Top entries assume that incomes of college and high-school graduates are uncorrelated aside from mortality experience;
bottom entries assume that they are perfectly correlated.

correlation. As already mentioned, the true correlation is a good deal
closer to the first. The table indicates a very substantial coefficient of
variation in the returns to college graduates, probably averaging over
2.0. As opposed to the variation in income (see Table 10), there is no
systematic tendency for this variation to increase with age.

Let us now bring together the discussion of these four parameters.
The coefficient of variation in returns is very large, probably averag-

---

I_h are uncorrelated, then

$$E[(SI_c - ESEI_c)(SI_hEI_h)] = ES^2EI_cEI_h - (ES)^2EI_cEI_h = EI_cEI_h\sigma^2(S),$$

and therefore

$$r_{min} = \frac{G(S)}{\sqrt{G(SI_c)G(SI_h)}}.$$

ing more than 2.0. The variation in costs is also large, although not as large as that in returns, and costs and returns are positively correlated. Consequently, the variation in returns per dollar of cost, equation (5), is probably lower, but not very much lower, than that in returns alone. Since returns are not perfectly correlated over time, the variation in the rate of return is less than that in returns per dollar of cost. The difference is not great, however, since the correlation of returns over time is apparently very high. The net effect would seem to be a rather high variation in the rate of return; the coefficient of variation is almost certainly higher than one and possibly a good deal higher.

One way to illustrate the magnitude of the variation is to point out that although a cohort of white males might receive a private rate of return of 12 per cent, many members will receive more than 25 or less than 0 per cent.[89] The existence of many low and even negative returns has been presumed by others from the wide overlapping of the distributions of the earning of college and high-school graduates.

Another way is to compare it with the variation in the rate of return to physical capital. Many persons have stressed that a dynamic competitive economy produces considerable variation in the gain from capital and some rough estimates by Stigler confirm this: the coefficient of variation in the returns per dollar of capital invested in a group of smaller corporate manufacturing firms was somewhere between one and two.[90] About the same variation was found in the return per dollar invested in a college education. But since the stability of the returns to education is apparently much greater,[91] the variation in rates of return on college education is very likely greater than that on manufacturing capital in smaller corporate firms.

A final question to be discussed is: How much of this large variation in the gain from a college education can be anticipated due to known differences in ability, environment, etc., and, therefore, should not be considered part of the *ex ante* risk? I have already argued that differences in gain due to race, sex, or urban-rural status should not be considered risk since they are, at least in part, anticipated and thus

[89] If rates of return were normally distributed and if the coefficient of variation equaled one, about one-third of the members would receive rates either above 24 or below 0 per cent.

[90] See G. J. Stigler, *Capital and Rates of Return in Manufacturing Industries*, Princeton for NBER, 1963, p. 63, footnote 14.

[91] Stigler found a correlation of only .7 between the adjacent, and much smaller correlations between the nonadjacent, average returns per dollar of capital in different manufacturing industries (*ibid.*, Table 18). Presumably the ranking among firms is even less stable.

affect behavior. One factor making it easy to anticipate differences even within a demographic group is the unusual stability of returns. On the other hand, differences in known measures of ability, such as IQ and grades, are small,[92] and have a rather small effect on earning (see section 2). Moreover, investors in education are much younger than investors in business capital; college students are generally in their early twenties, and are certainly not yet fully aware of their talents.

An important factor increasing the difficulty of anticipating the gain from college is that it is collected over a very long time. While business investments are often said to pay off within five or ten years, the payoff from college takes much longer: the unadjusted rate of return to the 1949 cohort of white male graduates is about 13 per cent; yet ten years after graduation it would still be negative and after a full fifteen years only about 6 per cent. A long payoff period increases risk along with low correlations between returns by reducing the value of information available when investing. Incidentally, the long payoff period increases the advantage of an education that is useful in many kinds of future economic environments. If "liberal" education were identified with such flexible education, as well it may be, there would be an important economic argument for liberal education, as well as arguments based on intellectual and cultural considerations.

[92] For example, the coefficient of variation in the IQ of college graduates is only 13 per cent (computed from Wolfle, *America's Resources*, Table G-2).

CHAPTER VI

Underinvestment in College Education?

This chapter adds several dimensions to the evaluation of the effects of college education on earnings and productivity by comparing private and social gains from college education with those from other investments. These comparisons permit a determination of how much is gained or lost by individuals and society from investing in the former rather than the latter, and are essential to determine whether there is underinvestment in college education; they also help determine whether the capital market difficulties, the lack of knowledge and liquidity, etc., outlined in Chapter III (see section 2) have been serious impediments to the flow of resources into college education.

1. Private Money Gains

In discussing whether the private gain from college exceeds that on other investments, a distinction must be made between the typical college graduate and the typical high-school graduate. Chapter IV indicated that the former gains more from college than the latter would, that he comes from a much higher socioeconomic background (see Table 5), and that he very likely finances his education with resources that would otherwise (in part at least) have been invested elsewhere, while the latter often would have to borrow, live frugally as a student, or work overtime (after school). For the sake of brevity, the discussion is limited to white male graduates, although interesting comparisons could be made with dropouts, nonwhites, and women.

The private rate of return after adjusting for differential "ability" seems to be more than 12 per cent to the cohort of white male college graduates. When comparing the rate on college with rates that would have been obtained if the resources spent on college had been invested elsewhere, there has been a rather surprising tendency to select rates on liquid investments bearing little risk, such as government bonds or savings accounts.[1] The discussion has just indicated (Chapter IV, section 4), however, that an investment in college education is subject to considerable risk, and is obviously extremely illiquid. Consequently, the gain from education should be compared with that on investments with equally large risk and illiquidity.

The earlier analysis indicated that the variation in the rate of return from corporate manufacturing investments is of the same general order of magnitude as that from college education. Stigler estimated the average rate of return on the former at a little over 7 per cent,[2] several percentage points higher than that on riskless assets, but still much lower than the 12+ per cent received by white male college graduates. Although this difference of some 5 percentage points might be explained by compensating differences in liquidity and taxation,[3] a more reasonable inference would be that the private money gain from college to the typical white male graduate is greater than what could have been obtained by investing elsewhere.

An estimate of the money gain could be found by discounting the adjusted income differentials between college and high-school graduates at a rate measuring alternative opportunities. If the 4 per cent riskless rate were used, the present value[4] of the gain to the 1949 cohort of white males would be more than $30,000; the more appro-

---

[1] See P. C. Glick and H. P. Miller, "Educational Level and Potential Income," *American Sociological Review*, June 1956, p. 310; and J. Morgan and M. H. David, "Education and Income," *Quarterly Journal of Economics*, August 1963, p. 435.

[2] G. J. Stigler, *Capital and Rates of Return in Manufacturing Industries*, Princeton for NBER, 1963, Table 10.

For each year from 1938 to 1957, a rate of return was defined for all corporate manufacturing firms as the ratio of after-tax profits to total capital. The simple average of these ratios equals about 7 per cent both during 1938–1947 and 1947–1957.

[3] Investors in firms could sometimes avoid the high personal income tax by converting ordinary income into capital gains; investors in education cannot. The fact that depreciation on physical capital can be explicitly deducted from taxable income while that on education cannot, at first glance, also seems to favor investment in firms. A closer look, however, raises some serious doubts (see Chapter II, section 1, and Chapter VII, section 2).

[4] By "present value" is meant the value at the time of entrance into college.

priate rate of 6 per cent would cut the gain to under $20,000, and the possibly still more appropriate rate of 10 per cent would cut it to under $4000. Although all these estimates are very much under the $100,000 figure often bandied about,[5] they are not insignificant. For example, even if the gain were "only" $3500 (a 10 per cent rate), average tuition and fees in 1949 could have been raised by more than 300 per cent without wiping it out.[6]

The typical high-school graduate is another story. Instead of more than 12 per cent, he would receive 10 to 11 per cent if he went to college. Moreover, instead of investing resources that could have been invested elsewhere he would have to finance much of his college education by borrowing from friends or relatives,[7] by living frugally, or by working after school and during vacations. Since households regularly pay from 8 to 18 per cent on bank and instalment credit loans and even more on others, the cost of borrowing and/or the preference for present consumption must be considered substantial. Consequently, even an 11 per cent rate of return from college would not bulk very large, especially when it is recognized that liquidity considerations would be important here because these persons presumably have a limited command of liquid assets.[8]

So while a college education seems to yield a net money gain to the typical white male college graduate, it may not to the typical white male high-school graduate. One should note, however, that the rapid growth in recent years of low-interest student loans subsidized by state and federal governments[9] certainly must increase the attractiveness of a college education. A study of the demand for these loans should shed considerable light on the conclusions reached here, and especially

---

[5] Derived by Glick and Miller, *American Sociological Review*, June 1956. For a critical comment on their estimate, see H. O. Houthakker, "Education and Income," *Review of Economics and Statistics*, February 1959, pp. 27–28.

[6] Tuition and fees are estimated at $230 per student per year in 1949 (see Appendix A, section 2b). They could have been raised to over $1000 without wiping out the gain.

[7] Or in recent years from governments. See later discussion.

[8] Thus, according to one study, lack of money is the major reason given for not going to college by high-school seniors from lower-income families, while it is a relatively minor reason given by seniors from higher-income families (see *Educational Status, College Plans, and Occupational Status of Farm and Nonfarm Youths: October 1959*, U.S. Bureau of Census, Series ERS (P-27), No. 30, Washington, 1961, Table D).

[9] As of September 1963, New York State alone had more than $72 million outstanding in loans (see *The New York Times*, September 22, 1963). By mid-1960 the National Defense Student Loan Fund amounted to almost $80 million (see A. Rivlin, *The Role of the Federal Government in Financing Higher Education*, Washington, 1961, p. 77).

on the capital market impediments to investment in college education.[10]

2. Social Productivity Gains

The social economic gain from education, the gain to society as opposed to individuals, could differ from the private gain because of differences between social and private costs and returns. Economists (and others) have generally had little success in estimating the social effects of different investments, and, unfortunately, education is no exception. One can, however, develop some lower and upper limits that effectively rule out many of the more fanciful assertions about the effects of education.

Total social as well as private costs would be the sum of direct and indirect costs. Direct costs are clearly greater to society than to students because some of the expenditures on students are paid out of public and private subsidies. Obviously, "free" state and municipal colleges use scarce resources and are not free to society. Indirect costs, on the other hand, would be greater to society only if the output of students foregone by society exceeded the earnings foregone by students, which is not so obviously true.

Direct social costs would be the sum of educational expenditures by colleges and the social cost of books and additional living expenses. While the latter can be approximated by their private cost, an estimate of educational expenditures is not obtained as easily since colleges spend money on athletic competitions, room and board, adult education, research, medical care, etc., as well as on education proper. In other words, they are multiproduct "firms" with a total expenditure much greater than that on the single product education. I have tried to approximate educational expenditures by eliminating expenditures on "noneducational activities," extension services, research, and "specialized instruction" from the total.[11]

Although social costs should obviously include capital as well as current costs, the fraction of educational expenditures paid by fees

[10] Although bearing low-interest rates, these loans are not "easy" in all respects; in particular, they usually require repayment within a much shorter period of time than it takes to collect the payoff from a college education (on the payoff period, see section 4 of Chapter IV).

[11] For definitions of these terms, see "Statistics of Higher Education, 1955–56," *Biennial Survey of Education in the United States, 1954–1956,* Washington, 1959, Chapter 4, section II, pp. 58–80. For a further discussion, see Appendix A, this volume, section 2c.

has usually been overestimated because only current expenditures have been considered. Since educational institutions are quite capital-intensive, expenditures are substantially raised and the fraction attributed to fees lowered when physical capital is included. For example, in 1950 the use value of capital in colleges was about 26 per cent of current expenditures, so that although fees were 42 per cent of current expenditures, they were only about 33 per cent of all expenditures. The full private contribution to all social costs has, however, been greatly underestimated because indirect costs are generally ignored, and they are mostly a private cost. If, for example, foregone earnings were used to represent indirect social costs, college students would be paying through tuition, fees, and foregone earnings almost three-quarters of all social costs.

Social and private economic returns from college would differ if a college education had different effects on earnings and productivity. A student generally must only determine the effect of a college education on his earnings, but society needs to determine its effect on national income. Thus if college graduates earn more partly because their productivity was systematically overestimated, private returns would tend to be larger than social ones. A more common criticism, however, is that earnings greatly understate the social productivity of college graduates (and other educated persons) because they are (allegedly) only partly compensated for their effect on the development and spread of economic knowledge. In technical language, social returns are said to be larger than private returns because of the external economies produced by college graduates.

As a first approximation, social returns will be measured by the before-tax earnings differentials, tax payments being one kind of external economy, and indirect social costs will be measured by the before-tax earnings foregone. The social rate of return, unadjusted for differential ability, would then be about 13 per cent to the 1939 cohort of urban, native white, male college graduates and 12.5 per cent to the 1949 cohort of white male college graduates. These are only slightly less than the private rates because differential tax payments almost offset the subsidies to college education. Similar results would be found for dropouts and for nonwhite, female, and rural college graduates.[12] Adjustments for IQ, grades, and other ability factors would have about the same effect on the social rates as they did on the private rates: relatively little for the typical college person, and

---

[12] For example, social rates of return to the 1939 cohorts of urban, native white male dropouts and urban, Southern nonwhite male graduates are estimated at 8.5 and 11 per cent, respectively, compared with private rates of 9 and 11.9 per cent.

a few percentage points for the typical high-school graduate (if he had gone to college).

The development of a more sophisticated estimate of the social gain is not easy because other external effects are very difficult to measure. The absence of any direct measurements forced me to use an indirect and not very reliable method. E. Denison estimated the contribution of physical capital, labor, increasing returns, and many other factors to economic growth in the United States. After deducting these contributions, a residual is left over that he calls the contribution of "advancement in knowledge." [13] By attributing all of the residual to education,[14] an upper limit to the social effect of education can be developed.[15]

According to Denison, about .58 percentage points of the 1.60 per cent average annual growth from 1929 to 1957 in national income per person employed is explained by the growth in knowledge,[16] and about .67 percentage points by the growth in education.[17] If the growth in knowledge was considered an indirect effect of the growth in education, the share attributed to education would almost double. This in turn implies that the estimated average rate of return on education would also almost double.[18]

If the contribution of different educational levels to the advance in knowledge were proportionate to their direct effects on earnings— possibly college graduates had a disproportionately large contribu-

---

[13] See his *Sources of Economic Growth in the United States,* New York, 1962.

[14] S. G. Strumilin, in an interpretation of economic growth in the Soviet Union, does consider the "residual" to be a "social" effect of education (see his "The Economics of Education in the U.S.S.R.," *International Social Science Journal,* 1962, No. 4, p. 642).

[15] Although a likely upper limit, it is not a necessary one because larger external economies from education might have been nullified by net external diseconomies from other sources.

[16] *Sources of Economic Growth,* Table 33. The amount (residual) attributed to knowledge would be different if different assumptions had been made about the importance of economies of scale, restrictions against the optimal use of resources, etc. For example, if all the increase in output per unit of input resulted from advances in knowledge, the contribution of such advances would rise to .93 percentage points.

[17] *Ibid.* The contribution of education is based on before-tax earning differentials liberally adjusted for ability (*ibid.,* Chap. 7).

[18] The increase in income attributable to an increase in education can be written as: $y = k \frac{C}{Y} = kI$, where y is the percentage increase in income, k is the effect on income of investing a dollar in education, and I is the fraction of income invested in education. If the effect of a given investment in education were to double, y and thus k would double. But since $r \cong k$, where r is the rate of return, a doubling of k would approximately double r.

tion—the unadjusted social rate of return to white male graduates would be estimated at close to 25 per cent. The initial estimate of the social rate, 13 per cent, and the 25 per cent provide a lower and an admittedly rough upper limit to the true rate, the difference between them measuring the ignorance of external effects. Although this difference is embarrassingly large, it does suggest that, contrary to many assertions, the private economic gain from education is much of the social economic gain. For the private gain is more than half of the apparent upper limit, and presumably a good deal more than half of the true social rate.

In recent years the federal government has been subsidizing investment in education through scholarships and loans,[19] and investment in business capital through accelerated depreciation, tax credits, and other means. Somehow the limited funds available must be allocated between these different kinds of investment. One determinant clearly should be, and hopefully is, their relative contribution to national income, a topic that will now be discussed briefly.

A first approximation to the social rate of return on business capital can be found by relating profits to capital, with profits including the corporate income and other direct taxes.[20] The before-tax rate of return on corporate manufacturing capital averaged about 12 per cent for both 1938–1947 and 1947–1957,[21] compared to an after-tax rate of 7 per cent. If the before-tax rate on all corporations were between 10 and 13 per cent and that on unincorporated firms between 4 and 8 per cent, almost the same as the after-tax rate on corporations, the rate on all business capital would be between 8 and 12 per cent.[22] The first approximation to the social rate of return to white male college graduates would be between 10 and 13 per cent after adjustment for differential ability. Since the rates to dropouts, women, and nonwhites would be a few percentage points lower, the rate to all college entrants would be between 8 and 11 per cent. The rates on business capital and college education seem, therefore, to fall within the same range.

A fuller treatment of external effects could, however, change the picture entirely. It has been seen that if all the unexplained residual

[19] See Rivlin, *Role of Federal Government,* Chapters 4 and 5.

[20] This method assumes only that direct taxes come *initially* out of the return on capital; it is consistent with any kind of *ultimate* incidence.

[21] Computed by adding the tax payments of corporate manufacturing firms to Stigler's after-tax profits.

[22] About 80 per cent of all tangible business capital seems to be in corporations (computed from Vol. II of *Studies in the National Balance Sheet of the United States* by R. Goldsmith, R. Lipsey, and M. Mendelson, Princeton for NBER, 1963).

for 1929–1957 were attributed to education, its estimated social rate would almost double; if, on the other hand, all was attributed to business capital, its estimated social rate would much more than double.[23] Consequently, depending on the allocation of the residual, that is, the "advance in knowledge," the estimated social rate on college education could be as much as twice and as little as less than half of that on business capital. Ignorance about the "residual," therefore, precludes at present any firm judgment about the relative social rates on business capital and college education.

3. Private Real Rates

A treatment of the full, as opposed to the economic, social rate of return on college education would involve a consideration of cultural advance, democratic government, etc., and is clearly far beyond the scope of this study. Even a treatment of the full private rate is exceedingly difficult and I shall be content simply to raise some questions and suggest a few very tentative answers.

In deciding whether to go to college, attitudes toward college life and studying, the kind of work college graduates do, and other psychic factors are relevant as well as the gain in earnings. Full or real returns and costs would be the sum of monetary and psychic ones, and the real gain would depend on the relation between these real returns and costs. The psychic gain from college, like the monetary gain, probably differs considerably between the typical college and high-school graduate. For presumably the former does and the latter does not go to college partly because of a difference in expected psychic gains.[24] Or to use more direct evidence, lack of interest is usually a major reason cited by high-school seniors in explaining why they were not going to college, and by college dropouts in explaining why they never finished.[25]

Quantitative estimates of psychic gains are never directly available and are usually computed residually as the difference between inde-

---

[23] The effect on the business rate is much greater than that on education because the estimated direct contribution of business capital to growth is much less than that of education (see Denison, *Sources of Economic Growth*, Table 33).

[24] For a similar argument applied to monetary gains, see section 2 of Chapter IV.

[25] See *Educational Status, College Plans, and Occupational Status of Farm and Nonfarm Youths: October 1959*, Tables D, and 12–16; also E. Roper, *Factors Affecting the Admission of High School Seniors to College*, Washington, 1949.

pendent estimates of monetary and real gains.[26] Unfortunately, independent estimates of the real gains to college graduates are not available. For example, they could not be measured by the monetary gains from other capital because there may also be psychic gains from such capital,[27] and, more importantly, because the real gains from college and other capital may differ owing to differences in access to the capital market or to other factors. One can use actual behavior to test whether real gains do differ. For if, say, college education were an unusually attractive investment, pressure would develop to invest more there, and while it could be offset in the short run by financing and other difficulties, these could be at least partially surmounted in the long run.

TABLE 12

Investment in College Education Relative
to Physical Capital for Selected Years

	Ratio of Investment in College to Gross Physical Investment	Ratio of Foregone Earnings to Gross Physical Investment
1920	.026	.016
1930	.076	.037
1940	.082	.040
1950	.103	.062
1956	.121	.071

Source: The numerators from T. W. Schultz "Capital Formation by Education," *Journal of Political Economy*, December 1960, Table 6; the denominators from Simon Kuznets, *Capital in the American Economy: Its Formation and Financing*, Princeton for NBER, 1961, Table R-4, p. 490.

Table 12 indicates that the gross investment in college education rose from about 2.5 per cent of that in physical capital in 1920 to about 8 per cent in 1940 and 12 per cent in 1956. Foregone earnings,

[26] See, for example, the estimates of "tastes for discrimination" in my *Economics of Discrimination*, Chapters 7 and 8.

[27] For example, Marshall alleged that much of the value of land in Great Britain resulted from the prestige attached to ownership (see his unpublished lecture, "Progress and Poverty," delivered March 6, 1883, and recently mimeographed by G. J. Stigler).

which are a rough measure of private investment, rose no less rapidly.[28] So the private real rate of return has apparently been higher on college education than on physical capital. Since the money rate has probably also been higher (see section 1), the evidence on real rates does not necessarily mean that the psychic rate has been higher on college education than on physical capital, but only that it could not have been much lower.

[28] Of course, gross investment in education may have risen faster because the cost rather than the quantity of education rose faster. Unfortunately, no one has developed a good measure of the quantity of education; the most reasonable available measure is the number of persons receiving a college education. Since 1940 the number of college graduates in the labor force has much more than doubled while the real value of the capital stock has increased by less than 70 per cent (see my Table 16 and Denison, *op. cit.*, Table 12).

CHAPTER VII

Rates of Return from High School Education and Trends over Time

The first section of this chapter investigates the effect of high-school education on earnings and productivity; the second investigates changes over time in the economic effects of higher education. The first considers the effect of differential ability on the apparently large rate of return from high school and thus on the apparently "decreasing returns" to additional years of schooling; the second considers whether the rapid secular increase in the number of high-school and college graduates in the United States has been accompanied by a secular decline in their rates of return.

1. The Rate of Return from High School Education

Rates of return were computed for the 1939 cohort of urban, native white, male high-school graduates and the 1949 cohort of all white male graduates using Census data and adjustments similar to those made for college graduates.[1] The best single private estimates, unadjusted for differential ability, average about 18 per cent, being 16 and

---

[1] See section 1 of Chapter IV and Appendix A.

20 per cent for the 1939 and 1949 cohorts, respectively. These are several percentage points greater than the corresponding estimates for college graduates.

TABLE 13

Average IQ at Several Educational Levels

Educational Level	Average IQ
High-school graduates	112.0
High-school dropouts	98.0
7–8 years of schooling	84.9

Source: Estimated from President's Commission on Higher Education, *Higher Education for American Democracy*, Washington, 1947, Volume VI, Table 11, p. 11. The data compiled by V. Benson give very similar results (see her "The Intelligence and Later Scholastic Success of Sixth Grade Pupils," *School and Society*, February 1942, p. 165, Table 1). Her data are especially interesting because the subsequent education of children given IQ tests in the sixth grade was determined. Therefore, the positive relation between IQ and education in her study cannot be considered a consequence of the education itself.

Table 13 suggests that the ability of high-school and elementary-school graduates differs considerably: the average IQ of high-school graduates is more than 30 per cent higher than that of persons with seven or eight years of schooling. A correction for differential ability might well have a larger effect on the estimated rate of return to high-school than to college graduates since the average IQ of the latter is only about 12 per cent higher (see Table 5). Unfortunately, adjusted high-school rates cannot be estimated very easily. For example, the unadjusted rate of return to high-school dropouts cannot be used because Table 13 indicates that their IQ is also much greater than that of elementary-school graduates; some confirmation is given by the fact that their unadjusted rate is only slightly below that to graduates.

Two estimates are available. Morgan and David have adjusted crude earnings differentials for father's education, personality, and several other variables.[2] The adjusted differential between high-school and elementary-school graduates is 64 per cent of the unadjusted differentials at ages 18 to 34 and 40 per cent at ages 35 to 74, while these ratios were 60 and 88 per cent between college and high-school graduates.[3] Thus their adjustments generally reduce the apparent gain from a high-school education by more than that from a college education.

A similar conclusion emerges from the study cited earlier of differentials between brothers.[4] Brothers averaging 11.8 years of schooling earned about $111 more (in 1939 prices) for each additional year of schooling than those averaging 8.9 years. This was about 73 per cent of the crude and 62 per cent of the corrected gains for high-school graduates of the same age in 1939.[5] Corresponding percentages for college graduates were 81 and 67.

The unadjusted rate of return to white male high-school graduates is greater than that to college graduates,[6] and the unadjusted rate to elementary-school graduates would be still greater. Such evidence might well suggest "diminishing returns" or "diminishing marginal product" from additional years of schooling. Adjustments for differential ability, however, seem to reduce the apparent rate more to high-school than to college graduates, and, I may add, probably still more to elementary-school graduates. So the appearance of diminish-

[2] See the full description in section 2 of Chapter IV.

[3] In line with the above expectation, the crude differential between high-school dropouts and elementary-school persons was not unaffected but was reduced by more than 60 per cent at ages 35 to 74 (computed from their Table III in "Education and Income," *Quarterly Journal of Economics*, August 1963; it was, however, increased slightly at the younger ages). One should point out, however, that the crude differentials between high-school graduates, dropouts, and elementary-school graduates are probably significantly understated in their survey. For example, they find that the present values of the earnings of white male nonfarmer high-school graduates and dropouts are about equal when only a 4 per cent interest rate is used, and dropouts actually earn more than graduates at ages 18 to 35 (see *ibid.*, Table IV). Yet not only the Census data but also other quantitative evidence (see, e.g., *School and Early Employment Experience of Youth*, Department of Labor, Bulletin 1277, Washington, 1960, pp. 32–33) and general observations suggest that the relative earnings of graduates are much larger than that.

[4] Donald E. Gorseline, *The Effects of Schooling upon Income*, Bloomington, 1932. See section 2 of Chapter IV for a discussion of this study.

[5] The brothers with higher and lower educations averaged about 43 and 44 years old, respectively (*ibid.*). Earning differentials between them were compared to differentials in 1939 between persons aged 35 to 44 and 45 to 54, and a simple average taken.

[6] However, as indicated in the discussion in Chapter IV, section 3, the results are different for nonwhites: for example, the unadjusted rate of return to southern, male, nonwhite high-school graduates in 1939 is a few percentage points lower than that to college graduates.

ing returns results at least in part from the nature of the correlation between ability and education. Fully adjusted rates, therefore, might show no diminishing returns and might even show "increasing returns" to additional years of schooling.

The very rapid secular growth in high-school education in the United States (see Table 14) may in the first place be mostly due to

TABLE 14

Investment in High School Education, College Education, and Physical Capital, 1900–1956
(current prices)

	Per Cent of 17-Year-Olds with 12 Years of Schooling (1)	Rate of Total Investment in High School to Gross Physical Investment (2)	Ratio of Fore-gone Earnings in High School to Gross Physi-cal Investment (3)	Ratio of Investment in High School to Investment in College (4)
1900	6.4	.021	.015	.900
1920	16.8	.041	.030	1.575
1930	29.0	.124	.071	1.625
1940	50.8	.146	.084	1.789
1950	59.0	.107	.066	1.033
1956	62.3	.133	.080	1.105

Source: Column 1: *Historical Statistics of the United States, Colonial Times to 1957*, Washington, 1960, Series H223–233, p. 207; numerators in other columns from T. W. Schultz, "Capital Formation by Education," *Journal of Political Economy*, December 1960, Table 5; denominators from sources given in Table 12.

compulsory school laws but is probably ultimately more directly related to anticipated private and social real rates of return. Evidence has already been presented indicating that the unadjusted private money rate of return to high-school education is very large, and although the adjusted rate may be much lower, it too is probably considerable. A first approximation to the unadjusted social money rate can be found by relating before-tax earning differentials to total costs: it is only slightly lower than the private rate for white males because differential tax payments almost offset public costs. The true social rate, moreover, would be much larger still if high-school education made an important contribution to the residual advance in knowledge (see the discussion in section 2 of Chapter V). So both the private and social rates of return seem sufficient to justify the large expansion of high-school education.

2. Trends in Rates of Return

Many issues of current importance depend on the secular trends in rates of return from education. For example, youngsters are now being exhorted to finish high school and even college partly because of a belief that relatively unskilled and uneducated persons are becoming increasingly obsolete in the American economy. This belief presumes that advances in technology have raised the gains from high-school and college education, especially since World War II, and perhaps even for a much longer period. On the other hand, economists have frequently alleged that the secular increase in the relative supply of more educated persons in the United States and elsewhere has reduced and will continue to reduce the gains from education.[7] In this section I try to provide some very preliminary answers to such questions by bringing together readily available evidence on secular trends.

After 1939

Column 1 of Table 15 provides estimated private rates of return, unadjusted for differential ability, to college graduates in 1939, 1949, 1956, 1958, 1959, and 1961. The estimates for 1939 and 1949 were computed from data in the 1940 and 1950 Census and presented in Chapter IV. Although from a common source, they are not strictly comparable since the 1940 Census gave the earnings of urban native white males, whereas the 1950 Census gave the incomes of all white males. The estimates for 1956 and 1958 are based on the incomes of all males rather than whites alone as in 1949; more importantly, they were collected in surveys that often give considerably different results from those obtained in the Census. The entries for 1959 are rough estimates based simply on comparisons between mean income differentials computed from the 1960 Census and from the 1958 survey for all males over age 25. The entries for 1961 are based on similar comparisons between median differentials at different age classes. A fuller treatment of the 1960 Census materials and the 1961 survey is cer-

---

[7] A forceful argument along these lines even in the context of the early postwar period can be found in S. Harris, *How Shall We Pay for Education?*, New York, 1948, pp. 61–72. For an earlier statement, see A. G. B. Fisher, "Education and Relative Wage Rates," *International Labour Review*, June 1932.

TABLE 15

Private Rates of Return from College
and High School Education
for Selected Years since 1939
(per cent)

Year of Cohort	College Graduates (1)	High School Graduates (2)
1939	14.5	16
1949	13+	20
1956	12.4	25
1958	14.8	28
1959 1961	} slightly higher than in 1958	

Source: For 1939, 1949, 1956, and 1958, see Appendix ·A. For 1959, see *U.S. Summary Detailed Characteristics*, U.S. Census of Population, Table 223; for 1961, see *Income of Families and Persons in the United States, 1961*, Current Population Reports, p. 60, No. 39, Table 28.

The 1959 estimates were based simply on a comparison of the differences between the mean incomes of all males of 25 and over in 1958 and 1959. Differentials between college and high-school graduates were higher in 1959 by 7 per cent and between the latter and elementary-school graduates by 11 per cent. Costs apparently rose by a slightly smaller amount during the same period. The 1961 estimates were based on comparisons of median income differentials at various ages in 1958 and 1961. They were generally higher in 1961, again by amounts probably slightly in excess of the rise in costs during the same three years. More precise comparisons may change these estimates somewhat, probably not much.

tainly warranted as more information on costs and incomes becomes available.

The rate of return apparently declined about 1.5 percentage points from 1939 to 1949 and then rose again in the late 1950s. Although these variations can hardly be considered statistically significant given the differences and errors in the basic data, the decline from 1939 to 1949 is consistent with extensive evidence of a general narrowing of skill differentials during the 1940s, and the rise from 1949 is consistent with the slight general widening during the 1950s. There apparently has been little net change in the private rate of return to male college graduates during the twenty-three years as a whole.

Private rates of return to high-school graduates for the same years are shown in column 2.[8] In contrast with the rates for college graduates, these rose throughout the period, by 4 points from 1939 to 1949, and by a whopping 8 points after 1949, so there was about a 12 point increase during the twenty-three years as a whole. Apparently, the economic position of high-school graduates remained about the same relative to college graduates and increased substantially relative to elementary-school graduates. Note, however, that since the rates in Table 15 are unadjusted for differential ability, the true rates would have moved differently since 1939 if the correlation between ability and education changed. One might well believe that the differential ability of high-school graduates rose over time because now only the physically handicapped, dullards, or least motivated persons fail to go to high school. Although this might explain the large rise in the unadjusted gain from high school, note that Morgan and David actually find a larger ratio of adjusted to unadjusted earnings differentials between high-school and elementary-school graduates at younger than at older ages. The ratios between college and high-school graduates, on the other hand, are smaller at younger ages.[9]

The movements in rates since 1939 were the net result of several changes with different effects. The substantial advance in technology and knowledge would tend to increase rates of return on education, even if the advance was "neutral" and did not change percentage differentials (see my argument in Chapter III, section 2), and even if the advance was itself an effect of education. Demand for well-educated persons has also risen since 1939 because of a shift in government and business toward complicated military hardware and systematic research.

On the other hand, a growth in the relative number of highly educated persons would, by itself, reduce rates of return on education. Table 16 indicates that the number of college and high-school graduates has increased at about the same rate since 1939, so there is apparently little reason from the supply side to expect much decline

---

[8] Since nonwhites are concentrated at lower educational levels, the last four estimates would be biased more when comparing rates of return from high school than from college. Comparisons made with the 1950 Census data indicate, however, that only a small upward bias could have resulted from including nonwhites.

[9] Computed from *Quarterly Journal of Economics,* August 1963, Table III.

TABLE 16

Percentage of Population
with High School and College Education
in 1940, 1950, and 1957

Year	High School Graduates	College Graduates
1940	12	5
1950	18	7
1957	22	9

Source: H. Miller, "Annual and Lifetime
Income in Relation to Education, 1939–1959,"
American Economic Review, December 1960,
Table 2.

in percentage earning differentials between them. Yet these changes
in supply would produce a decline in the rate of return from college
education. For the earnings of college and high-school graduates would
decline relative to less-educated persons, and thus absolute earning
differentials between college and high-school graduates would decline
even if percentage differentials were unchanged. And a decline in
absolute differentials would lower the rate of return from college
unless costs declined by an equal amount. Once again a change in
percentage differentials gives a wrong picture even of the direction of
change in rates of return.

A decrease in mortality would by itself—the earnings of survivors
taken as given—increase rates of return (see Chapter III, section 2).
Mortality among white adults was already so low in 1939, however,
that subsequent decreases could only increase rates by a minor amount.
To illustrate, suppose that no member of the 1939 cohorts ever died,
and that earnings beyond age 64 rose at a rate of 2 per cent per year.
The rate of return to white males in 1939 would have been less than
one-half of a percentage point above the rate computed with 1940
mortality conditions.

If adjusted rates behaved similarly to unadjusted ones, the rate of
return from college did not change on balance and that from high
school increased substantially after 1939. Therefore, advances in technology and other forces increasing the demand for educated persons
must have offset the increase in college graduates and more than offset
the increase in high-school graduates. Consequently, technological

advance and other changes apparently increased the demand for high-school graduates more than that for college graduates.

Before 1939

The growth in technology, shifts in demand, decline in mortality, growth in education, etc., clearly may not have occurred at the same rate in the early part of the century as they did subsequently. About technology and demand shifts, little can be said.[10] Mortality, however, definitely declined more rapidly in the early part of the century. For example, if the mortality of white males in 1901 had prevailed in 1939, rates of return to college and high-school education would have been about three-fifths of a percentage point lower than they were with 1939 mortality.

Although the relative number of both high-school and college graduates increased substantially before 1939, the former probably increased more rapidly. Supply changes alone, therefore, would produce a greater decline in the rate of return to high-school than to college graduates. Indeed, they would have *increased* the rate to college graduates if a widening percentage differential between college and high-school earnings more than offset a decline in the earnings of both relative to less-educated persons.[11]

Quantitative information before 1939 is extremely scanty and unreliable, and Tables 17 and 18 summarize the little information available. Table 17 presents absolute income differentials in both current and 1958 dollars between college and high-school graduates at scattered dates, while Table 18 presents similar differentials between high-school and elementary-school graduates. According to the 1926 survey,[12] real absolute differentials between college and high-school graduates declined substantially from the 1920s to the 1950s. Since real costs rose during this period, rates of return to college would have declined even more.[13] According to the same survey, however, real

---

[10] Denison's calculations suggest greater technological progress since the late 1920s only if Department of Commerce rather than Kendrick-Kuznets estimates of national product are used (see his *Sources of Economic Growth in the United States,* New York, 1962, p. 269).

[11] Note that once again a widening percentage differential may be consistent with a declining rate of return even if costs were unchanged.

[12] Everett W. Lord, *The Relation of Education to Income,* Indianapolis, 1928.

[13] These data constitute Renshaw's principal evidence of secular decline in rates of return from college education (see "Estimating the Returns to Education," *Review of Economics and Statistics,* August 1960, p. 322).

TABLE 17

Income Differentials between College and High School Graduates
at Various Ages and for Scattered Years since 1904
in Current and 1958 Dollars

	1904 Mean Earnings		1926 Median Incomes		1927 Mean Incomes		1956–1958 (current dollars)	
Age	Current Dollars (1)	1958 Dollars (2)	Current Dollars (3)	1958 Dollars (4)	Current Dollars (5)	1958 Dollars (6)	Mean Incomes (7)	Median Incomes (8)
25–34	—	—	1146	1870	834	1361	1915	1127
32	936	3019	—	—	—	—	—	—
30–34	—	—	1465	2390	—	—	1438	—
35–44	—	—	2821	4602	—	—	4068	2478

Source: Column 1: J. M. Dodge, "The Money Value of Technical Training," *Transactions of the American Society of Mechanical Engineers*, Vol. 25, 1904. Column 3: Lord, *Relation of Education and Income*. Column 5: Gorseline, *Effect of Schooling*. Column 7: Miller in *American Economic Review*, December 1960, Table 1, p. 965.

differentials between high-school and elementary-school graduates[14] widened greatly during the same period. These data do not necessarily imply, therefore, that rates of return to high-school graduates declined during the last thirty years.

While rates of return from college education may have greatly declined at the same time that rates from high school declined much less, if at all, the accuracy and comparability with later data of the 1926 survey are subject to doubt. For one thing, questionnaires were sent out through a single fraternity, and the response rate was low (about 50 per cent). Only 1750 persons in the final sample were college graduates, and many were business majors. Moreover, the differentials between high-school and elementary-school graduates seem unbelievably small compared to those between college and high-school graduates.

Several persons around the turn of the century studied the effect of education on incomes in a few cities, companies, specialties, or schools. They found much larger differentials between college, high-school, and elementary-school graduates than are found today (see Tables 17

[14] The survey clearly overstates these differentials because all persons with at least eight years of schooling are lumped together in the category I call "elementary-school graduates."

TABLE 18

Income Differentials between High School and Elementary School Graduates at Various Ages and for Scattered Years since 1900 in Current and 1958 Dollars

| Age | 1900–1906 Mean Earnings | | 1908 Mean Earnings | | 1927 Mean Incomes | | 1956–1958 Mean Incomes, 1958 Dollars | 1926 Median Incomes | | 1956–1958 Median Incomes, 1958 Dollars |
	Current Dollars (1)	1958 Dollars (2)	Current Dollars (3)	1958 Dollars (4)	Current Dollars (5)	1958 Dollars (6)	(7)	Current Dollars (8)	1958 Dollars (9)	(10)
20	300	980	275	862	—	—	—	—	—	—
21	425	1389	—	—	—	—	—	—	—	—
22	500	1634	425	1332	—	—	—	—	—	—
23	500	1634	—	—	—	—	—	—	—	—
24	625	2042	500	1724	—	—	—	—	—	—
25	900	2941	862	2702	—	—	—	—	—	—
25–34	494	1614	—	—	—	—	1222	316	515	1616
35–44	722	2359	—	—	—	—	1724	866	1413	1785
45–54	—	—	—	—	403	658	—	—	—	—

Source: Columns 1, 3: A. C. Ellis, *The Money Value of Education*, U.S. Office of Education Bulletin 22, Washington, 1917. Column 5: Gorseline, *Effects of Schooling*, Table XXXIV, p. 113. Columns 7, 10: Miller in *American Economic Review*, December 1960, Table 1, p. 965. Column 8: Lord, *Relation of Education and Income*, p. 8.

and 18). Since the real costs of schooling rose rapidly over time,[15] this evidence suggests a large decline in rates of return to both high-school and college education.

If the data before 1940 can be considered representative, which is questionable, rates of return on both high-school and college education declined rather significantly during the first forty years of the century, and then stopped declining and even rose during the next twenty years. Since at least the relative number of college graduates increased more rapidly after 1940 and since mortality declined more rapidly before, these very different trends would probably be explained by less rapid shifts in the demand for educated persons during the earlier period: advances in knowledge and shifts in demand for final products may have been less favorable to educated persons then.[16] This conclusion is sufficiently important that much more attention should be paid to the historical evidence.[17]

One can also learn much from comparisons of different countries. A particularly good example of an "autonomous" increase in the supply of higher education is provided by the influx of well-educated European Jews into Palestine during the twenties and thirties, an influx motivated by religious and cultural considerations, not by any economic demand for well-educated persons. The influx should have lowered the return to higher education, and recent evidence indicates private rates of return in Israel during the fifties of only about 6 and 9 per cent for high-school graduates and college persons, respectively.[18] An equally autonomous change has been the large-scale immigration of low-educated African and Asian Jews to Israel after its birth in 1948. This

---

[15] Total costs per student in 1947–1949 dollars were as follows in 1900 and 1950:

	High School	College
1900	320	1050
1950	1035	2415

See Schultz in *Journal of Political Economy*, December 1960, Tables 5 through 7. His figures were converted from current to 1947–1949 dollars with the Consumer Price Index.

[16] Historians usually do assume that the technological improvements accompanying the industrial revolution reduced the relative demand for highly skilled persons.

[17] Albert Fishlow has, in fact, studied the historical trends in the demand for and supply of educated persons in the United States. See his "Levels of Nineteenth-Century American Investment in Education," *Journal of Economic History*, 26, December 1966, pp. 418–436, as well as his "The American Common School Revival: Fact or Fallacy?" in H. Rosovsky, ed., *Industrialization in Two Systems: Essays in Honor of Alexander Gerschenkron*, New York, 1966.

[18] See R. Klinov-Malul, "The Profitability of Investment in Education in Israel," unpublished Ph.D. dissertation, Hebrew University, 1964, Chapter 3.

change should have increased the return to higher education, and, notwithstanding the equalitarian tradition in Israel, there is clear evidence of a significant increase after 1948.[19]

[19] See *ibid.*, Chapter 4; also V. Bahral, *The Effect of Mass Immigration on Wages in Israel* (mimeographed), Falk Project for Economic Research in Israel, 1962.

CHAPTER VIII

Age, Earnings, Wealth, and Human Capital

Virtually all the implications of the theory of investment in human capital developed in Part One depend directly or indirectly on the effect of human capital on the earnings and productivity of persons and firms. Consequently most of my empirical work has been concentrated on measuring and assessing these effects. Chapters IV through VI contain the results for various demographic groups and time periods in the United States.

Several investigators have examined a variety of other implications, and the additional empirical support given to the theory has been quite gratifying.[1] Thus Oi independently developed an analysis of the effect of investment in human capital on unemployment and turnover that is quite similar to ours, and tested it empirically in a number of ways.[2] Smith applied the analysis to the turnover of skilled personnel

---

[1] One criticism was made of this theory largely on the grounds of lack of realism and relevance (see R. S. Eckaus, "Investment in Human Capital: A Comment," *Journal of Political Economy*, October 1963). Instead of quarreling with details of his comment—and there are several that seem wrong or misleading—I would like to urge that the evidence provided by this chapter and the previous ones, by the studies mentioned here, and by many other studies indicates that the theory is quite useful in interpreting the real world.

[2] See Walter Y. Oi, "Labor as a Quasi-fixed Factor of Production," unpublished Ph.D. dissertation, University of Chicago, 1961, and "Labor as a Quasi-fixed Factor," *Journal of Political Economy*, December 1962.

in the military, and developed rules for increasing the efficiency of their expenditures on personnel.[3] Mincer applied the analysis in estimating the amounts spent on on-the-job training, and then used his estimates to understand the income and employment behavior of different groups.[4] In an earlier and pioneering article, Mincer had already developed and tested a theory that related the distribution of earnings to the distribution of investments in human capital.[5] Or to take a final and very different example, Clara Friedman has neatly used the human capital approach to show that virtually nobody enters the New York City public school teaching system with more than the minimum required schooling because the value of the additional pay given for additional schooling is less than the cost of postponed earnings.[6]

This chapter covers still another aspect: the effect of human capital on earnings and wealth at different ages. The first part deals with the steepness and shape of the well-known age-earnings profiles. Since these are relevant in studying the declining incomes of older persons or the low incomes of younger persons, the effect of learning on productivity, and many other life-cycle changes, a demonstration that their shape is determined by investment in human capital should be of considerable interest.

In recent years there has been a noticeable shift of emphasis in economic theorizing and data collection from income and flows to capital and stocks. This surely is the thrust of the permanent income and related hypotheses in consumption studies,[7] of the emphasis on the allocation of assets in monetary theory,[8] and of the attention paid to the capital aspects of expenditures on durable goods.[9] In line with

[3] See G. Smith, "Differential Pay for Military Technicians," unpublished Ph.D. dissertation, Columbia University, 1964.

[4] See J. Mincer, "On-the-Job Training: Costs, Returns, and Some Implications," *Investment in Human Beings*, NBER Special Conference 15, supplement to *Journal of Political Economy*, October 1962, pp. 50–59.

[5] See his "Investment in Human Capital and Personal Income Distribution," *Journal of Political Economy*, August 1958.

[6] See her "Differential Pay of New York City School Teachers," unpublished Ph.D. dissertation, Columbia University, 1962.

[7] See M. Friedman, *A Theory of the Consumption Function*, Princeton for NBER, 1957; and F. Modigliani and R. Brumberg, "Utility Analysis and the Consumption Function: An Interpretation of Cross-Section Data," in *Post-Keynesian Economics*, K. K. Kurihara, ed., New Brunswick, 1954.

[8] See J. Tobin, "Money, Capital and Other Stores of Value," *American Economic Review*, May 1961; or M. Friedman, "The Quantity Theory of Money—A Restatement," in *Studies in the Quantity Theory of Money*, M. Friedman, ed., Chicago, 1956.

[9] See R. W. Goldsmith, *A Study of Saving in the United States*, Princeton, 1955–1956.

this shift, life-cycle economic changes should be related not only or even primarily to changes in earnings and other income, but also to changes in human and other wealth. Accordingly, the second part of this chapter develops the concept of age-wealth profiles—the relation between age and the discounted value of subsequent earnings—and shows that their shape, like that of the underlying age-earnings profile, is determined by investment in human capital. A few applications illustrating the usefulness of age-wealth profiles and thus indirectly the importance of human capital conclude the discussion.

1. Age-Earnings Profiles

Table 19 shows the mean net after-tax incomes in 1939 and 1949 of males classified by age and years of schooling; the word "net" indi-

TABLE 19

Net After-Tax Incomes of White Males in 1939
and 1949, by Age and Years of Education
(dollars)

Age	16+ (1)	12 (2)	7 and 8[a] (3)
	1939		
14–21	29	360	457
22–24	1185	1136	925
25–29	1930	1494	1182
30–34	2839	1929	1453
35–44	3878	2488	1768
45–54	4361	2744	1935
55–64	3856	2527	1773
	1949		
14–21	42	705	795
22–24	1794	2151	1769
25–29	2929	2763	2185
30–34	4380	3218	2498
35–44	6295	3623	2778
45–54	7883	4215	2959
55–64	7329	4165	2711

Source: See Tables 2 and 3 and Appendix A, section 1.
[a] For 1939, 7 and 8 years of schooling; for 1949, 8 years.

cates that direct outlays on schooling have been subtracted from reported incomes. Although the analysis in this chapter does not at all depend on the use of such an income concept, I have done so because foregone income—an important part of the total cost of education—is implicitly subtracted from reported incomes. Economic analysis as well as consistent accounting would be made easier either if direct outlays were also subtracted or if foregone income was added back. Since the discussion in Chapter II indicates that *all* the costs of general on-the-job training and of certain other investments are implicitly subtracted from reported incomes, comparability among different kinds of human capital is most easily achieved by explicitly subtracting direct school outlays, which brings us to the net income concept used in Table 19.

The table clearly shows that average incomes at each age class are strongly related to education, a relation explored in the previous chapters. The table also shows that incomes tend to be relatively low at the beginning of labor force participation, rise throughout later ages until a common peak is reached in the 45 to 54 age class, and decline in the last age class. Although the peaks are reached in the same *class*, they are not necessarily reached at the same *age*. For example, if incomes continually increased to the peak age and continually declined thereafter, actual peak ages could be anywhere from 35 to 64, a spread of thirty years, and yet all the observed peaks might occur in the 45 to 54 age class.

Therefore, these data do not necessarily contradict the common notion that unskilled persons reach their peak earnings before skilled persons. This notion has been based, however, on misleading statistics. Since occupation changes with age, the more able tending to rise and the less able to fall in the occupational hierarchy, earnings in different occupations at a given moment in time might show an earlier peak in unskilled occupations merely because older unskilled workers are less able than younger ones. Education statistics are less affected because education is usually completed at an early age.

Table 19 gives the incomes of different cohorts at a moment in time, not those of a given cohort aging over time. Age-income profiles based on longitudinal or time series data can differ from those based on cross-sectional data because of business cycles, secular trends toward higher education, and occupation or life-cycle employment changes (see the discussion in the beginning of Chapter IV). Probably the most important, pervasive, and calculable difference results, however, from the secular growth in incomes, which implies, for example, that the cohort of college graduates aged 25 in 1939 received a higher real income at age 35 than did the cohort aged 35 in 1939. Since secular growth in the United States has been large, averaging almost 2 per cent per person per annum, the difference would be considerable.

The cross-sectional education profiles have been converted into time series profiles only by adjusting very simply for the secular growth in incomes. The income t years later of a cohort finishing its schooling in a base year was estimated by multiplying the base year income of the cohort with the same schooling and t years older by $(1.02)^t$, where 2 per cent is the assumed average annual growth in incomes. For example, the cohort of college graduates aged 35 to 44 in 1939 had an income of $3400, and the estimated income at age 35 of a cohort graduating from college in 1939 at age 22 would be $3400 multiplied by $(1.02)^{13}$. Chart 10 plots such time series profiles for college, high-school, and elementary-school graduates of 1939.

This adjustment for secular growth is inaccurate on several counts. Although 2 per cent is a good estimate of the average growth in real per capita income since the 1880s, the growth during the last twenty-five years, especially in after-tax incomes, has been less. Moreover, Chapter VI suggests that incomes of less-educated persons grew more rapidly before 1940 and possibly less rapidly after 1940 than those of more educated persons. Consequently, a more accurate adjustment of recent data would have a lower average rate of growth and different rates at different educational levels. Since, however, none of the conclusions reached in this chapter would be greatly affected, I have retained a simple 2 per cent adjustment. The rate of return estimates in Chapters IV through VI are more sensitive, and different adjustments were tried there.

The profiles in Chart 10 do not decline at older ages, but continue to rise through age 65, the last age covered by the data. This perhaps surprising conclusion can be checked with data from surveys taken at different times, which provide an independent measure of the change over time in a cohort's income. For example, college graduates aged 45 to 54 in 1939 would be 55 to 64 years old in 1949, and the real incomes of 45- to 54-year-old college graduates in the 1940 Census could be compared with those of 55- to 64-year-old college graduates in the 1950 Census. Such evidence is not altogether reliable since the income concept is not the same in different surveys, sampling and response errors abound, and so on; nevertheless, it can serve as a check. Table 20, which brings together data from the 1940 and 1950 Census, and from a Census survey in 1958, indicates that a cohort's income increases more with age than is shown by cross-section data. In particu-

CHART 10

"Time Series" Age-Earnings Profiles for Several 1939 Education Cohorts

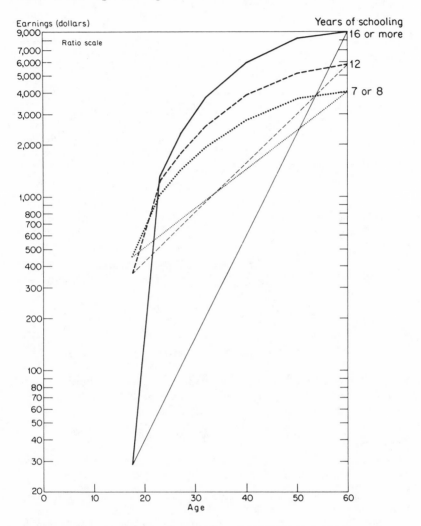

lar, there is no systematic tendency for time series profiles to decline in the last age class even though cross-section ones do.[10] The decline in the latter has been responsible for an erroneous inference about the

[10] The result may be due to selective retirement before the age of 65, since persons whose earnings would decline most might elect to retire early. I owe this point to J. Mincer.

TABLE 20

Estimated Incomes over Time of Cohorts
at Different Educational Levels
(dollars)

Age of Cohort in 1939	Income of Cohort in		
	1939	1949	1958
COLLEGE GRADUATES			
25–34	5155	8960	12,269
35–44	8386	11,543	10,966
45–54	9430	10,732	—
55–64	8338	—	—
HIGH SCHOOL GRADUATES			
25–34	3699	4812	6295
35–44	5380	5770	6510
45–54	5933	5798	—
55–64	5464	—	—
ELEMENTARY SCHOOL GRADUATES			
25–34	2848	3610	4337
35–44	3823	3896	3960
45–54	4182	3586	—
55–64	3833	—	—

Source: Tables 2 and 3 and Appendix A, section 1.

shape of the former[11] which has made for misunderstanding of the economic position of older workers. For example, their retirement at 65 has been misinterpreted because their earnings have been assumed to be way below their peak earnings rather than possibly higher than ever.

The time series and cross-section profiles would be identical in a

---

[11] Whether Marshall's statement that occupation profiles eventually turn down held for time series profiles in nineteenth-century England is not clear. Many related statements for the United States, however, make no allowance for growth and thus incorrectly jump from cross-section data to a longitudinal inference. To take one of many possible examples, H. Miller said, "When he [the average male worker] is in his forties or early fifties he has usually attained the peak of his earning power, and from that time until he is ready to retire from the labor market his annual earnings shrink until they are not any higher than those he received as a young man" (*Income of the American People*, New York, 1955, p. 64). He then refers to cross-section data that would not decline (at least up to the age of 65) if adjusted for the annual growth in earnings.

stationary economy since they differ only because of the growth in per capita earnings. If growth were due to the operation of forces, like neutral technological changes, that uniformly raised earnings at all ages, cross-sectional profiles would be unaffected, while time series profiles would decline to the former if growth ceased. If, on the other hand, growth were due to the embodiment of new technology in younger (that is, "newer") workers, or to other improvements in the economic effects of the human capital invested in successive cohorts with the same number of school years, cross-sectional profiles would be affected by growth and would approach the shape of the time series profiles if growth ceased. For example, if new technology were embodied in younger workers, they would have greater technological knowledge than older workers, so cross-sectional profiles would understate, while time series profiles would accurately measure, the effect of age on the earnings of workers with the same technological knowledge. So even though the time series profiles were derived from cross-sectional ones by adjusting for growth, they may more accurately describe the relation between age and earnings in a stationary economy. In particular, earnings may not decline before age 65 even in such an economy.

Although all the profiles in Chart 10 rise continuously, they do so at very different rates, the average rate of increase being positively related to education. This is apparent from the lines connecting incomes at ages 14 to 21 with those at 55 to 64, for they have slopes of 15, 7, and 5.5 per cent, respectively, for college, high-school, and elementary-school graduates. The analysis in Part One indicated that investment in human capital steepens age-earnings profiles because earnings are net of investment costs at younger ages and gross of returns at older ages. Indeed, the proposition could be turned around and if two profiles differed in steepness, the steeper could be said to indicate the presence of greater human capital. Consequently, the positive relation between steepness and education in Chart 10 seems to support this approach.

It does, but note that the data plotted there include the effects of all investments in human capital, including vocational and on-the-job training, health, knowledge of economic opportunities, and so forth, as well as education. College graduates could have more education than high-school graduates and less total capital because, for example, the latter had more on-the-job and vocational training. If so, high-school graduates would have lower net earnings at younger ages, higher earnings later on, and a steeper profile than college graduates. Since the contrary is indicated, the main inference must be that there is a positive correlation between education and total capital.[12] This inference is quite sensible because education is presumably an important part of the total, and other kinds of investment in human capital, such as health, migration, adult education, and on-the-job training, appear to be positively related to education (see Chapter IV, section 2).

TABLE 21

Annual Rates of Income Change between Successive Age Classes for 1939 Cohorts at Different Educational Levels

Education (years)	$t = 23$ $t' = 18$ (1)	$t = 27$ $t' = 23$ (2)	$t = 32$ $t' = 27$ (3)	$t = 40$ $t' = 32$ (4)	$t = 50$ $t' = 40$ (5)	$t = 60$ $t' = 50$ (6)	$t = 60$ $t' = 18$ (7)
16+	.43	.19	.10	.06	.03	.01	.05
12	.17	.09	.07	.05	.03	.01	.04
8	.14	.08	.06	.04	.03	.01	.04
Simple average	.25	.12	.08	.05	.03	.01	.04

Source: The data plotted in Chart 10. The entries are computed from the formula $\dfrac{Y_t - Y_{t'}}{Y_t + Y_{t'}} \times \dfrac{2}{t - t'}$, where Y_t is income at age t, and $Y_{t'}$ is income at age t'.

The entries in Table 21 bring out precisely what should be apparent from even a cursory glance at Chart 10; namely, the profiles are quite concave to the age axis, especially at younger ages and higher educational levels. The concavity is shown by the continual decline in annual rates of increase between successive age classes, the declines being strongest at younger ages and higher educational levels. In addition, rates of increase of earnings with age differ appreciably only at younger ages; for example, the rate of increase is 30 percentage points higher for college than for elementary-school graduates between ages 18 and 23, while they increase at about the same rate between 40 and 60.

The theory developed in Part One also explains these results remarkably well. Earnings are depressed "artificially" during the in-

[12] The net earnings of young persons in Chart 10 are overestimated because the direct costs of certain investments (such as migration and health) do not tend to be subtracted from earnings. The overestimate is probably not too large, however, because many direct costs (such as on-the-job training and education) are subtracted, and indirect costs are usually more important than direct costs. Moreover, earnings at older ages would include the return on all investments, and they are clearly directly related to education.

vestment period because costs are written off then, and rise unusually rapidly afterward because the depressant is released. A concave age-earnings profile results, especially near the investment period which is concentrated at younger ages. Since the total amount invested is positively correlated with education, more-educated cohorts would have more concave profiles, again especially at younger ages. So a simple theory of investment in human capital can explain the differences in concavity as well as in steepness.

2. Age-Wealth Profiles

As pointed out in the introduction, in recent years there has been a shift in both theoretical and empirical work from flows to stocks, which suggests that, in studying life-cycle behavior, attention should be paid to age-wealth profiles as well as to the more familiar age-earnings profiles. This section discusses the influence of investment in human capital on the shape of age and human-wealth profiles (little direct attention is paid to nonhuman wealth).

Although the market value of human wealth cannot be determined directly because, happily, there no longer is a market in human beings, an indirect estimate can be based on the rule that the value of an asset equals the discounted sum of the income stream yielded. In others words, the value of the human wealth "owned" at a particular age would equal the discounted sum of subsequent earnings. So the shape of the relation between age and the discounted sum of subsequent earnings, which is called an age-wealth profile, would be completely determined by interest rates and the shape of age-earnings profiles.

If interest rates were zero, age-wealth profiles would decline continuously because wealth would simply be the sum of subsequent earnings and, consequently, would have to decline with age regardless of the shape of age-earnings profiles.[13] If interest rates were infinitely large, wealth and earnings profiles would be identical; in particular, the former would rise as long as the latter did. With interest rates between these extremes, wealth profiles would peak somewhere between the initial and the peak earnings age, closer to the latter the higher the rates.[14]

---

[13] More precisely, they would rise only during periods of negative earnings. Since net earnings could be negative only during the investment period, even these rises would be at younger ages.

[14] See section 2 of Appendix B.

CHART 11

Age-Wealth Profiles of 1939 Graduates

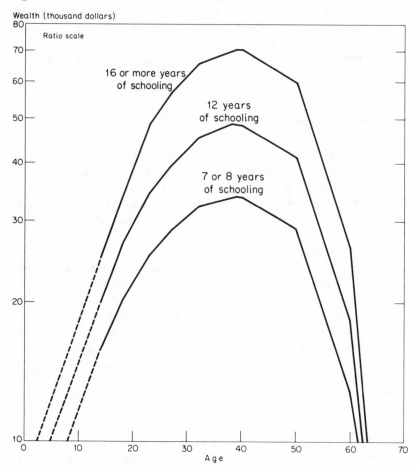

Wealth (thousand dollars)

Ratio scale

16 or more years of schooling

12 years of schooling

7 or 8 years of schooling

Age

Note: Earnings discounted at an 8 per cent rate.

Although time series profiles are clearly more relevant in calculating cohort wealth profiles than cross-sectional ones are, even the former have to be modified because they consider only the earnings of cohort members alive and participating in the labor force. They could be converted into the relevant cohort profiles with an adjustment for the fraction not participating at different ages. Since participation declines with age, the differences between time series and cohort profiles would be greater at older ages, especially at lower educational levels; in particular, the latter profiles would tend to turn down before age 65 even though the former did not. The peak in cohort earnings would be later, however, than that in cross-sectional earnings.

If a cohort earnings profile did not rise much, the wealth profile would necessarily decline continuously, at least if interest rates did not decline much with age. If earnings rose sufficiently, wealth would also rise, and the rate of increase in wealth would be positively related to, yet less than, that in earnings. Although wealth necessarily peaks before earnings, the peak wealth age would be later, the greater the increase and the later the peak in earnings.[15] Since the increase in earnings is related to investment in human capital, the increase in wealth and its peak age would also be related to this investment.

Chart 11 illustrates these effects by graphing the wealth profiles of the 1939 cohorts of college, high-school, and elementary-school male graduates.[16] All earnings have been discounted at an 8 per cent interest rate, about the average rate of return on business capital (see section 1 of Chapter V). Time series earnings were only adjusted for mortality, still by far the major cause of nonparticipation before age 65.

All the wealth profiles rise for about the first twenty years of labor force participation and then decline. The rates of increase are positively related to education, although the differences here are smaller than those in earnings. Wealth peaks at about age 39, some fifteen years before cohort earnings do. The peaks in wealth are not much affected by education because neither the peaks in earnings nor their rates of increase after the early thirties are much affected by education (see Table 21).

Investment in human capital explains not only these differences in wealth profiles, but also changes over time. For example, in the early nineteenth century wealth profiles usually peaked quite early, say at age 20 or so,[17] because mortality was high and workers were usually relatively unskilled. Unskilled workers with high mortality rates

---

15 For proofs of these assertions, see sections 2 through 4 of Appendix B.

16 Chart 11 was computed from earnings figures that are slightly different from and presumably less accurate than those used in section 1. Since the more correct figures would yield very similar wealth profiles, I have not bothered to make any corrections.

17 The value of a typical male Negro slave rose until he was in his early twenties, reached a peak there, and then declined for the rest of his life. (See R. Evans, Jr., "The Economics of American Negro Slavery, 1830–1860," *Aspects of Labor Economics*, Special Conference 14, Princeton for NBER, 1962, Table 12.) Since the value of slaves was determined by maintenance costs as well as productivity, the peak in the present value of subsequent productivity would have come still earlier, unless, as is unlikely, maintenance costs rose significantly during the late teens and early twenties. The present value of the earnings of unskilled free persons probably peaked at a similar age.

would have a flat or even declining (cohort) earnings profile,[18] and thus a continually declining wealth profile. The heavy investment in education, training, and health during the past hundred years has steepened the typical earnings profile and, consequently, shifted the typical peak wealth age to about 40.[19]

Before concluding, it might be wise to consider explicitly some applications of wealth profiles since they are less well known than earnings profiles and their importance may not be obvious to many readers. Two applications were chosen for their interest and timeliness. The first deals with the need to provide depreciation on human as well as physical capital and the second with life-cycle variations in savings.[20]

Many persons have suggested that a term accounting for the depreciation of human beings be subtracted from reported earnings. Irving Fisher, in his brilliant presentation of the conceptual foundations of the income and wealth concepts, said: "If it were true that income could never trench on capital, we could not reckon a laboring man's wages as income without first deducting a premium or sinking fund sufficient to provide for the continuance of this income after the destruction by death of the laborer." [21] If by "laboring man" is meant relatively unskilled, as seems reasonable, then Fisher's conclusion is supported by my analysis of age-wealth profiles. Since their earnings profile would not rise much with age, their wealth profile would tend to decline continuously. Wealth could be maintained constant, therefore, only if the rate of decline in wealth was subtracted from earnings at the same age and added to a depreciation or sinking fund.

In recent years emphasis has shifted from the laboring man to the educated man and from conceptual issues to more practical ones. Tax laws are said to discriminate against education and other kinds

---

[18] There is some evidence that the productivity of male Negro slaves did not change much between their twenties and fifties (see J. R. Meyer and A. H. Conrad, "The Economics of Slavery in the Ante Bellum South," *Journal of Political Economy*, April 1958, p. 106).

[19] For example, the profiles plotted in Chart 9 would have peaked several years earlier if mortality rates of the middle-nineteenth century had been used.

[20] I omit possibly the most well-known application, namely, to the relation between age and life insurance. This stimulated the pioneering book by L. Dublin and A. Lotka, *The Money Value of a Man*, New York, 1930, revised in 1940. Also see B. Weisbrod, "The Valuation of Human Capital," *Journal of Political Economy*, October 1961, pp. 425–436. A related application is to damage suits resulting from disability or death. An absorbing example is given in the best seller by L. Nizer, *My Life in Court*, New York, 1961, Chapter 5, section II, entitled "The Worth of a Man."

[21] *Nature of Capital and Income*, New York, 1930, p. 111. Fisher, however, argued against the use of this "ideal" definition of income.

of human capital because depreciation can be deducted only from the taxable income of physical capital.[22] Unquestionably, a more symmetrical tax treatment of these two classes of capital would be desirable. However, one should be aware that a good deal of depreciation on human capital occurs unknowingly. Thus, as pointed out elsewhere, part of the costs of human capital are "written off" immediately because foregone earnings are, in effect, deducted from accrued taxable income.[23] Since these indirect costs are about 75 per cent of the private costs of college education in the United States,[24] and an even higher percentage of general on-the-job training costs, the depreciation unknowingly permitted is considerable. Indeed, the present value of the amount so permitted would often be greater than that explicitly allowed on physical assets depreciated over a five- or ten-year or even longer period!

Some important relations between depreciation and human capital can be obtained using age-wealth profiles if true income were simply defined as the amount necessary to keep wealth intact.[25] Then the depreciation or "appreciation" necessary to convert reported into true earnings would simply equal the rate of change in wealth. Consequently, the depreciation could be said to be insufficient whenever wealth declined and excessive whenever it increased.

Since the wealth profile of unskilled workers would decline continuously, an explicit depreciation deduction is needed at each working age. The profiles of skilled workers, on the other hand, rise for a spell and the rises are larger and steeper, the greater the investment in human capital. Consequently, since their true earnings would actually be greater than reported earnings at younger ages and less only after the peak wealth age, an appreciation term would be required at all ages before the peak in wealth. So while tax laws can be said to discriminate against all unskilled and older skilled workers, they discriminate in *favor* of younger skilled workers. Of course, during the whole period of labor force participation there would be a net decline even in the wealth of skilled workers. But it would be relatively small: for example, using an 8 per cent interest rate, the average annual depreciation in the wealth of workers with a flat earnings profile (during an assumed forty-two-year earning period)

22 See T. W. Schultz, "Investment in Human Capital," *American Economic Review*, March 1961, p. 13, and R. Goode, "Educational Expenditures and the Income Tax," in *Economics of Higher Education*, S. J. Mushkin, ed., Washington, 1962.

23 See Chapter II, section 1, and Chapter V, section 1.

24 See Chapter IV, section 1.

25 Such an ideal definition is not necessary for our purposes, but it does simplify the discussion.

would equal 30 per cent of average earnings while that of the 1939 cohort of college graduates would equal only 18 per cent of their earnings.[26]

So death rather than investment in human capital appears to be the main reason why reported earnings, on the whole, overestimate true earnings. When the former is the principal determinant of wealth changes, as with unskilled workers, depreciation bulks large relative to earnings, but when the latter is more important, as with skilled workers, depreciation becomes less important. Probably the major explanation of this paradoxical conclusion is that much depreciation is unknowingly permitted on human capital.

In recent years studies of household behavior have been greatly influenced by the argument that current expenditures depend not only on current income but also on expected future income.[27] In particular, total consumption at any age would be affected by expectations about incomes at later ages. So life-cycle variations in consumption would not match those in earnings because the latter would be at least partly anticipated and then offset by appropriate savings and dissavings.[28] It shall be demonstrated that this new approach makes life-cycle changes in savings a function of age-wealth profiles and thus indirectly of the amount invested in human capital.

A lifetime consumption pattern is assumed to depend upon utility functions, expectations about earnings and other income, market interest rates, and planned bequests. Since savings are residually defined as the difference between income and consumption, savings are adjusted over a lifetime so as to make the consumption plan feasible. In particular, since earnings are high during the middle ages and low during the younger ages and retirement, the rate of savings would also be high during the middle ages and low or even negative during other periods. Broadly speaking, this pattern is usually found in empirical studies.[29]

More precise implications can be obtained by specifying the model more fully. In order to bring out clearly and simply the effects of

---

[26] See section 5 of Appendix B for a more general result.

[27] See especially Friedman, *Consumption Function*.

[28] This approach to life-cycle consumption patterns has been stressed by F. Modigliani and his associates. See Modigliani and Brumberg, in *Post-Keynesian Economics*, or F. Modigliani and A. Ando, "The Life Cycle Hypothesis of Savings," *American Economic Review*, March 1963.

[29] See Friedman, *Consumption Function*, Tables 8 and 9, and F. Modigliani and A. Ando, "The 'Permanent Income' and the 'Life Cycle' Hypothesis of Saving Behavior: Comparison and Tests," in *Consumption and Saving*, I. Friend and R. Jones, eds., Vol. II, Philadelphia, 1960, Table III-4.

human capital, several assumptions will be added that certainly have to be modified in a more complete analysis. Thus, let it be assumed that each cohort knows its earnings profile, that a single market interest rate applies to all transactions, that consumption is the same at all ages, and that after entry into the labor force the nonhuman wealth of a cohort can be changed only by its own savings and dissavings.[30] Each cohort starts out with wealth, partly in earning power and partly in property, and at "its" death leaves behind wealth, partly in the earning power of descendants and other subsequent cohorts and partly in property.

If its bequest, or terminal wealth, equaled the amount it was bequested, or initial wealth—that is, if there were zero generational or "social" savings—the rate of savings[31] at any age would exactly equal the rate of change of human wealth.[32] So savings would be negative from the initial to the peak human-wealth age, zero then,[33] positive at subsequent ages until retirement, and zero during retirement. A more reasonable assumption for the United States and other developed economies would be that social savings were positive, or that terminal wealth exceeded initial wealth. Then the initial dissavings would be smaller and of shorter duration, the zero savings rate would be reached before the peak wealth age, and a positive savings rate would continue into the retirement period.

Since the wealth profile of unskilled workers would decline continuously, they would have positive savings throughout their labor force period. Profiles of workers with investment in human capital, on the other hand, rise initially more sharply and longer, the greater the investment. So the magnitude and extent of the initial dissavings would be greater for cohorts with more human capital.

Since an initial period of dissavings would result in an initial decline in nonhuman capital, an increase in indebtedness, or some of both,[34] the large secular increase in human capital should have caused a secular increase in household indebtedness. Therefore, the

[30] These assumptions, as well as several others, are also made by Modigliani *et al.* in their quantitative work.

[31] Note that our concept of savings, unlike the usual ones, includes investment in the human capital of subsequent generations as well as accumulation of assets.

[32] In terms of the language just used, savings would equal the rate of depreciation or appreciation on wealth.

[33] Before retirement, only at the peak wealth age would permanent income, defined as the income accruing on wealth, equal actual income. So depreciation and thus savings equal zero when actual and permanent incomes are equal.

[34] Consequently, one can say that investment in human capital is substituted for investment in other capital.

observed increase in consumer credit and other debt may not have resulted simply from an increased demand for durables or from improvements in the market for credit, but probably also was a disguised effect of the secular increase in education and other human capital.

A change in the rate of population growth would probably change aggregate, although not necessarily social, savings because the relative number of persons at different ages would be affected. If savings rates were always greater at younger than at older ages, an increase in population growth would increase the aggregate savings rate. Such would tend to be the result in a world of unskilled workers because they would save more throughout the labor force period than during retirement.[35] Skilled workers, on the other hand, would have low and even negative savings rates at the youngest ages, and a larger population growth rate might actually reduce their aggregate savings rate. Therefore, the secular increase in human capital should have reduced the positive effect of a higher population growth rate on aggregate savings, and might even have led to a negative effect.

[35] This essentially is the model assumed by Kuznets in his discussion of the effect of population growth on aggregate savings. See his *Capital in the American Economy: Its Formation and Financing*, Princeton for NBER, 1961, Chapter III. Also see Modigliani and Ando in *American Economic Review*, March 1963, pp. 59–60.

CHAPTER IX

Summary and Conclusions

1. Summary

Most investments in human capital—such as formal education, on-the-job training, or migration—raise observed earnings at older ages, because returns are part of earnings then, and lower them at younger ages, because costs are deducted from earnings at that time. Since these common effects are produced by very different kinds of investment in human capital, a basis is provided for a unified and comprehensive theory. The analysis in Part One starts with a discussion of specific kinds of human capital, with the most attention paid to on-the-job training, because the latter clearly illustrates and emphasizes the common effects. This leads to a general theory applying to any kind of human capital.

The general theory has a wide variety of important applications. It helps to explain such diverse phenomena as interpersonal and interarea differences in earnings, the shape of age-earnings profiles—the relation between age and earnings—and the effect of specialization on skill. For example, because observed earnings are gross of the return on human capital, some persons earn more than others simply because they invest more in themselves. Because "abler" persons tend to invest more than others, the distribution of earnings would be very unequal and skewed even if "ability" were symmetrically and not too unequally distributed. Further, the conventional practice of adding returns to and subtracting costs from earnings serves to steepen age-earnings profiles and to increase their concavity as investment in human capital increases. Still another example, learning on and off the job has the same kind of effects on observed earnings as formal education, training, and other recognized investments in human capital, and can be considered one way to invest in human capital. Because all such activities have similar effects on earnings, the total amount invested in human capital and rates of return on this investment can, on certain reasonable assumptions, be estimated from information on observed earnings alone.

Some investments in human capital do not affect earnings because costs are paid and returns are collected not by the persons involved but by the firms, industries, or countries employing them. These investments, which are called "specific" investments, range from hiring costs to executive training and are of considerable importance. They help to explain the well-known fact that unemployment is greater among unskilled than skilled workers in the United States, for more specific capital is invested in the latter and employers have special incentive to continue them on the payroll. Similarly, incompletely vested pension plans may be used because they help to insure firms against a loss on their specific investment. The analysis further suggests that this type of investment is relatively more important in monopsonistic than in competitive firms.

Part Two investigates empirically the effect of one kind of human capital—formal education—on earnings and productivity in the United States. The basic technique used is to adjust data on the earnings or incomes of persons with different amounts of education for other relevant differences between them. Chapter IV determines the relation in recent years between earnings and college education, considering, among other things, college costs and the greater "ability" of college persons. The rate of return to an average college entrant is considerable, of the order of 10 or 12 per cent per annum; the rate is higher to urban, white, male college graduates and lower to college dropouts, nonwhites, women, and rural persons. Differences in the relative number of, say, white and nonwhite or urban and rural high-school graduates who go to college are consistent with the differences in their rates of return.

General observation indicates that college graduates tend to be more "able" than high-school graduates, apart from the effect of college education. This is indicated also by information gathered on

IQ, rank in class, father's education or income, physical health, ability to communicate, and several other distinguishing characteristics. A few studies permit some assessment of the relative importance of ability and education in explaining earning differentials between college and high-school persons. By and large, it appears, ability explains only a relatively small part of the differentials and college education explains the larger part. Apparently, moreover, the rate of return from college is positively related to the level of ability since there is evidence that ability plays a larger part in determining the earnings of college than high-school persons.

Gains from college education vary not only between groups, like men and women, but also substantially within given groups. Indeed, some calculations in Chapter IV indicate that the dispersion of rates of return among white male college graduates is as large as, and perhaps larger than, the very considerable dispersion in the returns per dollar of capital among smaller corporate manufacturing firms. A large dispersion makes it difficult for any individual to anticipate his gain from education, a difficulty that is compounded by a payoff period of some twenty to twenty-five years. This long payoff period provides an economic justification for flexible or "liberal" education since most of the benefits would be received when the economic environment was greatly different from that prevailing at the time of entry into the labor force.

In Chapter V attention is focused on the social gain from college education as measured by its effects on national productivity. The major difficulty here, one that always plagues economists, is in measuring the benefits and costs to society that are not captured or borne by college-educated persons. All that could be done was to derive—on the basis of crude information—lower and what is best labeled "possible" upper limits to the social rates of return, limits that unfortunately are wide apart. The more reliable lower limits thus derived do not differ much from the private rates of return, but the upper levels are almost double the latter. In the same chapter it is shown that private rates of return on college education exceed those on business capital. The evidence is insufficient to decide whether this, or the converse, is true of the social rates.

Chapter VI estimates private rates of return from high-school education. Before adjusting for differential ability, these private rates from high school turn out to be greater than those from college. But the "true" rates, after adjustment for ability, may not be, for ability apparently differs more between high-school and elementary-school students than between college and high-school students. A similar qualification applies to the crude evidence indicating that rates on elementary-school education are the highest of all.

A traditional view among economists—certainly the dominant one when I was a graduate student—is that changes in educational attainments have been largely autonomous, and that the secular increase in education has caused a decline in earning differentials and rates of return on education. Such evidence as there is, presented in Chapter VI, suggests indeed that the relative position of high-school and college graduates probably declined during the first forty years of the century under the impact of increases in their numbers. But the evidence is scattered and much less reliable than the information available for the past thirty years. The latter, presented in the same chapter, indicates that the rapid growth in the number of high-school and college graduates has not reduced their economic position. An alternative view, supported by this evidence, has therefore gained many adherents in recent years; namely, that educational attainments in good part adjust to, as well as influence, the demands of the economic system.

Chapter VII shows that investment in education in fact steepens and increases the concavity of age-earnings profiles, as predicted by the theory in Part One. Partly as an aside, the discussion also includes a critical examination of the common belief that earnings tend to turn down when persons reach their late forties or fifties; this belief is shown to be founded on an illusion, for it is based on data that do not take economic progress into account. The same chapter shows that the steepness of age-wealth profiles—the relation between age and the discounted value of subsequent earnings—is also increased by investment in education and other human capital. It is suggested that the apparent large secular increase in the peak wealth age in the United States resulted from a secular increase in the amount invested in such capital. The chapter concludes with some applications of these profiles, especially to life-cycle changes in savings, indebtedness, and consumption.

2. Future Research

I have no illusions that this study has more than scratched the surface of the research required on the economic effects of education and other investments in human capital. There is need for additional research on many different aspects of the gain from education and on other implications of the theoretical analysis in Part One. A few examples of possible research will be briefly mentioned.

Economists have been surprisingly ignorant of the quantitative effects of different kinds of ability on earnings and productivity, yet such knowledge is essential in estimating the gains from investment in human capital (and in resolving many other problems as well). The surveys utilized in this study show the feasibility and importance of determining these effects, and many more such attempts should be made in the future.

Only a limited amount could be said about the social gains from education because of ignorance about the external effects. This ignorance is closely connected with ignorance about the "residual" in calculations of the contribution of various factors to growth. Little progress can be achieved, therefore, in improving the estimation of these social gains until methods are discovered for reducing the residual.

To many underdeveloped countries the gains from education in the United States fifty years ago may be more relevant than the gains today because this country was much poorer then and many fewer persons were educated. The evidence available indicates a decline in the private gain from high-school and college education in the first forty years of the century, but a much more intensive study is required because this evidence is not very reliable. Fortunately, Albert Fishlow has already published a study of historical changes in the demand for and supply of educated persons in the United States, which throws considerably more light on trends in the gains from education.[1]

I have not tried to estimate gains to persons taking specialized programs in high school and college. Some literature is already available on the gains to various professionals, such as doctors, lawyers, engineers, or scientists,[2] and additional comparisons can and should be made between persons with B.A., M.A., or Ph.D. degrees, liberal arts or more specialized college majors, commercial or academic high-school programs, and so on. My estimates of the average gains to high-school and college persons would be useful as a yardstick to determine when gains were unusually large or small; for example, since

---

[1] A. Fishlow, "Levels of Nineteenth-Century American Investment in Education," *Journal of Economic History,* 26, December 1966, pp. 418–436; and "The American Common School Revival: Fact or Fallacy?" in H. Rosovsky, ed., *Industrialization in Two Systems: Essays in Honor of Alexander Gerschenkron,* New York, 1966.

[2] See, for example, M. Friedman and S. Kuznets, *Income from Independent Professional Practice,* New York, NBER, 1945; G. J. Stigler and D. Blank, *The Demand and Supply of Scientific Personnel,* New York, NBER, 1957; or W. L. Hansen, "The 'Shortage' of Engineers," *Review of Economics and Statistics,* August 1961.

average gains are large, the gains from particular specialties would have to be very large before they could be considered "excessive." [3]

There has been persistent interest, if little success, in measuring the differences in quality among high schools and colleges. One way to measure quality within an economic context is to relate expenditures on students and other variables in different schools to the (ability-adjusted) incomes of their graduates.[4] Such studies have already been undertaken on a small sample basis,[5] and, with sufficient persistence, additional information could be collected to expand the samples considerably.

Chapter VII presents empirical work dealing with other implications of the theory outlined in Part One, such as the shape of age-earnings and age-wealth profiles, differential unemployment, turnover of military personnel, differential pay of school teachers, and estimates of the amount invested in human capital. The theory is so rich in implications that many more could be investigated, and empirical work has already begun relating human capital to the turnover in employment of women, comparative advantage and United States exports, the elasticity of substitution between labor and physical capital, and several other problems.

Probably the most important application is to differences in incomes between regions and countries, either over time or cross-sectionally at a moment in time. The estimates presented here of the gains from education could be used to improve Denison's estimates of the contribution of education to economic growth in the United States. The major improvement, however, must await additional work on the external effects of education, work that, I fear, will be rather slow in coming.

A more immediate, and also important, application is to the personal distribution of incomes. This field has been afflicted with nu-

---

[3] This yardstick has been applied by H. G. Lewis to the medical profession with extremely interesting and surprising results: the rate of return to doctors (on their additional training compared to dentists) has apparently been no higher and perhaps lower than that to all college graduates. See his *Unionism and Relative Wages in the United States: An Empirical Inquiry*, Chicago, 1963.

[4] Another approach is from the cost side, and relates differences in expenditures to differences in curriculum, size, teaching staff, and other "real" inputs; in technical language, this approach in effect constructs "hedonic" cost indexes. An interesting initial study along these lines has been made by R. Calkins, "The Unit Costs of Programs in Higher Education," unpublished Ph.D. dissertation, Columbia University, 1963.

[5] See, e.g., the study by S. Hunt discussed in Chapter IV, "Income Determinants for College Graduates and the Return to Educational Investments," Ph.D. dissertation, Yale University, 1963.

merous theories that scarcely go beyond the skewness in the overall distribution of incomes although substantial empirical material on the anatomy of income distribution has been accumulated. The theory developed in section 3 of Chapter III combines the effects of investment in human capital and differential ability, and, unlike other theories, contains many implications about income distribution. The empirical work of Mincer, referred to earlier, as well as the fact that at least three-fifths of earnings are attributable either to investment in human capital or to differential ability,[6] is suggestive of the promise offered by this approach. I hope to present further work along these lines in the not too distant future.

3. Concluding Comments

In recent years the outpouring of work on education and other types of human capital has reached such a level that some persons have scornfully rejected it as simply another fad, while others have been repelled by a few reckless applications and by its use to justify all kinds of public policies. To those who believe in the great value of the concept, the excesses have been most unfortunate, although perhaps unavoidable. Probably no important development has ever sailed smoothly into the mainstream of economic thought.

One might, nevertheless, get discouraged were it not for the fact that peoples of the world differ enormously in productivity, that these differences are in turn largely related to environmental factors, and that the latter are in turn related to the accumulation of knowledge and the maintenance of health. The concept of investment in human capital simply organizes and stresses these basic truths. Perhaps they are obvious, but obvious truths can be extremely important. Indeed, I would venture the judgment that human capital is going to be an important part of the thinking about development, income distribution, labor turnover, and many other problems for a long time to come.

---

[6] Estimated by taking one minus the ratio of the average earnings of persons with no education to the average earnings of all persons.

Part Three

Economy-Wide Changes

Introduction

The concept of human capital is relevant not only to micro investments in education, training, and other skills and knowledge by individuals and firms, but also to understanding economy-wide changes in inequality, economic growth, unemployment, and foreign trade. The Introduction to the first edition indicates that research on the relation between human capital and economic growth stimulated much of the early interest in human capital. Throughout the first two editions are brief discussions of macro implications of human capital analysis, and the second Addendum to Chapter III is devoted mainly to income inequality. Still, these editions contain little systematic analysis at the macro level.

Research in recent years has increasingly appreciated that both economic growth and inequality are closely dependent on investments in different forms of human capital. This new section includes three of the several theoretical papers on these subjects I have written during the past ten years.

The first essay (joint with Nigel Tomes), on the rise and fall of families, analyzes inequality by building on the analysis in my Woytinsky Lecture, which was reprinted in the 2nd edition as an addendum to Chapter III. The new Chapter 10 assumes that parental investments in the human capital of their children depends on the children's abilities, and on the altruism, resources, and possibly also human capital of the parents. It uses these links between parents and children to analyze inequality of opportunity, or how parental background—their income, abilities and human capital—determines the human capital and earnings of children. The analysis helps explain why in all modern countries, the earnings of children are usually much closer to the average earnings of their generation than are the earnings of the parents relative to the average in their own generation.

Adam Smith opened the *Wealth of Nations* with a famous discussion of the relation between the division of labor and economic progress. The analysis of investment in human capital makes it possible to treat this

255

profound insight in a systematic fashion. The paper with Kevin Murphy reprinted here as Chapter 11 develops an analytical framework to consider various determinants of the division of labor by specialized skills. It shows that the extent of the division of labor is negatively related to the cost of coordinating different specialists in the production of output. Smith believed that the "extent of the market" is the main force limiting the division of labor, but we argue that this is not true in the modern economic world.

We show that economic growth stimulates greater specialization even if the extent of the market is unimportant. However, the analysis also demonstrates that specialization encourages economic progress. Under certain conditions specified in the chapter, continuing progress in per capita incomes would not be possible without the increased specialization and greater division of labor that accompanies growth. But the interaction between progress and specialization can produce rapid economic growth.

Parents choose not only how much to invest in each child, but also the number of children they have. In the mainly agricultural environments of undeveloped countries, the typical pattern is to have relatively many children and to invest little in each one. The reason is that education and other human capital investments are not very productive in these environments, whereas children can begin to contribute to farm output at an early age.

As an economy develops and the time of parents becomes more expensive, the advantages of having many children decline. Industrialization and the implementation of modern agricultural methods also raise the returns to education and other skills. The result is a shift in parental activities from rearing many children to investing much more in each one they have.

These are the issues considered in Chapter 12, co-authored with Kevin Murphy and Robert Tamura. We formulate a model of behavior and technology that shows why economic progress shifts parents toward much lower fertility levels and greater investments in the human capital of each child. This change can free an underdeveloped country from a "Malthusian"-type equilibrium with low per capita incomes and high birth rates, and can help propel its economy toward continuing growth in these incomes, with growing levels of human capital and low birth rates.

CHAPTER X

Human Capital and the Rise and Fall of Families[1]

Gary S. Becker and Nigel Tomes

1. Introduction

Ever since Pareto discovered that the distribution of larger incomes and
wealth is reasonably well approximated by a particular skewed distribution, since then called the "Pareto distribution," economists have continued to discuss inequality in the distribution of earnings, income, and
wealth among individuals and families. However, they have paid little
attention to the inequality within families over generations as determined by the relation between the incomes or wealth of parents, children, and later descendants. Schumpeter is the only major economist
who systematically considered intergenerational mobility with empirical
evidence as well as with theoretical analysis (see Schumpeter 1951).

Sociologists and other social scientists, on the other hand, have pre-

[1]Our research has been supported by National Science Foundation Grant no. SES
8208260. We received valuable assistance from Gale Mosteller and Michael Gibbs. We appreciate the useful comments at the Conference on the Family and the Distribution of
Economic Rewards and at seminars at Bar-Ilan University, Brigham Young University, the
University of Chicago, the Hebrew University, Institute des Etudes Politiques, the University of Pennsylvania, Purdue University, Stanford University, and the University of Western
Ontario. We especially thank Robert Willis for his helpful discussion at the Conference
on the Family and the Distribution of Economic Rewards. We have also benefited from
suggestions by Arthur Goldberger and Sherwin Rosen.

sented considerable empirical evidence on the occupations, education, and other characteristics of children and parents. Blau and Duncan (1967), in the influential book *The American Occupational Structure*, consider the effect of family background on the achievements of children. As long ago as 1889, John Dewey wrote, "[U]pon the average, children of parents who are exceptional, or who deviate from the mean, will themselves deviate from the mean only one third of their parents' deviation. . . . It is not likely that children of the poor would be better off, and children of the wealthier poorer in anything like the ratio of 2/3" (Dewey [1889, pp. 333–34]; this statement was brought to our attention by O. D. Duncan).

Although discussions of inequality among families have been almost entirely separate from discussions of inequality between generations of the same family, these inequalities are analytically closely related. In particular, regression away from the mean in the relation between, say, the incomes of parents and children implies large and growing inequality of income over time, while regression toward the mean implies a smaller and more stable degree of inequality. These statements are obvious in a simple Markov model of the relation between parents and children:

$$I_{t+1} = a + bI_t + \varepsilon_{t+1.} \tag{1}$$

where I_t is the income of parents, I_{t+1} is the income of children, a and b are constants, and the stochastic forces affecting the income of children (ε_{t+1}) are assumed to be independent of the income of parents.

Inequality in income will continue to grow over time if b is greater than or equal to unity, while inequality in income will approach a constant level if b is smaller than unity in absolute value. Clearly, the size of b also measures whether children of richer parents tend to be less rich than their parents and whether children of poorer parents tend to be better off than their parents. This example implies that, even in rigid and caste-dominated societies, many of the elite and underprivileged families would change places over generations unless inequality continued to grow over time ($b \geq 1$).

The degree of regression toward or away from the mean in the achievements of children compared to those of their parents is a measure of the degree of equality of opportunity in a society. The purpose of this paper is to analyze the determinants of unequal opportunities, sometimes called "intergenerational mobility," or, as in the title of our paper, "the rise and fall of families." We use all these terms interchangeably.

The many empirical studies of mobility by sociologists have lacked a framework or model to interpret their findings. We try to remedy this defect and to fill a more general lacuna in the literature by developing a systematic model that relies on utility-maximizing behavior by all participants, equilibrium in different markets, and stochastic forces with unequal incidence among participants.

An analysis that is adequate to cope with the many aspects of the rise and fall of families must incorporate concern by parents for children as expressed in altruism toward children, investments in the human capital of children, assortative mating in marriage markets, the demand for children, the treatment by parents of exceptionally able or handicapped children, and expectations about events in the next or in even later generations. Although these and other aspects of behavior are incorporated into a consistent framework based on maximizing behavior, we do not pretend to handle them all in a satisfactory manner. However, our approach indicates how a more complete analysis can be developed in the future.

The next section has a lengthy discussion of investments in the human capital of children. The discussion is lengthy because the relation between the earnings of parents and children is the major determinant of the rise and fall of most families. Section 3 moves on to consider the interaction between investments in human capital, transfers of material wealth (gifts and bequests) from parents to children, and the evolution of consumption over generations.

Section 4 considers the effect of the number of children on intergenerational mobility of consumption and wealth and also the effect on mobility of assortative mating in marriage markets.

Section 5 assembles about a dozen studies of the degree of regression to the mean between parents and children in income, earnings, and wealth. Available studies are few and are based on limited data, but the magnitudes of some basic parameters of our model are suggested by the evidence for the United States and other countries.

Much of our analysis of human capital is based on the model developed in Becker's Woytinsky Lecture (1967) to explain different investments among families. However, that lecture is mainly concerned with inequality and skewness in earnings and wealth and does not derive relations between the earnings and assets of parents and children. The approach in this paper is also based on a series of papers by us in the last decade that analyzes marriage, fertility, altruism of parents, and long-run equilibrium relations between parents and children (see esp. Becker 1974, 1981; Becker and Tomes 1976, 1979; Tomes 1981).

The present paper is closest in spirit to Becker and Tomes (1979), but these papers differ in important ways. We believe that the present discussion is a considerable improvement. We now distinguish human capital and earnings from other wealth, and we incorporate restrictions on the intergenerational transfer of debt. We assume now that parents' utility depends on the utility of children instead of on the permanent income of children. We also consider the effect of endogenous fertility on the relation between the wealth and consumption of parents and children. These improvements explain why the implications of the present paper are sometimes quite different from those of the earlier paper. In an essay devoted to critiquing parts of Becker (1981), Becker and Tomes (1984), and an earlier draft of this paper, Goldberger (1985) sometimes fails to see these differences between the current paper and our earlier work. We comment further on his critique elsewhere in this paper.

Since inequality over generations and inequality between families are closely related (as implied by eq. [1]), any adequate analysis of inequality must also consider marital patterns, fertility, expectations about future generations, and investments in human capital. Therefore, it is hardly surprising that a growing literature during the last 15 years has tried to integrate more realistic models of family behavior into models of the distribution of income and wealth.[2] Although this literature and our work have many similarities, the present paper is almost alone in relating the rise and fall of families to investments in human capital that interact with the accumulation of assets, the evolution of consumption, and the demand for children.

2. Earnings and Human Capital

Perfect Capital Markets

Some children have an advantage because they are born into families with greater ability, greater emphasis on childhood learning, and other favorable cultural and genetic attributes. Both biology and culture are transmitted from parents to children, one encoded in DNA and the other in a family's culture. Much less is known about the transmission of cultural attributes than of biological ones, and even less is known about the relative contributions of biology and culture to the distinctive endowment of each family. We do not need to separate cultural from ge-

---

[2] Among the important contributors to this literature are Stiglitz (1969), Blinder (1974), Conlisk (1974), Behrman and Taubman (1976), Meade (1976), Bevan (1979), Laitner (1979), Menchik (1979), Shorrocks (1979), Loury (1981), and Atkinson (1983).

netic endowments, and we will not try to specify the exact mechanism of cultural transmission. We follow our previous paper (Becker and Tomes 1979; see also, e.g., Bevan 1979) in assuming as a first approximation that both are transmitted by a stochastic-linear or Markov equation:

$$E^i_t = \alpha_t + hE^i_{t-1} + v^i_{t,} \tag{2}$$

where E^i_t is the endowment (or vector of endowments) of the ith family in the tth generation, h is the degree (or vector of degrees) of "inheritability" of these endowments, and v^i_t measures unsystematic components or luck in the transmission process. We assume that parents cannot invest in their children's endowment.

A priori restrictions on the magnitude or even on the sign of the inheritability of endowments are unnecessary since the degree of inheritability can be estimated from accurate information on the earnings of parents and children (and perhaps also grandparents). Yet the assumption that endowments are only partially inherited, that h is less than unity and greater than zero, is a plausible generalization to cultural endowments of what is known about the inheritance of genetic traits. This assumption implies that endowments regress to the mean: children with well-endowed parents tend also to have above-average endowments but smaller relative to the mean than their parents', whereas children with poorly endowed parents tend also to have below-average endowments but larger relative to the mean than their parents'.

The term α_t can be interpreted as the social endowment common to all members of a given cohort in the same society. If the social endowment were constant over time, and if $h < 1$, the average endowment would eventually equal $1/(1 - h)$ times the social endowment (i.e., lim $\bar{E}_t = \alpha/[1 - h]$). However, α may not be constant because, for example, governments invest in the social endowment.

Practically all formal models of the distribution of income that consider wages and abilities assume that abilities automatically translate into earnings, mediated sometimes by demands for different kinds of abilities (see, e.g., Roy 1950; Mandelbrot 1962; Tinbergen 1970; Bevan and Stiglitz 1979). This is useful in understanding certain gross features of the distribution of earnings, such as its skewness, but is hardly satisfactory for analyzing the effect of parents on their children's earnings. Parents not only pass on some of their endowments to children, but they also influence the adult earnings of their children by expenditures on their skills, health, learning, motivation, "credentials," and many other characteristics. These expenditures are determined not only by the abilities of children but also by the incomes, preferences, and fertility of parents as well as the public expenditures on education and other human capital of children and other variables. Since earnings are practically the sole income for most persons, parents influence the economic welfare of their children primarily by influencing their potential earnings.]

To analyze these influences in a simple way, assume two periods of life, childhood and adulthood, and that adult earnings depend on human capital (H), partly perhaps as a measure of credentials, and market luck (ℓ):

$$Y_t = \gamma(T_t, f_t) H_t \alpha + \ell_t \tag{3}$$

The earnings of one unit of human capital (γ) is determined by equilibrium in factor markets. It depends positively on technological knowledge (T) and negatively on the ratio of the amount of human capital to nonhuman capital in the economy (f). Since we are concerned with differences among families, the exact value of γ is not usually important because that is common to all families. Therefore, we assume that the measurement of H is chosen so that $\gamma = 1$.

Although human capital takes many forms, including skills and abilities, personality, appearance, reputation, and appropriate credentials, we further simplify by assuming that it is homogeneous and the same "stuff" in different families. Since much research demonstrates that investments during childhood are crucial to later development (see, e.g., Bloom 1976), we assume also that the total amount of human capital accumulated, including on-the-job training, is proportional to the amount accumulated during childhood. Then adult human capital and expected earnings are determined by endowments inherited from parents and by parental (x) and public expenditures (s) on his or her development:

$$H_t = \psi(x_{t-1}, s_{t-1}, E_t), \quad \text{with} \quad \psi_j > 0, \quad j = x, s, E. \tag{4}$$

Ability, early learning, and other aspects of a family's cultural and genetic "infrastructure" usually raise the marginal effect of family and public expenditures on the production of human capital; that is,

$$\frac{\partial^2 H_t}{\partial j_{t-1} \partial E_t} = \psi_{jE} > 0, j = x, s. \tag{5}$$

The marginal rate of return on parental expenditures (r_m) is defined by the equation

$$\frac{\partial Y_t}{\partial x_{t-1}} = \frac{\partial H_t}{\partial x_{t-1}} = \psi_x = 1 + r_m(x_{t-1}, s_{t-1}, E_t), \qquad (6)$$

where $\partial r_m/\partial E > 0$ by inequality (5).

Although the human capital of different persons may be close substitutes in production, each person forms a separate human-capital "market." Rates of return to him depend on the amount invested in him as well as on aggregate stocks of human capital. Marginal rates of return eventually decline as more is invested in a person because investment costs eventually rise as his forgone earnings rise. Also, benefits decline increasingly rapidly as his remaining working life shortens (see the more extended discussion in Becker [1975]).

Nonhuman capital or assets can usually be purchased and sold in relatively efficient markets. Presumably, therefore, returns on assets are less sensitive to the amount owned by any person than are returns on human capital. Little is known about the effect of abilities, other endowments, and wealth on returns from different assets, although some theory suggests a positive relation (see Ehrlich and Ben-Zion [1976]; see also the evidence in Yitzhaki [1984]). Our analysis only requires the reasonable assumption that returns on assets are much less sensitive to endowments and accumulations by any person than are returns on human capital (a similar assumption is made in Becker [1967, 1975]). A simple special case of this assumption is that the rate of return on assets is the same to all persons.

Much of the endowed luck of children (v_t) is revealed to parents prior to most of their investment in children. Therefore, we assume that rates of return on these investments are fully known to parents (as long as the social environment [α_t] and public expenditures [s_{t-1}] are known). Parents must decide how to allocate their total "bequest" to children between human capital and assets. We assume initially that parents can borrow at the asset interest rate to finance expenditures on children and that this debt can become the obligation of children when they are adults.

Parents are assumed to maximize the welfare of children when no reduction in their own consumption or leisure is entailed. Then parents borrow whatever is necessary to maximize the net income (earnings minus debt) of their children, which requires that expenditures on the human capital of children equate the marginal rate of return to the interest rate:

$$r_m = r_t, \quad \text{or} \quad \hat{x}_{t-1} = g(E_t, s_{t-1}, r_t), \qquad (7)$$

with $g_E > 0$ (by eq. [6]), $g_r < 0$, and also with $g_s < 0$ \qquad (8) if public and private expenditures are substitutes. Parents can separate investments in children (an example of the separation theorem) from their own resources and altruism toward children because borrowed funds can be made the children's obligation.

The optimal investment is given in chart 12 by the intersection of the horizontal "supply curve of funds," rr, with a negatively inclined demand curve (HH or $H'H'$). This figure clearly shows that better-endowed children accumulate more human capital; those with the endowment E accumulate ON units of expenditure, while those with $E' > E$ accumulate $ON' > ON$. Therefore, better-endowed children would have higher expected earnings because equation (3) converts human capital into expected adult earnings. The total effect of endowments on earnings, and the inequality and skewness in earnings relative to that in endowments, is raised by the positive relation between endowments and expenditures.

CHART 12.

Rates of return on parental expenditures on children.

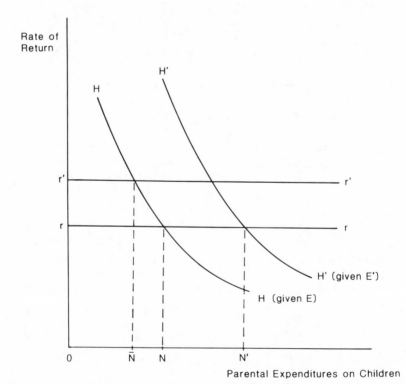

Clearly, an increase in the rate of interest reduces the investment in human capital and, hence, earnings. Compare ON and $O\tilde{N}$ in chart 12. The effect of an increase in public expenditures is less clear. If public expenditures are perfect substitutes dollar for dollar for private expenditures, the production of human capital would be determined by their sum $(x + s)$ and by E; an increase in public expenditures would then induce an equal decrease in private (parental) expenditures, and the accumulation of human capital would be unchanged. Even then, a sufficiently large increase in public expenditures would raise the accumulation of human capital because private expenditures cannot be negative.

Note that the human capital and earnings of children would not depend on their parents' assets and earnings because poor parents can borrow what is needed to finance the optimal investment in their children. However, the income of children would depend on parents because gifts and bequests of assets and debt would be sensitive to the earnings and wealth of parents. Indeed, wealthy parents would tend to self-finance the whole accumulation of human capital and to add a sizable gift of assets as well.

Although the earnings and human capital of children would not be directly related to parents' earnings and wealth, they would be indirectly related through the inheritability of endowments. The greater the degree of inheritability, the more closely related would be the human capital and earnings of parents and children. To derive the relation between the earnings of parents and children, substitute the optimal level of x given by equation (7) into the earnings-generating equation (3) to get

$$Y_t = \psi[\, g(E_t, s_{t-1}, r_t), s_{t-1}, E_t] + \ell_t = \phi(E_t, s_{t-1}, r_t) + \ell_t, \qquad (9)$$

$$\text{where } \phi_E = \psi_g g_E + \psi_E = \left(\frac{\partial Y}{\partial x}\right)\left(\frac{\partial x}{\partial E}\right) + \frac{\partial Y}{\partial E} > 0.$$

Since this equation relates E to Y, ℓ, g, and r, E_t can be replaced by E_{t-1} from (2) and then Y_t can be related to Y_{t-1}, ℓ_t, v_t, ℓ_{t-1}, and other variables:

$$Y_t = F(Y_{t-1}, \ell_{t-1}, v_t, h, s_{t-1}, s_{t-2}, r_t, r_{t-1}, \alpha_t) + \ell_t. \qquad (10)$$

Not surprisingly, the earnings of parents and children are more closely related when endowments are more inheritable (h). However, the relation between their earnings also depends on the total effect of endowments on earnings (ϕ_E). If this effect is independent of the level of endowments ($\phi_{EE} = 0$), then

$$Y_t = c_t + \alpha_t \phi_E + hY_{t-1} + \ell_t^*,$$

$$\text{where } \ell_t^* = \ell_t - h\ell_{t-1} + \phi_E v_t$$

$$\text{and } c_t = c(s_{t-1}, s_{t-2}, h, r_t, r_{t-1}).$$

(11)

The intercept c_t would differ among families if government expenditures (s_{t-1}, s_{t-2}) differed among them. The stochastic term ℓ_t^* is negatively related to the market luck of parents.

If the luck of adults and children (ℓ^*) is held constant, the earnings of children would regress to the mean at the rate of $1 - h$. However, the coefficient is biased downward by the "transitory" component of lifetime earnings of parents (ℓ_{t-1}) in OLS regressions of the actual lifetime earnings of children on the actual lifetime earnings of parents (Y_t on Y_{t-1}). If c_t is the same for all families, the expected value of the regression coefficient would equal

$$b_{t,t-1} = h\left(1 - \frac{\sigma_\ell^2}{\sigma_y^2}\right),$$

(12)

where σ_ℓ^2 and σ_y^2 are the variances of ℓ_t and Y_t. This coefficient is closer to the degree of inheritability when the inequality in the transitory component of lifetime earnings is a smaller fraction of the total inequality in lifetime earnings.

Families of particular races, religions, castes, or other characteristics who suffer from market discrimination earn less than do families without these characteristics. Persons with characteristics that are subject to discrimination earn less than do persons not subject to discrimination even when their parents' earnings are equal. Persons subject to discrimination would earn less—given the degree of inheritability—as long as discrimination reduces the earnings from given endowments, for discrimination then reduces the intercept in the equation that relates the earnings of parents and children ($c_t + \alpha_t \phi_E$ in eq. [11]).

Imperfect Access to Capital

Access to capital markets to finance investments in children separates the transmission of earnings from the generosity and resources of parents. Economists have argued for a long time, however, that human capital is poor collateral to lenders. Children can "default" on the market debt contracted for them by working less energetically or by entering occupations with lower earnings and higher psychic income. Such "moral hazard" from the private nature of information about work effort and employment opportunities can greatly affect the earnings realized from human capital. Moreover, most societies are reluctant to collect debts from children that were contracted by their parents, perhaps because the minority of parents who do not care much about the welfare of their children would raise their own consumption by leaving large debts to children.

To bring out sharply the effect of imperfect access to debt contracted for children, we assume that parents must finance investments in children either by selling assets, by reducing their own consumption, by reducing the consumption by children, or by raising the labor-force activities of children. Consider parents without assets[3] who would have to finance the efficient investment in human capital (say, ON in chart 12) partly by reducing their own consumption because they cannot contract debt for their children. A reduction in their own consumption would raise its marginal utility relative to the marginal utility of resources invested in children. This would discourage some expenditure on children. Consequently, both the amount invested in children and parental consumption are reduced by limitations on the debt that can be left to children. Clearly, richer parents would tend to have both higher consumption and greater investments in children.

Therefore, expenditures on children by parents without assets depend not only on endowments of children and public expenditures, as in equation (7), but also on earnings of parents (Y_{t-1}), their generosity toward children (w), and perhaps now also on the uncertainty (ε_{t-1}) about the luck of children and later descendants, as in

$$\hat{x}_{t-1} = g^*(E_t, s_{t-1}, Y_{t-1}, \varepsilon_{t-1}, w), \quad \text{with} g_Y^* > 0. \tag{13}$$

Public and private expenditures would not be perfect substitutes if public expenditures affected rates of return on private expenditures, as when tuition is subsidized. However, if they are perfect substitutes, g^* would depend simply on the sum of s_{t-1} and Y_{t-1}: an increase in public expenditures is then equivalent to an equal increase in parental earnings. The effect of children's endowments on investments is now ambiguous ($g_E^* \gtrless 0$) because an increase in their endowments raises the resources of children as well as the productivity of investments in their human capital. Expenditures on children are discouraged when chil-

---

[3] Even parents who accumulate assets over their lifetime may lack assets while investing in children.

dren are expected to be richer because that lowers the marginal utility
to parents of additional expenditures on children.

The demand curves for expenditures in chart 13 are similar to those
in chart 12 and are higher·in families with better-endowed children. The
cost of funds to a family is no longer constant or the same to all families.
Increased expenditures on children lower the consumption by parents,
which raises their subjective discount rates (the shadow cost of funds).
These discount rates are smaller to parents with higher earnings or more
poorly endowed children. Expenditures on children in each family are
determined by the intersection of supply and demand curves. An increase in parental earnings shifts the supply curve to the right and induces greater expenditures on children (compare S_1 and S'_1 in chart
13). The distribution of intersection points determines the distribution
of investments and rates of return and, hence, as shown in Becker (1967,
1975), the inequality and skewness in the distribution of earnings.

By substituting equation (13) into the earnings-generating equations
(3) and (4), we get

CHART 13.

Parental expenditures on children, with capital constraints.

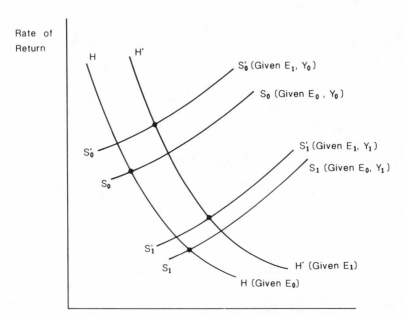

$$Y_t = \psi[\,g^*(E_t, Y_{t-1}, k_{t-1}),\, s_{t-1},\, E_t] + \ell_t \qquad (14)$$

$$= \phi^*(E_t, Y_{t-1}, k_{t-1}) + \ell_t,$$

where k_{t-1} includes w, s_{t-1}, and ε_{t-1}. Earnings of children now depend directly on the earnings of parents as well as indirectly through the transmission of endowments. Some authors (e.g., Bowles 1972; Meade 1976; Atkinson 1983) argue for a direct effect because "contacts" of parents are said to raise the opportunities of children; others argue for a direct effect because parents are said to receive utility directly from the human capital of children. Fortunately, the effects of parent earnings on access to capital can be distinguished analytically from its effects on "contacts" and "utility."

The indirect effect of parents' earnings on the earnings of children operates through the transmission of endowments and can be found by substituting E_{t-1} for E_t and then using equation (14) for E_{t-1}:

$$Y_t = F(Y_{t-1}, Y_{t-2}, \ell_{t-1}, v_t, h, \alpha_t, k_{t-1}, k_{t-2}) + \ell_t. \qquad (15)$$

The sum of both the direct and the indirect effects of parents' earnings is

$$\frac{\partial Y_t}{\partial Y_{t-1}} = \phi^*_{Y_{t-1}} + \frac{h\phi^*_{E_t}}{\phi^*_{E_{t-1}}} > 0. \qquad (16)$$

The indirect effect of grandparents' earnings, holding parents' earnings constant, is

$$\frac{\partial Y_t}{\partial Y_{t-2}} = -h\phi^*_{Y_{t-2}}\left(\frac{\phi^*_{E_t}}{\phi^*_{E_{t-1}}}\right) < 0. \qquad (17)$$

Earnings of grandparents and grandchildren are indirectly linked through the constraints on financing investments in children. That is, the earnings of parents are not sufficient to describe the effects on children of both the resources and the endowments of parents. Equation (17) shows that an increase in the earnings of grandparents lowers the earnings of grandchildren when parents' earnings and grandchildren's luck are held constant. Constraints on financing investments in children introduce a negative relation between the earnings of grandparents and grandchildren and raise the positive effect of parents' earnings on children's earnings.[4]

If Y_t were approximately linearly related to E_t and Y_{t-1}, then[5]

$$Y_t \cong c'_t + (\beta^* + h)Y_{t-1} - \beta^* h Y_{t-2} + \ell_t^*, \text{ with } \beta^* = \phi_Y^*. \quad (18)$$

The coefficient of parents' earnings exceeds the degree of inheritability by the marginal propensity to invest in the human capital of children (β^*). As in equation (12), OLS estimates of the coefficient of Y_{t-1} are biased downward by the transitory component of lifetime earnings. Ordinary least squares estimates of the relation between Y_t and Y_{t-1} tend toward[6]

$$\beta^* < b_{t,t-1}^* = \frac{b_{t,t-1 \cdot t-2}^*}{1 + h\beta^*} \leq \min(1, \beta^* + h, b_{t,\, t-1 \cdot\, t-2}^*), \quad (19)$$

where $b_{t,t-1 \cdot \, t-2}^*$ is the partial regression coefficient between Y_t and Y_{t-1}. Therefore, both partial and simple regression cofficients between the lifetime earnings of parents and children provide upper limits of the effect of capital market constraints on the propensity to invest in children. The biases in these OLS estimates can sometimes be overcome by

[4] Goldberger (1985, pp. 16–17) perhaps properly takes us to task for expressing too much "surprise" in our earlier work about a negative coefficient on grandparents' wealth (or income) because this is implied by our model (Becker and Tomes [1979] say that a negative coefficient "may seem surprising" [p. 1171]; Becker [1981] says "it is surprising" [p. 148]). However, we never claimed that an increase in grandparents' wealth would lower the wealth of grandchildren (Goldberger's discussion [1985, p. 2] is misleading about our claims). We have asked how persons who start with a presumed relation among the wealth of grandchildren, parents, and grandparents would interpret a negative coefficient on grandparents' wealth such as is found in Wahl's study (1985) reported in table 23.

[5] A similar equation is derived in Becker and Tomes (1979, eq. 25). However, the coefficient called β there refers to the propensity to bequeath all capital, including debt, to children, not to the propensity to invest in the human capital of children by parents who cannot leave debt. The approximation in eq. (18) would be linear in the logs of the earnings of children, parents, and grandparents if the endowment and earnings-generating equations are linear in logs. Then $\beta^* + h$ would give the percentage increase in the earnings of children per 1% increase in the earnings of fathers, and similarly for $-\beta^* h$.

[6] Equation (18) implies that

$$b_{t,t-1} \cong \beta^* + h - h[b^*_{(\beta \cdot y_{t-2} + \ell_{t-1}) \cdot y_{t-1}}]$$

$$\cong \beta^* + h - \frac{b\sigma_t^2}{\sigma_y^2} - h\beta^* b_{t-1,t}^*.$$

If the economy is in long-run equilibrium (see Becker and Tomes 1979), then $b_{t,t-1}^* = b_{t-1,t}^*$, $\sigma_{y_{t-1}}^2 = \sigma_{y_t}^2$, and the equality in eq. (19) follows. The relation between $b_{t,t-1}^*$ and the right-hand side of eq. (19) is derived in Becker and Tomes (1979, app. E).

the use of instruments for the lifetime earnings of parents, such as the lifetime earnings of uncles or of great-grandparents (see Goldberger 1979; Behrman and Taubman 1985).

The direct relation between the earnings of parents and children in equation (14) is likely to be concave rather than linear because obstacles to the self-financing investments in children decline as parents' earnings increase. When investments in the human capital of children are sufficient to lower marginal rates of return to the market rate on assets, further increases in parents' earnings raise the assets bequeathed to children but have no effect on the amount invested in the human capital of children (if rates on assets are independent of parents' earnings). Presumably, "contacts" of parents and the direct utility to parents from the human capital of children are more important in richer families. Hence, capital constraints have different implications for the curvature of the relation between the earnings of parents and children than do these alternative explanations.

Becker and Tomes's (1979) discussion implies that, because β^* and h enter symmetrically, even knowledge of the true values of the coefficients attached to parents' and grandparents' incomes in an equation such as (18) could not identify β^* and h without other information, such as which coefficient is larger. Earnings in rich families not subject to capital constraints are related by the simple equation (11), which does not include β^*. Therefore, h would be known if the coefficient on parents' earnings in rich families is known. Then β^* and h could be distinguished in equation (18) by using this information on h.

In earlier drafts of the present paper we unwisely denote β^* by β, although β in Becker and Tomes (1979) refers to a different concept. Since the coefficient β^* measures the marginal propensity to invest in the human capital of children by capital constrained parents who are prevented from making the wealth-maximizing investment in their children, β^* does not enter the earnings-generating equation for richer families (eq. [11]) who are not so constrained. Put differently, β^* is zero in richer families. There is no general presumption about the size of β^* relative to h even in low-income families because β^* depends on public transfers to children, incomes, and other variables.

The coefficient β in our earlier work (see, e.g., Becker and Tomes 1979) measures the marginal propensity to bequeath wealth to children when parents can leave debt to children and when human wealth is not distinguished from other wealth. Our earlier work and Section 3 of the present paper show that this propensity depends on the generosity of parents toward children and may not be sensitive to the level of income. However, it is likely to be large in most families (see Sec. 3). Such a presumption motivated the assumption in our earlier work that $\beta > h$, an assumption used to identify β and h from the coefficients in an equation such as (18).

Goldberger (1985, pp. 19–20) correctly states that we did not provide an independent way to evaluate this assumption. The present paper makes progress toward the goal of identification because h can be determined from knowledge of the coefficients in the equation for the earnings of parents and children in (richer) families who leave positive bequests to children. Given h, β^* (or a more general relation between β^* and parents' earnings) can be determined from knowledge of the coefficients on parents' or on grandparents' earnings in the earnings equation for poorer families who are capital constrained. Even β—the marginal propensity of parents to bequeath wealth to children—might be determined from information on the relation between the consumption of parents and children in richer families (see the next section).

Rich families can more readily self-finance a given investment in children than can poor and middle-level families. Richer families also have better than average endowments, which raises the wealth-maximizing investment in human capital by richer families above that by poorer families. Empirical observations strongly indicate that richer families come closer to financing the optimal investment in the human capital of children than do poorer families. This indicates that the wealth effect on investments in children dominates the endowment effect. The wealth effect would dominate if endowments regress strongly to the mean, for then the endowments of richer children would be much below those of their parents and the endowments of poorer children would be much above those of their parents. The evidence considered in Section 6 does suggest that endowments relevant to earnings do regress strongly to the mean.

If returns on assets are not highly sensitive to earnings and endowments, the greater resources available to rich families to finance wealth-maximizing investments in children imply that equilibrium marginal rates of return on investments in children are lower in richer families than they are in more capital constrained poor and middle-level families even though endowments and average rates of return are higher in richer families. Equilibrium marginal rates then tend to decline, perhaps not monotonically, as earnings of parents rise. Eventually, marginal rates on human capital would equal the rate of return on assets, and then marginal rates would be relatively constant as parents' earnings rose. Poorer children are at a disadvantage both because they inherit lower endowments and because capital constraints on their parents limit the market value of the endowments that they do inherit.

If marginal rates are lower in richer families, a small redistribution of human capital away from these families and toward children from poorer families would raise the average marginal rate of return across different families. This would raise efficiency even though endowments and the average productivity of investments in children are greater in richer families (see also Becker 1967, 1975). The usual conflict between "equity," as measured by inequality, and efficiency is absent because a redistribution of investments toward less advantaged children is equivalent to an improvement in the efficiency of capital markets.

Larger public expenditures on the human capital of children in families subject to capital constraints raise the total amount invested in these children even when public and private expenditures are perfect substitutes. The reason is that public expenditures increase the total resources of a family if taxes are imposed on other families. An increase in family resources in capital constrained families is shared between parents and investments in children in a ratio determined by the marginal propensity to invest (β^*). If public and private expenditures are perfect substitutes, the fraction $1 - \beta^*$ of government expenditures on children is offset by compensatory responses of their parents. That is, to further equity toward other family members, even constrained parents redistribute some time and expenditures away from children who benefit from government expenditures to siblings and themselves. Compensatory responses of parents apparently greatly weaken the effects of public health programs, food supplements to poorer pregnant women, some Head Start programs, and social security programs (see the discussion in Becker [1981, pp. 125–26, 251–53]).

We saw earlier in Section 2 that the total investment in children in families with positive bequests to children is unaffected by public expenditures on children that are perfect substitutes for parents' expenditures. Parents reduce their own expenditures to offset fully such public expenditures. However, public and private expenditures may not be perfect substitutes. If, for example, public expenditures raise rates of return on family expenditures, increased public expenditures could even raise family expenditures because a "substitution effect" works against the "redistribution effect."

Goldberger criticizes us (1985, pp. 9–10; Simon [in press] repeats Goldberger's criticism) because we emphasize redistribution or income effects at the expense of substitution effects when discussing various public programs. Since our first joint paper we have explicitly noted that government programs may have substitution effects by changing rates of return on parental investments in children (see Becker and Tomes 1976, p. S156). However, we have emphasized the redistribution effects of many programs—including Head Start programs, welfare, aid to pregnant women, and social security—because the redistribution effects are clear, while substitution effects are not clear, even in direction. For example, what is the substitution effect of a social security program? Or is there evidence that Head Start programs raise rather than lower marginal rates of return on parents' expenditures? (See Becker 1981, p. 126.) Although tuition subsidies to education may appear to raise rates of return on parents' expenditures on education, actually they might lower marginal rates of return when combined with rationing of places (see Peltzman 1973).

Redistributions of expenditures within families induced by government subsidies can explain why many programs appear to have weak effects on participants (see the discussion in Becker [1981, pp. 125–26, 251–53]). Of course, weak effects on participants do not imply that substitution effects are negligible or that they reinforce redistribution effects, but weak effects do imply that these programs do not have strong offsetting substitution effects.

Capital constrained parents could finance expenditures on children by reducing their life-cycle savings if children could be counted on to care for elderly parents. In many societies, poorer and middle-income-level parents are supported during old age by children instead of by the sale of gold, jewelry, rugs, land, houses, or other assets that could be accumulated by parents at younger ages. Our analysis suggests that these parents choose to rely on children instead of on assets because rates of return on investments in children are higher than they are on other assets.

In effect, poorer and middle-level parents and children often have an implicit contract, enforced imperfectly by social sanctions, that parents invest in children in return for support during old age. Both parents and children would be made better off by such contracts if investments in children yield a high return, where included in the yield is any insurance provided by children against an unusually long old age.

3. Assets and Consumption

Our analysis implies that bequests and gifts of assets to children do not rise rapidly until marginal rates of return on investments in children are reduced to the rate on assets. Further increases in contributions from parents then mainly take the form of assets rather than of human capital because returns on assets are less sensitive to the amount accumulated. These conclusions imply that most bequests to children are found in a relatively small number of richer families and that the ratio of assets to human capital of children would rise as parents' wealth rose. The empirical evidence clearly indicates that assets and income from nonhuman capital are much more important in richer than in poorer families.

Empirical studies also indicate that the proportion of income saved remains reasonably constant or that it rises as income, including "permanent" income, increases (see the studies reviewed in Mayer [1972]). However, these studies provide flawed measures of savings because investments in human capital and "capital gains or losses" from intergenerational increases or decreases in endowments are not considered savings. Lower- and middle-income families invest primarily in their children's human capital. Endowments tend to increase from parents to children at lower income levels and to decrease from parents to children at higher levels because of regression to the mean in endowments. Therefore, empirical studies understate relative savings by lower- and middle-income families because both intergenerational capital gains and investments in human capital are relatively larger in these families. We believe that an appropriate concept of savings may well show that the fraction saved declines as permanent income rises. After all, this would be expected if equilibrium marginal rates of return on investments in children decline as income increases.

Our conclusion that most bequests of assets are found in a relatively small number of richer families does not presuppose "class" differences in altruism or other class differences in the propensity to save, as in Kaldor (1956) and Pasinetti (1962), or as used in Atkinson (1983). In our analysis, all families have the same intrinsic tendency to save and leave estates because they are assumed to have the same altruism toward children. Still, apparent "class" differences in savings would exist because poorer families save mainly in the human capital of children, which are not recorded as savings or bequests.

The assets of a person are determined by bequests from parents and by his own life-cycle accumulations. We assume that parents choose bequests by maximizing their expected utility, subject to the expected earnings and life-cycle asset accumulation of children. To develop further our analysis of bequests, we must turn to an explicit treatment of utility maximization by parents. We continue to assume, until the next section, that each adult has one child without marriage.

Suppose that the utility function of parents is additively separable in their own consumption and in various characteristics of children. Most of our analysis does not depend on a specific measure of these characteristics as long as they are positively related to the total resources of children. However, we can simplify the relation between the consumption by parents and children by assuming that parents' utility depends on the utility of children as in

$$U_t = u(Z_t) + \delta U_{t+1},$$ (20)

where Z_t is the consumption of parents and δ is a constant that measures the altruism of parents.

If the preference function given by equation (20) is the same for all generations and if consumption during childhood is ignored, then the utility of the parent indirectly would equal the discounted sum of the utilities from the consumption of all descendants:

$$U_t = \sum_{i=0}^{\infty} \delta^i u(Z_{t+i}).$$ (21)

The utility of parents depends directly only on the utility of children, but it depends indirectly on all descendants because children are concerned about their descendants.

We assume that parents succeed in maximizing their "dynastic" utility, as represented by equation (21). This rules out bargaining by children to obtain larger transfers than those that maximize parents' utility. A more general assumption is that parents maximize a weighted average of their own and their children's utility, with weights determined by bargaining power (see the normative use of this assumption in Nerlove, Razin, and Sadka [1984]); however, this generalization would not change any major conclusions.

With perfect certainty about rates of return and incomes in all generations, the first-order conditions to maximize utility are the usual ones. For example, with a constant elasticity of substitution in consumption,

$$u'(Z) = Z^{-\sigma},$$ (22)

where $\sigma > 0$, and

$$\ln Z_{t+1} = \frac{1}{\sigma} \ln(1 + r_{t+1})\delta + \ln Z_t,$$ (23)

where r_{t+1} measures the marginal rate of return to investments in children in period t. With an exponential utility function,

$$u'(Z) = e^{-pZ}, \quad p > 0,$$ (24)

and

$$Z_{t+1} = \frac{1}{p}\ln (1 + r_{t+1})\delta + Z_t. \qquad (25)$$

If parents could finance expenditures on their children with debt that becomes the obligation of children, the marginal cost of funds would equal the rate on assets in all families. Then equation (23) or equation (25) implies that the relative or absolute change in consumption between generations would be the same in all families that are equally altruistic (δ) and that have equal degrees of substitution (σ or p). Each family would maintain its relative or absolute consumption position over generations, and consumption would not regress to the mean. Stated differently, any degree of relative or absolute inequality in consumption in the parents' generation would then be fully transmitted to the children's generation.

Nevertheless, the earnings of children would still regress to the mean, regardless of the altruism of parents, as long as endowments are not fully inherited by children (see Sec. 2). Consumption does not automatically regress to the mean when earnings do because parents can anticipate that their children would tend to earn less or more than they do. They can use debt and assets to offset the effect on wealth of the expected regression in earnings.

Therefore, although earnings may regress to the mean, well-being as measured by consumption would not regress at all if parents have full access to capital markets to finance investments in their children's human capital. The assets bequeathed to children would rise and the debt bequeathed would fall as parents' earnings rose. This crucial distinction between regression across generations in earnings and consumption appears to have been ignored in the extensive literature on the mobility of families.

Still, the main implication of equations such as (23) and (25) is disquieting, namely, that all initial differences among families in consumption and total resources are fully transmitted to future descendants. Surely, the resources of the current generation are essentially independent of the resources of their distant ancestors. Several forces are responsible for the decay over time in the influence of the past on consumption and total resources. These include difficulties in transmitting debt to children, uncertainty about the future, the effect of parents' wealth on fertility, and imperfect assortative mating. We consider these variables in turn.

Consumption is fully separated from earnings only when children can be obligated for debts created by parents. If debt cannot be created for children (see the discussion in Sec. 2), parents without assets could not offset any upward regression in the endowments and earnings of their children. Parents would face a complicated maximization problem because capital constraints may be binding only for some descendants. The results of utility maximization can be summarized by endogenously determined subjective discount rates and marginal rates of return for each generation of a family that guide as well as reflect the decisions for that generation. These shadow prices exceed the rate on assets whenever constraints on access to debt prevent borrowing from children. Discount rates of (richer) parents with sufficient assets to raise or lower their bequests to children would equal the rate on assets.

We argue in Section 2 that equilibrium marginal rates of return of constrained parents tend to decline as their earnings become larger. Then equation (23) or equation (25) implies that the relative or absolute growth in consumption between generations would also decline as the earnings of parents rose. However, the relative or absolute growth in consumption between generations would be constant among richer families who receive a marginal rate of return equal to the rate on assets. Therefore, the consumption of children would regress more rapidly upward to the mean in poor families than downward to the mean in rich families. This produces a convex relation between the consumption of parents and children. At the same time, earnings regress more slowly upward in poor families than they regress downward in rich families.

Assets bequeathed to children in richer families act as a buffer to offset any regression to the mean in the earnings of children. The richest families could maintain their consumption over time compared to less rich families only by increasing their bequests sufficiently to offset the stronger downward regression in the earnings of the richest children. As a result, bequests could regress away from the mean.

Our analysis of consumption has assumed perfect certainty, although uncertainty about much of the luck of future generations is not fully insurable or diversifiable. If each generation knows the yields on investments in the human capital of children and in bequests to children, but may not have perfect certainty about the earnings of children and is still more uncertain about subsequent generations, then the first-order condition for maximization of expected utility is

$$\varepsilon_t u'(Z_{t+1}) = \left(\frac{\delta^{-1}}{1 + r_{t+1}}\right) u'(Z_t), \tag{26}$$

where ε_t refers to expectations taken at generation t before any new information about earnings and other wealth of descendants is acquired between t and $t + 1$.

With the exponential function, this first-order condition becomes

$$Z_{t+1} = c + \frac{1}{p}\ln (1 + r_{t+1})\delta + Z_t + n_{t+1}, \qquad (27)$$

where c is a positive constant and where n_{t+1}, the distribution of fluctuations in Z_{t+1} around $\hat{Z}_{t+1}$, does not depend on Z_t. If the capital market permitted all families to finance the wealth-maximizing investments in their children, $r_{t+1} = r_a$ in all families, where r_a is the asset rate. Then equation (27) implies that the growth in consumption follows a random walk with drift (Kotlikoff, Shoven, and Spivak [1986] derive a similar result when the length of life is uncertain). More generally, equation (27) shows that, if the utility function is exponential, uncertainty adds a random term to consumption but does not basically change the implications of our analysis concerning the degree of regression to the mean in consumption.

A second-order approximation to the left-hand side of equation (26) readily shows that the effect of uncertainty on the degree of regression toward the mean with more general utility functions than the exponential depends on the signs and magnitudes of second- and higher-order derivatives of the utility function.[7] Uncertainty could induce regression toward the mean in consumption even when there would be none with certainty. However, uncertainty could also induce regression away from the mean, or greater rates of regression toward the mean at higher rather than at lower levels of consumption, with utility functions that otherwise seem as empirically relevant as those having opposite implications. Consequently, we cannot make any strong statement concerning the effect of uncertainty on the degree of regression toward the mean in the consumption of parents and children.

---

[7] If r_{t+1} is constant, a second-order approximation to u'_{t+1} in eq. (26) gives

$$\frac{d\hat{Z}_{t+1}}{dZ_t} = \left(\frac{u''_t}{u'_t}\right)\left[\frac{u'_{t+1} + \dfrac{vu'''_{t+1}}{2}}{u''_{t+1} + \dfrac{vu''''_{t+1}}{2}}\right]$$

where u'''_{t+1} is the third derivative, u''''_{t+1} is the fourth derivative of utility from consumption in the $t+1$ first generation, and v is the given variance of n_{t+1} around $\hat{Z}_{t+1}$. The term on the left-hand side is more likely to be less than one (regression toward the mean) when $(u)''''$ is large relative to $(u)'''$.

4. Fertility and Marriage

Regression toward the mean in marriage and the positive effect of wealth on fertility help explain why differences in consumption and total resources among richer families do not persist indefinitely into future generations. Here we only sketch out an analysis. The implications of fertility and marriage for consumption and bequests are also discussed in Becker and Tomes (1984) and Becker and Barro (1985).

Let us first drop the assumption that all parents have only one child and generalize the utility function in equation (20) to

$$U_p = u(Z_p) + a(n) n U_c, \tag{28}$$

with $a' < 0$, where U_c is the utility of each of the n identical children and $a(n)$ is the degree of altruism per child. The first-order condition for the optimal number of children is that the marginal utility and marginal cost of children are equal. The marginal cost of children to parents equals net expenditures on children, including any bequests and other gifts. The marginal costs are determined by the circumstances and decisions of parents.

The previous section showed that the consumption and total resources of wealthy families may not regress down because these families can offset the downward regression in the earnings of their children by sufficiently large gifts and bequests. Fortunately, this unrealistic implication does not hold when the number of children can vary. Richer families tend to spend some of their greater resources on additional children. This reduces the bequest to each child below what it would be if they did not increase the number of children (see the proofs in Becker and Barro [1985]). A positive response of fertility to increases in wealth causes consumption and wealth per child to regress down, perhaps rapidly.

Poor and middle-income families without assets who are prevented from leaving debt to their children must trade off between earnings of each child, number of children, and parent consumption. The human capital invested in each child and, hence, the earnings of each child would then be negatively related to the number of children, as found in many studies (see, e.g., Blake 1981). The degree of regression to the mean in earnings among these families would be lower if fertility and parents' earnings are negatively related than if they are unrelated.

We do not have much to add to our previous analysis (see Becker and

Tomes 1976; Becker 1981, chap. 6; Tomes 1981) of responses to differences between children. This analysis implies that richer families invest more human capital in better-endowed children and that they compensate other children with larger gifts and bequests. Poorer families who primarily invest in human capital face a conflict between the efficiency of greater investments in better-endowed children and the equity of greater investments in less well endowed children.

Despite the claim that observed differences between siblings in earnings is helpful in determining the degree of intergenerational mobility in earnings (see, e.g., Brittain 1977, pp. 36–37), there is no necessary connection between the relation among siblings and the degree of intergenerational mobility. The reason is that differences in earnings between siblings is determined by characteristics within a single generation, such as the substitution between siblings in the utility function of parents, whereas intergenerational mobility in earnings is determined by differences across generations, such as the regression toward the mean of endowments (for a further discussion, see Tomes [1984]).

Regression to the mean in marriage—called imperfect positive assortative mating—also increases the degree of regression to the mean in earnings, consumption, and assets. However, the effect of marriage is less obvious than it may appear because parents often can anticipate the marital sorting of children. For example, wealthy parents would use gifts and bequests to offset some of the effects on the well-being of their children of the tendency for rich children to marry down, just as they use gifts and bequests to offset the effect of the regression downward in endowments. Although a full analysis of the interaction between the behavior of parents and expectations about the marriages of children is complicated by bargaining between in-laws on the gifts to be made to their children (some issues are discussed in Becker [1981, chap. 7] and Becker and Tomes [1984]), one cannot be satisfied with the many models that simply ignore expectations about children's marriages (see, e.g., Stiglitz 1969; Pryor 1973; Blinder 1976; Atkinson 1983).

Fertility and marriage have not been fully integrated into our analysis of intergenerational mobility—we only would insert "fully" into Goldberger's statement that "it's fair to say that [fertility and marriage are] not integrated into his intergenerational system" (1985, p. 13). However, the discussion in this section, the discussion of fertility in Becker and Barro (1985), and that of marriage in Becker and Tomes (1984) indicate to us that a utility-maximizing approach can integrate fertility, marriage, and intergenerational mobility into a common framework with useful implications.

5. Empirical Studies[8]

Only a few empirical studies link the earnings or wealth of different generations because of difficulties in gathering such information and because of insufficient interest by social scientists. Tables 22 and 23 present estimates from several studies of the degree of regression to the mean in earnings, income, and wealth, with coefficients of determination (when available), the number of observations, and notes about other variables (if any) included in each regression.

Table 22 has evidence on the earnings or incomes of sons and fathers from three studies based on separate data sets for the United States and one study each for England, Sweden, Switzerland, and Norway.[9] Although the average age of fathers and sons is quite different except in the Geneva study, both Atkinson (1981) and Behrman and Taubman (1983) present evidence that such differences in age do not greatly affect the estimated degree of regression to the mean.

The point estimates for most of the studies indicate that a 10% increase in father's earnings (or income) raises son's earnings by less than 2%. The highest point estimate is for York, England, where son's hourly earnings appear to be raised by 4.4%. However, the confidence intervals are sizable in all studies except Malmö because fathers' earnings "explain" a small fraction of the variation in the earnings of sons. Moreover, response errors and the transitory component in father's earnings (or income) may severely bias these regression coefficients.[10] Furthermore, the analysis in Section 2 indicates that transitory variations in lifetime earnings, and the omission of the earnings of grandparents biases these regression coefficients downward. However, the error from omitting grandparents' earnings would be small if parents' earnings do not have a large effect (see eq. [18]) and if the transitory in lifetime earnings is not large.

---

[8] We are indebted to Robert Hauser for bringing to our attention several studies of intergenerational mobility that use the data on Wisconsin high school graduates and for guiding us through various adjustments that correct for response and measurement errors in these studies.

[9] These studies have various limitations. Hauser et al. (1975) sample families in only one state (Wisconsin) and only include sons who graduated from high school; all fathers in the Behrman and Taubman (1983) sample are twins; fathers in the Atkinson (1981) sample had modest earnings in the city of York; fathers in the de Wolff and van Slijpe (1973) study are from the city of Malmö; Soltow (1965) uses a very small sample from one city in Norway; and Girod (1984) surveys students in the canton of Geneva.

[10] These estimates may also be biased (the direction is not clear) because information is not available on hours worked and nonpecuniary income from employment (see the discussion in Becker and Tomes [1984, n. 13]).

Hauser et al. (1975) reduce response errors and the transitory component by using a four-year average of parents' income and a three-year average of son's earnings, while Hauser (in press) uses a four-year average of parents' income and a five-year average of son's earnings during his initial period of labor-force participation. Tsai (1983) not only averages incomes of parents over several years but also uses a retrospective report on their income in 1957. At Hauser's suggestion, we have corrected for the response errors in father's earnings by using the analysis in Bielby and Hauser (1977). Behrman and Taubman (1983) exclude sons who have less than four years of work experience because their earnings do not represent well their lifetime earnings. De Wolff and van Slijpe (1973) and Freeman (1981) reduce the importance of the transitory component by using the average income in father's occupation as an estimate of his lifetime earnings.

Despite these adjustments for response errors and transitory incomes, point estimates of the regression coefficients for earnings and incomes are rather low in all the studies (except for large incomes in Sweden). Moreover, a study in progress by Elizabeth Peters (1985) that uses data from the National Longitudinal Survey (the same survey used by Freeman [1981]) also finds a small coefficient (below .2) when a simple average of four years of son's earnings is regressed on a simple average of five years of father's earnings.

Some indirect evidence of sizable regression toward the mean in lifetime earnings is provided by life-cycle variations in earnings. By definition, endowments are fixed over a lifetime. Therefore, earnings should be more closely related over the life cycle than across generations because endowments are imperfectly transmitted from parent to child (endowments are not a "fixed effect" across generations). Stated differently, relative to other members of his cohort, a person is usually much more similar to himself at different ages than is a father similar to his son when they are of the same age. The correlation coefficient between the "permanent" component of male earnings at different ages has been estimated from a seven-year panel to be about .7 in the United States (see Lillard and Willis 1978, table 1). The inheritability of endowments from fathers to sons is surely less, probably much less, than is the correlation between the permanent component of earnings at different ages.

The evidence in table 22 suggests that neither the inheritability of endowments by sons (h) nor the propensity to invest in children's human capital because of capital constraints (β^*) is large. For example, if the regression coefficient between the lifetime earnings of fathers and sons is $\leq .4$ and if the transitory variance in lifetime earnings is less than one-third of the variance in total lifetime earnings, then both h and β^*

TABLE 22

Regressions of Son's Income or Earnings on Father's Income or Earnings in Linear, Semilog, and Log-linear Form

Location and Son's Year	Father's Year	Variables			Coefficient	t	R^2	N	ε	Author
		Dependent	Independent	Other						
Wisconsin: 1965–67	1957–60	E	IP	None	.15	8.5	.03	2069	.13	Hauser, Sewell, and Lutterman (1975)
*	1957–60	Log E	IP	None	.0006	10.6	.05	N.A.	.09	Hauser (in press)†
1974	1957–60	Log E	Log IP	None	.28‡	15.7	.09	2493	.28	Tsai (1983)†
United States, 1981–82	1981–82	Log E§	Log E§	None	.18	3.7	.02	722	.18	Behrman and Taubman (1983)
United States: 1969 (young white)	When son was 14	Log H	Log $F3$	"	.16	3.2	...	1607	.16	Freeman (1981)
1966 (older white)	When son was 14	Log H	Log $F3$	"	.22	7.3	...	2131	.22	Freeman (1981)
1969 (young black)	When son was 14	Log H	Log $F3$	"	.17	1.9	...	634	.17	Freeman (1981)
1966 (older black)	When son was 14	Log H	Log $F3$	‖	.02	0.4	...	947	.02	Freeman (1981)

York, England:									
1975–78	Log H	Log W	None	.44	3.4	.06	198	.44	Atkinson (1981)
1975–78	Log W	Log W	None	.36	3.3	.03	307	.36	Atkinson (1981)
Malmö, Sweden,				.08	1.8	.19	545	.17″	* de Wolff and van
1963	Log I	ICD	None	.12	2.4	.19	545	.13	Slijpe (1973)
				.69	10.9	.19	545	.79	
Geneva, Switzerland,									
1980	IHH	IHH	None	.31	4.1	.02	801	.13	Girod (1984)
Sarpsborg, Norway,									
1960	Log I	Log I	None	.14	1.2	.01	115	.14	Soltow (1965)

NOTE.—ε = elasticity of son's income or earnings with respect to father's income or earnings; E = earnings; H = hourly earnings; I = income; B = income in three-digit occupation; ICD = income-class dummy; IHH = household income; IP = parents' income; W = weekly earnings.

*First 5 years in the labor force.

†Also Robert M. Hauser (personal communication, October 2, 1984).

‡Adjusted for response variability.

§Adjusted for work experience. Sons with work experience of 4 years or less were excluded. The regression was weighted so that each father had equal weight.

‖Work experience, three dummies for region of residence at age 14, five dummies for type of place of residence at age 14, and a dummy for living in one parent/female home at age 14.

″The elasticities are values between pairs of income classes.

would be less than .28 if $h = \beta^*$; moreover, $h \leq .6$ if $\beta^* = 0$, and $h \leq 0$ if $\beta^* \geq .4$ (see n. 4).

If capital constraints completely disappeared, would the same families dominate the best-paid and most prestigious occupations? (For this fear, see the often-cited article by Herrnstein [1971].) The answer is no: families in the best occupations would change frequently even in "meritocracies" because endowments relevant to earnings are not highly inheritable—h is less than .6 and may be much less. Another way to see this is by noting that, if the relation between the lifetime earnings of fathers and sons is no larger than .4, practically all the advantages or disadvantages of ancestors tend to disappear in only three generations: "from shirtsleeves to shirtsleeves in three generations." Parents in such "open" societies have little effect on the earnings of grandchildren and later descendants. Therefore, they have little incentive to try to affect the earnings of descendants through family reputation and other means.

In particular, any lifetime "culture of poverty" tends to disappear between generations because characteristics that determine earnings are variable between generations. For example, children of parents who earn only half the mean can expect to earn above 80% of the mean in their generation, and their own children can expect to earn only slightly below the mean.

Yet, family background is still important. For example, even if the degree of regression to the mean is 80%, children of parents whose earnings are twice the mean tend to earn 30% more than the children of parents whose earnings are only 50% of the mean. A 30% premium is large relative to the 10%–15% premium from union membership (see Lewis 1986) or to the 16% premium from two additional years of schooling (see Mincer 1974). Children from successful families do have a significant economic advantage.

Families who are poor partly because of discrimination against their race, caste, or other "permanent" characteristics may advance more slowly. Clearly, blacks in the United States have advanced much more slowly than have immigrants, partly because of public and private discrimination against blacks. Although many have studied changes over time in the average position of blacks relative to whites (see, e.g., the excellent recent study by Smith [1984]), few have studied the relation between earnings of sons and fathers in black families. The evidence in table 22 suggests that older blacks regress more rapidly to the mean than do older whites, although the evidence may be spurious because response errors are higher and apparently more complicated for blacks (see Bielby, Hauser, and Featherman 1977). Opportunities for younger blacks clearly have improved during the last 20 years. The evidence in table 22 that younger blacks regress more slowly suggests that discrimination raises the regression toward the mean in earnings (see the theoretical discussion in Sec. 2).

Goldberger points out (1985, pp. 29–30) that our earlier work uses much higher illustrative values for β than the values of β^* suggested by the empirical evidence in this section. But β and β^* are different: to repeat, β refers to the propensity to bequeath wealth to children by families who are not capital constrained. Therefore, low β^*'s are not inconsistent with high β's. A low β^* combined with a low h does imply sizable intergenerational mobility in earnings, whereas a high β implies low intergenerational mobility in wealth and consumption among families that bequeath wealth to their children (we ignore the distinction between the wealth and consumption of children and the wealth and consumption per child; see Secs. 3 and 4).

We readily admit (see Sec. 1) that the distinction in the present paper between earnings, wealth, and consumption as well as our attention to intergenerational capital constraints and fertility behavior have greatly clarified our thinking about intergenerational mobility. However, since a low β^* is not inconsistent with a high β, we see no reason why the empirical evidence of a low β^* "would occasion the tearing of [our] hair and the gnashing of [our] teeth" (Goldberger 1985, pp. 29–30). Moreover, aside from fertility and marriage, we still expect high values for β (see Sec. 3).

Table 23 presents evidence from three studies for the United States and Great Britain on the relation between the wealth of parents and children. Harbury and Hitchens (1979) and Menchik (1979) use probates of wealthy estates, while Wahl (1985) uses data on wealth from the 1860 and 1870 censuses. The estimated elasticity between the assets of fathers and sons is about .7 in the United States for probated assets in recent years but is less both for assets of living persons in the nineteenth century and for probated assets in Britain.

Wahl finds a small negative coefficient for grandparents' wealth when instruments are used for both parents' and grandparents' wealth but a positive coefficient for grandparents' wealth when their actual wealth is used. The theoretical analysis incorporated into equation (18) does imply a small negative coefficient for grandparents' wealth when the effect of parents' wealth is not large, as is the case in her study. However, Behrman and Taubman (1985) usually find small positive (but not statistically significant) coefficients on grandparents' schooling in their study of years of schooling for three generations. Their findings may be inconsistent with our theory, although equation (18) does imply a negligible coefficient for grandfathers' schooling when the coefficient on parents' schooling is small—it is less than .25 in their study.

The data in tables 22 and 23 are too limited to determine with confi-

TABLE 23

Regressions of Son's Wealth on Father's and Grandfather's Wealth

Location and Son's Year	Father's Year	Notes	Coefficient for Father's Wealth	Coefficient for Grandfather's Wealth	R^2	N	Author
United States: Up to 1976	1930–46	*†	.69 (7.5)	...	.29	173	Menchik (1979)
	1860	†	.76	...	.25	199	Menchik (1979)
1860	1860	‡§	.21 (1.6)	.05 (2.0)	.46	45	Wahl (1985)
1860	1860	‖§	.26 (2.1)	-.008 (-1.6)	.14	106	Wahl (1985)
1870	1870	‡§	.30 (5.5)	.05 (2.4)	.27	46	Wahl (1985)
1870	1870	‖§	.46 (2.1)	-.03 (-1.6)	.10	125	Wahl (1985)

Great Britain:							
1934, 1956–57	1902, 1924–26	†	.48 (3.7)	...	...	...	Harbury and Hitchens (1979)
1956–57, 1965	1916, 1928	†	.48 (5.3)	...	...	...	Harbury and Hitchens (1979)
1973	1936	†	.59 (8.4)	...	...		Harbury and Hitchens (1979)

NOTE.—*t*-statistics are in parentheses.

*Menchik also includes the following as explanatory variables: number of years between death of parents and child, number of child's siblings (plus one), and stepchild dummy.

†Log-linear regression.

‡Wahl uses an instrument for parent's wealth. The following variables are used to create the instrument: age of household head (and age squared), occupational and regional dummies, residence farm/nonfarm, and whether parent is bloodline. Grandparent's wealth is actual wealth.

§Wahl uses data for parents and maternal grandparents instead of for fathers and grandfathers.

‖Wahl uses instruments for both parent's and grandparent's wealth. She creates the instruments by using the list given in the daggered note above.

dence whether wealth or earnings regress less rapidly to the mean, although wealth appears to regress less rapidly. Wealth would regress slowly if parents bequeath assets to children to buffer the total wealth and consumption of children against regression in their earnings. However, wealth would regress rapidly if wealthier parents have sufficiently more children than do poorer parents. Wahl (1985) does find a strong positive relation in the nineteenth century between the fertility and the wealth of parents.

Capital constraints on investments in children probably declined during this century in the United States and in many other countries because fertility declined, incomes rose, and government subsidies to education and to social security grew rapidly. Evidence in Goldin and Parsons (1984) is consistent with sizable capital constraints on poor families in the United States during the latter part of the nineteenth century. These families withdrew their children from school at early ages in order to raise the contribution of teenage children to family earnings. A weakening of capital constraints in the United States is also indicated by the decline over time in the inequality in years of schooling and by the declining influence of family background on education attainments of children (Featherman and Hauser 1976).

There is evidence that the influence of family background on the achievements of children is greater in less developed countries than it is in the United States. For example, father's education has a greater effect on son's education in both Bolivia and Panama than in the United States. Moreover, the influence of father's education apparently declined over time in Panama as well as in the United States (see Kelley, Robinson, and Klein 1981, pp. 27–66; Heckman and Hotz 1985).

6. Summary and Discussion

This paper develops a model of the transmission of earnings, assets, and consumption from parents to children and later descendants. The model is based on utility maximization by parents concerned about the welfare of their children. The degree of intergenerational mobility, or the rise and fall of families, is determined by the interaction of utility-maximizing behavior with investment and consumption opportunities in different generations and with different kinds of luck.

We assume that cultural and genetic endowments are automatically transmitted from parents to children, with the relation between the endowments of parents and children determined by the degree of "inheritability." The intergenerational mobility of earnings depends on the inheritability of endowments. Indeed, if all parents can readily borrow to finance the optimal investments in children, the degree of intergenerational mobility in earnings essentially would equal the inheritability of endowments.

However, poor families often have difficulty financing investments in children because loans to supplement their limited resources are not readily available when human capital is the collateral. Such capital market restrictions lower investments in children from poorer families. Intergenerational mobility in earnings then depends not only on the inheritability of endowments but also on the willingness of poor families to self-finance investments in their children.

The degree of intergenerational mobility in earnings is also determined by the number of children in different families. Additional children in a family reduce the amount invested in each one when investments must be financed by the family. Consequently, a negative relation between family size and the earnings of parents also reduces the intergenerational mobility of earnings.

Assets act as a buffer to offset regression to the mean in the endowments and, hence, in the earnings of children. In particular, successful families bequeath assets to children to offset the expected downward regression in earnings.

Parents with good access to capital markets can transfer assets or debt to nullify any effect of regression to the mean in earnings on the consumption of children. This effectively separates the relation between the consumption by parents and children from inheritability of endowments and regression to the mean in earnings. Consumption in poorer and middle-level families who do not want to leave bequests tends to regress upward because equilibrium marginal rates of return on investments in the human capital of children tend to be higher in families with low earnings. Consumption and total resources in richer families that do leave bequests to children regress down to the mean, mainly because fertility is positively related to parents' wealth. In this way, larger families dilute the wealth bequeathed to each child. Imperfect assortative mating also tends to cause consumption and wealth to regress to the mean.

We have examined about a dozen empirical studies relating the earnings, income, and assets of parents and children. Aside from families victimized by discrimination, regression to the mean in earnings in the United States and other rich countries appears to be rapid, and the regression in assets is sizable. Almost all earnings advantages and disadvantages of ancestors are wiped out in three generations. Poverty would not seem to be a "culture" that persists for several generations.

Rapid regression to the mean in earnings implies that both the inheritability of endowments and the capital constraints on investments in children are not large. Presumably, these constraints became less important as fertility declined over time and as incomes and subsidies to education grew over time.

In this paper and in previous work we claim that a theory of family behavior is necessary to understand inequality and the rise and fall of families. In making the claim, however, we have not intended to downgrade the importance of empirically oriented studies. Indeed, we have always viewed them as a necessary complement to theoretical analysis. We apologize if our claims for maximizing theory could be interpreted as denying the value of empirical and statistical work that is not explicitly based on a model of maximizing behavior.

We still claim, however, that our model of family behavior is useful in understanding the effect of public policies and other events on inequality and the rise and fall of families. Here we part company with Goldberger (1985), who denies whether our theory adds much to formulations not based on a model of maximizing behavior. He claims (see esp. pp. 30–33) that our theory has few implications that differ from simple regressive models of the earnings or incomes of different generations of a family. Perhaps some perspective about the validity of his claim can be acquired through a brief summary of a few implications of our analysis.

1. Earnings regress more rapidly to the mean in richer than in poorer families. Moreover, even though endowments of children and earnings of parents are positively related, a small redistribution of investment in human capital from richer to poorer families would tend to raise the overall efficiency of investments. The reason is that investments by poorer families are constrained by limited access to funds.

2. Unlike earnings, consumption would regress more rapidly to the mean in poorer than in richer families if fertility is not related to parents' wealth. Indeed, consumption then would not tend to regress at all among rich families who leave gifts and bequests to their children.

3. However, our analysis also implies that fertility is positively related to the wealth of parents. This dilutes the wealth that can be left to each child and induces a regression to the mean among rich families in the relation between consumption per child and the consumption of parents.

We do not know of any other analysis of the family that has these implications, regardless of the approach used. The implications have not been tested empirically, but Goldberger (1985) mainly questions the novelty of the implications of our analysis, not its empirical validity. Additional implications are obtained by considering the effect of public programs.

Becker and Tomes (1979, pp. 1175–78) show that a progressive income tax could raise the long-run relative inequality in after-tax income. The standard deviation clearly falls, but average incomes also fall eventually because parents reduce their bequests to children. Goldberger's useful calculations (1985, pp. 24–25) support our analytical proof that an increase in the degree of progressivity could actually lead to an increase in after-tax inequality. His calculations suggest, however, that a couple of generations would elapse before relative inequality might even begin to increase. He overstates the delay before which inequality might begin to increase, and he understates the likelihood of an eventual net increase, by not considering the effect of greater progressivity on the contribution to inequality of the unsystematic component of the tax system (see Becker and Tomes 1979, pp. 1177–78).[11]

We are not concerned with inequality in this paper, but we believe that the model developed here also implies that after-tax inequality might increase when the degree of progressivity increases. Income taxes alter behavior in our analysis partly by affecting the coefficients in equations such as (11), (18), and (27). Empirical or regressive models that start with such equations or with other equations not derived from an explicit model of behavior across generations would have difficulty in analyzing the effects of income taxes on the coefficients in these equations because such models usually provide insufficient guidance to how these coefficients are determined.

This conclusion applies to other policies as well and to various changes in the environment faced by families. Indeed, the issues are not special to inequality and intergenerational mobility but apply to efforts to understand all social behavior.

To illustrate with a different public program, consider the effects of

[11] Although Goldberger admits that we only claim a possible long-run increase in inequality, he criticizes the statement that "perhaps this conflict between initial and equilibrium effects explains why the large growth in redistribution during the last fifty years has had only modest effects on after-tax inequality" (Becker [1981, p. 156]; a similar statement is in Becker and Tomes [1979, p. 1178]; Goldberger omits the "perhaps" in our statement and says we "conjecture"). He asks, "Is it true that over the past fifty years, the mean and variance of disposable income both fell? If not, what explanation has his model [i.e., Becker-Tomes] provided?" (1985, pp. 26–27). These are strange questions. We were not foolish enough to contend that only the tax system affected the growth of incomes during the past 50 years nor did we try to assess how other forces affected inequality. Since we could prove with our model that a progressive income tax need not lower inequality in the long run, and since inequality apparently did not decline significantly during the past 50 years, we speculated about whether progressive income taxes did lower inequality over this period. Surely, that speculation could be very relevant in forcing a reassessment of the common belief that progressive taxes lower inequality. Of course, other changes during this period could have masked a negative effect of income taxes on inequality, but this has to be proven rather than simply assumed.

public debt and social security on the consumption of different generations of a family. Barro (1974) uses a model of parent altruism that is similar to the model of altruism in this paper, when fertility is fixed, to question whether social security and public debt have significant effects on consumption. Parents who make positive bequests to children do not raise their consumption when they receive social security or revenue from the issue of public debt. Instead, they raise their bequests to offset the effect of these programs on the consumption of children. However, the consumption of altruistic parents who are constrained from leaving debt to children is raised by social security and public debt, and the consumption of their children is lowered (see Drazen 1978).

To avoid misunderstanding, we hasten to add that we do not claim that all public programs are neutralized through compensatory reductions within families. This is not true for poorer families in this example or for all families when fertility can vary (see Becker and Barro 1985). Moreover, we have shown that progressive income taxes reduce the incentive to invest in children. We claim not neutrality but that our analysis of family behavior is helpful in understanding the effects of various public programs on the rise and fall of families.

Systematic empirical evidence is necessary before this and other claims can be evaluated. We close by reiterating our belief that such evidence will confirm that the analysis of family behavior within a utility-maximizing framework provides many insights into the rise and fall of families in modern societies.

References

Atkinson, A. B. "On Intergenerational Income Mobility in Britain." *Journal of Post Keynesian Economics* 3, no. 2 (1981): 194–217.

———. *Social Justice and Public Policy.* Cambridge, Mass.: MIT Press, 1983.

Barro, Robert J. "Are Government Bonds Net Wealth?" *Journal of Political Economy* 82, no. 6 (1974): 1096–1117.

Becker, Gary S. "Human Capital and the Personal Distribution of Income: An Analytical Approach." Woytinsky Lecture no. 1. Ann Arbor: University of Michigan, Institute of Public Administration, 1967.

———. "A Theory of Social Interactions." *Journal of Political Economy* 82, no. 6 (1974): 1063–93.

———. *Human Cpital.* 2d ed. New York: Columbia University Press (for NBER), 1975.

———. *A Treatise on the Family.* Cambridge, Mass.: Harvard University Press, 1981.

Becker, Gary S., and Barro, Robert. "A Reformulation of the Economic Theory of Fertility." Discussion Paper no. 85-11. Chicago: Economics Research Center, NORC, October 1985.

Becker, Gary S., and Tomes, Nigel. "Child Endowments and the Quantity and Quality of Children." *Journal of Political Economy* 84, no. 4, pt. 2 (1976): S143–S162.

———. "An Equilibrium Theory of the Distribution of Income and Intergenerational Mobility." *Journal of Political Economy* 87, no. 6 (1979): 1153–89.

———. "Human Capital and the Rise and Fall of Families." Discussion Paper no. 84-10. Chicago: Economics Research Center, NORC, October 1984.

Behrman, Jere, and Taubman, Paul. "Intergenerational Transmission of Income and Wealth." *American Economic Review* 66, no. 2 (1976): 436–40.

———. "Intergenerational Mobility in Earnings in the U.S." Mimeographed. Philadelphia: University of Pennsylvania, Center for Household and Family Economics, 1983.

———. "Intergenerational Earnings and Mobility in the United States: Some Estimates and a Test of Becker's Intergenerational Endowments Model." *Review of Economics and Statistics* 67, no. 1 (1985): 144–51.

Bevan, D. L. "Inheritance and the Distribution of Wealth." *Economica* 46, no. 184 (1979): 381–402.

Bevan, D. L., and Stiglitz, J. E. "Intergenerational Transfers and Inequality." *Greek Economic Review* 1, no. 1 (1979): 6–26.

Bielby, William T., and Hauser, Robert M. "Response Error in Earnings Functions for Nonblack Males." *Sociological Methods and Research* 6, no. 2 (1977): 241–80.

Bielby, William T.; Hauser, Robert M.; and Featherman, David L. "Response Errors of Black and Nonblack Males in Models of the Intergenerational Transmission of Socioeconomic Status." *American Journal of Sociology* 82, no. 6 (1977): 1242–88.

Blake, Judith. "Family Size and the Quality of Children." *Demography* 18, no. 4 (1981): 421–42.

Blau, Peter M., and Duncan, Otis Dudley. *The American Occupational Structure.* New York: Wiley, 1967.

Blinder, Alan S. *Toward an Economic Theory of Income Distribution.* Cambridge, Mass.: MIT Press, 1974.

———. "Inequality and Mobility in the Distribution of Wealth." *Kyklos* 29, no. 4 (1976): 607–38.

Bloom, Benjamin S. *Human Characteristics and School Learning.* New York: McGraw-Hill, 1976.

Bowles, Samuel. "Schooling and Inequality from Generation to Generation." *Journal of Political Economy* 80, no. 3, pt. 2 (1972): S219–S251.

Brittain, John A. *The Inheritance of Economic Status.* Washington, D.C.: Brookings Institution, 1977.

Conlisk, John. "Can Equalization of Opportunity Reduce Social Mobility?" *American Economic Review* 64, no. 1 (1974): 80–90.

Dewey, John. "Galton's Statistical Methods." *Publications of the American Statistical Association* 1, no. 7 (1889): 331–34.

Drazen, Allan. "Government Debt, Human Capital and Bequests in a Life-Cycle Model." *Journal of Political Economy* 86, no. 3 (1978): 505–16.

Ehrlich, Isaac, and Ben-Zion, Uri. "Asset Management, Allocation of Time, and Returns to Saving." *Economic Inquiry* 14, no. 4 (1976): 558–86.

Featherman, David L., and Hauser, Robert M. "Changes in the Socioeconomic Stratification of the Races, 1962–1973." *American Journal of Sociology* 82, no. 3 (1976): 621–51.

Freeman, Richard B. "Black Economic Progress after 1964: Who Has Gained and Why?" In *Studies in Labor Markets,* edited by Sherwin Rosen. Chicago: University of Chicago Press (for NBER), 1981.

Girod, Roger. "Intra- and Intergenerational Income Mobility: A Geneva Survey (1950–1980)." Paper presented at the meeting of the International Sociological Association Research Committee on Stratification, Budapest, September 1984.

Goldberger, Arthur S. "Family Data Analysis: Assortment, Selection, and Transmission." Proposal to the National Science Foundation, Washington, D.C., 1979.

———. "Modelling the Economic Family." Woytinsky Lecture. Ann Arbor: University of Michigan, Institute of Public Administration, 1985.

Goldin, Claudia, and Parsons, Donald O. "Industrialization, Child Labor, and Family Economic Well-Being." Mimeographed. Philadelphia: University of Pennsylvania, Department of Economics, 1984.

Harbury, C. D., and Hitchens, D. M. W. N. *Inheritance and Wealth Inequality in Britain.* London: Allen & Unwin, 1979.

Hauser, Robert M. "Earnings Trajectories of Young Men." In *Social Stratification in Japan and the United States,* edited by D. J. Treiman and K. Tominaga. In press.

Hauser, Robert M.; Sewell, William H.; and Lutterman, Kenneth G. "Socioeconomic Background, Ability, and Achievement." In *Education, Occupation and Earnings,* edited by William H. Sewell and Robert M. Hauser. New York: Academic Press, 1975.

Heckman, James J., and Hotz, V. Joseph. "The Labor Market Earnings of Panamanian Males." Mimeographed. Chicago: University of Chicago, 1985.

Herrnstein, Richard J. "I.Q." *Atlantic* 228, no. 3 (1971): 43–58.

Kaldor, Nicholas. "Alternative Theories of Distribution." *Review of Economic Studies* 23, no. 2 (1956): 83–100.

Kelly, Jonathan; Robinson, Robert U.; and Klein, Herbert S. "A Theory of Social Mobility, with Data on Status Attainment in a Peasant Society." In *Research in Social Stratification and Mobility,* vol. 1, edited by Donald J. Treiman and Robert V. Robertson. Greenwich, Conn.: JAI, 1981.

Kotlikoff, Laurence J.; Shoven, John; and Spivak, Avia. "The Effect of Annuity Insurance on Savings and Inequality." In *Journal of Labor Economics* 4, no. 3 (1986).

Laitner, J. P. "Household Bequests, Perfect Expectations, and the National Distribution of Wealth." *Econometrica* 47, no. 5 (1979): 1175–93.

Lewis, H. Gregg. *Union Relative Wage Effects: A Survey.* Chicago: University of Chicago Press, 1986.

Lillard, Lee A., and Willis, Robert J. "Dynamic Aspects of Earning Mobility." *Econometrica* 46, no. 5 (1978): 985–1012.

Loury, Glenn C. "Intergenerational Transfers and the Distribution of Earnings." *Econometrica* 49, no. 4 (1981): 843–67.

Mandelbrot, Benoit. "Paretian Distributions and Income Maximization." *Quarterly Journal of Economics* 76, no. 1 (1962): 57–85.

Mayer, Thomas. *Permanent Income, Wealth, and Consumption*. Berkeley: University of California Press, 1972.

Meade, J. E. *The Just Economy*. Albany: State University of New York Press, 1976.

Menchik, Paul L. "Inter-generational Transmission of Inequality: An Empirical Study of Wealth Mobility." *Economica* 46, no. 184 (1979): 349–62.

Mincer, Jacob. *Schooling, Experience and Earnings*. New York: Columbia University Press (for NBER), 1974.

Nerlove, Marc; Razin, Assaf; and Sadka, Efraim. "Some Welfare Theoretic Implications of Endogenous Fertility." Mimeographed. Philadelphia: University of Pennsylvania, Department of Economics, 1984.

Pasinetti, Luigi L. "Rate of Profit and Income Distribution in Relation to the Rate of Economic Growth." *Review of Economic Studies* 29, no. 4 (1962): 267–79.

Peltzman, Sam. "The Effect of Government Subsidies-in-Kind on Private Expenditures: The Case of Higher Education." *Journal of Political Economy* 81, no. 1 (1973): 1–27.

Peters, Elizabeth. "Patterns of Intergenerational Mobility." Mimeographed. Boulder: University of Colorado, 1985.

Pryor, F. L. "Simulation of the Impact of Social and Economic Institutions on the Size Distribution of Income and Wealth." *American Economic Review* 63, no. 1 (1973): 50–72.

Roy, A. D. "The Distribution of Earnings and of Individual Output." *Economic Journal* 60, no. 239 (1950): 489–505.

Schumpeter, Joseph A. *Imperialism and Social Classes*, translated by Heinz Norden. New York: Augustus M. Kelley, 1951.

Shorrocks, A. F. "On the Structure of Inter-Generational Transfers between Families." *Economica* 46, no. 184 (1979): 415–25.

Simon, Herbert. "Rationality in Psychology and Economics." *Journal of Business* 59, no. 4, part 2 (Oct. 1986): S209–24.

Smith, James P. "Race and Human Capital." *American Economic Review* 74, no. 4 (1984): 685–98.

Soltow, Lee. *Toward Income Equality in Norway*. Madison: University of Wisconsin Press, 1965.

Stiglitz, J. E. "Distribution of Income and Wealth among Individuals." *Econometrica* 37, no. 3 (1969): 382–97.

Tinbergen, Jan. "A Positive and a Normative Theory of Income Distribution." *Review of Income and Wealth* 16, no. 3 (1970): 221–34.

Tomes, Nigel. "The Family, Inheritance, and the Intergenerational Transmission of Inequality." *Journal of Political Economy* 89, no. 5 (1981): 928–58.

———. "Inequality within the Family and Regression to the Mean." Mimeographed. London: University of Western Ontario, Department of Economics, 1984.

Tsai, Shu-Ling. "Sex Differences in the Process of Stratification." Ph.D. dissertation, University of Wisconsin, 1983.

Wahl, Jenny Bourne. "Fertility in America: Historical Patterns and Wealth Effects on the Quantity and Quality of Children." Ph.D. dissertation, University of Chicago, 1985.

Wolff, P. de, and van Slijpe, A. R. D. "The Relation between Income, Intelligence, Education and Social Background." *European Economic Review* 4, no. 3 (1973): 235–64.

Yitzhaki, Shlomo. "On the Relation between Return and Income." Mimeographed. Jerusalem: Hebrew University, 1984.

CHAPTER XI

The Division of Labor, Coordination Costs, and Knowledge[1]

Gary S. Becker and Kevin M. Murphy

1. Introduction

Adam Smith begins his study of the wealth of nations [1965] with three chapters on the causes and consequences of the division of labor among workers. His very first sentence claims that, "The greatest improvement in the productive powers of labor, and the greater part of the skill, dexterity, and judgment with which it is anywhere directed or applied, seem to have been the effects of the division of labor." A little later he adds that, "It is the great multiplication of the productions of all the different arts, in consequence of the division of labor, which occasions, in a well-governed society, that universal opulence which extends itself to the lowest ranks of the people" [page 11].

We believe that the priority Smith gives to the division of labor among

[1] We had valuable comments from Ronald Findlay, Sergio Rebello, Andrei Shleifer, Robert Tamura, Robert Vishny, two referees, and from participants in seminars at the University of Chicago, Duke University, the University of Iowa, Queens University, Pennsylvania State University, the Stockholm School of Economics, and the Conference on Human Capital and Economic Growth, Institute for the Study of Free Enterprise Systems, University of Buffalo, May 26 and 27, 1989. Support from the Lynde and Harry Bradley Foundation, NICHD grant #1 Ro1 HD22054, and NSF grant #SES85-20258 is gratefully acknowledged. David Meltzer and Rebecca Kilburn provided very useful research assistance.

workers is an enormous insight. But we differ with his claim, followed by many later economists, that the degree of specialization is limited mainly by the extent of the market. Specialization and the division of labor are also influenced by several other factors that often are far more significant than the extent of the market.

A variable of great importance is the cost of combining specialized workers. Modern work on principal-agent conflicts, free-riding, and the difficulties of communication implies that the cost of coordinating a group of complementary specialized workers grows as the number of specialists increases.

The productivity of specialists at particular tasks depends on how much knowledge they have. The dependence of specialization on the knowledge available ties the division of labor to economic progress since progress depends on the growth in human capital and technologies.

The contribution of this paper is to show how specialization and the division of labor depend on coordination costs, and also on the amount and extent of knowledge. We explore implications of these relations for economic progress, industrial organization, and the activities of workers.

Section 2 develops a simple model of specialization among complementary tasks that links the division of labor to coordination costs, knowledge, and the extent of the market. Sections 3, 4, and 5 then separately consider in greater detail coordination costs, human capital, and market size. Section 6 models economic growth through endogenous increases over time in both human capital and the division of labor.

Section 7 shifts the focus from the division of labor among tasks needed to produce one good to that between workers who contribute to current consumption, and teachers who engage in roundabout production by raising the human capital of others. In an efficient allocation, teachers have more human capital than workers, and teachers who contribute to the production of consumer goods in the more distant future have greater human capital than teachers engaged in less roundabout production.

A recent paper by Yang and Borland [1991] also relates the division of labor to "transactions" costs and learning through specialization. However, since they do not consider how general knowledge affects the division of labor, they have a very different interpretation of the relation between specialization and economic progress.

2. Division of Labor Among Tasks

We follow Smith in recognizing that a very large number of tasks and processes are combined to produce even the most commonplace goods,

such as pins or nails. All workers perform many tasks that could be re-
fined into numerous distinct subtasks. For example, labor economics is
a specialized field, but some economists concentrate on labor supply,
others only consider the labor supply of married women, and others are
narrower still, as they analyze the labor supply of young black mothers
on welfare. Even finer labor specialties would emerge under appropriate
conditions and incentives.

To model the unlimited divisibility of tasks, we assume that a contin-
uum of tasks along a unit interval must be performed to produce the
only good (Y) in the economy. "Must be performed" is modeled by the
Leontief production function,

$$Y = \min_{0 \leq s \leq 1} Y(s), \tag{1}$$

although much weaker assumptions about the complementarity among
tasks would yield similar results about the division of labor. The rate of
production from the sth task ($Y(s)$) equals the product of the working
time devoted to $s(T_w(s))$ and the productivity of each hour ($E(s)$):

$$Y(s) = E(s) T_w(s). \tag{2}$$

A worker who does not specialize and performs all the tasks himself
allocates his working time and investments in specific human capital
among tasks to maximize the common output on each one. However, it
is possible for workers to do better by specializing in subsets of the tasks,
and then combining their outputs with that of other workers who specialize in other tasks. The increasing returns from concentrating on a
narrower set of tasks raises the productivity of a specialist above that of
a jack-of-all-trades. For example, a doctor who specializes in surgery is
more productive than one who performs an occasional operation because surgical skills are honed by operating, and because the specialist
has greater incentive to invest in surgical knowledge.

We call a "team" a group of workers who cooperate to produce Y by
performing different tasks and functions. They can be either part of the
same firm, or they can engage in transactions across different firms. "Cooperation" and "team" should not be taken to signify that team members
have the same goals and do not have conflicting interests, for conflicts
among members are an important consideration in our analysis.

Instead of assuming that workers have intrinsic comparative advantages at different tasks (as in the Roy model [1951]), we follow Murphy
[1986], Becker [1991, Chapter 2], and Smith too [1965] in assuming
that all workers are intrinsically identical. Specialization is what pro-

duces most comparative advantages; they do not arise at birth or in childhood. Although intrinsic differences are not negligible, we have no doubt—nor did Smith—that produced differences among workers are far more important.

Since the distribution of s does not have a natural metric, it is innocuous for our purposes to assume that all tasks are equally difficult and have the same degree of interdependence with other tasks. Therefore, each of the intrinsically identical members of an efficient team concentrates on an equal set of tasks, $w = 1/n$, where n is the team size. Output on each task depends on the size of the set and also on the general knowledge (H) available:

$$Y = Y(H,w), \ Y_h > 0, \ Y_w < 0. \tag{3}$$

Increasing returns to specialization is captured by the assumption that $Y_w < 0$, for otherwise there is no gain from specialization.

To illustrate the process with a specific example, assume that

$$E(s) = dH^\gamma T_h^\theta(s), \tag{4}$$

where $\theta > 0$ determines the marginal productivity of T_h, the time devoted to acquiring task-specific skills. General knowledge (H) is assumed to raise the productivity of the time spent investing in skills ($\gamma > 0$). The total time devoted to the sth skill is $T(s)$, so

$$T_h(s) + T_w(s) = T(s). \tag{5}$$

Time is allocated between "investing" (T_h) and "working" (T_w) to maximize output, which implies that

$$Y(s) = A(\theta)H^\gamma T(s)^{1+\theta}, \tag{6}$$

where $A = d\theta^\theta (1 + \theta)^{-(1+\theta)}$.

If each person allocates one unit of working time uniformly among a set $w = 1/n$ of tasks, then $T(s)w = T(s)(1/n) = 1$. Substitution into equation (6) then gives output on each task as a function of team size:

$$Y = AH^\gamma n^{1+\theta}. \tag{7}$$

Output per team member equals

$$y = Y/n = B(H,n) = AH^\gamma n^\theta. \tag{8}$$

Clearly, B rises with the size of the team as long as $\theta > 0$; that is, as long as investments in task-specific skills have a positive marginal productivity.

This example can be generalized to include learning-by-doing and other considerations. But it would still retain the implication that per capita output grows with team size, so that the gains from specialization are limited only by the extent of the market. If N people in a market could work with each other, equation (8) implies that output per person is maximized when $n = N$: when everyone in the market becomes part of the same team. Since each member specializes in tasks of width $w = 1/N$, the division of labor is then limited only by N, market size.

Sometimes the division of labor is limited by the extent of the market, but more frequently in the modern world it is limited by other forces. Our analysis will place the extent of the market in proper perspective by considering it along with other forces that affect the degree of specialization.

Conflict among members generally grows with the size of a team because members have greater incentives to shirk when they get a smaller share of output (see, e.g., Holmstrom [1982]). Moreover, efforts to extract rents by "holding-up" other members also grows as the number of members performing complementary tasks increases (see Chari and Jones [1991]). Further, the chances of a breakdown in production due to poor coordination of the tasks and functions performed by different members, or to communication of misleading information among members, also tends to expand as the number of separate specialists grows. In addition, coordination costs depend on whether workers trust each other, whether contracts are enforced, and whether governments maintain stable and effective laws.

Principal-agent conflicts, hold-up problems, and breakdowns in supply and communication all tend to grow as the degree of specialization increases. We call these problems part of the cost of "coordinating" specialists, and assume that the total coordination cost per member (C) depends on n (or w):

$$C = C(n), \quad C_n > 0. \tag{9}$$

Net output per team member (y) is the difference between benefits and costs:

$$y = B - C = B(H,n) - C(n), \quad B_n > 0, C_n > 0. \tag{10}$$

If B were independent of n, autarchy or one-member "teams" are efficient as long as C rises with n. If C were independent of n, the division of labor is limited only by N, the extent of the market, as long as B rises with n. With both $B_n > 0$ and $C_n > 0$, an efficient team generally has more than one member and less than all workers in the market. The efficient amount of specialization is obtained by differentiating equation (10) with respect to n to get the first-order condition:

$$B_n \geq C_n, \tag{11}$$

where $B_{nn} - C_{nn} < 0$ is the second-order condition, and we assume that $B_n > C_n$ for small n. If $B_n > C_n$ for all $n \leq N$, the division of labor would be limited only by the extent of the market; otherwise, the optimal n^* $< N$ is found where $B_n = C_n$. The efficient division of labor is then limited by coordination costs, not by market size.

The rest of the paper assumes that actual teams are efficient and maximize income per member. We believe that this is a good approximation in competitive product and labor markets, although competition may not be sufficient to achieve efficient teams when members are in different firms. Still, contractual arrangements and buyouts can offset locational and other "externalities" across firms, and would limit the discrepancies between actual and efficient teams.

3. Coordination Costs

A few examples might help clarify the relation between specialization and coordination costs. Most pediatricians in a city, or even in a single HMO, do not specialize in particular childhood diseases. No doubt they would learn more about a disease through specialization, but the additional knowledge would require greater expenses in coordinating their care with that of other pediatricians. For parents often do not know what is wrong with their children, and would need to see several pediatricians to get adequate care if each were highly specialized. Yet we would expect to find, and do observe, more specialization in childhood diseases that require extensive knowledge to detect and treat, such as liver diseases and cancer.

If each historian specialized in the events of only a few years, they would become more expert on developments during these shorter time periods. But since events over a few years are not isolated from those in prior and subsequent years, each one would then have to coordinate his research with that of several other specialists. Such coordination costs can be greatly reduced by specialization in larger and more self-contained periods.

Economists and lawyers working on the relation between law and economics can coordinate their research, but coordination costs are reduced when economists also become lawyers or lawyers also become economists, as with the increasing number of persons who take advanced degrees in both law and economics. Yet it is not surprising that joint degrees are more common in law and economics than in health economics, since the investment required for a medical degree is much greater than for a law degree.

The family in most traditional societies has an extensive division of labor between husbands, wives, children, and sometimes other kin. Extensive specialization was made easier by the altruism and caring among family members. These lowered coordination costs by reducing the tendency for members to shirk and try to extract greater shares of their family's production (see the discussion in Becker [1991, Chapter 2]).

A rather enormous literature has studied the comprehensive division of labor found in insect colonies. Although genetically based, the degree of specialization does respond to changes in the environment. For example, the division of labor by age among honeybees is less extensive in smaller colonies—a measure of the extent of the market. The division of labor among bees also responds to the spatial organization of colonies, the demands of brood rearing, difficulties of communicating food sources, and other determinants that often can reasonably be considered to be "coordination" costs (see Winston [1987, pp. 101–7]).

An analysis of the cost of coordinating specialized tasks and functions provides insights into many aspects of the organization of firms and industries. Specialized members of a team who are employed by the same firm get coordinated by the rules of the firm, whereas specialists who are employed by different firms have their activities coordinated by contracts and other agreements that govern transactions across firms. Companies that cut the material for a dress manufacturer or supply car doors to General Motors are part of the "teams" producing particular dresses or General Motors cars. In market economies of the modern era, even firms involved in producing the simplest goods, such as pencils, use many downstream and upstream firms to produce these goods, so that modern teams are very large.

Companies are less "vertically" integrated when it is cheaper to coordinate specialized team members through market transactions. This is why companies are more specialized when they can economize on transactions costs by locating near each other—as the computer industry locates in Silicon Valley, the United States clothing industry was once concentrated on the West Side of Manhattan, and much of the small arms industry during the mid-nineteenth century squeezed into a small area of Birmingham (see Allen [1929]).

An important function of entrepreneurs is to coordinate different types of labor and capital: economists like John Bates Clark [1899] believed that this is their main function. Economic systems that encourage entrepreneurship would have lower costs of coordination, and presumably a more widespread division of labor among workers and firms. Since centrally planned economies throttle entrepreneurship as well as weaken the capacity of markets to coordinate transactions, workers and firms should be less specialized in these economies than in market economies. Unfortunately, there is no systematic evidence on the degree of specialization among workers in the formerly Communist economies of Eastern Europe, although there is abundant evidence that firms were large and carried vertical integration to ridiculous extremes, or so it appears in comparisons with market economies.

In a stimulating article many years ago, Hayek [1945] stressed the importance to an economy of coordinating efficiently the specialized knowledge of different participants: ". . . the problem of a rational economic order is . . . the utilization of knowledge which is not given to anyone in its totality," and "Through [the price system] not only a division of labor but also a coordinated utilization of resources based on an equally divided knowledge has become possible." Hayek's insight is that the cost of coordinating specialized workers is smaller, and hence the division of labor is greater, in economies that make effective use of prices and markets to coordinate tasks and skills across firms.

Hayek did not emphasize an even more significant implication of his analysis, although he must have been aware of it. The specialized knowledge at the command of workers is not simply given, for the knowledge acquired depends on incentives. Centrally planned and other economies that do not make effective use of markets and prices raise coordination costs, and thereby reduce incentives for investments in specialized knowledge.

4. Knowledge and Specialization

The division of labor and specialization both within and between countries increased enormously during the past several centuries as much of the world became vastly richer. Sixteenth century European cities had perhaps a few hundred occupations, whereas a telephone directory for even a small American city now lists thousands of specialized services. Probably no more than 15 percent of physicians in the nineteenth century were specialists—neither general practitioners nor pediatricians— while in recent years over 75 percent of United States physicians specialize.[2] The first three economic journals started in the United States were general purpose journals—the *Quarterly Journal of Economics* in 1886, the *Journal of Political Economy* in 1892, and the *American Economic Review* in 1911—whereas most of the many journals established in recent years are highly specialized: the *Journal of Applied Econometrics*, the *Journal of Legal Studies*, and the *Journal of Economic Demography* are a few examples.

Engineers of the early nineteenth century were not highly specialized. But the growth of industries based on new technologies and greater knowledge of science during the nineteenth and twentieth centuries led to many engineering specialties. The British Institute of Civil Engineering started in 1818; the mechanical engineers started their own society in 1847; the electrical engineers in 1871; the automobile engineers in 1906; and so on until chemical and other specialized societies emerged during the past 70 years (see Buchanan [1989]).

The engineering, medical, and economics examples illustrate that much of the growth in specialization over time has been due to an extraordinary growth in knowledge. We assume as in equation (8) that an increase in the knowledge embodied in the human capital of workers not only raises the average product per team member, but also raises the marginal product of a larger team:

$$\frac{\partial}{\partial H}\left(\frac{\partial B}{\partial n}\right) = B_{nh} > 0. \tag{12}$$

The presumption built into equation (4) is that general knowledge is usually complementary with investments in task-specific knowledge.

By differentiating the first-order condition (11) that maximizes income per worker with respect to H, one gets

$$\frac{dn^*}{dH} = \frac{B_{nh}}{C_{nn} - B_{nn}} > 0, \tag{13}$$

where $B_{nn} - C_{nn} < 0$ is the second-order condition. The inequality in (12) signs these derivatives, and it is necessary if our model is to explain why economic development and the growth in knowledge raise specialization and the division of labor.

Equation (13) indicates that teams get larger and workers become

---

[2] See Peterson and Pennell [1962] and Shapiro [1989]. Note, however, that U.S. physicians are much more specialized than those in Canada and Western Europe (see Fuchs and Hahn [1990]).

more specialized and expert over a smaller range of skills as human capital and technological knowledge grow. Adam Smith recognizes the relation between specialization and knowledge when he states that the division of labor ". . . is generally carried further in those countries which enjoy the highest degree of industry and improvement . . ." [1965, p. 5]. However, in his discussion the causation went from the division of labor to greater knowledge, while in ours it also goes from greater general knowledge to a more extensive division of labor and greater task-specific knowledge.

The "jack-of-all-trades" is less useful than the specialist in economies with advanced technologies and an extensive human capital base. Although workers in modern economies have considerable knowledge of principles and have access to complicated technologies, a typical worker also commands a very much smaller share of the total knowledge used by the economy than do workers in simpler and more backward economies.

It is the extensive cooperation among highly specialized workers that enables advanced economies to utilize a vast amount of knowledge. This is why Hayek's emphasis on the role of prices and markets in combining efficiently the specialized knowledge of different workers is so important in appreciating the performance of rich and complex economies.

An "expert" has been facetiously defined as "someone who knows more and more about less and less." Highly specialized workers are surely experts in what they do, and yet know very little about the many other skills found in a complex economy. Modern expertise comes partly at the expense of narrowness, and of ignorance about what other people do.

Equation (12) also helps determine how workers with different knowledge get allocated to different sectors. The costs involved in "coordinating" specialists surely differ greatly among sectors; for example, costs are relatively low in dense urban communities, and in industries where suppliers and downstream firms locate near each other and communicate easily. The effects of higher coordination costs on specialization and the division of labor are exacerbated by the optimal allocation of workers among sectors.

An efficient allocation "assigns" workers whose productivity is least affected by coordination costs to the high cost sectors. This implies that workers with lower human capital would be assigned to the high cost sectors if greater coordination costs lower the marginal product of human capital (see Becker [1991, Appendix]). The first-order condition for n and the envelope theorem show that this is the case since

$$\frac{\partial^2 y}{\partial H \partial \lambda} = \frac{\partial (B_h)}{\partial \lambda} = B_{hn} \frac{\partial n^*}{\partial \lambda} < 0, \tag{14}$$

where λ is a coordination-cost-raising parameter, with $c_{n\lambda} > 0$, $B_{hn} > 0$ by equation (13), and $\partial n^*/\partial \lambda$ is clearly <0. This analysis explains, among other things, why earnings are usually higher in large cities even after adjusting for observable measures of human capital—such as years of schooling and experience (see, e.g., Fuchs [1967])—because unobserved human capital is also attracted to cities by the lower coordination costs.

5. Extent of the Market

Adam Smith recognized that specialization had costs as well as benefits since it made workers "stupid" and "ignorant."[3] But Smith forcefully stated his belief that the division of labor is limited mainly by the extent of the market. The modern literature on specialization within a profession [Baumgardner, 1988], increasing returns and specialization in international trade [Krugman, 1987], the degree of brand proliferation [Lancaster, 1975], and on the economic gains from population growth (e.g., Simon [1977] and Locay [1990]) has followed this emphasis on the limitations to the division of labor imposed by the extent of the market.

In our formulation also, the division of labor is limited by market size when n^*, the optimal number of team members, is greater than or equal to N, the number of workers in the market. In that case, each worker specializes in different skills, so that each has some monopoly power ex post (see Gros [1987] and Baumgardner [1988]). This may well describe the position of many specialists in small towns and rural areas.

However, every reasonably large metropolitan area has several, often many, persons who have essentially the same specialized skills and compete in the same market. Pediatricians in the same HMO or psychiatrists

---

[3] "The man whose life is spent performing a few simple operations has no occasion to exert his understanding or to exercise his invention . . . and generally becomes as stupid and ignorant as it is possible for a human creature to become" [Smith, 1965, p. 734].

Due to this and similar statements, some scholars have seen a serious contradiction in Smith's approach to the division of labor: Book I extols its advantages, while Book IV points out its corrupting influence (e.g., see the discussion in Marx [1961] and West [1964], but see Rosenberg [1965]). But surely there is no necessary contradiction between Smith's recognition that the division of labor entails major costs, and his belief that the division of labor is crucial in promoting the wealth of nations. The contradiction is with Smith's belief that the division of labor is limited mainly by the extent of the market.

who work out of a psychoanalytic institute have closely related skills and seek patients in the same geographic market. Any publisher in a major city has access to many copy editors and translators with very similar skills.

The division of labor cannot be limited mainly by the extent of the market when many specialists provide essentially the same skills. Our claim is that instead it is usually limited by the costs of coordinating workers with different specialties, as in the examples discussed in Section 3.

We recognize that it is possible to reinterpret our examples by emphasizing quality differences among specialists who only appear to have the same skills, or by claiming they are in separate local markets. By the same token, however, the illustrations provided by Smith and others to support the emphasis on the extent of the market can often be reinterpreted in terms of coordination costs. For example, the division of labor may be greater in cities than in small towns not because markets are larger in cities, but because it is easier to coordinate specialists in more densely populated areas.

There even seems to be a problem with Smith's justly famous example of a pin factory, where workers specialize in various functions, including drawing out, straightening, and cutting the wire. Why didn't the several factories that made pins in Smith's England combine their activities, get a larger scale and market, and specialize more within each factory? If the answer is that the cost of combining these factories exceeded the gain from a greater division of labor, then specialization was limited by these costs of "coordination," not by the extent of the market.[4] Again, the answer may be that the pins were of very different qualities, or that each factory catered to a separate local market, although pins were cheap to ship and Smith does not mention the quality of pins.

Perhaps the most significant difference between our approach and that based on market size lies in the divergent interpretations of the enormous growth in specialization as countries develop. We claim that the huge increase in scientific and other knowledge and decline in coordination costs raised the benefits from greater specialization. The alter-

---

[4] Stigler's important elaboration of the connection between the division of labor and the extent of the market [1951] recognizes that the Smithian view appears to lead to specialized producers and monopolistic suppliers. He asks, ". . . why does the firm not abandon the functions subject to increasing returns, allowing another firm (and industry) to specialize in them to take full advantage of increasing returns?" [p. 188]. His answer that "these functions may be too small to support a specialized firm or firms" [p. 188] is inadequate because a firm need not specialize *only* in these functions. Each firm could be the sole provider of some functions subject to increasing returns and one of several providers of functions subject to decreasing returns.

native view suggested by Smith's approach is that declines in transportation costs raised the effective size of markets. Surely both sets of forces were operating, although the expansion in knowledge and decline in coordination costs seem by far to be the more fundamental forces. Indeed, some of the growth in markets was not even exogenous, but rather the search for larger markets was induced by the increase in knowledge and decline in coordination costs that raised the gain from larger teams with more specialized members.

6. The Growth in Specialization and Knowledge

However, the growth in knowledge also is not exogenous, for it depends on investments in new technologies, basic research, and human capital. The incentive to invest in knowledge depends partly on the degree of specialization and the level of task-specific skills. In other words, there is not a one-way correlation between knowledge and the division of labor, but mutual determination.

To show in a simple way the interaction between the division of labor, the accumulation of knowledge, and economic growth, we consider the functional form given by equation (8) after netting out a constant elasticity coordination cost function:

$$y_t = A_t H_t^\gamma n_t^\theta - \lambda_t n_t^\beta. \tag{15}$$

The first-order condition for optimal n implies that

$$n_t^* = \left(\frac{\theta}{\beta \lambda_t}\right)^{1/(\beta-\theta)} A_t^{1/\beta-\theta} H_t^{\gamma/(\beta-\theta)}, \tag{16}$$

where $\beta > \theta > 0$ is the second-order condition. Replacing n in equation (15) by the right-hand side of equation (16) gives optimal output as a function of general knowledge and various parameters:

$$y_t^* = k_t A_t^{\beta/(\beta-\theta)} H_t^{\gamma\beta/(\beta-\theta)}, \tag{17}$$

with

$$k_t = \lambda_t^{-\theta/(\beta-\theta)} \left[\left(\frac{\theta}{\beta}\right)^{\theta/(\beta-\theta)} - \left(\frac{\theta}{\beta}\right)^{\beta/(\beta-\theta)}\right] > 0. \tag{18}$$

Equation (17) divides the change in per capita income into the growth in human capital (H), the growth in technology (A), and the decline in coordination costs (λ):

$$\frac{d \log y}{dt} = \frac{\gamma\beta}{\beta - \theta} \frac{d \log H}{dt} + \frac{\beta}{\beta - \theta} \frac{d \log A}{dt} - \frac{\theta}{\beta - \theta} \frac{d \log \lambda}{dt}. \quad (19)$$

There is not a separate entry for coordination costs in the usual growth accounting calculus, so $-(\theta/\beta - \theta)$ $(d \log \lambda/dt)$ would be considered part of the "residual" along with the effects of the growth in A, and some of the effects of changes in H.

To endogenize the accumulation of human capital, we consider a simple one-sector model where the human capital of period $t + 1$ is just the unconsumed output of period t (the next section considers a separate human capital sector):

$$H_{t+1} = y_t - c_t = A_t H_t^\gamma n_t^\theta - \lambda_t n_t^\beta - c_t, \quad (20)$$

where c_t is consumption in t.

If $\gamma < 1$, diminishing returns to the accumulation of knowledge discourage further investment as this stock of knowledge grows. Admittedly, knowledge is not subject to diminishing returns in the same obvious way as is physical capital because greater knowledge raises the productivity of further investment in knowledge. However, as knowledge continues to grow, limited human capacities tend to make it harder to pack more knowledge into a person without running into diminishing returns. This is why $\gamma < 1$ seems to be a plausible assumption.

Autonomous technological progress in the neoclassical model offsets the diminishing returns to a higher capital-labor ratio. In our model the induced expansion in the division of labor as human capital grows raises the marginal product of additional knowledge. Equation (17) shows that the total elasticity of output with respect to human capital exceeds γ since $\beta > \beta - \theta$. The reason is that an increase in H has an indirect effect on y through the induced increase in n. This indirect effect is stronger the larger θ is relative to β: the bigger is n's effect on the productivity of specialized production compared with its effect on coordination costs. As it were, greater specialization enables workers to absorb knowledge more easily, which offsets to some extent the tendency toward diminishing returns from the accumulation of knowledge.

The model is completed with a conventional separable utility function defined over consumption into the indefinite future:

$$U = \frac{1}{\sigma} \sum_{t=0}^{\infty} \alpha^t c_t^\sigma, \qquad \text{with } \sigma < 1. \quad (21)$$

Present consumption is transformed into future consumption through the production of human capital. If the rate of return on investment in human capital is denoted by r, the first-order conditions for optimal consumption over time are

$$\alpha(c_{t+1}/c_t)^{1-\sigma} = R_t = 1 + r_t, \qquad t = 0, 1, \ldots \qquad (22)$$

With the given inherited knowledge stock, H_0, the first-order conditions in equations (16) and (22), and the production function in equation (15) determine the optimal path over time of c, H, and y. These variables converge to constant values at a steady state if the rate of return continues to fall without limit as capital grows, they converge to a steady-state growth path if the rate of return becomes independent of the capital stock, and they grow at increasing rates if the rate of return rises as capital grows.

Since a higher H_{t+1} means equally lower c_t (given y_t), the transformation between c_{t-1} and c_t gives the rate of return on changes in H_t. By the envelope theorem this equals the derivative of y^* in equation (17) with respect to H:

$$R_t = -\frac{dy_{t+1}}{dc_t} = \frac{dy_{t+1}}{dH_{t+1}} = \frac{\beta\gamma}{\beta - \theta}k_t A_t^{\beta/(\beta-\theta)} H_t^{[\beta\gamma/(\beta-\theta)]-1}, \qquad (23)$$

where k is defined in equation (20).

The rate of return falls, is constant, or rises with higher H, as $\beta\gamma \gtreqless \beta - \theta$. If $\beta\gamma = \beta - \theta$, and A and λ are constant over time, steady-state growth in y, H, and c starts from any initial H_0 at a rate equal to

$$1 + g = \frac{c_{t+1}}{c_t} = \frac{y_{t+1}}{y_t} = \frac{H_{t+1}}{H_t} = (R\alpha^{-1})^{1/1-\sigma}. \qquad (24)$$

If $\beta\gamma < \beta - \theta$, and A is constant, the economy converges to a stationary state ($g = 0$). If $\beta\gamma > \beta - \theta$, and A is constant, rates of growth in Y, H, and c all increase over time. In Yang and Borland's model [1991] the growth rate must eventually decline because gains from a greater division of labor are eventually exhausted.

Equations (16) and (24) show that output per capita, knowledge, and the division of labor all grow together over time. Growth in these variables is interdependent, as causation runs from knowledge to the division of labor and output, as well as from the division of labor to knowledge and output. The equilibrium rate of growth at all moments is Pareto optimal since there are no externalities in the model.

Rates of growth in output and human capital are higher when the level of technology (A) is greater. These growth rates may be quite re-

sponsive to better technology because the induced expansion in specialization raises the exponent of A to $\beta/\beta - \theta > 1$.

Equations (18) and (23) show that rates of return on investments in
knowledge depend on the cost of coordinating specialized workers (λ).
Countries with lower coordination costs due to stabler and more efficient laws, or other reasons, not only have larger outputs, but they also
tend to grow faster because lower costs stimulate investments in knowledge by raising the advantages of a more extensive division of labor.

7. The Division of Labor Between Sectors: Teachers and Workers

Workers specialize in the production of different goods as well as in different tasks required to produce a single good. For example, an experienced steel worker who has accumulated considerable skill at firing blast
furnaces would be much less productive in the computer software industry. The discussion in previous sections of the advantages from specialization at tasks implies that workers become specialized to particular sectors partly because they become skilled at the tasks specific to a sector.

In discussing specialization across sectors, we continue to assume that
all workers are identical to start, but they become different by investing
in different skills at particular tasks. Each good is produced by teams
that perform a very large number of specialized complementary tasks,
where the productivity of each team depends on parameters of the relevant production function and the human capital of team members.

To analyze specialization across sectors, we consider the production
function in each sector that has optimized out the endogenous team
size. Output depends explicitly only on the human capital of team members, but implicitly it also depends on coordination costs and other parameters that determine specialization and the division of labor. The
marginal products of human capital partly depend on the benefit and
cost parameters that determine the optimal division of labor in each
sector. Differences across sectors in these marginal products lead to sec-
toral differences in the human capital per worker. There is abundant
evidence that years of schooling per worker differ greatly among industries (see Gill [1989] and Mincer and Higuchi [1988]).

Given our emphasis on the relation between the division of labor, the
accumulation of knowledge, and economic progress, the discussion of
specialization across sectors concentrates on differences between the
consumption and investment sectors. We drop the assumption of Section 6 that human capital is simply unspent consumer goods, and introduce more realistic assumptions about the way human capital is produced.

To simplify the presentation, we consider only a special case of the production function for consumer goods in equation (17): $\beta\gamma = \beta - \theta$, and A and k are both normalized to unity. Therefore,

$$C_t = N_{ct}H_{ct}. \tag{25}$$

The term H_{ct} refers to the human capital of each person in the consumption sector in period t, N_{ct} is the number of these persons—we call this the number of "workers" in period t—and C_t is the aggregate output of consumer goods.

All persons who help produce human capital are called "teachers." We assume that human capital lasts for only one period, and that teachers in period t produce the human capital of both workers and teachers in period, or "cohort," $t + 1$. All persons in each cohort spend their "youthful" time as students acquiring the human capital that prepares them to become workers or teachers when they become adults. The human capital acquired by a student depends on the human capital of her teachers, and the number of teachers per student.

The human capital acquired by students is assumed to be proportional to the human capital of teachers (H_T), where the factor of proportionality depends on the number of teachers per student (τ):

$$H_{t+1} = F(\tau_t)H_T, F' > 0, F'' < 0, \tag{26}$$

where we shall show that ε, the elasticity of F with respect to τ, must fall as τ increases. Since this is a reduced form, H_T is the human capital of each teacher in a human capital production "team," and τ is the number of students per member of each team.

The assumption $F' > 0$ means that an increase in "class size"—a decrease in τ—reduces the human capital acquired by each student. This relation may not hold for all values of τ, but obviously it pays to economize on teachers when fewer teachers do not lower the human capital produced per student. Although many empirical studies do not find that larger classes reduce the learning of students (see the review in Hanushek [1989]), a good recent study by Card and Krueger [1990] finds that workers earn more if they went to schools with smaller classes. Moreover, an experiment conducted by Tennessee that randomly assigned students to classes of different sizes also found that smaller classes improved performance (see Finn and Achilles [1990]).

It is somewhat surprising that the concavity of F and the assumption that output in both the consumption and human capital sectors are proportional to the human capital of persons employed in each sector do not imply that students who prepare for different sectors acquire the same amount of human capital. Instead, the production functions in equations (25) and (26) imply a finely calibrated inequality between the human capital of workers and teachers in *efficient* allocations of persons and investments.

The teachers of workers in period j were students in period $j - 1$, their teachers were students in $j - 2$, and so on, continuing backwards until one comes to the persons in the initial period who indirectly taught the workers in j. In essence, C_j is not simply produced by the workers in that period and their teachers, but also by the whole sequence over time of teachers who helped train these workers.

We define the jth "lineage" as this sequence of teachers and students in successive periods that ends in period j because the students in j become workers then. A lineage is a "team" of teachers, students, and workers in different periods who combine to produce consumer goods. The human capital of workers in later periods is produced with more "roundabout" methods, and hence has longer lineages, than the human capital of workers in earlier periods.

The roundabout methods used to produce human capital can be seen by substituting repeatedly into equation (26) to express the human capital of persons in period t who belong to the jth lineage as

$$H_{jt} = H_{j0}F\left(\frac{N_{j0}}{N_{j1}}\right) \cdots F\left(\frac{N_{jt-1}}{N_{jt}}\right), j = 0, \ldots, \infty, \ t \leq j, \tag{27}$$

where $N_{jt'}$ is the number of teachers in lineage j in period t' ($<t$), and H_{j0} is the human capital of the N_{j0} initial teachers in this lineage. By substituting equation (27) into (25), we get

$$C_j = H_{jj}N_{jj} = H_{j0}F\left(\frac{N_{j0}}{N_{j1}}\right) \cdots F\left(\frac{N_{jj-1}}{N_{jj}}\right)N_{jj}. \tag{28}$$

We only consider accumulations of human capital that are efficient, that maximize consumption in any period, given consumptions in all other periods. It is obvious that the teacher-student ratios within a lineage then cannot be constant over time because marginal products in the lineage would be zero for all members. The negative effect on the production of human capital from having an additional student in a lineage would exactly cancel the positive effect of subsequently having an additional teacher. The Appendix shows that efficient teacher-student ratios would fall over time within each lineage, so that teaching in a lineage would become less intensive as the lineage becomes closer to training workers who produce consumer goods.

Another important implication is due both to the concavity of the human capital production function with respect to the teacher-student ratio and the constant returns to scale in the consumption sector with respect to the number of workers. As a result of these assumptions, it is efficient to provide students who are further removed from becoming workers with more extensive training, so that teacher-student ratios would be higher in the more roundabout lineages (see the Appendix). Consequently, the human capital of members of more roundabout lineages grows over time relative to those of less roundabout ones.

Even though the economy only has one consumption good and homogeneous human capital, the efficient accumulation of human capital creates an infinite number of sectors or lineages. Members of a particular sector would be specialized to that one partly because their human capital would be too little for the more roundabout sectors and too much for the less roundabout ones.

In addition, workers and teachers specialize in particular tasks within their sectors. Since more roundabout lineages have greater human capital, the analysis in Section 2 of the effects of human capital on the degree of specialization implies that members of the more roundabout sectors tend to specialize in a narrower range of tasks.

The distribution of human capital evolves over time. The human capital within each lineage grows at decreasing rates, but the slower-growing lineages are culled out over time when their members produce consumer goods, and the faster-growing lineages expand in size. Since lower-order lineages disappear over time, all human capital in later periods is "descended" from the teachers of persons in a small number of highly roundabout lineages in the initial period.

Inequality in the distribution of human capital at any moment expands over time because the human capital of sectors with greater human capital (the higher-order lineages) grows faster. However, the inequality would fall over time because the sectors with the least human capital (the lower-order lineages) are culled out and eliminated. We have not been able to reach any general conclusions about the net effect of these opposing forces on charges over time in the distribution of human capital.

What is rather remarkable about these rich implications concerning teacher-student ratios and the growth of human capital in different lineages is that they apply to *any* efficient path over time. Several additional properties hold if the economy is in a steady-state equilibrium, with consumption and human capital in each lineage growing at the same constant rate. For example, the inequality in this distribution of human capital across lineages tends to be greater when the steady-state growth rate is higher. However, we do not want to emphasize steady-state properties, for it is not clear that a steady state exists, given the restrictions on the teacher-student function implied by an efficient equilibrium.

8. Summary

This paper considers specialization and division of labor both within and between sectors. Workers concentrate on different tasks and combine their activities in "teams" to produce each sector's output. A more extensive division of labor raises productivity because returns to the time spent on tasks are usually greater to workers who concentrate on a narrower range of skills.

The traditional discussion of the division of labor inaugurated by Adam Smith emphasizes the limitations to specialization imposed by the extent of the market. Limited markets sometimes curtail the division of labor, but we claim that the degree of specialization is more often determined by other considerations. Especially emphasized are various costs of "coordinating" specialized workers who perform complementary tasks, and the amount of general knowledge available.

On this view, specialization increases until the higher productivity from a greater division of labor is just balanced by the greater costs of coordinating a larger number of more specialized workers. Consequently, principal-agent conflicts, hold-up problems, communication difficulties, and other costs of combining specialized workers into productive teams play a major part in our approach. Since teams may include workers in different firms, costs of coordination also depend on the efficiency of markets and how well contracts are enforced.

Greater knowledge tends to raise the benefits from specialization, and thus tends to raise the optimal division of labor. This helps explain why workers become more expert on narrower ranges of tasks as knowledge grows and countries progress. Increased specialization in turn raises the benefits from investments in knowledge, so that the growth in tandem of specialization and investments in knowledge may allow an economy to continue to develop.

The paper also considers the division of labor between workers who produce consumer goods and teachers who produce human capital. The analysis distinguishes among teachers of workers in the initial period, teachers of the teachers of workers in the following period, and so on for teachers engaged in more and more roundabout production of workers. We show than an efficient economy has a finely etched division of labor, where teachers have more human capital than workers, and teachers in higher-order lineages—in more roundabout production—have greater human capital than teachers in lower-order ranges.

Adam Smith's emphasis on the importance of specialization and the division of labor to economic progress is not simply an influential landmark in the development of economics. An analysis of the forces determining the division of labor provides crucial insights not only into the growth of nations, but also into the organization of product and labor markets, industries, and firms.

Appendix

Equation (28) implies that the marginal products of workers in any lineage are

$$\frac{dC_j}{dN_{jk}} = \frac{C_j}{N_{jk}} \left\{ \varepsilon\left(\frac{N_{jk}}{N_{jk+1}}\right) - \varepsilon\left(\frac{N_{jk-1}}{N_{jk}}\right) \right\}, k < j \tag{29}$$

$$\frac{dC_j}{dN_{jj}} = \frac{C_j}{N_{jj}} \left\{ 1 - \varepsilon\left(\frac{N_{jj-1}}{N_{jj}}\right) \right\}, k = j > 0, \tag{30}$$

where $\varepsilon(\tau) = F'(\tau) \times \tau/F(\tau)$, is the elasticity of the human capital production function with respect to the teacher-student ratio. Marginal products in the final period of a lineage are positive only if this elasticity is less than one in the period before the end of the lineage. Moreover, equation (29) shows that marginal products will not be positive in periods prior to the end unless in each lineage the elasticities with respect to the teacher-student ratio are increasing over time.

In addition, the marginal products in equation (29) would rise with a reduction in the number of members in a lineage only if the elasticity of human capital with respect to the teacher-student ratio falls as the ratio increases. Then a reduced number of members in the kth period raises the elasticity when they are teachers (since the teacher-student ratio falls) and lowers the elasticity when they are students (since the teacher-student ratio rises). Both effects imply that marginal products are positive only when the teacher-student ratio is falling over time within each lineage.

These results also have strong implications for differences across lineages. An optimal allocation of the labor force between lineages requires that the marginal rates of substitution between persons in any periods i

and k be the same for members of all lineages (say j and m). By equations (29) and (30) this implies that

$$\left(\frac{N_{ji}}{N_{jk}}\right)\frac{\varepsilon_{jk} - \varepsilon_{jk-1}}{\varepsilon_{ji} - \varepsilon_{ji-1}} = \frac{N_{mi}}{N_{mk}}\frac{\varepsilon_{mk} - \varepsilon_{mk-1}}{\varepsilon_{mi} - \varepsilon_{mi-1}}, \tag{31}$$

where ε_{jk} is $\varepsilon(N_{ji}/N_{jl+1})$, and $\varepsilon_{jj} = 1$ for all j and k. When $i = j = 1$, $k = 0$, and $m = 2$, equation (31) becomes

$$\left(\frac{N_{11}}{N_{10}}\right)\frac{\varepsilon_{10}}{1 - \varepsilon_{10}} = \left(\frac{N_{21}}{N_{20}}\right)\frac{\varepsilon_{20}}{\varepsilon_{21} - \varepsilon_{20}}. \tag{32}$$

Since ε_{21} must be less than one for the marginal product of workers in this lineage to be positive in period two, then $\varepsilon_{20} < \varepsilon_{10}$ to satisfy equation (32). Given that elasticities decline with the teacher-student ratio, this ratio must be higher in period 0 for the second than for the first lineage.

Similar conditions hold over longer horizons. Not only must the teacher-student ratio decline over time within a lineage, but it also increases as a lineage becomes more roundabout. This implies that human capital grows faster over time in more roundabout lineages.

References

Allen, George C. *The Industrial Development of Birmingham and the Black Country, 1860–1927* (London: George Allen & Unwin Ltd., 1929).

Baumgardner, James R. "The Division of Labor, Local Markets, and Worker Organization." *Journal of Political Economy* XCVI (June 1988), 509–27.

Becker, Gary S. *A Treatise on the Family,* enlarged edition (Cambridge, MA: Harvard University Press, 1991).

Buchanan, R. A. *The Engineers: A History of the Engineering Profession in Britain, 1750–1914* (London: Jessica Kingsley Publishers, 1989).

Card, David, and Alan B. Krueger. "Does School Quality Matter? Returns to Education and the Characteristics of Public Schools in the United States." NBER Working Paper, May, 1990.

Chari, V. V., and Larry E. Jones. "A Reconsideration of the Problem of Social Cost: Free Riders and Monopolists." Federal Reserve Bank of Minnesota, June, 1991.

Clark, John B. *The Distribution of Wealth: A Theory of Wages, Interest and Profits* (New York: Macmillan, 1899).

Finn, Jeremy D., and Charles M. Achilles. "Answers and Questions About Class Size: A Statewide Experiment." *American Educational Research Journal* XXVII (Fall 1990), 557–77.

Fuchs, Victor R. "Differentials in Hourly Earnings by Region and City Size,

1959." Occasional paper #101 (New York: NBER), 1967. An excerpt was published in *Monthly Labor Review* XC (January 1967), 22–26.

Fuchs, Victor R., and James H. Hahn. "How Does Canada Do It? A Comparison of Expenditures for Physicians' Services in the United States and Canada." *New England Journal of Medicine* CCCXXIII (September 27, 1990), 884–90.

Gill, Indermit. "Technological Change, Education and Obsolescence of Human Capital: Some Evidence for the U.S." Ph.D. thesis, University of Chicago, 1989.

Gros, Daniel. "Protectionism in a Framework with Intra-industry Trade: Tariffs, Quotas, Retaliation, and Welfare Losses." *International Monetary Fund Staff Papers* XXXIV (March 1987), 439–76.

Hanushek, Eric A. "The Impact of Differential Expenditures on School Performance." *Educational Researcher* XVIII (May 1989), 45–51, 62.

Hayek, F. A., "The Use of Knowledge in Society." *American Economic Review* XXXV (September 1945), 519–30.

Holmstrom, Bengt. "Moral Hazard in Teams." *Bell Journal of Economics* XIII (Fall 1982), 324–40.

Krugman, Paul R. "The Narrow Moving Band, the Dutch Disease, and the Consequences of Mrs. Thatcher: Notes on Trade in the Presence of Dynamic Scale Economics." *Journal of Development Economics* XXVII (1987), 41–55.

Lancaster, Kelvin. "Socially Optimal Product Differentiation." *American Economic Review* LXV (September 1975), 580–85.

Locay, Luis. "Economic Development and the Division of Production Between Households and Markets." *Journal of Political Economy* XCVIII (October 1990), 965–82.

Marx, Karl. *Capital* (Moscow: Foreign Languages Publishing House, 1961).

Mincer, Jacob, and Yoshio Higuchi. "Wage Structures and Labor Turnover in the United States and Japan." *Journal of the Japanese and International Economics* II (1988), 97–113.

Murphy, Kevin M. "Specialization and Human Capital." Ph.D. thesis, University of Chicago, 1986.

Peterson, P. Q., and M. Y. Pennell. *Health Manpower Source Book*, Section 14: Medical Specialists (Washington, DC: United States Public Health Service, 1962).

Rosenberg, Nathan. "Adam Smith on the Division of Labour: Two Views or One?" *Economica* XXXII (May 1965), 127–39.

Roy, Andrew D. "Some Thoughts on the Distribution of Earnings." *Oxford Economic Papers* N.S. III (June 1951), 135–46.

Shapiro, David B., *Reference Data on Physician Manpower* (Chicago: American Medical Association, 1989).

Simon, Julian. *The Economics of Population Growth* (Princeton, NJ: Princeton University Press, 1977).

Smith, Adam. *The Wealth of Nations* (New York: Modern Library, 1965).

Stigler, George J. "The Division of Labor is Limited by the Extent of the Market." *Journal of Political Economy* LIX (June 1951), 185–93.

West, E. G., "Adam Smith's Two Views on the Division of Labour." *Economica* XXXI (February 1964), 23–32.

Winston, Mark K., *The Biology of the Honeybee* (Cambridge MA: Harvard University Press, 1987).

Yang, Xiaokai, and Jeff Borland. "A Microeconomic Mechanism for Economic Growth." *Journal of Political Economy* XCIX (June 1991), 460–82.

CHAPTER XII

Human Capital, Fertility, and Economic Growth[1]

Gary S. Becker, Kevin M. Murphy, and Robert Tamura

1. Introduction

Economic growth has posed an intellectual challenge ever since the beginning of systematic economic analysis. Adam Smith claimed that
growth was related to the division of labor, but he did not link them in
a clear way. Thomas Malthus developed a formal model of a dynamic
growth process in which each country converged toward a stationary per
capita income. According to his model, death rates fall and fertility rises
when incomes exceed the equilibrium level, and the opposite occurs
when incomes are less than that level. Despite the influence of the Malthusian model on nineteenth-century economists, fertility fell rather
than rose as incomes grew during the past 150 years in the West and
other parts of the world.

The neoclassical model of growth responded to the failure of the Malthusian model by essentially ignoring any link between population and
the economy. Adjustments in this model take place not in the popula-

[1] Our research was supported by National Science Foundation grant SES-8520258 and
by National Institute of Child Health and Human Development grant SSP 1 R37 HD22054.
We had helpful comments from Edward Prescott, Sherwin Rosen, and Henry Wan and
useful assistance from David Meltzer.

tion growth rate, but in the rate of investment in physical capital. The physical capital stock grows more slowly when per capita income exceeds its equilibrium level, and it grows more rapidly when per capita income is below equilibrium.[2]

Neither Malthus's nor the neoclassicists' approach to growth pays much attention to human capital. Yet the evidence is now quite strong of a close link between investments in human capital and growth. Since human capital is embodied knowledge and skills, and economic development depends on advances in technological and scientific knowledge, development presumably depends on the accumulation of human capital.

Evidence for the twentieth-century United States supports this reasoning. Gross investment in schooling grew much more rapidly in the United States between 1910 and 1950 than gross investment in physical capital (Schultz 1960). Denison (1985) found that the growth in years of schooling between 1929 and 1982 "explained" about 25 percent of the growth in U.S. per capita income during the period. The experiences of nearly one hundred countries since 1960 suggest that education investments in 1960 are an important variable explaining subsequent growth in per capita incomes (see Barro 1989). Considerable circumstantial evidence also indicates that countries grow more rapidly when education and other skills are more abundant.

Our model of growth takes this evidence seriously and departs from both the Malthusian and neoclassical approaches by placing investments in human capital at the center. Crucial to our analysis is the assumption that rates of return on investments in human capital rise rather than decline as the stock of human capital increases, at least until the stock becomes large. The reason is that education and other sectors that produce human capital use educated and other skilled inputs more intensively than sectors that produce consumption goods and physical capital. This leads to multiple steady states: an undeveloped steady state with little human capital and low rates of return on investments in human capital, and a developed steady state with much higher rates of return and a large and perhaps growing stock of human capital.

Our analysis contains elements of both the Malthusian and neoclassical models since fertility is endogenous and rates of return on investments in physical capital decline as its stock increases. The endogeneity of fertility also leads to multiple steady states: a "Malthusian" undevel-

---

[2] The convergence of per capita income in the neoclassical growth model may help explain the experience of the developed countries (see Dowrick and Nguyen 1989). However, for the entire world, it fails badly.

oped steady state with high birth rates and low levels of human capital, and a developed steady state with much lower fertility and abundant stocks of human and physical capital.

Multiple steady states mean that history and luck are critical determinants of a country's growth experience. In our formulation, initial levels of human capital and technology, and subsequent productivity and other shocks, determine whether a country grows richer over time or stagnates at low income levels. Many attempts to explain why some countries and continents have had the best economic performance during the past several centuries give too little attention to accidents and good fortune.

Our approach relies on the assumption that higher fertility of the present generation increases the discount on per capita future consumption in the intertemporal utility functions that guide consumption and other decisions. Therefore, higher fertility discourages investments in both human and physical capital. Conversely, higher stocks of capital reduce the demand for children because that raises the cost of the time spent on child care.

Section 2 sets out the basic assumptions of our analysis and derives its main implications in an informal way. Section 3 provides a more rigorous discussion of a special case without physical capital, but with endogenous fertility and rates of return on human capital that are independent of its stock. Section 4 formally treats the case with both physical and human capital and the case in which the human capital sector uses educated and other skilled inputs more intensively than other sectors.

Section 5 discusses several broad implications of the analysis. Among other issues, it explains why the brain drain occurs invariably from less developed to developed countries, whereas less developed countries import as well as export financial and other tangible capital. We also discuss the "takeoff" period, in which increases in physical and human capital and decreases in fertility are unusually rapid.

Section 6 summarizes the discussion and offers a few concluding comments.

2. Basic Properties of the Model

This section first presents several basic assumptions about human capital and fertility and then derives in an informal way the properties of two stable steady-state positions. At one, human capital is negligible and fertility is high, while at the other, human capital is widespread and perhaps growing over time and fertility tends to be low.

The production and rearing of children are very time intensive. This implies that higher wage rates—due perhaps to greater human or physical capital per worker—induce a substitution effect away from fertility by raising the cost of children.

A second assumption about fertility is more novel and comes from recent work by Becker and Barro (1988) on dynastic families. It states that the discount rate applied by the present generation to the per capita consumption of subsequent generations depends negatively on the fertility of the present generation. Becker and Barro motivate the assumption with a utility function of parents who are altruistic toward their children. The discount rate between generations is determined by the degree of parental altruism toward each child. Diminishing marginal utility implies that the discount rate applied to the utility of each child declines as the number of children increases.

A simple formulation is

$$V_t = u(c_t) + a(n_t) n_t V_{t+1}, \tag{1}$$

with $u' > 0$, $u'' < 0$, and $a' < 0$; V_t and V_{t+1} are the utilities of parents and each child; c_t is parental consumption; and n_t is the number of children. The degree of altruism per child, $a(n)$, is negatively related to the number of children.

We assume that the production of human capital is human capital intensive and uses relatively more human capital per unit of output than the consumption, child rearing, and physical capital sectors do. By contrast, the production of physical capital is assumed to use physical capital as intensively as the consumption sector. The evidence does indicate that the education sector uses much highly educated labor as teachers and researchers, whereas the production of physical capital does not seem to use especially large amounts of physical capital.

In neoclassical models, the rate of return on physical capital investments is assumed to fall as the per capita stock of physical capital increases. A corresponding assumption for human capital is less plausible since human capital is knowledge embodied in people. The benefit from embodying additional knowledge in a person may depend positively rather than negatively on the knowledge he or she already has. There is a similar assumption behind the mastery learning concept in education pedagogy, where learning of complicated mathematics and other materials is more efficient when the building blocks of elementary concepts are mastered (see Bloom 1976).

A positive effect of the stock of human capital on investments in human capital is also part of the "neutrality" assumption in the literature on the life cycle accumulation of human capital (see the pioneering paper by Ben-Porath [1967]; see also Heckman [1976] and Rosen [1976]), the relation between parents' human capital and the learning of children (Becker and Tomes 1986), and the perpetual economic growth analysis in recent growth models (Becker and Murphy 1988, 1989; Lucas 1988; Tamura 1988, 1989).

The main implication of our two assumptions about human capital investments is that rates of return on human capital do not monotonically decline as the stock of human capital increases. Rates of return are low when there is little human capital, and they grow at least for a while as human capital increases. Eventually, they may begin to decline as it becomes increasingly difficult to absorb more knowledge (see the discussion in Becker and Murphy [1989]).

To discuss the implications of these assumptions about human capital and fertility, consider charts 14 and 15. Human capital per worker at time $t(H_t)$ is plotted along the horizontal axis and human capital at time $t + 1$ (H_{t+1}) is plotted along the vertical axis; physical capital is ignored for the present. The rate of return on investments in human capital, $R_h(H)$, rises with H, and it is relatively low at the origin, where $H = 0$. The discount rate on future consumption, $[a(n)]^{-1}$, is high at that point because $a(n)$ depends negatively on fertility (n), which tends to be high when H is low because the time spent bearing and rearing children is then cheap. Therefore, the discount rate on the future would exceed the rate of return on investment when $H = 0$:

$$[a(n_u)]^{-1} > R_h \text{ when } H = 0. \tag{2}$$

This inequality is a necessary and sufficient condition for a steady state when $H = 0$ (at U), for it guarantees that the economy does not want to invest when there is no human capital. Moreover, the steady state is locally stable, for the inequality must continue to hold for small positive values of H. Hence, the economy returns over time to $H = 0$ for some values of $H > 0$. As H increases, R_h also increases and $a(\cdot)$ falls as n falls, so that eventually they become equal. Then investment in H becomes positive, but the economy continues to return over time to the steady state with $H = 0$, as long as the amount invested is less than the capital that wears out.

However, the amount invested in human capital continues to rise as the stock of human capital increases because the rate of return continues to rise, and the demand for children falls as they become more expensive. Therefore, a steady state emerges when H is sufficiently large that it satisfies the condition

$$[a(n^*)]^{-1} = R_h(H^*), \tag{3}$$

where n^* is the steady-state fertility rate. If rates of return eventually fall as H gets large, H^* refers to a constant level of H, as at L in chart 14. However, if R_h asymptotes to a constant level, then H^* refers to a constant rate of growth in H, shown by the curve $h'h'$ in chart 15.

The policy functions hh and $h'h'$ in charts 14 and 15 give human capital in period $t + 1$ as a function of the amount in t. The steady states at $H = 0$ and $H = H^*$ are stable locally since hh and $h'h'$ are below the steady-state line $H_{t+1} = H_t$ for all $H < \hat{H}$ and are above the steady-state

CHART 14.

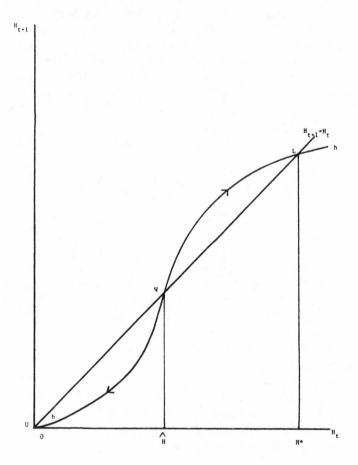

CHART 15.

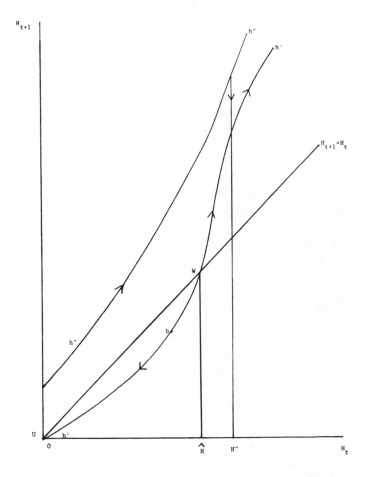

line for all $H > \hat{H}$. The point W at which $H = \hat{H}$ is a third steady state, but it is unstable; negative deviations ($H < \hat{H}$) lead over time toward $H = 0$, and positive deviations ($H > \hat{H}$) lead toward H^*.

The steady-state level $\hat{H}$ is nonoptimal when the program is not globally concave. The unstable steady state $\hat{H}$ is then replaced by a threshold human capital stock $\tilde{H} \neq \hat{H}$. At $\tilde{H}$, a parent is indifferent between reducing and raising the human capital of her children.

It is easy to incorporate physical capital into the story. With the usual assumption that the rate of return on physical capital is very high when there is little physical capital, the equilibrium stock of physical capital is positive at the steady state with $H = 0$. The equilibrium rate of return on investments in physical capital equals the endogenous discount rate

$$[a(n_u)]^{-1} = R_k \text{ when } H = 0, K = K_u, \qquad (4)$$

where R_k is the rate of return on investments in K.

The per capita amount of physical capital at the steady state with $H = H^*$ is likely to be larger than at the steady state with $H = 0$ because the discount rate is lower, although the equilibrium per capita stock of physical capital depends also on the degree of complementarity or substitution in production between K and H. However, if H grows at a constant rate in this steady state, so too would the equilibrium stock of physical capital.

The lower and upper stable steady states correspond to undeveloped and developed economies, respectively, where the lower one has smaller per capita incomes, lesser amounts of both human and physical capital per capita, and higher birth rates. Our analysis implies that rates of return on human capital (R_h) tend to be higher in developed economies, whereas rates of return on physical capital (R_k) may be greater or smaller in developed economies depending on birth rates in both steady states and the rate of growth of consumption in the developed steady states.

An undeveloped economy is stuck there unless sufficiently big favorable technology or other shocks raise the policy function above the steady-state line at $H = 0$ or increase the stock of human capital above $\hat{H}$. Similarly, an economy would remain developed unless war or other disasters destroy enough human capital to lower it sufficiently below $\hat{H}$ or reduce the policy function below the stead-state line. Even temporary shocks can permanently jar an economy into development if it accumulates enough human capital ($> \hat{H}$) before the shocks are over. By the same token, however, temporary shocks could push an economy toward permanently low incomes if it disinvests enough human capital ($H < \hat{H}$) before the shocks cease.

Human capital has a more fundamental role than physical capital in determining these steady-state equilibria because R_h rises, at least for a while, as H increases, while R_k falls with K. Given the human capital investment function, the initial level of per capita human capital determines where the economy ends up, regardless of the initial stock of physical capital. Although the stock of physical capital may affect the rate of return on investments in human capital, we show in Section 4 that an increase in physical capital could either raise or lower the return on human capital, depending on the degree of substitution between H and K in both production and consumption.

3. Fertility and Growth

The next two sections use specific models to illustrate the type of steady-state equilibrium and dynamics discussed in Section 2. This section highlights fertility, especially the time intensity of rearing children and the effect of the number of children on the rate of discount of future consumption. To concentrate on these properties, we ignore physical capital and assume simple production functions in the consumption, human capital, and fertility sectors.

We also assume that everyone is identical and lives for two periods, childhood and adulthood, works T hours as an adult, and spends all his or her childhood time investing in human capital. A person chooses to have n children at the beginning of the adult period, where v hours and f units of goods are spent rearing each child (v and f are constants) and each child is endowed with H^0 units of productive skills. The human capital of children depends on the endowments and human capital (H) of their teachers-parents and the time (h) spent on teaching. Assuming a Cobb-Douglas production function and H^0 and H as perfect substitutes, we have

$$H_{t+1} = Ah_t(bH^0 + H_t)^\beta. \tag{5}$$

The coefficient A measures the productivity of investments, b gives the number of H^0 units that are equivalent to one unit of H, and $\beta \le 1$ measures the effect of scale on the production of human capital.

The consumption sector also has a Cobb-Douglas production function:

$$c_t + fn_t = Dl_t(dH^0 + H_t), \tag{6}$$

where c is per capita adult consumption, D measures the productivity of this sector, l is the time spent by each adult producing consumer goods, and d is the rate of exchange between H^0 and H. We assume that the consumption sector has constant returns to scale in the effective amount of time, $l(dH^0 + H)$. By summing over the time allocated to fertility, consumption, and investment, we get the time budget equation

$$T = l_t + n_t(v + h_t). \tag{7}$$

This section concentrates on the effects of fertility by assuming that $b = d = 1$ to eliminate any comparative advantage from using human capital in the human capital sector instead of in the consumption sector. Both sectors have a comparative advantage relative to the production of children. It is also assumed that $\beta = 1$: the economy accumulates human capital without running into diminishing returns.

Parents maximize the dynastic utility function in equation (1) (or state planners maximize the intergeneration utility function in [1]) with respect to fertility and the time spent investing in human capital. We simplify the utility function with

$$a(n) = \alpha n^{-\varepsilon}, \, u(c) = \frac{c^{\sigma}}{\sigma}, \tag{8}$$

where $0 \le \varepsilon < 1$ and $0 < \sigma < 1$, α is the degree of pure altruism (when $n = 1$), and ε is the constant elasticity of altruism per child as their number increases.

The arbitrage condition between per capita consumption in periods t and $t + 1$ is

$$\frac{u'(c_t)}{au'(c_{t+1})} = \alpha^{-1} n_t^{\varepsilon} \left(\frac{c_{t+1}}{c_t} \right)^{1-\sigma} \ge R_{ht} = 1 + r_{ht}, \tag{9}$$

where r_h is the rate of return on investments in human capital, and equality holds when investments are positive. The rate of return is determined from

$$R_{ht} = A(T - vn_{t+1}) \tag{10}$$
$$= A(l_{t+1} + h_{t+1} n_{t+1}).^{3}$$

It is not surprising that the rate of return depends positively on the productivity of investments (A). Since the rate of return measures the effect

---

[3] To calculate the Euler equation for human capital investment, rewrite the Bellman equation using the learning technology (eq. [5]), the budget constraint (eq. [6]), and the time constraint (eq. [7]) to yield

$$V_t(H_t) = \max \left[\frac{(D(dH^0 + H_t)\{T - n_t[v + H_{t+1}A^{-1}(bH^0 + H_t)^{-\beta}]\} - fn_t)^{\sigma}}{\sigma} \right.$$
$$\left. + \alpha n_t^{1-\varepsilon} V_{t+1}(H_{t+1}) \right].$$

Differentiating with respect to H_{t+1} produces

$$-c_t^{\sigma-1} D(dH^0 + H_t) n_t A^{-1} (bH^0 + H_t)^{-\beta} + \alpha n_t^{1-\varepsilon} V'_{t+1} \le 0.$$

Using the envelope theorem provides

$$V'_{t+1} = c_{t+1}^{\sigma-1} D\{T - n_{t+1}[v + H_{t+2} A^{-1} (bH^0 + H_t)^{-\beta}}$$

on c_{t+1} of increasing H_{t+1}, it also depends on the productivity of greater H_{t+1}, which depends on l_{t+1}, $n_t^+{}_1$, and h_{t+1}.

The first-order condition for maximizing utility with respect to fertility comes from differentiating V_t in equation (1) with respect to n_t:

$$(1 - \varepsilon)\alpha n_t^{-\varepsilon} V_{t+1} = u'(c_t)[(v + h_t)(H^0 + H_t) + f]. \tag{11}$$

The second-order condition requires that $\varepsilon + \sigma < 1$ and $u'' < 0$ (see Becker and Barro 1988). The left-hand side of equation (11) gives the marginal utility from an additional child, and the right-hand side gives the sum of time and goods costs of producing and rearing a child. Costs depend on the endogenous time spent investing in children as well as the fixed time (v) and goods (f) inputs.

At the steady state with $H = 0$, equation (9) becomes the strict inequality

$$n_u^\varepsilon > \alpha A(T - vn_u), \tag{12}$$

with n_u being the steady-state fertility rate. This inequality will hold when parents have a sufficiently large family. The first-order condition for fertility in equation (11) simplifies in the steady state with $H = h = 0$ to

$$\frac{(T - vn_u)H^0 - fn_u}{vH^0 + f} = \frac{\sigma(1 - \alpha n_u^{1-\varepsilon})}{(1 - \varepsilon)\alpha n_u^{-\varepsilon}}. \tag{13}$$

The left-hand side gives the financial rate of return from children in the steady state: the ratio of adult consumption to the consumption forgone to produce a child. The rate of return from children is greater when endowments are larger and the time (v) and goods (f) spent to produce children are smaller. Therefore, parents have many children when they are cheap to produce and yet are reasonably well endowed with earning power. A sufficiently high rate of return from having children would induce parents to have enough children to discourage any investments

---

$$- \beta H_{t+2} A^{-1}(dH^0 + H_{t+1}) bH^0 + H_{t+1})^{-(1 + \beta)}]\}.$$

When $\beta = 1$ and $b = d$, the last two terms in square brackets drop out, leaving

$$V'_{t+1} = c_{t+1}^{\sigma-1} D(T - n_{t+1} v).$$

Substituting this into the Euler equation yields

$$-c_t^{\sigma-1} + \alpha n_t^\varepsilon c_{t+1}^{\sigma-1} A(T - vn_{t+1}) \leq 0.$$

in the children's human capital. Then $H = 0$ would be a steady-state equilibrium.

This steady state must be stable for some positive values of H. Since the rate of return on investments is strictly less than the discount rate when $H = 0$, it must also be less for some $H_t > 0$. Then $H_{t+1} = 0$, and the economy returns to the steady state in one generation. Clearly, the steady state is also stable for some H_t with positive investment when $H_{t+1} < H_t$.

An increase in the stock of human capital raises per capita income and hence has a positive income effect as well as a negative substitution effect on the demand for children. The income effect dominates in economies with little human capital if components of f—necessities such as food, housing, and clothing—are the main cost of rearing children, as determined from

$$\frac{f}{v(H^0 + H_t) + f} > 1 - \sigma. \tag{14}$$

A positive relation between fertility and per capita income is a Malthusian property that helps stabilize the steady state with $H = 0$. Higher fertility when $H > 0$ raises the discount on future consumption and lowers the rate of return on investments. Both effects reduce the incentive to invest and help return the economy to the steady state.

However, our analysis implies that the Malthusian assumption of a positive relation between fertility and income is a myopic view of the effects of development on fertility that may hold when countries have only a little human capital, but does not hold when they manage to reach a moderate stage of development. Even if parents do not invest in children, the cost of the time input must rise as H increases, which reverses the inequality in (14) when H is large enough. Then the substitution effect begins to dominate the income effect, and fertility declines with further increases in H. Eventually, the rate of return on investment in children becomes as large as the discount rate, and parents start investing in children ($h > 0$). The amount invested at first is insufficient to maintain the stock of human capital, and the economy returns over time to the steady state (see point b in chart 15).

Investments rise further as the stock of human capital increases further. If investments are sufficiently productive (A) and there are appropriate values of v, ε, and σ (see eq. [18] below), the amount invested would exceed the initial stock for sufficiently high initial stocks of H. Then H_t does not decline over time toward $H = 0$, but instead continues to grow over time. As H grows, the endowment H^0 becomes negligible relative to time costs, $(v + h)H$. The economy converges to a steady-state growth path (see Tamura [1989] for a discussion of the stability of this path), with a constant fertility rate (n^*), a constant time (h^*) spent investing in H, and a constant rate of growth over time in both H and c (g^*).

The steady-state values n^* and h^* are determined from the first-order conditions for n and h when f and H^0 are negligible:

$$(1 - \varepsilon)\alpha n^{*-\varepsilon}V_{t+1} = u'(c_t)(v + h^*)H_t, \tag{15}$$

$$A\alpha n_*^{-\varepsilon} \frac{dV_{t+1}}{dH_{t+1}} = u'(c_t), \tag{16}$$

where dV_{t+1}/dH^*_{t+1} is evaluated along the steady-state path with

$$1 + g^* = \frac{c_{t+1}}{c_t} = \frac{H_{t+1}}{H_t} = Ah^*. \tag{17}$$

Dividing equation (16) by (15) and substituting $\sigma = d\log V_{t+1}/dH_{t+1}$ and $h^* = (1 + g^*)/A$, we get

$$1 + g^* = \frac{\sigma v A}{1 - \sigma - \varepsilon} \tag{18}$$

and

$$h^* = \frac{\sigma v}{1 - \sigma - \varepsilon}. \tag{19}$$

The steady-state fertility rate is found by substituting into equations (9) and (10):

$$\alpha n^{*-\varepsilon}(T - v n^*) = A^{-1}(1 + g^*)^{1-\sigma}. \tag{20}$$

Steady-state growth exists if the combination of A, v, σ, and ε on the right-hand side of equation (18) exceeds one. Equations (18) and (20) show that an increase in the productivity of investments (A) raises both steady-state growth and fertility. Higher fixed-time costs of children (v) or a more elastic altruism function (ε) reduces n^* and raises g^* as families substitute away from children when they become more expensive and toward greater investment in each child.

Greater altruism (α), and lower adult mortality that expands adult time (T), both raise n^* but do not affect g^* (see Meltzer [1989] for a general discussion of the effects of mortality within this model). Note, however, that the absence of any effect of α and T on g^* results from the constant elasticity form assumed for $u(c)$ and $a(n)$. With other functional forms, increases in α or T could either raise or lower the steady-state growth rate.

The analysis implies that fertility and the steady-state rate of growth in per capita incomes could be either negatively or positively related among countries, or over time in a given country, depending on why growth rates differed. If g^* differed mainly because the productivity of investments differed, n^* and g^* would be positively related; if g^* differed mainly because the cost of children differed, g^* and n^* would be negatively related; and if g^* differed mainly because adult mortality or the degree of altruism toward children differed, g^* and n^* might well be unrelated. Studies of growth rates among countries since 1950 find that they are very weakly negatively related to fertility rates (see Barro 1989). This suggests that growth rates do not differ mainly because of differences in the productivity of investments in human capital.

Our analysis does imply that the *level* of per capita income and fertility would be strongly related. This is easily seen by comparing n_u in equation (13) with n^* in equation (20): $n_u > n^*$ for all values of $g^* \geq 0$. Therefore, countries with low levels of human capital that have not undergone much development would have higher fertility than developed countries with much human capital. It is well known that the negative relation among countries between the fertility rate and the level of per capita real income is very strong (see, e.g., the evidence in Tamura [1988, 1989]).

Since we have been assuming that the value function V is concave, the optimal human capital in period $t + 1$ is a continuous function of the human capital in t. With the steady state at $H = 0$ stable for some $H > 0$ and the steady-state growth path stable for some H, there must also be a steady state with a constant positive level of H and a constant n; in chart 15, this steady state is at W where $H = \hat{H}$, and the policy function intersects the line $H_{t+1} = H_t$. These steady-state values of H and n are determined from the first-order conditions in equation (19) with $g = 0$ and a first-order condition for n.

A comparison of equation (20) when $g = 0$ with equation (12) shows that $n_d < n_u$. Even if n and H are positively related for H near $H = 0$, n must decline below its level at $H = 0$ before the steady state at $H = \hat{H}$. Moreover, equation (20) shows that $n^* < n_d$: fertility is lower when H is growing at a constant rate than when H is constant. The economy substitutes away from children as human capital and the time cost of raising children increase.

When a steady state with $H = 0$ exists, the steady state with positive human capital is locally and globally unstable (see Tamura [1989] for a formal proof). As chart 15 shows, the economy moves over time to $H = 0$ for all $H < \hat{H}$, and it moves to steady-state growth for all $H > \hat{H}$. The instability of this steady state results from the negative relation between fertility and human capital. The decline in fertility when H increases above $\hat{H}$ lowers the discount rate on future consumption and also raises the rate of return on investments. Both forces raise investments and next period's human capital relative to this period's. With $H_{t+1} > H_t$, fertility falls further and the process continues.

Indeed, if this interaction between n and H is strong enough, the value function becomes convex. Then the function that relates H_{t+1} to H_t has a jump at some capital stock $\tilde{H}$. The lower leg lies below the steady-state line, with $H_{t+1} < H_t$ for all $H_t < \tilde{H}$. The upper leg lies above the steady-state line, with $H_{t+1} > H_t$ for all $H_t > \tilde{H}$. Although $\tilde{H}$ is not a steady-state solution to the first-order conditions because this solution does not maximize utility if V is convex, $\tilde{H}$ does have the properties of an unstable steady state.

The policy functions become discontinuous even for "normal" values of the parameters. The discontinuous relation between H_{t+1} and H_t at $H = \tilde{H}$ is matched by a discontinuous relation between n_t and H_t at $H = \tilde{H}$. The jump in investment when H increases slightly beyond $H = \tilde{H}$ goes together with a fall in fertility. Since the interaction between n and H produces the convexity of V, it is no surprise that they both are discontinuous functions of the human capital stock. However, all the adjustment from a switch between the decay regime and the growth regime occurs through investments and fertility, leaving consumption unaffected (see Tamura [1989] for a formal proof). These results can be seen in chart 17 below.

4. Comparative Advantage in the Production of Human Capital

In modern economies, the human capital sector relies on skilled and trained labor more than the consumption sector does. The teaching sector has highly educated employees, while many services and some goods rely on unskilled labor. Our analysis captures this difference in a simple way if the endowment (H^0) is less important in the production of human capital, that is, if $b < d$ in the production functions for H and c in equations (5) and (6).

If H is small relative to H^0 and if β in equation (5) is close to one, rates of return increase as a person accumulates more human capital. Therefore, the economy should be more efficient with specialization in the accumulation of human capital: teachers in the human capital sector should have more human capital than workers in the consumption sector. However, such specialization may not be feasible if the capital market, especially the market between generations, is undeveloped. Teachers may be unable to borrow the resources to finance very great investments in human capital. This paper makes the strong assumption that because of such capital market difficulties, specialization is not feasible and everyone has the same human capital, even when returns increase as a person accumulates more human capital (Becker and Murphy [1989] analyze efficient specialization between teachers and workers).

We introduce physical capital into the analysis by assuming that physical capital is accumulated consumer goods that do not wear out. The consumption sector is assumed to use physical capital more intensively than the human capital sector, and we treat the simple case in which human capital does not use any physical capital at all. The Cobb-Douglas function in equation (6) is extended to include physical capital:

$$c + fn + \Delta K = D[l(dH^0 + H)]^\gamma K^{1-\gamma}, \tag{21}$$

where ΔK is the net (and gross) investment in physical capital. The human capital production function is still given by equation (5), with $\beta \le 1$.

If the human capital sector uses human capital much more intensively than the consumption sector—if b is much less than d—the rate of return on investments in human capital would be low when $H = 0$ and would rise for a while as H increases, even if $\beta < 1$. The rate of return on H when $H = 0$ would be below the discount rate on future consumption even with moderate levels of fertility, and hence of the discount rate. Therefore, the comparative advantage of the human capital sector in using human capital raises the likelihood of a stable steady state at $H = 0$.

The equilibrium conditions for the steady state are

$$R_k = \alpha^{-1} n_u^\varepsilon > R_h, \tag{22}$$

with

$$R_k = 1 + (1 - \gamma)(c_u + fn_u) K_u^{-1} \tag{23}$$

and

$$R_h = A(T - vn_u) \frac{(bH^0)^\beta}{dH^0}. \tag{24}$$

Clearly, for a sufficiently small b, $R_h < \alpha^{-1}n_u^\varepsilon$ for any positive value of n_u. Since the rate of return on K goes to infinity as $K \to 0$, K_u must be positive. Therefore, the rate of return on physical capital must exceed that on human capital at this steady state.

When H is larger relative to H^0, b, and d, the comparative advantage of the human capital sector in the use of H becomes unimportant. With $\beta = 1$, the economy approaches a steady-state growth path as H increases, where fertility is constant and human capital, physical capital, and per capita consumption all grow at the rate g^*, given by

$$1 + g^* = \frac{H_{t+1}}{H_t} = \frac{K_{t+1}}{K_t} = \frac{c_{t+1}}{c_t} = \frac{\tilde{\sigma}vA}{1 - \sigma - \varepsilon}, \tag{25}$$

with $\tilde{\sigma} = \gamma\sigma$.

The slight difference between the right-hand side of this equation and the right-hand side of equation (18) is that $\partial \log V / \partial \log H = \gamma\sigma < \sigma$ along the steady-state growth path when consumption depends also on physical capital. The ratio of K to H, constant along the steady-state path, is determined by the condition

$$A(T - vn^*) = R_h = R_k = \alpha^{-1}n^{*\varepsilon}(1 + g^*)^{1-\sigma}. \tag{26}$$

Since the discount rate on future consumption $[a(n)]^{-1}$ depends negatively on fertility, the interest rate with steady-state growth would be less than in the undeveloped steady state if fertility were sufficiently lower in the growth equilibrium to make the right-hand side of equation (26) less than the middle term of equation (22). This implies that the rate of return on $K(R_k)$, which equals the interest rate, could be larger or smaller in steady-state growth compared with the undeveloped equilibrium. An increase in the steady-state growth rate due to a change in A or another parameter could mean a lower interest rate and rate of return on physical capital if fertility fell enough. These results are quite different from those in the neoclassical model, where interest rates and rates of return on physical capital are positively related to the growth rate because the discount rate is assumed to be constant.

Since R_h, the rate of return on human capital, equals R_k in the growth equilibrium but is less than R_k in the undeveloped equilibrium, R_h must increase relative to R_k as an economy moves between these equilibria. Indeed, R_h must be higher in the steady-state growth equilibrium than in the undeveloped equilibrium even if R_k and the interest rate are lower. The reason is that R_k can be lower only if fertility is lower, but lower fertility implies that R_h is higher; compare the left-hand side of equation (26) with the right-hand side of equation (24) when $\beta = 1$ and $b < d$.

As H and K get larger, fertility is encouraged by an income effect, but it is discouraged by a substitution effect from the higher cost of time. Fertility would be lower in the growth equilibrium than in the undeveloped equilibrium if the substitution effect dominates: if parents want few children when they are expensive. Empirically, fertility is much lower in richer than in poorer countries, which suggests that the substitution effect does dominate. The lower fertility in richer countries implies that interest rates and rates of return on physical capital might also be lower in richer countries.

The phase diagram in chart 16 helps analyze the stability of the steady-state growth equilibrium and the dynamic paths of human capital and physical capital. The point U is the steady state with $H = 0$ and $K > 0$, and the slope of the ray Op gives the ratio of K to H along the steady-state growth path. The isocline $\dot{K} = 0$ is the locus of all combinations of K and H that lead to zero investment in K; similarly, for the isocline $\dot{H} = 0$. Since U is a steady-state equilibrium, both isoclines go through U.

An increase in K discourages investment in K because R_k declines as K increases. An increase in H has conflicting effects on the incentive to invest in K. It encourages investment because K and H are complements in production (see eq. [21]) and if an increase in H reduces fertility. However, an increase in H would discourage investment in K if it lowers the marginal utility of future consumption by raising investment in H. We assume that, on balance, an increase in H encourages investment in K, so that the isocline $\dot{K} = 0$ is positively sloped, as in chart 16.

An increase in K has conflicting effects on investments in H since it raises the cost of the time spent investing in H, but it also raises the marginal utility of future consumption by reducing investment in K and perhaps by reducing fertility. For given fertility, the net effect of an increase in K on investment in H depends on the elasticity of substitution in production compared to that in consumption.[4] Chart 16 assumes that,

[4] Let α be the discount factor (we assume fertility is fixed), w_t the wage in period t, and c_t the corresponding level of consumption. The first-order condition for human capital with log utility is simply

$$\frac{w_t}{c_t} = A\alpha \, \frac{w_{t+1}}{c_{t+1}},$$

on balance, an increase in K discourages investment in H. So $\dot{H} = 0$ is positively sloped since an increase in H raises R_h and hence investment in H.

The isoclines $\dot{H} = 0$ and $\dot{K} = 0$ intersect not only at U but also at an unstable steady state at W. An economy that begins to the right of the stable manifold M through W grows over time toward the path given by Op (see curve b in chart 16), whereas an economy that begins to the left of M declines over time toward point U with $H = 0$ (see curve a). Only economies that begin along M end up at W. The increasing returns to H and the likely decline in n as H increases are what destabilize the steady state at W. These effects could be strong enough to make the value function V convex, and hence the relation between n_t, H_{t+1}, and H_t discontinuous, although the relation between c_{t+1} and H_t is continuous (chart 17 gives an example).

The curve b in chart 16 shows that H grows faster than K when an economy starts off near the steady state at W. Then the ratio of K to H falls as the steady-state growth path Op is approached. Human capital in the United States apparently did grow faster than physical capital since the turn of the century (Schultz 1960), and human capital now accounts for a large fraction of all U.S. capital (see the estimates in Jorgenson and Fraumeni [1989]).

If a war or other disaster destroys some physical capital, rates of return on K and investments in K increase. Investments in H also increase if the isoclines for $\dot{H}$ are positively sloped. If the economy had been on the growth path, H and K would grow more rapidly over time after the disas-

---

and the first-order condition for physical capital is simply

$$\frac{1}{c_t} = \alpha \, \frac{r^k_{t+1}}{c_{t+1}},$$

where r^k_{t+1} is the marginal product of capital in period $t + 1$. Rewriting these equations as

$$\left(\frac{H_{t+1}}{H_t}\right)\left(\frac{w_t H_t}{c_t}\right) = A\alpha\left(\frac{w_{t+1} H_{t+1}}{c_{t+1}}\right)$$

and

$$\frac{k_{t+1}}{c_t} = \alpha \, \frac{k_{t+1} r^k_{t+1}}{c_{t+1}},$$

we see that if human capital grows at the fixed rate $A\alpha$, the first equation will be satisfied since labor's share is fixed with Cobb-Douglas functions. If the savings rate is constant, then k_{t+1}/c_t is constant, and the second equation will be satisfied since capital's share is also fixed.

CHART 16.

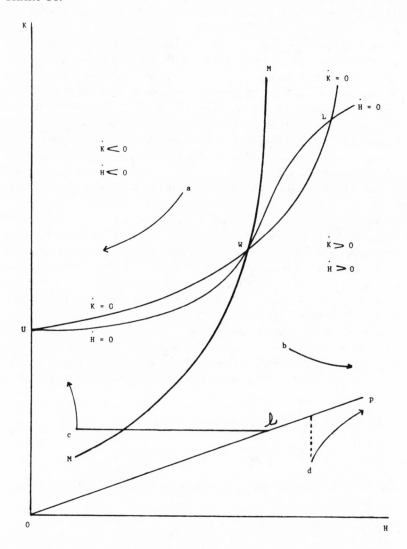

ter than they did before. This implies that the stock of human capital would be greater at any future year than it would have been without the destruction of physical capital. Since the ratio of K to H approaches the same equilibrium ratio that existed before the disaster, K must at some future year also exceed the level it would have reached had the disaster not occurred. Since both H and K exceed the levels they would have

CHART 17.

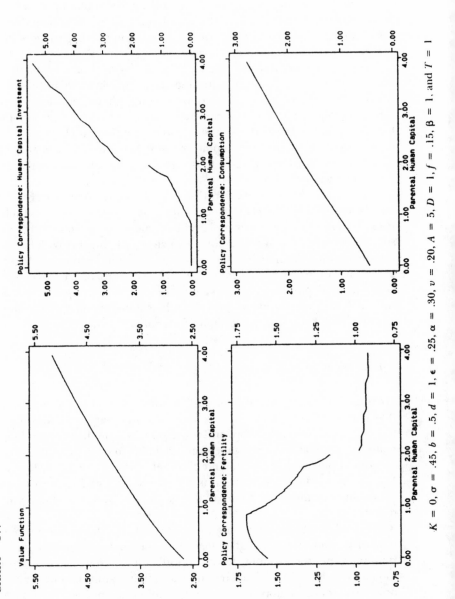

$K = 0, \sigma = .45, b = .5, d = 1, \epsilon = .25, \alpha = .30, \upsilon = .20, A = .5, D = 1, f = .15, \beta = 1, \text{ and } T = 1$

had, per capita income must also eventually surpass the levels it would have reached!

It might appear from this conclusion that destruction of physical capital should be encouraged, for per capita incomes eventually exceed the levels they would have reached. But initial declines in per capita income dominate any eventual increase for the generation that experiences the disaster since its dynastic utility is reduced.

The story is quite different when a disaster destroys human capital, as when a conqueror kills off the educated class. Since investments in both H and K are discouraged, the economy would always have lower per capita incomes than if H had not been destroyed. Indeed, if enough human capital is destroyed—if the economy is moved in chart 16 from point l on the growth path to a point c that is to the left of the manifold M—the economy never returns to the growth path. Instead, it sinks toward the undeveloped steady state at U.

If the coefficient β in equation (5) is less than one, the rate of return on H eventually falls as H increases. Then a steady-state growth equilibrium does not exist, but it is replaced by a stable steady state with constant levels of H, K, and n (see point L in charts 14 and 16). With $\beta < 1$, the slope of the isocline $\dot{H} = 0$ in chart 16 begins to decrease as H gets larger and intersects $\dot{K} = 0$ again at point L. The ratio of K to H is lower at L than at W but is higher than along the growth path Op. The steady state at L, like the steady-state growth path, is stable for all initial quantities of H and K that are to the right of the manifold M.

5. Discussion

Malthus did not pay much attention to human capital, as he assumed that parents were concerned only about the number of children they have. His conclusion that ebbs and flows in birth (and death) rates help maintain wage rates at a constant level is valuable in understanding long-run developments in England and elsewhere prior to his time. But the Malthusian world was shattered forever by the persistent growth in incomes and decline in birth rates that began in the West during the nineteenth century.

The undeveloped steady state in our model has Malthusian properties, for human capital is negligible, fertility is high, and changes in birth rates may help the economy to return to this steady state when it is not too far away. However, our analysis indicates that Malthusians have a myopic view that is inappropriate when economies manage to diverge enough from the undevelopment "trap." Economies would continue to develop and diverge from that steady state if technological and other shocks either raise the policy functions above the steady-state line or raise the stocks of human and physical capital sufficiently, for example, if human capital is raised above the unstable steady-state amount H in charts 14 and 15. Improved methods to use coal, better rail and ocean transports, and decreased regulation of prices and foreign trade are some changes that helped trigger the early growth of the West (see the discussion in Rosenberg and Birdzell [1986]).

Considerable luck is needed in the timing and magnitude of shocks to give a sufficiently big push to investments in human and physical capital. But very unlikely configurations of events do occur in the course of thousands of years of history. We believe that the West's primacy, which began in the seventeenth century, was partly due to a "lucky" timing of technological and political changes in the West.

Even temporary events, if they are strong enough, can permanently wrench an economy away from undevelopment. If temporary events lead to favorable initial conditions, the economy continues to grow even without the stimulus of major additional innovations or other events similar to those that got the process started. Suppose that a sequence of events raised the policy function temporarily from $h'h'$ in figure 2 to $h''h''$. The economy moves along this function and accumulates H'' units of human capital by the time these events cease and the policy function returns to $h'h'$. If new technologies had raised the demand for human capital, the stimulus would cease when these technologies were fully exploited, as long as no further technological advances emerge. Nevertheless, the economy continues to invest in human capital because it had accumulated enough for the process to become self-generating. Analytically, growth displays "state" or "path" dependence, and initial conditions count (see Arthur [1988] for a good discussion of such path dependence in the location of "silicon valleys"; see also David [1985]).

According to our analysis, at some point in the growth process, economies experience periods of particularly rapid accumulation of human and physical capital and declines in birth rates and family size. This happens near the unstable steady states at W in charts 14, 15, and 16 and near the points of discontinuity in chart 17. These periods of rapid change are reminiscent of the "takeoff" in Rostow's theory of growth (see Rostow [1963] for an empirical evaluation of his analysis). Takeoffs in our approach are driven by increasing returns to investments in human capital and increased costs of children as capital is accumulated. An economy that starts at point W is posed either to take off toward sustained economic growth or to fall back toward stagnation.

Needham (1969) presents a well-known discussion of why the industrial revolution did not begin in medieval China, even though that country was much more advanced technologically than medieval Europe. He emphasizes the policies of the mandarin bureaucrats (a view criticized by Chao [1986]; see also Jones's [1988] criticisms of Needham), but he also recognizes the delicacy and instability of the prior European equilibrium: "These many diverse discoveries and inventions had earthshaking effects in Europe, but in China the social order of bureaucratic feudalism was little disturbed by them. The *built-in instability* of European society must therefore be contrasted with a homeostatic equilibrium in China" (p. 214; our italics).

Our analysis implies that rates of return on education and other human capital are higher in developed than in undeveloped countries, both absolutely and relative to rates on physical capital. Rates of return on physical capital may be either higher or lower in developed countries, depending on fertility and rates of growth in consumption. Consequently, we readily explain why the "brain drain" of educated and skilled persons almost invariably occurs from poorer to richer countries, such as the Indian academics, engineers, and doctors who migrate to the United States. Although tangible capital flows in both directions, it is not clear whether, as implied by our analysis, physical capital goes both to richer countries that grow rapidly and do not have particularly low fertility and to poorer countries that do some growing and have high fertility.

An increased stock of human capital raises investments in developing new technologies by expanding the education-intensive research and development industry. Since our analysis implies that human capital grows sharply with development, it readily explains why systematic research and development activities are confined to richer countries.

The rapid growth in the labor force participation of married women is one of the more striking changes induced by economic development during the past half century. Our formal model has only one sex, but it easily incorporates the strong division of labor between married men and women in undeveloped countries, where women spend most of their time bearing and raising many children and doing other work that is complementary to child care. The large decline in birth rates and rise in wage rates as countries develop encourage married women to spend much more of their time in the labor force, which greatly weakens the traditional division of labor.

It has been known for a long time that recovery from wars and other disasters is usually remarkably rapid. John Stuart Mill (1848, p. 74) remarked on "what has so often excited wonder, the great rapidity with which countries recover from a state of devastation, the disappearance in a short time, of all traces of mischiefs done by earthquakes, floods, hurricanes, and the ravages of war." He argues that recovery is rapid only when most of the population is left "with the same skill and knowledge which they had before" (p. 75).

Chart 16 shows that a wartime destruction of physical capital in a country that starts along the growth path (Op) stimulates more rapid investment in this capital. It may well also stimulate more rapid investment in human capital; see curve d in chart 16 and the discussion in Section 4. Then per capita incomes eventually exceed what they would have been had the war not happened, although it still lowers the dynastic utility of the generations alive at the time. This analysis can explain the rapid recovery and then vigorous growth in Germany and Japan after World War II, which suggested to many people the erroneous conclusions that countries benefit from wartime destruction of their physical capital stock.

We can also explain Mill's proviso that knowledge and skills survive. Countries recover from modest reductions in their knowledge, but large enough losses bring a cumulative decline as both physical capital and human capital slide toward an undeveloped state. This happens in chart 16 if human capital is reduced below the manifold through the unstable steady state W (see point c). Wartime destructions of physical and human capital have different consequences because human capital is knowledge embodied in people. When too much knowledge is destroyed, an economy loses the foundation for further accumulations of knowledge—whether embodied in people or disembodied in technologies—which is the essence of economic growth.

6. Concluding Remarks

Our analysis of growth assumes endogenous fertility and a rising rate of return on human capital as the stock of human capital increases. Societies can save across generations by the birth of many children, by great investment in each child, and by long-term accumulation of physical capital. When human capital is abundant, rates of return on human capital investments are high relative to rates of return on children, whereas when human capital is scarce, rates of return on human capital are low relative to those on children. As a result, societies with limited human capital choose large families and invest little in each member; those with abundant human capital do the opposite.

This increasing incentive to invest in human capital as the amount of human capital increases leads to two stable steady states. One has large families and little human capital, and the other has small families and large and perhaps growing human and physical capital. A country may switch from the first "Malthusian" equilibrium to the second "development" equilibrium if it has reasonably prolonged good fortune and policies that favor investment.

There is still only a meager understanding of the growth process: of why some countries and regions have grown more rapidly than others and why the growth leaders are not the same in different historical periods. Our analysis appears to highlight important variables in growth and development: investments in human capital, choices over family size and birth rates, interactions between human capital and physical capital, the existence of several stable steady-state equilibria, and the crucial role of luck and the past. Perhaps this analysis will push the understanding of growth a few steps forward.

References

Arthur, Brian. "Urban Systems and Historical Path Dependence." In *Cities and Their Vital Systems: Infrastructure Past, Present, and Future*, edited by Jesse H. Ausubel and Robert Herman. Washington: Nat. Acad. Press, 1988.

Barro, Robert J. "Economic Growth in a Cross Section of Countries." Working Paper no. 3120. Cambridge, Mass.: NBER, September 1989.

Becker, Gary S., and Barro, Robert J. "A Reformation of the Economic Theory of Fertility." *Q.J.E.* 103 (February 1988): 1–25.

Becker, Gary S., and Murphy, Kevin M. "Economic Growth, Human Capital and Population Growth." Paper presented at the conference on the Problem of Development: Exploring Economic Development through Free Enterprise, sponsored by the Institute for the Study of Free Enterprise Systems, State Univ. New York, Buffalo, May 1988.

———. "Human Capital, the Division of Labor and Economic Progress." Manuscript. Chicago: Univ. Chicago, 1989.

Becker, Gary S., and Tomes, Nigel. "Human Capital and the Rise and Fall of Families." *J. Labor Econ.* 4, no. 3, pt. 2 (July 1986): S1–S39.

Ben-Porath, Yoram. "The Production of Human Capital and the Life Cycle of Earnings." *J.P.E.* 75, no. 4, pt. 1 (August 1967): 352–65.

Bloom, Benjamin S. *Human Characteristics and School Learning.* New York: McGraw-Hill, 1976.

Chao, Kang. *Man and Land in Chinese History: An Economic Analysis.* Stanford, Calif.: Stanford Univ. Press, 1986.

David, Paul A. "Clio and the Economics of QWERTY." *A.E.R. Papers and Proc.* 75 (May 1985): 332–37.

Denison, Edward F. *Trends in American Economic Growth, 1929–1982.* Washington: Brookings Inst., 1985.

Dowrick, Steve, and Nguyen, Duc-Tho. "OECD Comparative Economic Growth

1950–85: Catch-up and Convergence." *A.E.R.* 79 (December S1989): 1010–30.

Heckman, James J. "A Life-Cycle Model of Earnings, Learning, and Consumption." *J.P.E.* 84, no. 4, pt. 2 (August 1976): S11–S44.

Jones, Eric L. *Growth Recurring: Economic Change in World History.* New York: Oxford Univ. Press, 1988.

Jorgenson, Dale W., and Fraumeni, Barbara M. "Investment in Education." *Educational Researcher* 18 (May 1989): 35–44.

Lucas, Robert E., Jr. "On the Mechanics of Economic Development." *J. Monetary Econ.* 22 (July 1988): 3–42.

Meltzer, David O. "Length of Life, Human Capital and Economic Growth." Paper presented at the conference on the Family, Gender Differences and Development, Economic Growth Center, Yale Univ., New Haven, Conn., September 1989.

Mill, John Stuart. *Principles of Political Economy, with Some of Their Applications to Social Philosophy.* London: Parker, 1848.

Needham, Joseph. *The Grand Titration: Science and Society in East and West.* London: Allen and Unwin, 1969.

Rosen, Sherwin. "A Theory of Life Earnings." *J.P.E.* 84, no. 4, pt. 2 (August 1976): S45–S67.

Rosenberg, Nathan, and Birdzell, L. E. *How the West Grew Rich: The Economic Transformation of the Industrial World.* New York: Basic Books, 1986.

Rostow, Walt W., ed. *The Economics of Take-off into Sustained Growth: Proceedings of a Conference Held by the International Economic Association.* New York: St. Martin's, 1963.

Schultz, Theodore W. "Capital Formation by Education." *J.P.E.* 68 (December 1960): 571–83.

Tamura, Robert. "Fertility, Human Capital and the 'Wealth of Nations.' " Ph.D. dissertation, Univ. Chicago, 1988.

———. "Fertility, Human Capital and the 'Wealth of Nations.' " Working paper. Iowa City: Univ. Iowa, 1989.

Appendix A

Sources and Methods

This appendix sets out some of the sources and methods used in deriving the rates of return and other figures presented in the study. It should be read by all persons planning to use the findings since the basic data are quite imperfect and many adjustments could have been made differently. First, the methods used to estimate incomes at different levels of education are presented, and then those used to estimate costs.

1. Incomes

a. The Basic Data

The basic income data came from the 1940 and 1950 Censuses and from the surveys of 1956 and 1958.[1] M. Zeman estimated mean earnings by age and education in 1939 from data in the 1940 Census that

[1] See *Sixteenth Census of the United States: 1940, Population, Education, Educational Attainment by Economic Characteristics and Marital Status*, Bureau of the Census, Washington, 1947, Tables 29 and 31. *United States Census of Population, 1950*, Special Reports, *Education*, Vol. IV, part 5, Chapter B, Bureau of the Census, Washington, 1953, Table 12. *Income of Families and Persons in the United States* for 1956 and 1958, Current Population Reports, Consumer Income, Bureau of the Census, Series P-60, nos. 27 and 33, Washington, 1958 and 1960.

351

gave the distribution of persons by income class.[2] I used the 1950 Census to make my own estimates of incomes in 1949, and H. Miller estimated means from the 1956 and 1958 surveys.[3] Zeman used incomes near the midpoints of all closed income classes as the means of these classes, and Lorenz distributions to estimate the means of the $5000-and-over class. Miller used the midpoints of all closed classes and the single figure $20,000 as the mean of the $10,000-and-over class. I used essentially the midpoints of all closed classes and Pareto distributions to estimate means in the open-end class, except that the maximum mean in the open-end class was limited to $27,000, the minimum to $15,000, and obviously incorrect figures were eliminated. The same

TABLE A-1

Open-End Means Used in Calculating 1949 Incomes
(dollars)

	Years of Education			
Age	8	12	13–15	16+
14–15	15,000	—	—	—
16–17	15,000	—	—	—
18–19	15,000	15,000	—	—
20–21	15,000	15,000	15,000	—
22–24	15,000	15,000	15,000	16,826
25–29	15,213	15,213	15,068	17,157
30–34	15,782	15,782	15,915	16,926
35–44	17,971	17,971	19,231	22,349
45–54	22,739	22,739	25,446	27,000
55–64	26,656	26,656	27,000	27,000

Source: See text.

means were used for elementary-school graduates as for high-school graduates.[4] These estimates are shown in Table A-1.

My estimates for 1949 differ from those of Houthakker and Miller[5]

[2] See his "A Quantitative Analysis of White–Non-White Income Differentials in the United States in 1939," unpublished Ph.D. dissertation, University of Chicago, 1955, Tables 13 and 16.

[3] See his "Annual and Lifetime Income in Relation to Education, 1939–1959," *American Economic Review*, December 1960, Table 1.

[4] So few elementary-school graduates are in the open-end class that estimates based on Pareto distributions were unstable. Moreover, because so few are in this class, it does not greatly matter which means are used.

[5] H. S. Houthakker, "Education and Income," *Review of Economics and Statistics*, February 1959, pp. 24–28, and Miller, *op. cit.*

primarily because of the different treatment of the open-end class. They use the same open-end mean at all age and educational levels, Miller $20,000 and Houthakker $22,000, while mine rises significantly with age and education. There is little question that actual open-end means do rise with age and education, so that they overestimate incomes at lower levels relative to those at higher ones. Table A-2 indi-

TABLE A-2

Three Estimates of Before-Tax Income Differentials
between Education Classes in 1949
(dollars)

| | Income Differences between Persons with: | | | | | |
| | 12 and 8 Years of School | | | 16+ and 12 Years of School | | |
Age	Houthakker	Miller	Becker[a]	Houthakker	Miller	Becker[a]
22–24	417		413	−522		−378
25–29	642	706	638	201	876	228
30–34	819		810	1577		1439
35–44	1023	1026	993	3135	3030	3416
45–54	1438	1442	1551	3631	3427	4753
55–64	1504	1538	1890	3280	3107	4051

Source: Houthakker, *Review of Economics and Statistics*, February 1959, Table 1, p. 25; and Miller, *American Economic Review*, December 1960, Table 1, p. 966.
[a] Whites only.

cates, however, that at most ages all three studies show similar income differentials between education classes. Zeman and Miller exclude persons with no income although they should be included in estimating cohort incomes for exactly the same reason that dead members of a cohort are included (via mortality adustments).

I have assumed that persons attend college only from ages 18 to 22½ and high school only from 14 to 17. Actually, of course, high school and college are also attended at earlier and, especially after World War II, later ages. Moreover, the Census only tries to ascertain the highest grade completed and excludes partial years of schooling. Together, these facts imply that some persons over age 22½ with 16+ years of schooling would still be in school and, therefore, at best working only part time; similarly, for high-school graduates over age 18 and those with 13 to 15 years of school over age 20. Consequently, reported incomes at certain ages would not completely measure full-time incomes; data on the fraction of persons reporting no income, shown in Table A-3, suggest that in 1949 the bias is significant for

TABLE A-3

Fraction of White Males Reporting No Income in 1949, by Age and Education Class

	Years of Education				
Age	8 (1)	9–11 (2)	12 (3)	13–15 (4)	16+ (5)
14–15	.778	—	—	—	—
16–17	.569	.595	—	—	—
18–19	.227	.333	.239	—	—
20–21	.129	.108	.102	.240	—
22–24	.065	.046	.052	.116	.123
25–29	.043	.030	.026	.046	.045
30–34	.035	.024	.020	.019	.022
35–44	.033	.025	.023	.020	.020
45–54	.041	.036	.035	.029	.025
55–64	.065	.060	.059	.046	.041

Source: *1950 Census of Population, Education*, Vol. II, Table 12.

16+ years of schooling at ages 22 to 29, for 13 to 15 years at ages 20 to 24, for 12 years at ages 18 to 21, for 9 to 11 years at ages 16 to 19, and for 8 years at ages 14 to 17, while of lesser significance at other ages. Therefore, all persons with zero income have been included at these other ages, while only 2 per cent of persons who have 16+ school years aged 22 to 29, 13 to 15 years aged 20 to 24, and 12 years aged 18 to 21 are assumed to have no income (persons aged 14 to 19 with 8 and 9 to 11 years of schooling are discussed later).

b. Under- and Overreporting

From a comparison of Census and national income data, S. Goldsmith concluded that the Census underreports all types of income, the bias being greatest for dividends, interest, and other kinds of property income, and least for wages and salaries.[6] Her study suggests that wages and salaries were underreported by about 10 per cent. The 1940

[6] See Selma Goldsmith, "The Relation of Census Income Distribution Statistics to Other Income Data," *An Appraisal of the 1950 Census Income Data*, Studies in Income and Wealth 23, Princeton for NBER, 1958.

data cover only wages and salaries, so they were simply uniformly increased by 10 per cent to correct for the apparent Census bias. Since the understatement is probably greater at higher earning levels, the adjustment is probably too large at lower age-education classes and too small at upper classes.

To increase comparability with the 1940 Census, property incomes in the 1950 Census and the two Census surveys should be excluded. Since Table A-4 indicates, however, that aggregate earnings are about

TABLE A-4

Comparison of Incomes Reported by Census
and Commerce for 1946 and 1954
(dollars)

Source and Type of Information	1946	1954
Total earnings OBE series, adjusted	135.1	218.8
Total income CPS	129.8	217.7

Source: S. Goldsmith, in *An Appraisal of 1950 Census Income Data*, Table 2.

equal to the total incomes reported by the Census, the underreporting of earnings just about offsets the inclusion of property and other "unearned" income. Therefore, at the aggregate level at least, Census incomes can be used to measure true earnings. Although property income would be a larger percentage of total incomes at higher age-education levels, as noted above, the underreporting of earnings probably also rises with age and education. Hence the unadjusted data may not greatly overestimate earning differentials between different levels.

c. Unemployment

Earnings of less-educated persons are usually more affected by business cycles, partly because their employment is more volatile and partly because wages fluctuate more than salaries. Incomes reported in Census and other surveys refer to particular stages of business cycles, while rates of return depend on lifetime earnings accruing over several full cycles. The 1950 Census and the 1956 and 1958 surveys cover relatively normal times and are probably only slightly affected, but the 1940 Census covers a period of sizable unemployment and might be seriously biased. Accordingly, I have tried to correct the 1940 Census data for their departure from "normality."

First, the average unemployment rate of wage and salary workers was estimated for each educational level in 1940, and the average duration of unemployment of all persons unemployed less than a year was computed.[7] If the average duration did not depend on education and if unemployed persons earned the same when employed as others, one could estimate what earnings would have been if nobody were unemployed.[8] Column 3 of Table A-5 presents these estimates which

TABLE A-5

Adjustment for Unemployment in 1939, by Education Class

Education (years)	Per Cent Unemployed (wage and salary workers) (1)	Duration of Unemployment (years) (2)	Employment Adjustment (3)	Earnings Adjust- ment (4)
7–8	20.37	.63	1.08	1.08
12	14.10	.63	1.06	1.08
13–15	10.54	.63	1.04	1.07
16+	5.92	.63	1.02	1.07

Source: Column 1: *1940 Census of Population, Education*, Table 17, p. 76. Column 2: Computed from *1940 Census of Population, The Labor Force (Sample Statistics), Occupational Characteristics*, Washington, 1943, Table 17, pp. 199 and 202. Column 4: Based on figures in *ibid.*, Tables 3 and 6; and *Employment, Payroll, Hours and Earnings*, Bureau of Labor Statistics, L.S. 53-2884 and L.S. 53-0902.

show that unemployment did increase percentage earning differentials between educational levels.

Deviations of actual wages and actual salaries in 1939 from "normal" levels were determined by assuming that normal levels in 1939 equaled a simple average of actual levels from 1937 to 1941. Wage earners were separated from salary earners at each educational level with the help of Census information. If actual wages and salaries devi-

[7] Persons unemployed more than a year presumably do not have any wages or salaries and, therefore, are already excluded from Zeman's figures.

[8] Actually only abnormal unemployment should be eliminated as unemployment is normally also higher among less-educated persons. Only a small bias results, however, because normal unemployment was a small part of the total in 1939.

ated from normal values by the same percentage at each educational level, normal wages and salaries in 1939 could then be easily determined. Ratios of normal to actual values are shown in column 4.

The coefficients in columns 3 and 4 were applied uniformly to all age classes, even though the incidence, at least of unemployment, is greater at younger ages. Although earnings of less-educated persons were raised by relatively large percentages, they were not raised by relatively large absolute amounts because the level of earnings is positively related to education. Accordingly, the adjustments for the depressed conditions of 1939 had a surprisingly small effect on rates of return.

d. Coverage in 1939

The 1940 Census only reports the incomes of native whites with less than $50 of income other than wages and salaries. About one-third of all whites and more than half of the college graduates are omitted. The latter are especially underrepresented because independent professionals are excluded and most of them are college graduates. To rectify this underrepresentation, I estimated separately the earnings and number at different ages of independent dentists, lawyers, and physicians.

Table A-6 presents these estimates along with the earnings and number of college graduates computed from the Census. The relative number and earnings of independent professionals rise strongly with age. Column 5 presents estimates of the average earnings of both groups combined, which are weighted averages of the earnings of each, the weights being their relative numbers. A comparison of columns 3 and 5 shows that the combined average is not very different from the Census average before age class 45 to 54. Since rates of return are dominated by earnings at younger ages, the omission of independent professionals would have little effect on these rates: it would lower the rate to college graduates by less than 1 percentage point.

Although the inclusion of independent professionals increases the coverage of college graduates to about the same levels as other education classes, considerable biases might result since more than one-third of all whites are still excluded. The biases offset each other to some extent, however, because presumably foreign-born persons earn less than natives and natives with property income earn more than other natives. Probably the net effect is to lower rates of return from high-school and college education since the relative importance of the

Average Earnings of Census College Graduates and Independent
Doctors, Dentists, and Lawyers in 1939

	Independent Professionals		Census College Graduates		Earnings of Both Groups Combined (dollars) (5)
			Earnings (adjusted for unemployment) (dollars)		
Age	Earnings (dollars) (1)	Number (2)	(3)	Number (4)	
25–29	2174	15,631	1997	177,400	2011
30–34	3285	38,762	2878	161,800	2957
35–44	4491	108,476	3782	187,060	4042
45–54	5028	72,278	4185	97,920	4543
55–64	4238	45,690	3782	42,120	4019

Source: Columns 1 and 2 computed from William Weinfeld, "Income of
Physicians, 1929–49," *Survey of Current Business*, July 1951, Tables 1 and 16;
"Income of Lawyers, 1929–49," *Survey of Current Business*, August 1949, Tables 1
and 10; and "Income of Dentists, 1929–48," *Survey of Current Business*, January
1950, Tables 2 and 9; columns 3 and 4 from *1940 Census of Population, Education*.

foreign born is smaller at higher educational levels. Fortunately, as
Table A-7 suggests, the biases are probably not very large because the
relative number of persons excluded is much smaller at younger ages
for all education classes.

e. Taxes

Census and other surveys report before-tax incomes whereas incomes
net of direct personal taxes are needed to estimate private rates of
return. Internal revenue data were used in 1949 to find the average
fraction paid in taxes at each income class, including the open-end
class.[9] Means of after-tax incomes at all age-education levels were
estimated from the after-tax incomes in each income class. Although
there was little change in tax schedules between 1949 and 1956 to
1958, the fraction of income paid in taxes increased from 7.5 to over
10 per cent between 1949 and 1956 because of the growth in money
incomes. At each age-education class the fraction of income taxed in

[9] See *Statistics of Income for 1949*, Part I, Washington, 1954, Table 8. The separate
returns for women were excluded.

TABLE A-7

Fraction of Native Whites and Urban Whites Included
in 1939 Data, by Age and Education

Age	Ratio of Native Whites Included and Independent Professionals to All Native Whites, by Years of Education				Ratio of Urban White Males Included[a] to All Urban White Males, by Years of Education			
	7–8 (1)	12 (2)	13–15 (3)	16+ (4)	7–8 (5)	12 (6)	13–15 (7)	16+ (8)
18–19	.964	.758	.490	.582	—	—	—	—
20–21	.826	.850	.636	.589	.705	.740	.479	.495
22–24	.840	.863	.757	.696				
25–29	.843	.841	.795	.754	.728	.773	.724	.675
30–34	.822	.798	.745	.785	.671	.720	.675	.717
35–44	.776	.718	.651	.836	.589	.606	.570	.718
45–54	.704	.621	.553	.742	.488	.491	.480	.612
55–64	.604	.521	.443	.698	.386	.395	.369	.549

Source: Numerators are from Table A-6 and sources cited there; denominators of columns 1, 2, and 4 are from *1940 Census of Population, Education*, Table 29, pp. 14 f; denominators of columns 5, 6, 7, and 8 are from *1940 Census of Population*, Vol. IV: Characteristics by Age, Part 1 (U.S. Summary), Washington, 1943, Table 18, pp. 78 and 81.

[a] Also includes rural independent professionals aged 25 and over.

1956 and 1958 was assumed to equal the fraction taxed in 1949 multiplied by the ratio of the aggregate tax rates. A more sophisticated adjustment would not have much effect on the results.

Only about 1.5 per cent of income was paid in direct personal taxes in 1939.[10] Urban males with seven or more years of schooling presumably paid a somewhat larger fraction: native whites, perhaps about 4 per cent, and nonwhites, about 2 per cent. As mentioned in Chapter IV, 1939 cohorts received the bulk of their incomes not in 1939 but in the 1940s, 1950s, and 1960s, and would be subject to the higher rates prevailing then. The after-tax incomes of 1939 cohorts were also estimated assuming that they paid the same fraction in taxes at each age-education level as 1949 cohorts did.

[10] Taxes paid were found in *Statistics of Income for 1939*, Part I, Washington, 1942; adjusted gross income was estimated by C. H. Kahn, *Business and Professional Income under the Personal Income Tax*, Princeton for NBER, 1964, Chapter 5.

f. Urban-Rural Distribution

The 1940 Census covers all urban persons while the other surveys cover rural persons as well. If elementary, high-school, and college graduates were differently distributed by place of residence, the rates of return could be biased since money incomes are related to size of place of residence. Table A-8 indicates that they had about the same

TABLE A-8

Distribution of Persons of Different Educational Levels, by Size of Place of Residence, 1939

	Urban Population (*per cent*)			Urban as Per Cent of Total (4)
Years of Education	Over 250,000 (1)	25,000–250,000 (2)	2500–25,000 (3)	
7–8	40.6	29.6	29.8	50.1
12	37.3	32.5	30.2	66.9
16+	39.1	30.9	30.1	76.4

Source: Columns 1–3 from Table 18; column 4 from *1940 Census of Population, Education*, Table 29, pp. 147–151.

distribution among urban areas; more educated persons, however, were less likely to live in rural areas. Consequently, the rates would have an upward bias in 1949 and later years because rural incomes are lower than urban ones even when education is held constant. The bias is small, however, because relatively few persons between the crucial ages of 18 and 45 are in nonurban areas.

g. Hours of Work

Hours of work may differ among education classes for a variety of reasons: some persons retire earlier, have the opportunity to work more hours during any week, take longer vacations, and so on. Perhaps rates of return should be estimated from earnings per hour rather than the annual earnings presented in the Census and other reports. Fortunately, this difficult question does not have to be answered since average weekly hours of work apparently do not vary

TABLE A-9

Average Hours Worked in
1939, by Educational Level

Years of Education	Average Hours Worked
9–11	44.0
12	44.5
13–15	45.1
16+	44.7

Source: *1940 Census of Population, Labor Force (Sample Statistics), Occupational Characteristics,* Table 3 (all employed persons) and Table 9 (wage and salary workers only).

greatly among education classes. Table A-9 presents estimates from the 1940 Census based on the assumption that within occupations average hours of work did not vary systematically by education. In his study, Finegan also finds no significant relation between hours of work and education.[11]

2. Costs

a. Earnings of Students

Earnings of students cannot be estimated directly from the Census reports since these do not separate student earnings from those of full-time participants in the labor force with the same number of completed school years. If "full-time" students spend three-quarters of the available working time at school and, therefore, have one-quarter (summers) available for employment, the simplest assumption is that they could earn about one-quarter of what they would earn if they were not attending school. That this is a surprisingly good assumption is brought out by Table A-10, which presents three largely independent estimates of the earnings of college students. The first simply assumes that they earn one-quarter of the earnings of high-school graduates aged 18 to 21; the second comes from a study giving the

[11] A. Finegan, "A Cross-Sectional Analysis of Hours of Work," *Journal of Political Economy,* October 1962. He does find a relation when income is held constant.

TABLE A-10

Alternative Estimates of Fraction of
Earnings of High School Graduates of
Same Age Received by College Students

Source of Estimate	Fraction
Becker	.250
Costs of attending college	.349
Labor force participation	.236

Source: The denominator of the second
estimate is my estimate of the average earnings
of high-school graduates aged 18 to 21 in 1949;
the numerator is determined from *Costs of
Attending College*, Table 8, p. 48. The third
estimate is largely derived from "The Employment of Students, October 1960," in *Monthly
Labor Review*, July 1961, Tables C and E. Since
the labor force participation surveys were
taken in October, they tend to understate
the relative participation of college students
because they participate more during the
summer. I have assumed that the relative
participation of college students during the
summer is the same as their relative earnings
during the summer (derived from *Costs of
Attending College*, Table 8), while the participation of nonstudents is the same throughout the
year. The overall participation rate of college
students relative to nonstudents aged 18 to 24
could then be estimated from the formula

$$p = \frac{3}{4}s + \frac{1}{4}(3r)s,$$

where p is their overall relative participation,
s is their relative participation during the non-
summer months, and $3r$ is the participation
of college students during the summer relative to the rest of the year. According to the
sources cited, $3r = 1.413$ and $s = .214$; therefore $p = .236$.

earnings of a sample of college students during the academic year
1952–1953; the third is based partly on this sample and largely on
the actual labor force participation of nonstudents and students between age 18 and 24. The last estimate indicates that college students

work about one-quarter as much as nonstudents of the same age, while a comparison of the first and second estimates suggests that they earn about one-quarter as much as high-school graduates of the same age.[12] Consequently, the assumption that college students earn about one-quarter of the amount earned by high-school graduates of the same age is apparently fairly accurate, probably more so than some subtler assumptions that have been used.[13]

The 1940 Census and the 1956 and 1958 surveys do not give the earnings of persons younger than 18, so I simply assumed that the average earnings of elementary-school graduates increase from ages 14 to 18 at the same rate as from ages 18 to 21. The 1950 Census does give the incomes of persons aged 14 to 17 classified by education level. Column 1 of Table A-11 presents the mean incomes at ages 14 to 15 and 16 to 17 of all persons who have completed eight years of schooling, while column 2 presents much higher estimates obtained by extrapolating the rate of increase between ages 18 to 19 and 20 to 21. Since the Census usually understates incomes immediately following the typical age of entrance into the labor force (see the earlier discussion in section 1a), most of those with zero incomes among college persons aged 20 to 29 and high-school persons aged 16 to 21 were omitted. Column 3 of Table A-11 gives the average incomes of elementary-school graduates at ages 14 to 17 when zero incomes are assumed to be only 5 per cent of the total. These figures are actually higher than those based on extrapolation because about 78 per cent of 14- to 15-year-olds and 57 per cent of 16- to 17-year-olds with eight years of

---

[12] The ratio is somewhat higher in the second estimate because the earnings of students (in the numerator) are based on the academic year 1952–1953, while the earnings of high-school graduates (in the denominator) are based on 1949. An adjustment for the strong general rise in earnings between 1949 and 1952–1953 would lower the ratio to about .29. The difference between .25 and .29 is probably explained by the fact that the average age of college students is somewhat greater than 20, and their average ability is greater than that of high-school graduates. The .25 estimate, in effect, adjusts costs for the differential ability of college students, while the .29 estimate does not.

[13] Schultz's estimate of the earnings foregone by college students in 1950 is a good deal larger than that implicit in ours (see his "Capital Formation by Education," *Journal of Political Economy,* December 1960, Tables 1 and 2), partly because he uses the actual age distribution of college students and partly because he assumes (wrongly, I believe) that they forego forty weeks of income. (I am indebted to Schultz for very helpful discussions and correspondence on alternative estimating methods.) Blitz's estimates are even higher than Schultz's (see Rudolph C. Blitz, "A Calculation of Income Foregone by Students: Supplement to 'The Nation's Educational Outlay,'" in *Economics of Higher Education,* Selma J. Mushkin, ed., Washington, 1962, Appendix B, pp. 390–403). Albert Fishlow made very detailed estimates of opportunity costs in "Levels of Nineteenth-Century American Investment in Education," *Journal of Economic History,* 26, December 1966, pp. 418–436.

TABLE A-11

Alternative Estimates of Earnings of Persons Aged 14 to 17
with Eight Years of Schooling, 1949
(dollars)

Age	Including All Persons with Zero Incomes (1)	Extrapolated from Earnings at Ages 18–19 and 20–21 (2)	Assuming Only 5 Per Cent Have Zero Incomes (3)
14–15	104	333	431
16–17	258	525	558

Source: *1950 Census of Population, Education*, Table 12.

schooling reported no income in 1949. Yet more than 7 per cent of
the elementary-school graduates over age 22 reported no income.[14]

The earnings of high-school students were assumed to equal one-
quarter the estimated earnings of elementary-school graduates aged
14 to 17. Another estimate is presented in Table A-12 that is derived
largely from surveys of labor force participation by students and nonstudents aged 14 to 17. This estimate indicates somewhat smaller
actual, though larger foregone, earnings than ours does.[15]

b. Direct Private Costs

Information on current expenditures, tuition, and enrollments for
1940 and 1950 were taken from a special study[16] rather than directly
from the biennial surveys of the Office of Education because the study
apparently presents more consistent and comparable data.[17] Informa-

[14] Many of the persons who leave school after only completing the eighth grade
were still in school at ages 14 to 15 and even 16 to 17 (see *School and Early Employment Experience of Youth*, Dept. of Labor, No. 1277, Washington, 1960, Tables
5 and 6). Moreover, the same study indicates that teen-agers not in school have a lot
of "unexplained time," i.e., time when they were not in the labor force, in training,
sick, etc. (see *ibid.*, Table 20). Possibly these considerations explain the extraordi-
narily large fraction reporting no income.

[15] Schultz's estimates (*Journal of Political Economy*, December 1960, Table 5) of
both actual and foregone earnings are again much larger than ours.

[16] See *Current Operating Expenditures and Income of Higher Education in the
United States, 1930, 1940 and 1950* (called *COEIHE* in later references), a Staff Tech-
nical Paper of the Commission on Financing Higher Education, Columbia University
Press, New York, 1952, Tables 3, 58, 83, 91, and 115.

[17] See *ibid.*, Introduction, pp. iii to ix.

TABLE A-12

Alternative Estimates of Fraction
of Earnings of Elementary School
Graduates of the Same Age Received
by High School Students

Source of Estimate	Fraction
Becker	.25
Labor force participation	.21

Source: The second estimate was obtained
in the same way as the third estimate in Table
A-10. The sources are *Employment of Students,*
Current Population Reports, Labor Force,
October 1955 (Series P-50, No. 64), Tables 1
and C; and Special Labor Force Report No.
16, "The Employment of Students, October
1960," *Monthly Labor Review,* July 1961, Tables
C and E. I had to assume that the relative
summer participation of high-school students
was the same as that of college students.

tion from the biennial surveys improved considerably during the 1950s
and was used for 1956 and 1958.

Gross tuition and fees would equal reported tuition and fees plus
contributions by the federal government to the tuition of veterans.
An estimate of tuition paid for extension courses was subtracted since
enrollment figures exclude extension students. The estimate assumed
that extension tuition was the same fraction of all tuition as current
expenditures on extension were of all current expenditures.[18]

The tuition paid by students would be lower than the tuition received by colleges because of scholarships from colleges and other
sources. The 1952–1953 national sample provides information on
scholarships received from both sources: together they averaged about
20.7 per cent of tuition.[19]

Figures on enrollment usually include part-time along with full-

[18] These ratios were .073 in 1939 and .053 in 1949 (see *ibid.,* Tables 3 and 91).
[19] See *Costs of Attending College,* Table 8. Scholarships from colleges averaged
about 13.9 per cent of tuition, which is close to the 12.5 per cent estimate for
1953–54 of John F. Meck (see his *Testimony Before the House Ways and Means
Committee, 1958,* General Revenue Revisions, Vol. 78, 85th Congress, 2nd Session,
Washington, 1958, p. 1065).

time students, and accordingly overestimate the number of full-time equivalents. A special study in 1958 indicated that part-timers were about 24 per cent of all male college students.[20] If part-timers averaged about half the course load of full-timers (they probably averaged somewhat less),[21] the number of full-time equivalents would be about 88 per cent of the total enrollment. All the college enrollment figures, therefore, have been multiplied by 0.88.

All these adjustments transformed the crude figures into full-time tuition charges and payments for nonextension students; payments were $112 per student in 1939, $228 in 1949, $209 in 1956,[22] and $242 in 1958, and charges averaged about 25 per cent higher because of college and other scholarships. In recent years the Office of Education surveyed the tuition charged full-time students in a large number of colleges, and found an average of $296 in 1956–1957 and $319 in 1957–1958.[23] This is generally consistent with my estimates for these years considering the bias in favor of more expensive schools in the Office of Education survey, and the slight. upward biases in my estimates of full-time equivalents and extension tuition.

The 1952–1953 survey gives the average outlay by college students on books and supplies, travel between home and school, and capital (e.g., typewriters) used in schoolwork. These were assumed to be the only other private direct costs and to be the same fraction of tuition in other years as they were in 1952–1953. In that year books and sup-

[20] *Total Enrollment in Institutions of Higher Education, First Term, 1959–60,* Washington, 1962, Table 1.

[21] According to some estimates, part-time undergraduate students average about two-sevenths and part-time graduate students about three-fifths of the load of full-timers; together they would average about one-third. For these estimates, see R. W. Wallers, "Statistics of Attendance in American Universities and College, 1949," *School and Society,* December 1949, and S. Mushkin and E. McLoone, *Student Higher Education: Expenditures and Sources of Income in 16 Selected States,* Washington, 1960.

[22] The decline from 1949 to 1956 was quite unexpected, but turned out to be rather easily explained. While average tuition per student increased somewhat in private colleges, it decreased substantially in public ones, and the fraction of students in public colleges increased from .51 in 1949 to .56 in 1956. (See "Statistics of Higher Education: Receipts, Expenditures and Property, 1949–50," Section II of *Biennial Survey of Education in the United States, 1948–50,* Washington, 1952, Table 2, and "Statistics of Higher Education: Receipts, Expenditures and Property, 1955–56," Volume II of *Biennial Survey of Education in the U.S., 1954–56,* Washington, 1959, Table X; and *Statistical Abstract of the U.S.-1961,* Table 157.) Average tuition declined in the public institutions partly because the relative number of veterans declined and public institutions were sometimes permitted to charge veterans going to school under the G.I. Bill more than other students.

[23] W. Robert Bokelman, *Higher Education Planning and Management Data, 1957–58,* Washington, 1958, Table 34.

plies were 22.5 per cent of tuition, travel 23.9 per cent, and capital 7 per cent.[24]

High-school tuition was set equal to zero. The other direct costs of high-school students—transportation, books, etc.—were estimated by assuming that the ratio of these costs to expenditure per student by high schools equaled one-half the observed ratio for college students. The use of one-half is quite arbitrary and perhaps a somewhat different ratio would be more justifiable. However, a considerable change in the values assumed for these other direct costs would not have much effect on the estimated rates of return from high school.

c. Direct Social Costs

Direct social costs equal the sum of current educational expenditures, capital used up on education, and property taxes that would have been levied if schools were not tax-exempt. Educational expenditures are much smaller than total expenditures by schools, since schools are multiproduct institutions (especially at the college level) that do extension work, house and feed students, organize athletic contests, conduct research, and so on. I have excluded from the total what the biennial survey calls "noneducational" expenditures, extension, organized research, and expenditures on "organized activities relating to instructional departments." One might argue that some research and organized activities expenditures should be included since these directly benefit students and make it easier to acquire a good faculty. Expenditures on them were only about 13.6 per cent of other educational expenditures in 1939, but rose to 29 per cent in 1949.[25] Including these expenditures as educational costs would- have lowered the estimated rate of return about .75 of a percentage point in 1949—a relatively small difference.

The amount of tangible capital per school was estimated from an unpublished study by Robert Rude.[26] Only 80 per cent of all colleges in his sample reported their capital, so his figure for college capital may be too low; but since those not reporting were quite small, the bias is probably not large. Capital per student was obtained by divid-

---

[24] See *Costs of Attending College,* Table 8. Ten per cent of the capital was assumed to be used up during a single school year. This assumption is discussed in the next section.

[25] See *COEIHE,* Tables 58 and 83.

[26] See his unpublished manuscript, "Assets of Private Nonprofit Institutions in the United States, 1890–1948," National Bureau of Economic Research, 1954. There is evidence that Rude overestimated the relative value of land (see an unpublished discussion by Z. Griliches).

ing the amount per school by the number of students per school. The fraction of all capital used on "noneducational" activities (extension, housing, etc.) is assumed to be the same as the fraction of all current expenditures on these activities. If "current" expenditures on research and other noneducational activities include an allowance for capital overhead, some of the capital used on noneducational activities would be subtracted twice.[27] About 37 and 48 per cent of college capital in 1939 and 1949, respectively, was excluded from Rude's estimates.[28]

The Office of Education combines expenditures of high schools and elementary schools. The expenditures of each could be estimated from the formula

$$wX + (1 - w)\alpha X = Y,$$

if w and α were known, where X is the expenditure per student in high schools, Y is the combined expenditure per student, w is the fraction of students in high schools, and $1/\alpha$ is the ratio of expenditures per student in high schools to those in elementary schools. Now w is regularly reported and α is occasionally reported. For example, it was stated that $1/\alpha$ equaled about 1.74 in 1939–1940,[29] and I have used this ratio to estimate X, the expenditure per high-school student. High-school capital was assumed to be the same fraction of the combined capital as it was of the combined expenditures. Finally, noneducational expenditures and capital were assumed to be the same fraction of high school as they were of the combined elementary- and high-school expenditures and capital.

The opportunity cost of capital used in education, which measures the rate of return on other capital plus the rate of depreciation on

---

[27] On the other hand, if the current expenditures on research and other "noneducational" activities do not include any allowances for current "overhead," some of the general administrative expenditures and other such "overhead" should be allotted to these activities and excluded from my figures. I did not, however, try to make any adjustment for this.

[28] The breakdown is as follows:

	1939	1949
Noneducational	19.1	21.9
Extension	7.3	5.3
Research	5.6	14.2
Organized activities	5.5	7.1

(See COEIHE, Tables 58, 83, and 115.)

[29] See Statistical Summary of Education, 1939–40, Vol. II of the Biennial Survey of Education in the United States, 1938–40, Washington, 1943, Table 42, footnote 1, p. 44. In 1941–1944 it was put at 1.70 (see Statistical Summary of Education, 1941–42, Vol. II of the Biennial Survey of Education in the United States, Table 38, p. 34).

capital in education, was assumed to be 10 per cent of its value per annum. Usually, rates of interest rather than rates of return have been used in measuring opportunity costs, even though the latter seem more appropriate in determining social as well as private costs. In any case, the estimated opportunity cost of capital would not have been much lower if interest rates had been used.

Schools are exempt from property taxes while private businesses are not. In order to compare social rates of return on investments in business and education, either actual property taxes should be added to the net incomes of businesses or implicit taxes to the cost of education. The implicit annual property tax on educational capital was taken as 1.5 per cent of its value.[30] This amounted to $18 per student in 1939 and $21 in 1949, and was added to other educational costs.

[30] See Blitz, in *Economics of Higher Education*, p. 161.

Mathematical Discussion of Relation between Age, Earnings, and Wealth

1. This appendix derives some relations between the earnings and wealth profiles that were used in section 2 of Chapter VII. If the function $E(j)$ stands for earnings at age j, and $r(t, E)$ for the instantaneous interest rate at time t and the earnings function E, wealth at age j would be given by

$$W(j) = \int_{t=j}^{t=\infty} E(t) e^{-\int_{q=j}^{q=t} r(q, E)\, dq}\, dt. \tag{1}$$

The properties of this very general integral equation are not easily discovered and a number of simplifications are introduced. Interest rates are assumed to be independent of the date or earnings function, so

$$r(t, E) = r. \tag{2}$$

Earnings are assumed to grow at a constant rate for m years and then to equal zero, or

$$E(j) = a e^{bj} \quad 0 \leq j \leq m$$
$$= 0 \quad j > m, \tag{3}$$

where b is the rate of growth.

Time series earnings are often converted into cohort earnings through an expected labor force period that depends on mortality conditions: cohort earnings would equal time series earnings during this period and zero thereafter. Equation (3) can be so interpreted, with m the expected labor force period, and ae^{bj} earnings during the period. Time series earnings profiles in the United States can be approximated by a simple exponential function, although, as shown in the text, a fuller analysis would certainly have to incorporate a declining rate of growth. The labor force period method of adjusting for mortality, although widely used, is not always accurate and the more appropriate survivorship method is used in the text; the former is, however, a first approximation and its use considerably simplifies the mathematical analysis.

Substituting equations (2) and (3) into (1) gives

$$W(j) = \int_j^m ae^{bt}e^{-r(t-j)}\, dt, \qquad (4)$$

and wealth can be explicitly computed as

$$W(j) = \frac{a}{b-r}\left[e^{(b-r)m}e^{rj} - e^{bj}\right], \quad b \neq r \qquad (5)$$

$$= ae^{rj}(m - j), \quad b = r. \qquad (5')$$

Several relations between this wealth function and length of life (m), the rate of growth in earnings (b), and the rate of interest (r) are worked out in the following sections. It is assumed that $b \neq r$, although similar results can easily be proved for $b = r$.

2. The peak wealth age—the age at which wealth is maximized—is positively related to m, b, and r. Differentiating equation (5) yields

$$\frac{\partial W}{\partial j} = \frac{a}{b-r}\left[re^{(b-r)m}e^{rj} - be^{bj}\right], \qquad (6)$$

and

$$\frac{\partial^2 W}{\partial j^2} = \frac{a}{b-r}\left[r^2 e^{(b-r)m}e^{rj} - b^2 e^{bj}\right] < 0 \quad \text{if } \frac{\partial W}{\partial j} = 0.$$

Accordingly, wealth is maximized when

$$re^{(b-r)m}e^{rj} = be^{bj}, \qquad (7)$$

and the peak age simply equals

$$\hat{j} = m - \frac{\log b/r}{b - r}.$$ (8)

Hence

$$\frac{\partial \hat{j}}{\partial m} = 1 > 0,$$

$$\frac{\partial \hat{j}}{\partial b} = -\frac{1}{(b-r)^2} \left[1 - \left(\frac{r}{b} + \log \frac{b}{r} \right) \right] > 0$$ (9)

$$\frac{\partial \hat{j}}{\partial r} = -\frac{1}{(b-r)^2} \left[1 - \left(\frac{b}{r} + \log \frac{r}{b} \right) \right] > 0,$$

since

$$1 < \frac{r}{b} + \log \frac{b}{r}, \quad \text{for all } \frac{b}{r} > 0.$$

A few numerical calculations can illustrate the orders of magnitude involved. If m is taken as 42 years—about the average number spent in the labor force by persons experiencing 1940 mortality rates—r as 8 per cent and b as 3 per cent—roughly the average annual growth in the earnings of 1939 college graduates between ages 30 and 60—$\hat{j}$ would equal 22.4 years, or 40 years if age 18 rather than age 0 were considered the initial year. If b equaled 2.7 per cent—roughly the average growth in earnings of 1939 elementary-school graduates between ages 30 and 60—$\hat{j}$ would equal 20.5 years, or 2 years less than college graduates. If r were 4 per cent, $\hat{j}$ would be 14 and 12 for these college and elementary-school graduates respectively, much lower than when $r = .08$, but still a difference of 2 years. A reduction of m to 36 years—the average time spent in the labor force after age 18 by nineteenth-century slaves—would reduce all peak ages by about 6 years, regardless of the values of b and r.

3. Equations (5) and (6) imply that

$$\frac{\partial W}{\partial j} \bigg/ W = \frac{re^{(b-r)m}e^{rj} - be^{bj}}{e^{(b-r)m}e^{rj} - e^{bj}}$$ (10)

$$= \frac{re^{(b-r)(m-j)} - b}{e^{(b-r)(m-j)} - 1}.$$

By equation (3)

$$\frac{\partial E}{\partial j} \bigg/ E = b;$$ (11)

so it follows from (10) and (11) that

$$\frac{\partial W}{\partial j} \bigg/ W < \frac{\partial E}{\partial j} \bigg/ E. \tag{12}$$

Since earnings reach a peak at age m, later than the peak in wealth, equation (12) implies that the ratio of peak to initial values is greater for earnings than wealth.

The rate of change in wealth is positively related to, as well as less than, the rate of change in earnings, or

$$\frac{\dfrac{\partial W}{\partial j} \bigg/ W}{\partial b} > 0. \tag{13}$$

For

$$\frac{\dfrac{\partial W}{\partial j} \bigg/ W}{\partial b} = \frac{-e^{gx} + 1 + gxe^{gx}}{(e^{gx} - 1)^2} > 0, \tag{14}$$

where $x = m - j$ and $g = b - r$, only if

$$e^{gx}(1 - gx) < 1. \tag{15}$$

If $|gx| \geq 1$, equation (15) clearly holds; if $|gx| < 1$, then

$$\frac{1}{1 - gx} = 1 + gx + (gx)^2 + \cdots, \tag{16}$$

and the infinite series expansion of e^{gx} shows that equation (15) must hold. Therefore equation (13) is proven.

Although the rate of change in wealth is greater the greater the rate of change in earnings, the ratio of peak to initial wealth is a smaller fraction of the ratio of earnings at the peak wealth age to initial earnings the greater the rate of increase in earnings. That is,

$$\frac{\partial \left[\dfrac{W(\hat{j})/W(0)}{E(\hat{j})/E(0)} \right]}{\partial b} = k < 0. \tag{17}$$

Since

$$\frac{W(j)}{W(0)} = \frac{e^{(b-r)m}e^{rj} - e^{bj}}{e^{(b-r)m} - 1}, \tag{18}$$

and

$$\frac{E(j)}{E(0)} = e^{bj}, \tag{19}$$

$$\frac{W(j)/W(0)}{E(j)/E(0)} = \frac{e^{(b-r)(m-j)} - 1}{e^{(b-r)m} - 1}. \tag{20}$$

By equation (8)

$$m - \widehat{j} = \frac{\log b/r}{b - r},$$

so

$$k = \frac{e^{\log b/r} - 1}{e^{(b/r)m} - 1} = \frac{b/r - 1}{e^{(b-r)m} - 1}. \tag{21}$$

Hence

$$\frac{\partial k}{\partial b} < 0$$

only if

$$e^{gm} - 1 - gme^{gm} < 0,$$

or only if

$$e^{gm}(1 - gm) < 1. \tag{22}$$

Equation (22) is simply equation (15) again; therefore (17) has been proven.

4. The equation

$$\frac{\partial W}{\partial x} \bigg/ W = \frac{ge^{gx}}{e^{gx} - 1} \tag{23}$$

gives the rate of decline in wealth as the number of remaining years in the labor force (x) declines. Equations (10), (11), and (23) imply that

$$\frac{\partial W}{\partial x} \bigg/ W + \frac{\partial W}{\partial j} \bigg/ W = b = \frac{\partial E}{\partial j} \bigg/ E, \tag{24}$$

or

$$\frac{\partial W}{\partial x} \bigg/ W = \frac{\partial E}{\partial j} \bigg/ E - \frac{\partial W}{\partial j} \bigg/ W. \tag{25}$$

The difference between the rates of change in earnings and wealth with respect to age is simply equal to the rate of decline in wealth as the number of remaining years declines.

Equation (23) indicates that wealth declines more rapidly the fewer the years remaining, and declines infinitely fast as these years approach zero. As they go to infinity—life becomes indefinitely long—the rate of decline in wealth approaches $b - r$ if $b > r$, and 0 if $b < r$. Therefore, equations (23) and (24) imply that

$$\lim_{x \to \infty} \frac{\partial W}{\partial j} \Big/ W = \min (b, r). \qquad (26)$$

The rate of change in wealth with age approaches the rate of change in earnings only if the latter were less than the discount rate; otherwise the discount rate would be approached, a somewhat surprising result.

5. According to the definition used in the text, the rate of "depreciation" at age j is

$$D(j) = -\frac{\partial W(j)}{\partial j}, \qquad (27)$$

while the rate of "appreciation" is $-D(j) = \dfrac{\partial W(j)}{\partial j}$. The average rate during the whole period of labor force participation is given by

$$\bar{D} = \frac{1}{m} \int_0^m D(j)\, dj = \frac{-1}{m} \int_0^m \frac{\partial W}{\partial j}\, dj$$

$$= \frac{1}{m} [W(0) - W(m)] = \frac{1}{m} W(0), \qquad (28)$$

since $W(m) = 0$.

Average depreciation divided by average earnings gives the ratio

$$d = \frac{\bar{D}}{E} = \frac{\dfrac{1}{m} W(0)}{E} = \frac{\displaystyle\int_0^m E e^{-ri}\, dj}{\displaystyle\int_0^m E\, dj}, \qquad (29)$$

which is the ratio of the present values at the initial age of earnings discounted at the market rate to earnings discounted at a zero rate. This ratio is obviously positively related to the market rate, approaching zero for an infinite, and unity for a zero, rate.

"Permanent" earnings are defined either as

$$E_p(j) = E(j) - D(j), \qquad (30)$$

or as

$$E_p(j) = rW(j), \tag{31}$$

so

$$E(j) = D(j) + rW(j), \tag{32}$$

and, therefore, equation (29) can be written as

$$d = \frac{\bar{D}}{\bar{E}} = \frac{\dfrac{1}{m} W(0)}{r\bar{W} + \dfrac{1}{m} W(0)}. \tag{33}$$

Hence d would be smaller the smaller the ratio of initial to average wealth. Section 2 of Chapter VII implies that the latter, in turn, would be smaller the faster the rate of increase in earnings because the rate of increase in wealth is positively related to the rate of increase in earnings.

Author Index

Subject Index